W9-AEM-779

www.wadsworth.com

www.wadsworth.com is the World Wide Web site
for Wadsworth and is your direct source to dozens
of online resources.

At *www.wadsworth.com* you can find out about
supplements, demonstration software, and student
resources. You can also send email to many of our
authors and preview new publications and exciting
new technologies.

wadsworth.com
Changing the way the world learns®

Fifth Edition

COLLEGE STUDY SKILLS

Becoming a Strategic Learner

Dianna L. Van Blerkom
University of Pittsburgh at Johnstown

THOMSON
™
WADSWORTH

Australia • Canada • Mexico • Singapore • Spain • United Kingdom • United States

College Study Skills: Becoming a Strategic Learner, Fifth Edition
Dianna L. Van Blerkom

Publisher: Carolyn Merrill
Editorial Assistant: Amy Hurd
Technology Project Manager: Joe Gallagher
Editorial Assistant, Editorial Production: Kate Hedgpeth
Print/Media Buyer: Mary Beth Hennebury
Permissions Editor: Bob Kauser
Project Manager: Carol O'Connell, Graphic World Publishing Services

Text Designer: Susan Gerould, Perspectives
Photo Manager: Sheri Blaney
Cover Designer: Janet Wood
Cover Printer: Phoenix Color
Compositor: Graphic World, Inc.
Printer: Globus Printing
Cover Photo: © BananaStock/Alamy Images

Printed in the United States of America
1 2 3 4 5 6 7 09 08 07 06 05

For more information about our products, contact us at:
Thomson Learning Academic Resource Center
1-800-423-0563
For permission to use material from this text or product, submit a
request online at **http://www.thomsonrights.com**
Any additional questions about permissions can be submitted by email
to **thomsonrights@thomson.com.**

Thomson Higher Education
25 Thomson Place
Boston, MA 02210-1202
USA

Asia (including India)
Thomson Learning
5 Shenton Way
#01-01 UIC Building
Singapore 068808

Australia/New Zealand
Thomson Learning Australia
102 Dodds Street
Southbank, Victoria 3006
Australia

Canada
Thomson Nelson
1120 Birchmount Road
Toronto, Ontario M1K 5G4
Canada

UK/Europe/Middle East/Africa
Thomson Learning
High Holborn House
50–51 Bedford Road
London WC1R 4LR
United Kingdom

Latin America
Thomson Learning
Seneca, 53
Colonia Polanco
11560 Mexico
D.F. Mexico

Spain (including Portugal)
Thomson Paraninfo
Calle Magallanes, 25
28015 Madrid, Spain

Library of Congress Control Number: 2005920660

ISBN 0-534-64540-2

In loving memory of my parents,
Rachel and Simon Adelman

BRIEF CONTENTS

CONTENTS

ACTIVITIES CONTENTS

Chapter 6

Chapter 7

Chapter 8

Chapter 9

Chapter 10

Chapter 11

TO THE INSTRUCTOR

Do you find yourself carrying handouts to class all the time? After years of carrying text excerpts, student examples, and exercises to supplement the text I used, I decided to write *College Study Skills: Becoming a Strategic Learner*. This fifth edition provides all of these resources and more, so you can concentrate on the students in your class instead of spending your time looking for supplemental materials. A wide variety of active learning strategies are also included in this text. Not all of them will work for every student in every situation. In fact, most students will find that no single strategy will work for all their courses; they may need to use different strategies for different courses. By giving students an opportunity to try a number of different strategies, they'll be able to find the ones that work best for them.

Why is study skills instruction important? Many college students say that no one ever really taught them how to study. Although they probably did learn some study skills during their twelve years of schooling, they may not have learned the learning strategies that are necessary for college success. College courses are often more difficult, more intensive, cover more material at a faster pace, and focus on topics that are completely unfamiliar to new college students. Some or all of these differences may contribute to the difficulties that some students have during their first year in college. As a result, some students are dissatisfied with their grades or their performance in their courses, but they don't know what to do to correct this problem. Often they experience anxiety and frustration and may even begin to doubt whether they have the ability to succeed in college. For many of these students, simply learning how to study and how to learn strategically in college makes the difference between failure and success. Other students benefit by increasing their motivation, boosting their self-esteem, or learning better ways to study so that they can enjoy their college experience more. Becoming strategic learners can help them achieve both their academic and their personal goals in college. If students apply what they are learning, they should see an improvement in their grades, have more time for other responsibilities or for leisure activities, feel less stressed about their academic work, feel better about themselves, and perhaps even begin to enjoy learning.

In order to succeed in college, students must learn to apply the strategies they are learning to real course material. Practicing these strategies on material in psychology, history, biology, and sociology, for example, will help students learn to modify and adapt the strategies to the lectures, texts, exams, and assignments for their other courses. This transfer experience will help motivate students to use these new strategies in their other courses, one of the goals of learning skills courses.

UNIQUE FEATURES OF THE TEXT

You might expect to find many of the important aspects of this book in any comprehensive study strategies text. However, I feel that there are many features unique to this text:

- Emphasis on strategic learning throughout.

- Over 100 student examples help students using the text to connect to effective study strategies illustrated by their peers.

- Excerpts from college textbooks in many disciplines help students practice new skills immediately.

- Quick Start Strategy Pages that provide an early introduction to many of the essential skills and strategies students need to succeed in college.

- Exercises and applications for practice of the concepts being taught.

- "Hands-on and experiential approach," which supports best theories about how students really learn.

- Provides longer selections for practice, which simulates the real college experience better than short excerpts found in competing texts.

- Well written and engaging with a modern and student-friendly design.

- Flexible, straightforward format and organization that appeals to a variety of instructors—full-time or part-time faculty, counselors, residence life personnel, or anyone in academic assistance.

- Boxed feature, "Tip Blocks," in each chapter for traditional and nontraditional students.

IMPORTANT ASPECTS OF THE BOOK

This text provides a step-by-step approach to college learning skills. By breaking each of the topics down into smaller units, students will be able to master each of the steps before moving on to the next. Each chapter includes instruction in the skill, student examples, exercises for practice, and activities for self-evaluation.

Instruction

This text provides clear, easy-to-read explanations of how to study. Strategies for setting goals, managing time, improving concentration, taking notes, reading and understanding textbooks, organizing text information, and preparing for and taking tests are included. Because every student learns differently, a number of different strategies for taking lecture notes, preparing "To Do" lists, and preparing study sheets (just to name a few) are described in the text. Students are encouraged to try all of the strategies and then permitted to select the ones that work best for them. But learning to study effectively and efficiently requires more than just knowing a new skill; it also requires using that skill. In many cases, understanding why particular strategies work helps motivate students to use them in their other courses.

Explanations and rationales for using these strategies are also presented so that students understand why one strategy may work in particular situations while others may not.

Examples

More than 100 examples, prepared by students who were enrolled in learning skills classes, have been included in the text to show students how to use the strategies that are presented. For many students, seeing an example of what they have to do makes it much easier to do it right the first time. Since there are many ways to develop a study sheet, take notes, or even keep track of assignments, a number of different examples are shown for each of the different strategies discussed in the text. These models help students understand how to use the strategies and may also motivate them to complete their assignments.

Practice

One of the most important goals of any successful learning skills course is getting students to transfer what they learn to other course work. In order to help students achieve this goal, well over 100 activities have been designed to let students practice what they have learned. Each of the activities has been strategically placed within the chapter so that students can practice the new strategy immediately after it has been introduced. In addition, a number of the activities encourage students to practice older strategies as they are learning new ones. Many of these activities are based on excerpts from other college textbooks. In this way, students are afforded practice with material that is similar to the course material they are currently using. Finally, many of the activities require students to practice the strategies using their own course materials. In this way, students transfer the skills they have learned to their other courses while at the same time increasing their understanding of the material for their other courses. In many cases, this leads to overall higher success, something that helps students see the real value of study skills instruction.

Self-evaluation

Many of the activities are designed to help students monitor their own learning. The "Where Are You Now?" activities provide a quick check of the number of effective strategies students have prior to beginning each unit and the number they have made a part of their repertoire at the end of the unit. Some instructors choose to have students complete the end-of-chapter activity at a later date to allow more time for the students to incorporate the strategies. In addition, activities throughout the book ask students to evaluate many of the strategies that are presented in the text. It is only through self-evaluation that students can actually prove to themselves that one method of study is working for them. Once students know that a strategy is effective, they are more likely to continue to use it.

CHANGES IN THE FIFTH EDITION

The fifth edition of *College Study Strategies: Becoming a Strategic Learner* contains new information, activities, and student examples in every chapter. Although additional changes were made in all chapters in this fifth edition, only the most significant changes are listed below.

Chapter Changes

- Chapter 4, Memory and Learning, has been moved up to the first section of the text (previously was Chapter 9) to help students gain an understanding early in the semester of how they learn and process information into long-term memory. This should help them realize that they need to take good lecture notes, mark and take notes on their text material, and use the Five-Day Study Plan and active study strategies when preparing for exams.

- Chapter 9 (previously Chapter 8, Taking Text Notes) has been renamed Organizing Text Information to better reflect the new emphasis on organizing text information in the process of taking notes. It now includes new material and many new examples and activities.

- Chapter 12, Preparing for Essay Exams, and Chapter 14, Preparing for Final Exams, have been reorganized for better clarity.

New Features

- Quick Start Strategy Pages can be found prior to Chapter 1. These pages contain an overview of over 50 critical strategies for Succeeding in College, Managing Time, Taking Lecture Notes, Text Reading, Preparing for Exams, and Taking Exams.

- Graphic Displays have been added to every chapter to highlight key information in a visual format for ease in learning.

- A more active and interactive Web site has been designed for the fifth edition.

- Many new student examples have been added throughout the text.

- Full-size calendars and forms have been added back into the fifth edition.

New Sections

- Plagiarism (Chapter 1)

- Improving Your Academic Standing (Chapter 1)

- Being Open to Change (Chapter 2)

- Calculating Your GPA (Chapter 2)

- Managing Multiple Projects (Chapter 3)

- Creating Interest in the Task (Chapter 6)

- Why You Need to Organize Text Information (Chapter 9)

- Math and Science Problem Cards (Chapter 10)

- Taking Math Exams (Chapter 11)

- Calculating Your Course Grade (Chapter 14)

Revised Sections

- Learning Styles (Chapter 1)

- Decision Making (Chapter 1)

- Self-regulated Learning (Chapter 1)
- Levels of Interaction (Chapter 1)
- Characteristics of Goals (Chapter 2)
- Identifying Time Needed for Study (Chapter 3)
- Information Processing (Chapter 4)
- General Memory Strategies (Chapter 4)
- Repetition and Rehearsal Strategies (Chapter 4)
- Note-taking Systems (Chapter 5)
- Editing Your Notes (Chapter 5)
- Minimizing Distractions (Chapter 6)
- Differences in High School and College Textbooks (Chapter 7)
- How to Mark Your Textbook (Chapter 8)
- Predicting Questions in the Margin (Chapter 8)
- Mapping and Charting (Chapter 9)
- Five-Day Study Plan (Chapter 10)
- Active Preparation and Review Strategies (Chapter 10)
- Study Sheets (Chapter 10)
- Self-Tests (Chapter 10)
- Coping with Test Anxiety (Chapter 11)
- General Test-Taking Strategies (Chapter 11)
- Specific Test-Taking Strategies (Chapter 11)
- Practicing Essay Answers (Chapter 12)
- Setting Up a Final Exam Plan (Chapter 14)

Text Excerpts

- New and updated text excerpts throughout the book.
- More text excerpts have been included in the fifth edition.

Activities

- More group and journal activities have been added to each chapter.
- Many new activities throughout the text.

Supplementary Materials

Instructor's Manual
The Instructor's Manual includes an overview of each chapter, key terms and definitions, teaching suggestions, course materials and handouts, journal activities, quiz questions, and multiple-choice, essay, and discussion questions. Also included are excerpts from other college textbooks, additional student examples, and transparency masters.

College Study Skills *Web Site*
Students using this text will have access to the *College Study Skills* book-specific Web site. In addition to the answers to the end-of-chapter review questions, students will have access to text excerpts and four entire chapters from

college textbooks for transfer practice activities, handouts on additional topics related to college success such as calculating your GPA, calendars and forms, a self-scoring version of the learning style inventory, sample lectures for note-taking practice, word cards, crossword puzzles, chapter quizzes, Internet exercises, Web links, college success links, and many other special features.

College Success Factors Index

This unique online survey is the perfect tool that allows you to track the progress of your students in the course—and at the same time shows students what they need to work on to succeed. The CSFI is housed in a password-protected area of the Wadsworth Web site; passwords can be ordered as a bundle item with this textbook. Contact your Thomson Wadsworth representative for more information.

ACKNOWLEDGMENTS FOR THE FIFTH EDITION

Many people have been instrumental in making the fifth edition of *College Study Skills: Becoming a Strategic Learner* possible. I am especially appreciative of the innovative ideas, concrete suggestions, and wonderful support of my editor, Carolyn Merrill. I am also appreciative of the assistance provided by Kate Hedgpeth and the rest of the Wadsworth team: Elise Kaiser and Mary Beth Henneburg. Carol O'Connell makes the production process run smoothly and has been invaluable in getting this book into print. Thank you all. As always, my husband, Mal, has been my greatest support. In addition to writing the first half of Chapter 4, he is always willing to help out at home, provide objective feedback, and remind me that I should be working. I am grateful to my students who have been eager to share their own strategies for success. Their enthusiasm, encouragement, and personal success have continued to motivate me both in and out of the classroom. After teaching for more than twenty years, I am still learning from them. Many of the new topics and expanded coverage are a direct result of their requests, insight, and suggestions.

I have been very fortunate to have had a group of reviewers who shared their time, expertise, and wonderful suggestions for shaping this fifth edition. Thank you for your feedback on the strengths and weaknesses of the text and your excellent suggestions. Your insight and experience in teaching college learning skills and college success courses have been invaluable in creating this fifth edition:

Current Reviewers
Bill Buskist, Auburn University
Margaret Hebert, Eastern Connecticut State University
Rita McReynolds, Mississippi State University
Cindy O'Neal, Central Oregon Community College
Craig Winchell, Louisiana State University

Reviewers of Previous Editions
Karen L. Aguirre, Miami-Dade, South Campus
Charlotte Babcock, Northern Arizona University
Jackie Barton, Blue Mountain Community College
Vanneise Collins, University of Arkansas, Monticello
Nancy I. Crook, North Central Technical College
Muriel Davis, San Diego Mesa College
Bobby Decuir, University of Louisiana, Lafayette
Samantha Fey, Cape Fear Community College

Teresa Hall, Santa Monica College
Lois Mary Hassan, Henry Ford Community College
Howard Hayward, Lewis University
Faith Heinrichs, Central Missouri State University
Cynthia A. Hilden, Blue Mountain Community College
Carlotta W. Hill, Oklahoma City Community College
Judy Jenkins, Volunteer State Community College
Jim Kalat, North Carolina State University
Michelle Kalina, Sierra College
Linda Kleemann, Lewis and Clark Community College
Clare J. Landry, Rockford College
Marlene J. Lang, University of South Dakota
Dawn Leonard, Charleston Southern University
Virda Lester, Tuskegee Institute
Terri Massie-Burrell, Towson University
James V. Muniz, University of Scranton
Mary Ostrander, Central Oregon Community College
Mary Pepe, Valencia Community College
Helene Selco, Cornell University
Sharon R. Stevens, Oklahoma City Community College
Sharon Sundin, Southwest Texas State University
Doug Winborn, Middle Tennessee State University

TO THE STUDENT

This text introduces and explains many useful study strategies that will help you achieve your academic goals. If you're using this text before or during your first semester in college, you should be well prepared for the challenges ahead of you. If you've already attended one or more semesters in college, you may be enrolled in a study skills course because you weren't satisfied with your previous academic performance. By learning and applying new study strategies, you can improve your academic performance.

Did you take driver's education in high school? When I ask my students that question, most indicate that they have and that, for the most part, it's still taught in much the same way as it was when I took it. You do the "book part"—learning how to operate the car and the "rules" for safe driving. You then do the "car part"—you actually practice driving in the driver's education car. To be a good driver, you need to do both well. Becoming a successful student isn't that different. You need to do the "book part" (learning new skills and strategies) and the "car part" (applying those strategies to your own college assignments). If you use the new strategies to complete your reading assignments, take your lecture notes, and prepare for and take exams, you'll be successful in college. By trying out each of the new strategies for managing your time, setting goals, taking text notes, and preparing essay answers, for example, you can evaluate the effectiveness of each method and choose the one that works best for you—you can become a strategic learner.

Once you put your newly learned strategies into practice, you should begin to see your grades improve in each of your courses. This kind of improvement does not result from just being told what to do differently but rather from hard work and persistence in applying effective learning strategies to your own course material. Becoming a successful student takes time and effort—there are no miracles involved. If you're willing to learn new skills and strategies and are also motivated to use them when doing your own course assignments, you, too, can achieve your goals.

Speaking of goals, I have four goals for you in your use of this text. First, I want you to learn new strategies that will make learning and studying much more effective. Second, I want you to use those strategies in your own course work, so that you can achieve your academic goals. Third, I want you to feel better about yourself both as a student and as a person—I want you to have self-confidence. Fourth, I want you to actually learn to enjoy school. Instead of dreading a class, an assignment, or even an exam, I'd like you to look forward to them because you'll know how to be successful in taking notes, writing that report, and preparing for and taking that exam. If you apply what you're learning, you should see an improvement in your grades, have more time for leisure activities, feel less stressed about your academic work, feel better about yourself, and, perhaps, even begin to enjoy learning.

HOW TO USE THIS BOOK

There are many resources available in this text to help you make a successful transition to college learning. Each of the following text resources will provide you with additional information to help you achieve your goals.

Concept Maps

The concept maps on the first page of the chapter are designed to give you a brief introduction to the main topics in the chapter. Think about what you already know about each of the topics before you begin reading the text. You may also find that they can serve as a template for your own map of the chapter. See Chapter 9 for more information on how to map the information in your textbook.

College Success Factors Index

If your instructor has ordered the College Success Factors Index with your textbook, you can go to www.success.wadsworth.com to find the link to CSFI, which will let you see how you compare with other students in areas proven to be determinants of college success by completing the 80 self-scoring statements. Then read about each of the factors to see how you can be even more successful in college.

Quick Start Strategy Pages

Just before Chapter 1, you'll find a series of Quick Start Strategy pages. These pages contain an introduction to many of the critical strategies you'll need to succeed in college. The topics include: Succeeding in College, Managing Time, Taking Lecture Notes, Text Reading, Preparing for Exams, and Taking Exams. After you complete the assessment on the first page, look through the strategies and select some to use today. If you need more information on how to use a particular strategy, you'll be able to find it by checking the index at the end of the text or by going to that chapter in the book. These strategy pages are designed to help you get off to a great start this semester.

Where Are You Now? Activities

By completing the "Where Are You Now?" activities before reading the chapter, you can evaluate your current strategy use related to the topics in each chapter. Once you identify your strengths and weaknesses, you can focus on those areas where you need the most assistance. You may notice after completing one of these activities that they provide you with an overview of some of the strategies that will be discussed in the chapter. After you complete the chapter or even two or three weeks later, complete the activity again in the text (using a different color pen) or do it online at the *College Study Skills* Web site (http://info.wadsworth.com/vanblerkom5).

Tip Blocks

The Tip Blocks found in each chapter include additional strategies for both traditional and nontraditional students. You'll find practical suggestions in each chapter that will save you time, help you apply your strategies to your other course work, or give you tips for making studying more interesting and challenging.

Student Examples

The student examples shown in the text serve as models for many of the strategies that are described in each chapter. Although it's become almost a cliché, a picture is worth a thousand words to students who aren't sure how to take lecture notes, create recall questions, and set up study sheets, just to name a few of the applications you may find useful in this text. Occasionally, poor examples are included that contain common errors students make. These examples are designed to keep you from making those same mistakes.

Transfer Activities

Each chapter contains two or three transfer activities. Many are group or self-monitoring activities. These activities help you learn to apply the new strategies described in the chapter to your other college course work. By using the strategies in your own work, you'll be able to determine which are the most effective for you, while at the same time improving your performance in your other courses.

Self-Monitoring Activities

Each chapter contains self-monitoring activities. By completing these activities you can learn how to monitor your learning. These activities help you monitor your performance in your other course work and the strategies that you're using. Knowing whether or not you're using effective strategies can help you make changes, if they're necessary, in order to be more successful in college.

Group Activities

The group activities in each chapter are designed to encourage collaborative work. Many students enjoy working with others and find that they learn much more when working in a group. Sharing ideas, resources, and strategies all help you succeed in college. If you haven't already discovered the advantages of collaborative work, you may find that these activities will demonstrate how effective it can be.

Journal Activities

The journal activities in each chapter are designed to help you reflect on your learning experiences as you move through the text and your course work. By writing about how you applied each of the strategies to your own work, you can evaluate how effective they were in helping you achieve your goals. You may also find that noting any changes that you would make the next time you used the strategy can help you monitor your own learning and your progress toward success. Many students find that writing about their progress is very motivating and provides them with feelings of accomplishment as well.

Terms You Should Know

At the end of each chapter, you'll find a list of terms you should know. In college, you're expected to understand all of the new terminology presented in the text and in lecture. As you move through the text, write each term on the front of an index card and then write the definition (found within the chapter) on the back. Dig through the text and your lecture notes for any additional terms you should know and make flash cards for them, too. Recite the definitions until you know them all without looking.

College Study Skills Book-Specific Web Site

The *College Study Skills: Becoming a Strategic Learner* book-specific Web site contains a wealth of information to help you succeed in college. You'll find answers to the multiple-choice and completion items from the end of chapter reviews. There are handouts on topics such as calculating your GPA, forms for setting goals and action planning, and calendars for time-management activities. You'll also find a self-scoring form of the Learning Style Inventory described in Chapter 1. There are sample lectures and text excerpts for note-taking practice and practice tests for objective and essay exams. You'll also have access to four entire text chapters from a variety of academic disciplines. You'll have word cards and crossword puzzles to help you learn the course terminology. Internet links, college success links, and many other features can be found on this Web site. Check it out at http://info.wadsworth.com/vanblerkom5.

Review Questions

The review questions at the end of each chapter are designed to help you monitor your learning. You'll find a list of key terms you should know, and both completion and multiple-choice questions. You'll be able to check the answers to both the completion and multiple-choice items on the Web site listed above. Please keep in mind, though, that these questions don't cover all of the important information in the chapter. They're designed to provide you with some feedback on your reading comprehension and learning, but you need to predict additional questions to prepare for quizzes and exams. I recommend predicting about 35 to 40 additional questions for each chapter. By using the review questions as models, you should be able to generate these additional questions on your own or within a study group.

A FINAL NOTE

It's always exciting and rewarding when students tell me that the strategies in this book helped them. I'm especially delighted to hear about their success in their freshman year. I'm often as happy, I think, as they are when they make the Dean's List. If you were successful during your first semester, first year, or even during your college career because of your use of this text, I'd love to hear from you, too. Drop me a note and let me know how *College Study Skills: Becoming a Strategic Learner* helped you. Also, if you have any suggestions for how this book can be improved in order to help other students succeed in college, please let me know. You can contact me by writing to:

Dianna Van Blerkom
Thomson/Wadsworth
10 Davis Drive
Belmont, California 94002

Introduction

How do you study now? What strategies do you plan to use to be successful this semester? Jot down your strategies under each of the topics before you go on.

Succeed in College?
-
-
-

Manage Your Time?
-
-
-

Take Lecture Notes?
-
-
-

Read Your Textbook?
-
-
-

Prepare for Exams?
-
-
-

Take Exams?
-
-
-

On the next six pages, you'll find over 50 great strategies to help you get off to a great start this semester. Look them over. How many of your strategies were included? Go back and put a check mark next to each of the strategies you already use. Then put a star next to each strategy that you would like to use to be more successful in college. Pick a few strategies from each page that you plan to start using right now and list them on page Q8. Each week, as you learn to use more new strategies in this course, add to your list.

College Success

- **ATTEND ALL CLASSES.** One of the best ways to be successful in college is to attend all classes. Although you will be tested on material from the course text, most of the test questions will come from lectures.

- **TAKE A LIGHTER COURSE LOAD.** If this is your first semester in college, start off with a lighter course load. This semester your goal is to do well. When you're a sophomore, junior, or senior, you can more easily take more credits.

- **BECOME AN ACTIVE LEARNER.** Unlike high school, in college you can't learn all of the material by just reading over it a couple of times. You need to write and recite the information to get it into long-term memory.

- **PARTICIPATE IN CLASS.** If you feel a bit uncomfortable participating in class, set a goal to either ask or answer one question during each class. Once you begin participating, you'll feel more a part of the class and will become more actively involved in the learning process.

- **GET TO KNOW YOUR INSTRUCTORS.** Take a few minutes and stop to talk with your instructor before or after class or during office hours. Ask a question about the material or check on your progress in the course. If you talk with your instructors, you may feel more comfortable asking for help when you need it.

- **STAY UP TO DATE WITH YOUR WORK.** Many new college students have difficulty keeping up with all of the reading that's assigned in college classes. It's critical for you to do each assignment before you attend the next class. If you get behind in your reading, you may never have time to catch up. The workload in college just increases as the semester progresses.

- **BE RECEPTIVE TO CHANGE.** If the strategies that you used in high school aren't working, ask your instructor, tutor, or learning center staff for suggestions for different ways to learn. Even though the strategies that they suggest may not seem like they'll work, you must be willing to give them a chance. If you don't make changes in the way you take notes, read your texts, or prepare for exams, for example, you won't see changes in your performance.

- **WORK HARD THIS SEMESTER.** Forget about doing all of your assignments in the evening. If you're taking 15 credits this semester, you'll need a *minimum* of 30 hours (2 hours outside of class for every hour in class) to do your work. If you want high grades, if you work slowly, or if you're taking difficult courses, you'll need more time to do your work well.

- **DROP A CLASS WHEN NECESSARY.** Don't be afraid or ashamed to withdraw from a class when you know you aren't going to pass it. You don't earn credits for failed courses but they really pull down your grade point average. Check your college calendar to make sure you know the last day you can drop a class. Then check with your course instructor before making your decision.

Managing Your Time

- **KEEP A TIME LOG.** The first step in good time management is to evaluate how you use your time now. Write down how you spend your time every hour, every day for one week. Then go back and count how many hours you spent studying, attending class, eating, sleeping, commuting, getting ready for class, watching TV, surfing the net, chatting, reading and writing e-mail, socializing, and so on.

- **CREATE A FIXED COMMITMENT CALENDAR.** Write in all of your fixed commitments (things you do on a regular basis) on a 24-hour/weekly calendar. Then identify the time you have available for study. If you work and attend class full time, you may have very few empty blocks. If not, you should have plenty of time for study and social activities.

- **CALCULATE HOW MUCH TIME YOU NEED FOR STUDY.** You need a *minimum* of two hours outside of class for every hour you're in class (a 2-to-1 study ratio) to complete your work. However, if you want to earn high grades, have difficult classes, or work slowly, for example, you need to increase your study ratio to 3 to 1, 4 to 1 or even 5 to 1.

- **KEEP A STUDY LOG.** Take a few minutes each day to keep track of how much time you are spending on your work. Write down each class and how many hours (or parts of hours) you study. At the end of the week add up your totals for each class. Are you spending the appropriate amount of time on every course?

- **CREATE A SEMESTER ASSIGNMENT CALENDAR.** During the first week of classes, take some time and write all of your assignments, quizzes, and exams on a calendar so you can see what's due on any day and for at least two weeks in advance. Rather than consulting your course syllabi one at a time every day, having a semester view of what you have to do and when it's due will help you plan more effectively.

- **USE DAILY "TO DO" LISTS.** Make out a list of what you plan to do for tomorrow every evening. Break tasks down, set priorities, and separate academic and personal goals.

- **SCHEDULE YOUR STUDY TIME.** Plan to study in one-hour blocks (50 minutes for study and a 10-minute break). Schedule study time throughout the day so that you can complete at least two of your study tasks before dinner. Use time between classes to get a start on your next assignment.

- **SWITCH SUBJECTS.** If you have long study blocks (three or more hours), start with one task, such as reading 10 pages of Sociology, and then switch off after an hour or so to working on your English paper. After another hour (and break), switch to something else or back to more Sociology. Switching subjects increases your motivation and keeps you working longer.

Taking Lecture Notes

- **READ THE CHAPTER BEFORE THE LECTURE.** You'll get more out of attending class lectures if you read the chapter (or at least skim through it) before the lecture. You'll build background about the topics, get a sense of how the material is organized, and become familiar with important names and technical terms, which will help you better understand the lecture and take better notes.

- **REVIEW YOUR NOTES FROM THE LAST LECTURE.** As you're sitting in class waiting for your professor to begin, take a few minutes and review the last set of notes you took. Most course instructors pick up just where they left off at the end of the last class. Your review will help you get a better sense of how the new information is connected to what you already have in your notes.

- **SIT IN THE FRONT OF THE CLASSROOM.** There are many advantages to sitting in the front of the classroom. The obvious ones are that you'll see and hear better, but you'll also find that you tend to be more actively involved in the class when you sit near the front. You'll also find that you have many fewer distractions, so you'll be able to concentrate more on the lecture.

- **BE AN ACTIVE LISTENER.** Getting involved in the lecture is essential to understanding the material you're hearing. Pay attention and tell yourself you want to listen. Participate by asking and answering questions in class and taking notes.

- **TAKE NOTES.** If you're a new college student, you may think that sitting back and listening carefully to the lecture will help you learn the material. That may be true; however, you won't be able to get it into long-term memory by just listening. You must take notes so you'll have a record of the information from which to study.

- **WRITE DOWN MAIN POINTS AND DETAILS.** As you take notes, listen for the main points (topics) that your instructor is presenting and write them next to the margin. Then indent a little and write down as many details as you can. Until you learn more about how to take lecture notes, just write as much as you possibly can during each class.

- **EDIT YOUR NOTES AFTER THE LECTURE.** As soon as possible after the lecture, edit your notes. Think back to the lecture, use your textbook, or get together with a classmate or study group to fill in gaps, check for accuracy, clarify meaning, and improve the organization in your notes. Write questions about the important information in the margin of your notes.

- **REVIEW YOUR NOTES.** At the end of the week and before exams, you need to review your notes to put the information into long-term memory and to keep it accessible. Instead of reading over your notes, write or recite the information using the headings and questions in the margin as cues.

Reading Your Textbook

- **PREVIEW THE CHAPTER BEFORE YOU READ.** Read the title, introduction, and headings; glance at graphics; and read the summary. A two- to five-minute preview will increase your comprehension, build interest, and reduce the total time it takes to read the chapter.

- **DIVIDE THE CHAPTER INTO CHUNKS.** Break the chapter into 10- or 15-page chunks. Dividing the chapter into smaller reading segments increases your comprehension and improves your concentration and memory.

- **SPACE YOUR READING.** If you have a 40-page chapter to read for your Wednesday afternoon class, space your reading out over two or three days. Read one chunk on Monday after class, two chunks on Tuesday, and the last ten pages on Wednesday morning.

- **USE A READING/STUDY SYSTEM.** Use a reading/study system such as P2R, SQ3R, or S-RUN-R to read your text assignments. Each of these systems includes strategies to use before reading, during reading, and after reading.

- **MARK THE TEXT OR TAKE NOTES AS YOU READ.** Highlight or take notes at the end of each paragraph or headed section. Don't start marking until you've at least finished reading one sentence and work toward reading a whole paragraph before marking. Marking and note taking condense the material and help you identify the important information.

- **PREDICT QUESTIONS IN THE MARGIN.** At the end of each headed section go back and write questions about the important material that you highlighted or noted in the margin. Then underline the answers. Predicting and writing questions increases comprehension dramatically for most students.

- **PAUSE TO MONITOR YOUR COMPREHENSION.** Pause at the end of every headed section or page and think about what you just read. Recite or mumble the main points or concepts that were presented.

- **QUIZ YOURSELF TO TEST YOUR UNDERSTANDING AND MEMORY.** After you finish reading, go back and quiz yourself on the material. Recite the answers to the questions that you wrote or cover your marking or notes and using the heading as a cue, try to recite the details.

- **EVALUATE YOUR READING.** Check your understanding of the material by discussing it with a classmate, friend, or study group. If you can't talk about it, you didn't understand it. Test your marking and notes by comparing them with those of other classmates or by checking with your professor. Did you identify all of the important information? Were there questions on the test from your text that you missed in your marking or notes?

Preparing for Exams

- **GATHER INFORMATION ABOUT THE EXAM.** About a week before the exam, make sure you know what chapters and lectures the exam will cover. You'll also be able to prepare better if you know how many questions will be on the exam, what types of questions will be asked, and the point value of each part of the exam.

- **SPACE YOUR STUDY.** Space out your study using the Five-Day Study Plan. Cramming the night before the exam simply isn't very effective in storing information in long-term memory. Study for about two hours a day for four to six days depending on how much material is on your exam, for a total of about eight to ten hours (or more).

- **DIVIDE THE MATERIAL.** Divide the material you need to learn into chunks. For an exam covering four chapters, focus on one chapter (and accompanying lecture notes) each day and plan a final review on day five.

- **PLAN DAILY REVIEWS.** After studying a new chapter, go back and review the material that you created for the previous chapters. Daily repetition will help you learn the information, form more cues to remember it, and keep it fresh in memory.

- **MAKE WORD CARDS.** Although you are rarely required to write out definitions of the technical terminology, you do need to know them. Most exam questions involve technical terms in the questions and/or in the answers. Make out a set of word cards for each chapter with the term, name, event, theory, or even formula on one side of an index card and the definition or identification on the back and practice them until you know them.

- **PREDICT QUESTIONS.** You should also predict your own test questions. Write questions in the margin of your text and lecture notes or put them on index cards and practice them every day during your study plan. You may also find it useful to create your own self-tests using the same format as your actual exam (multiple choice, true/false, matching, or essay).

- **MAKE STUDY SHEETS.** Study sheets are one-page compilations of all of the important information about one topic. Pretend you are allowed to take one 8½-by-11" sheet of paper into the test with anything you want on it about one topic (of course you'll make four to seven per chapter). Study sheets help you build layers of cues to learn and recall the information.

- **SELF-TEST TO MONITOR YOUR LEARNING.** Don't just read over the material as you review it each day; test yourself by reciting from memory. Recite the answers to your word and question cards. Recite the information on your study sheets by looking only at the topic. Recite the information in your notes by covering the details and reciting using the headings as cues.

Taking Exams

- **READ DIRECTIONS CAREFULLY.** If you want to do well on exams in college, you must read the directions to every section of the exam carefully. Not all tests are the same and not all sections of the same test have the same directions.

- **REDUCE YOUR ANXIETY.** It's common to feel nervous before an exam, but some students become so anxious that it interferes with their test performance. Take a minute or two at the beginning of the exam to calm down. Take a deep breath, do a few relaxation exercises, and tell yourself you will do well because you're well prepared.

- **BUDGET YOUR TIME.** Preview the exam to see how many questions you have to answer, what types they are, and their respective point values. Then divide your time based on the point value of each section of the exam.

- **ANSWER THE EASIEST QUESTIONS FIRST.** Instead of wasting a lot of time trying to come up with answers that you simply don't know or can't figure out, answer the easiest questions (the ones you know immediately) first. Then go back and figure out the answers to the more difficult questions afterward.

- **ELIMINATE WRONG ANSWERS.** When taking multiple-choice exams, don't look for the right answer. Instead, try to eliminate all of the wrong answers. The only response left should be the correct one.

- **UNDERLINE KEY WORDS.** Underline keywords in the question that help you focus in on what the question is asking. You may also find it helpful to underline or circle the word or words that make a statement incorrect. Professors often make statements wrong by substituting an incorrect word or phrase for the correct one.

- **DO A MEMORY SEARCH.** When you don't know an answer immediately, don't give up. Do a memory search to try to find a cue to it in your long-term memory. Ask yourself what chapter it came from, what topic it involved, what study sheet it was on, and similar questions. You'll be surprised at how the information will suddenly pop into your head once you find the right cue.

- **GUESS STRATEGICALLY.** When you can't figure out an answer, don't just leave a blank or make a random guess. Instead, use strategic guessing. Look for patterns, put all true or all false for the ones you don't know, or count your responses in case your professor uses a balanced answer key. You won't get them all correct, but you can pick up a few points.

- **PLAN BEFORE ANSWERING ESSAY QUESTIONS.** Before you start writing out your essay answer, take a few minutes to plan in the margin. You'll be able to gather your thoughts and organize them. You'll be able to evaluate the quality of your answer before you even begin.

Strategies for Success

In the spaces below, list the strategies that you plan to use right now to get this semester off to a great start!

College Success:

_____

_____

_____

Managing Your Time:

_____

_____

_____

Taking Lecture Notes:

_____

_____

_____

Reading Your Text:

_____

_____

_____

Preparing for Exams:

_____

_____

_____

Taking Exams:

_____

_____

_____

"In the beginning of the semester, I was dead set against changing my ways. I thought my study methods were tried and true and would work in college the same as they did in high school. I was wrong. I was studying, taking notes, and writing papers the wrong way. Now that I've learned new study methods, I've changed my habits, and I am getting higher grades in college than I ever did in high school."

Carlos Becerra
Student

GETTING READY TO LEARN

In this chapter you will learn more about:

- Characteristics of successful students
- Using your learning style to enhance performance
- Getting motivated to learn
- Making the transition to learn
- Making the most of your college resources

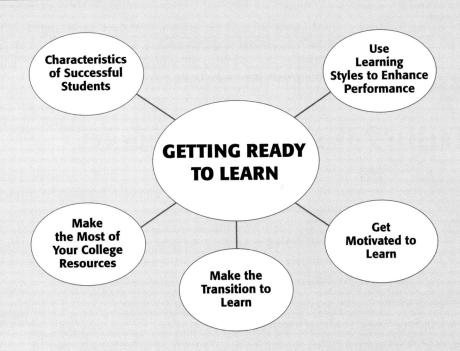

Activity 1-1

Where Are You Now?

Take a few minutes to answer *yes* or *no* to the following questions.

	YES	NO
1. Do you know how to increase your motivation?	____	____
2. Do you know where to go on your campus to get financial aid, a tutor, and information on clubs and organizations?	____	____
3. If you miss class, do you expect your professor to go over the material with you at a later date?	____	____
4. Do you know your preferred learning style?	____	____
5. Do you plan to take a lighter course load during your first semester in college?	____	____
6. Do you attend class regularly and stay up-to-date with your assignments?	____	____
7. Do you experience stress about getting your assignments done on time?	____	____
8. Do you make decisions without thinking about the outcome?	____	____
9. Have you really thought about why you are in college?	____	____
10. Do you expect college to be the same as high school?	____	____
Total Points	____	

Give yourself 1 point for each *yes* answer to all questions except 3, 7, 8, and 10 and 1 point for each *no* answer to questions 3, 7, 8, and 10. Now total up your points. A low score indicates that you need some help adjusting to college. A high score indicates that you already have realistic expectations.

CHARACTERISTICS OF SUCCESSFUL STUDENTS

What makes some students succeed in college and others fail? Faculty, administrators, and students have discussed that question for years. Although there is no exact formula for success, research indicates that there are some factors that do lead to success. Successful students are actively involved in their learning. In addition, successful students are more likely to plan, monitor, and evaluate their learning—they are strategic learners. Finally, successful students take responsibility for their own learning—they are independent learners.

Becoming an Active Learner

How do you typically prepare for a quiz or an exam? When I ask my students that question at the beginning of the semester, most say they read over the material. Is that what you said? You may be thinking that reading over the material worked well for your high-school exams. Unfortunately, you'll have to use more active study strategies for college exams, because they contain much more information and occur much less frequently. Many college exams cover two to three hundred pages of text and four weeks of lecture material. You can't learn all of that information just by reading over it a few times. Instead, you need to identify, organize, and condense the information. Next, you need to use active study strategies such as taking notes, predicting questions, making word and question cards, developing study sheets, participating in study groups, and self-testing to learn the material.

Active learners talk and listen, write, read, and reflect on (think about) what they are learning.[1] Talking about the information and listening to others discuss the information in a study group, for example, gets you actively involved in the learning process. In addition to reviewing the information, you are elaborating on it by putting it in your own words. You can also learn by reading actively. Active reading involves previewing, highlighting, predicting questions, and thinking critically about the material, all of which force you to interact with the printed word. These strategies help you activate your prior knowledge (what you already know about the topic), identify the key information, check your understanding of it, and form connections within the material. Writing summaries, taking notes, developing concept maps and study sheets, and writing out answers to predicted essay questions help you organize and synthesize (combine the parts into a whole) the information as you learn it. Reflecting on the information helps you gain a deeper understanding of the material and form connections between the new information and your prior knowledge. Getting actively involved in your learning is the first step toward succeeding in college. You'll learn many active learning strategies in the remainder of this text.

Activity 1-2

How Do You Compare to Successful Students? (Optional)

 If your instructor has ordered the College Success Factors Index with your textbook, you can go to www.success.wadsworth.com and see how you compare with other students in areas proven to be determinants of college success by completing the 80 self-scoring statements. Then read about each of the factors to see how you can be even more successful in college.

Becoming a Strategic Learner

Another way to be more successful in college is to become a strategic learner. According to Weinstein and Hume, **"Strategic learners** are students who view studying and learning as a systematic process that is, to a good degree, under their control."[2] Weinstein's model of strategic learning involves three main components: skill, will, and self-regulation.

---

[1]Chet Meyers and Thomas B. Jones, *Promoting Active Learning: Strategies for the College Classroom* (San Francisco: Jossey-Bass, 1993).

[2]Claire E. Weinstein and Laura M. Hume, *Study Strategies for Lifelong Learning* (Washington, DC: American Psychological Association, 1998).

Skill

Strategic learners possess a wide variety of skills to aid their learning. These **skills** include knowledge about yourself as a learner, knowledge about different types of academic tasks, knowledge about strategies for learning, prior content knowledge, and knowledge about the contexts in which that knowledge could be useful.[3] Let's look at the first three of these components briefly.

You already know many things about yourself as a learner. You know which subjects you excel in, which types of classes you like, and which types of assignments you do best. You know something about your ability as a student from your grades in high school or scores on standardized tests. However, you may not know much about your learning style—about how you learn best—and you probably aren't aware of many of the study and learning strategies that you'll need to use to be successful in college.

After completing twelve years of formal schooling, you have a great deal of knowledge about completing academic tasks. You know how to do math problems, write a paper, and read a chapter in a textbook, just to name a few. However, some of the tasks that you'll be asked to complete in college are different from anything you've done before; they will require you to complete new tasks, to complete some tasks differently, and, possibly, to apply new strategies for learning.

Although you've learned some study strategies in the past, you'll need to develop many new ones to succeed in college. Many of the tasks you will be asked to complete will be new to you. In addition to the increased amount of information you'll have to learn, you also will be expected to understand the material rather than just memorize it. To achieve these goals, you must learn new strategies and learn how to match them appropriately to the task.

Will

Just knowing how to prepare for an exam or take lecture notes, though, is not enough. A strategic learner must have the will to put that knowledge into practice. **Will** involves setting goals, selecting appropriate study strategies, and believing in your own ability and in the study strategies that you have chosen. In addition, strategic learners are motivated—they are willing to work hard to achieve their goals. In this chapter you'll learn more about getting motivated, and in Chapter 2 you'll learn how goal setting plays a key role in helping you become a strategic learner.

Every semester I have students in my classes who are very successful in college. Some of them excel because they are very bright and have a great deal of prior knowledge and use successful study strategies. Others, however, do not have the same skill level as the first group of students, but they still do very well in all of their classes. When I talk to them after class or in my office, it becomes very clear that they work much harder than some of their classmates. They are more motivated; spend more time on their work; have clear, well-defined study and career goals; and have a positive attitude toward school.

Have you ever met a student who didn't do well in college? Most people assume that the students who fail or quit are those who can't do the work or don't have enough ability to succeed. However, most studies indicate that it is just as often the brightest students (as defined by test scores or academic histories) who do not succeed. Why does this happen? Look around your own classroom. You probably will

---

[3]Claire E. Weinstein, Strategic Learning/Strategic Teaching: Flip Sides of a Coin, in Pintrich, Brown, and Weinstein, Eds., *Student Motivation, Cognition, and Learning: Essays in Honor of Wilbert J. McKeachie* (Hillsdale, NJ: Lawrence Erlbaum, 1994).

notice that some students are absent. Not attending class, not doing reading assignments, not preparing for exams and many other similar factors contribute to college failure. These activities depend on your willingness to do what is necessary to be successful in college. Will is an equally important factor in college success.

Self-Regulation

Finally, strategic learners are **self-regulated learners.** They manage their time well, monitor their learning, evaluate the results of their effort, and approach learning in a systematic way.[4] Self-regulated learners plan before starting a task, select strategies that they know are appropriate for the task, and monitor their own learning as they are completing the task and after the task is completed. Self-regulated learners know what they have to do to be successful. They set goals and design plans that help them complete their work on time. They also know a wide variety of study skills and strategies and choose the appropriate strategies for each task and testing situation. For example, self-regulated learners prepare differently for multiple-choice and essay exams. They use different strategies for completing a reading assignment that will be followed by a quiz and one for which they must only attend class and take notes.

Finally, self-regulated learners monitor their learning. They pause to check their understanding when reading, ask questions in class when they don't understand something, compare lecture notes with friends, and self-test before exams. Self-regulated learners also make adjustments when they find their strategies are not working.

Self-regulated learners are self-directed, not other-directed. They are what we often call **independent learners**—they take the initiative for their own learning. In high school, your parents and teachers often took the responsibility for your learning; they made sure that you completed your assignments, remembered to study for exams, and often felt responsible if you were not successful. Your teacher may have told you what to study, given you a review sheet to memorize, or reviewed all of the information the day before the test. College professors believe that you need to learn how to learn without your parents or your teachers telling you what to study, when to study, how to study, or even how long to study. You have to learn to do that on your own—you have to become an independent learner.

If you miss class, *you* are responsible for the material and the assignment. Don't expect your teaching assistant (TA) or professor to repeat the lecture for you privately at your convenience. Instead, you should ask another student for the notes. If you fail a quiz or exam, you need to see your professor to talk about your performance. Don't expect your professor to call you in for a conference. Instead, you need to take the initiative and schedule the appointment. Your professors expect you to take the responsibility for your education.

However, being an independent learner doesn't mean you have to do everything on your own. If you don't understand the material in your text or class lecture, see your TA or your professor for help. Go with specific questions, if possible. You can also request a tutor or see someone in your college learning center. With a little help, you can be a more successful student.

You'll have the opportunity to use many new learning strategies in many of the text activities, and, I hope, you will use them in your other course work. By using the strategies in your own work, monitoring their effectiveness, and making changes when necessary, you can become a strategic learner.

---

[4]Claire E. Weinstein and Laura M. Hume, *Study Strategies for Lifelong Learning* (Washington, DC: American Psychological Association, 1998).

Activity 1-3

Discuss Strategies for Success

Make a list of at least ten strategies that college students need to use to be successful. Then share your ideas with a group of your classmates. As a group, select the ten strategies or activities that are most representative of successful students. Think about how many of the strategies you currently use and select three that you plan to use this semester to increase your success.

USE LEARNING STYLES TO ENHANCE PERFORMANCE

Your learning style also affects your ability to succeed in college. Researchers in education and psychology have been investigating the issue of learning styles since the 1950s. In this section, you'll discover more about how you learn best, how to match learning strategies to specific tasks and subject areas, and how using your preferred and non-preferred learning style will affect your performance in college.

What Are Learning Styles?

The term **learning style** refers to the preferred way that you acquire, process, and retain information—the way you learn best. We learn new tasks in different ways; we each have our own style or preference for learning. The time of day you study, the kinds of strategies you use, whether you work alone or with a group, and even the place you study are all aspects of your learning style.

However, your learning style involves more than these factors. Researchers have explored the nature of learning styles in many different ways. Some relate learning style to cultural factors that affect the expectations that teachers, parents, and students have about learning in the classroom and at home. Others have investigated the relationship of learning styles to whether we are left-brained or right-brained learners (whether we tend to process information in a linear, analytical manner like a computer or in a more holistic, visual manner like a kaleidoscope).[5] Many learning styles are based on Kolb's theory that some people approach new situations through "feeling" and others through "thinking."

Activity 1-4

What's Your Learning Style?

Complete the Learning Style Inventory in Figure 1.1A (on page 8) or use the self-scoring inventory on the *College Study Skills* Web site (http://info.wadsworth.com/vanblerkom5). As you read each of the statements, check *yes* or *no* to indicate the response that describes you best. Then use the information in Figure 1.1B to determine your preferred learning style.

---

[5]Sharon L. Silverman and Martha E. Casazza, *Learning & Development: Making Connections to Enhance Teaching* (San Francisco: Jossey-Bass, 2000).

Characteristics of Learning Modalities

The Learning Style Inventory in Figure 1.1 is an informal inventory that can provide you with information about your preferred learning modality (learning through the senses). Are you a visual learner, an auditory learner, a kinesthetic learner, or do you have preferences in two areas. As you read through the following descriptions, you may find that you have some of the characteristics of each style. You probably do. We all have some strengths in each of the three learning modes. As you discovered by completing the inventory on page 8, however, one of the styles is your preferred style for learning new information.

Visual Learners

If you found that you're a **visual learner,** you learn best by seeing things. Reading; looking at pictures, diagrams, and charts; and watching films, videos, and demonstrations are all ways that you can learn new information. You probably have found that you understand your professor's lecture better if you read the text chapter ahead of time. Note-taking strategies such as outlining, mapping, and charting, which will be discussed in Chapter 9, work well for visual learners. Think about how you study for exams. You probably reread your text and lecture notes, rewrite your notes, take notes, and fill in study guides or make study sheets. During an exam, you may be able to "see" the correct answer in your mind's eye. Have you ever closed your eyes and pictured the information on the textbook page, the chalkboard, or your study sheets? Many new strategies for visual learners can be found in Figure 1.2 and in Chapters 4 and 10. Check them out now if your current study methods aren't paying off.

Auditory Learners

If you're an **auditory learner,** you learn best by hearing information. Unlike the visual learner, you probably prefer to go to your class and listen to the lecture before you read the text chapter. Do you understand the text much more easily after you hear the professor's lecture? Reading difficult text passages out loud is also a good idea for the auditory learner. Discussing the course material, mumbling information as you read and study, asking and answering questions out loud, and listening to study notes on tape are some strategies that you may already use if your preferred learning style is auditory. You may find that you can actually "hear" the professor's lecture when you try to recall the specific point you need to answer a test question. Many new test-preparation and memory strategies that are designed for auditory learners are included in Figure 1.2 and Chapters 4 and 10.

Kinesthetic Learners

If you're a **kinesthetic learner,** you learn best by doing things. You prefer hands-on tasks that allow you to touch and feel. Try some of the strategies listed in Figure 1.2 now. Many of the strategies used by visual and auditory learners also appeal to kinesthetic learners. For example, in Chapter 9 you'll learn a strategy called **mapping**— creating visual diagrams or representations of written and oral information. Whereas the visual learner can recall the information from a concept map by seeing it, the kinesthetic learner will be able to remember it by the feel of how he or she created it. Kinesthetic learners also learn well from doing experiments, taking self-tests, or replicating the tasks they will later have to perform in the testing situation. Many auditory learners use flash cards to recite definitions or information about a topic. The kinesthetic learner also learns well from making up the flash cards as well as from the action of self-testing. In Chapter 10, you'll learn how to create study sheets, make up self-tests, construct models, and work problems in order to prepare for upcoming exams.

FIGURE 1.1A
Learning Style Inventory

As you read each of the following statements, put a check mark for *yes* or *no* to indicate the response that describes you best.

	YES	NO
1. I remember things better if someone tells me about them than if I read about them.	_____	_____
2. I'd rather read about "tapping" (extracting the sap from) trees than take a field trip and actually tap a tree.	_____	_____
3. I enjoy watching the news on television more than reading the newspaper.	_____	_____
4. I'd rather build a model of a volcano than read an article about famous volcanoes.	_____	_____
5. When I'm having trouble understanding my text chapter, I find that reading it out loud helps improve my comprehension.	_____	_____
6. If I had to identify specific locations on a map for an exam, I would rather practice by drawing and labeling a map than reciting the locations out loud.	_____	_____
7. I tend to better understand my professor's lecture when I read the text material ahead of time.	_____	_____
8. I would rather take part in a demonstration of how to use a new computer program than read a set of directions on its use.	_____	_____
9. If someone asked me to make a model for a class project, I would rather have someone explain how to make it than rely on written directions.	_____	_____
10. If I were preparing for an exam, I'd rather listen to a summary of the chapter than write my own summary.	_____	_____
11. I would prefer my professor to give me written directions rather than oral directions when I have to do a writing assignment.	_____	_____
12. I'd rather listen to the professor's lecture before I read the chapter.	_____	_____
13. If I had to learn to use a new software program, I'd prefer to read the written directions rather than have a friend describe how to use it.	_____	_____
14. If I have trouble understanding how to complete a writing assignment, I prefer to have written directions than have someone explain how to do it.	_____	_____
15. I like to listen to books on tape more than I like to read books.	_____	_____
16. When I have to learn spelling or vocabulary lists, I prefer to practice by reciting out loud rather than writing the words over and over again.	_____	_____
17. If I had a choice, I would prefer to watch a video of someone else doing chemistry experiments than actually perform them myself.	_____	_____
18. When I have trouble with a math problem, I prefer to work through the sample problems rather than have someone tell me how to do them.	_____	_____

Note: A self-scoring version of this inventory is available on the *College Study Skills* Web site.

FIGURE 1.1B
Scoring Instructions

Your responses in both the *yes* and *no* columns are important in determining your preferred learning style. Tally your responses using the following scoring key and then use the chart to total your responses.

1. Circle your *yes* and *no* responses as they appear in the boxes below. Not all numbers will be circled.

Auditory				Visual			Kinesthetic			
Yes:				Yes:			Yes:			
1	3	5	9	2	7	11	4	6	8	18
10	12	15	16	13	14	17				
No:				No:			No:			
6	7	11	13	1	3	4	5	2	10	16	17
14	18			8	9	12	15				

2. Then total your circled *yes* and *no* answers in the chart below.

	A (Auditory)	V (Visual)	K (Kinesthetic)
Number of *yes* responses			
Number of *no* responses			
Total points			
Cutoff score	8	8	5

3. Total your scores for each column.

4. Compare your total with the cutoff score.

5. If your score is equal to or higher than the cutoff score, then you show a preference for that style of learning. The higher your score is, the stronger your preference for that style of learning. You may find that you have high scores in two areas; that's okay. You may learn well using more than one learning style. Note: Your total points for the A, V, and K columns should add up to 18.

Integrated Learning Styles

Although each of us has a preferred learning style, most of us learn information by using a combination of learning styles. In fact, some courses, assignments, or exams may require you to use one or more of your less preferred learning styles in order to complete the task. When you are forced to complete a hands-on activity, for example, you may find that using a kinesthetic approach is more successful. Even though it's not your best way to learn *most* material, it is the best way to learn *that* material. Although my preferred learning style is visual, I always call the computer help desk when I run into a problem with a computer program. The advantage for me is that the technical support personnel tell me how to fix my problem, and they stay on the line and assist me as I complete each of the steps on the computer. By using my two less preferred learning styles together, I learn better than by using my preferred style. Of course, using a computer program is a hands-on task, so actually completing the task on the computer is the best way to learn to do it. Even a student who is a visual learner will perform better on a rock-identification exam by going to the rock lab and iden-

FIGURE 1.2

Active Learning Strategies for
Visual, Auditory, and Kinesthetic
Learners

Visual	Auditory	Kinesthetic
Read and highlight your text.	Read difficult passages out loud.	Take notes as you read your text assignments.
Visualize pictures, charts, and diagrams.	Recite the main points at the end of every headed section of the text.	Predict questions in the margin at the end of each headed section.
Outline information.	Explain information out loud.	Create word, question, and problem cards and practice them in groups of 10 or 15.
Map information.		
Create charts and study sheets.	Discuss the text assignment or lecture material with a study partner or study group.	Make up puzzles or games (like Jeopardy or the Match game) to learn text and lecture material.
Read related material.		
Rewrite your lecture notes.	Tape the lectures from your most difficult class and play them again when you commute or do household chores.	Practice labeling diagrams, recreating maps, and filling in charts to learn information for exams.
Color code your notes and study sheets.		
Write out steps in a process for solving math and science problems.	Cover the details in your lecture notes and recite from the headings.	Construct diagrams, models, and problem cards to practice math and science material.
Create study sheets.	Recite out loud the answers to questions in the margin or word and question cards.	Make up self-tests in the same format as the actual test and take them.
Write word and question cards.		
Write questions in the margin and underline the answers.	Teach the material to someone or something else.	Participate in study groups and review sessions.
		Work problems.
Create visual images to connect information to acronyms and acrostics.	Create a taped self-test and recite the answers before listening to the correct ones.	Take end-of-chapter and online tests to prepare for exams.
Use the method of loci to recall information.	Explain the steps for solving math and science problems.	Develop acronyms and acrostics to recall information and practice using them.
	Create rhymes, poems, and songs to recall information.	

tifying the rocks for practice. This kinesthetic activity is much more effective than simply looking at the pictures of the rocks and reading about their characteristics. As an auditory learner, you may prefer to recite material to learn it; however, you probably will also benefit from writing recall questions in the margin of your note page (see Chapter 5 or Chapter 9) so that you can do that oral review. By using visual and kinesthetic strategies, you can make the best use of your auditory learning style.

Using a combination of auditory, visual, and kinesthetic strategies will help you benefit from all the ways that you can learn information. As you learn about note-taking, text-reading, and test-preparation strategies in later chapters, keep your preferred learning style in mind. However, the most successful students are often the ones who can use strategies that take advantage of all of the ways they learn or those who can switch styles depending on the demands of the course or the assignment.

Activity 1-5

Find Out More About How You Learn Best

Rank the four responses to each item according to the following scale in order to determine more about how you learn best: 4 = best, 3 = good, 2 = fair, 1 = poor.

1. I learn best when I study

   _____ in the morning.
   _____ in the afternoon.
   _____ in the evening.
   _____ late at night.

2. I learn best when I study

   _____ in complete quiet.
   _____ with soft background noise.
   _____ with moderate levels of noise.
   _____ in a noisy environment.

3. I learn best when I study

   _____ by myself.
   _____ with my regular study partner.
   _____ with a small group.
   _____ in a large-group review session or recitation class.

4. When I take exams, I generally

   _____ just guess to get done.
   _____ pick the first answer that looks right.
   _____ read all the possible answers before I choose one.
   _____ eliminate incorrect responses before I select the correct answer.

Other Characteristics of Learning Styles

The inventory in Activity 1-5 should help you find out more about how you learn best. One of the interesting outcomes of completing this activity is that many students find that they aren't always aware of some of the characteristics of their own learning style. In fact, you may want to experiment with some of these issues in order to test your responses further. For example, you may have indicated that you learn best when you study in the morning, but in fact you actually do most of your work in the late evening. This may be a habit you established in high school or for some other reason. However, now that you know that you learn best in the morning, you should change your time schedule to work earlier in the day. When and where you work are often dependent on each other, so look at your rankings to items 1 and 2. If you find that you often do your assignments late at night, it may be because that's the only time you can find a quiet place to study.

Your response to question 3 may explain why you work best when you're asked to do group projects, or why, for you, they're often something you dread. Many students study best when they work by themselves, whereas others find that everything falls into place when they work in groups. Although question 4 appears to focus on how you should take a test, it really assesses how impulsive (acting without thinking) or reflective (thinking before acting) you are in learning situations. If you tend to be impulsive, you may have more difficulty completing certain types of academic tasks—especially problem-solving tasks. Students who are more reflective tend to think through things more slowly and carefully. Reflective learning styles are generally more suited to academic learning and success. If you tend to be an impulsive learner, you can learn to be more reflective by using many of the learning strategies that will be presented in the remainder of the text.

Activity 1-6

What Type of Learner Are You?

 Find out more about what kind of learner you are by taking the quiz at the Personality Type Web site (www.personalitytype.com). This interactive quiz, based on the MBTI, is short, easy, and self-scoring. After identifying your type, be sure to take some time to explore the information available on the Web site.

A Word of Caution

The results of the learning style inventories that you completed in Activities 1-4 and 1-5 may not be accurate. These are informal surveys that have not been scientifically tested. In addition, these (and all) learning-style inventories are self-report questionnaires. That means that you determine your own score. Your mood, the way you interpret the statements, and how you feel at the time you do the activity all affect your score. You may want to do the inventories again, perhaps later in the semester or even next semester, to verify your results.

As you take different types of courses, experience different instructional modes, and complete different kinds of projects, tests, and assignments, you'll be forced to use many auditory, visual, and kinesthetic study strategies. Using your less preferred styles over and over again strengthens those styles. Once you know they do work, at least in certain situations, you'll tend to use them more often and feel more comfortable when working in those styles, too. When faced with a new learning task, try working within your preferred learning style first, but if that doesn't work, don't give up. Instead, try using one of your less preferred learning styles. Through experimentation you'll find the right learning style and the most effective learning strategies for each of your courses and academic tasks.

If you are intrigued by some of the ways of looking at learning styles that were discussed earlier, go to your college learning center, counseling center, or testing center and ask to take a formal learning style inventory. Some of the more common ones (which are much too long and complex to include here) are the LSI (Kolb's Learning Style Inventory); the 4MAT System developed by Bernice McCarthy; the Learning Style Inventory by Dunn, Dunn, and Price; and the MBTI (the Myers-Briggs Type Indicator).

Why Your Learning Style Is Important

Staci, a former student, shared her frustrations about one of her courses. She said, "No matter what I do, it just doesn't work." What she meant was that no matter how much she studied, she continued to fail her exams. Have you ever felt that way? Soon after Staci began working with a tutor, her grades improved. Two things occurred that made a difference for her. First, her tutor was able to explain the material in a manner that better matched her learning style; the tutor modified his style of instruction to match her style of learning. Second, Staci changed her study strategies to better match the instructor's teaching and testing style.

Do you tend to do well in some classes but have difficulty in others? For instance, let's say you are taking History and Biology this semester. Given the same level of effort and time spent in preparation, you may think that you should do equally well in both courses. However, if you earned an A in History but got only a C in Biology, you probably would feel frustrated and confused. Even though college biology probably is harder than high school biology, that may not be the reason for your poor performance. You may have more difficulty in college biology because the instructor's teaching style did not match your learning style or because you didn't use the appropriate strategies when preparing the biology assignments. The chart in Figure 1.2 includes a variety of active learning strategies. Check the index to find more information on how to use these strategies. Pick one or two from your preferred learning style to start using right now.

Activity 1-7

Evaluate Your Instructors' Teaching Styles

Use the chart to evaluate three of your instructors' teaching styles. Check the appropriate space if your instructor uses any of these activities. Then count the check marks for visual, auditory, and kinesthetic activities to determine your professors' preferred teaching styles. Do your professors' teaching styles match your learning style?

Instructional Mode	Instructor's Name:	Instructor's Name:	Instructor's Name:
1. Lectures			
2. Writes on board			
3. Uses transparencies			
4. Shows videos			
5. Uses handouts			
6. Includes discussions			
7. Does experiments			
8. Does demonstrations			
9. Gives directions orally			
10. Gives directions in writing			
11. Uses group activities			
Instructor's preferred teaching style			
Your preferred learning style			

Many professors teach the way that they learn best; they use their preferred learning style. Professors who are auditory learners typically lecture and involve students in class discussions. Visual learners present material primarily through handouts, videos, and transparencies and by writing key information on the chalkboard. Kinesthetic learners often teach through demonstrations, class activities, experiments, and other hands-on methods. If you learn best through the method that your professor uses, you probably feel very comfortable, in control, or "in your element" in that particular course. If, on the other hand, your learning style doesn't match your professor's teaching style, you may feel uncomfortable in class, have difficulty completing assignments, and perform poorly on exams. This mismatch can lead to frustration and even failure.

Understanding how you learn best can also improve your concentration. When you're working in your preferred learning mode, you probably find that you are better able to concentrate on your study tasks. Approaching a task from your preferred style results in a better fit or match—studying feels right. When things are "going well" during a study session, you'll probably complete your work efficiently and effectively. Working outside of their preferred style or using a learning style that does not fit the task may be the reason you put in a lot of time on your studies but don't get the results you expect.

GET MOTIVATED TO LEARN

Psychologists have been trying to explain why some people work hard at a task while others choose not to do so. Think of a task that you recently completed. Did you put all your energy into completing it? Did you understand what you were trying to accomplish? Did you continue working on the task even though it was difficult? How you answered each of these questions may give you a better understanding of how motivation affects college success. Motivation affects whether or not you do your work, which study strategies you decide to use, when you do your work, how long you work on a task, how well you concentrate on it, how much effort you expend doing it, and what you learn from completing the task. **Motivation** can be described as something that energizes, directs, and sustains behavior toward a particular goal. Understanding more about the factors that influence motivation and the strategies that can be used to increase it can help you be more successful in college.

Activity 1-8

How Motivated Are You?

List three academic tasks that you worked on recently. On a scale of 1 to 10 (with 1 being the least effort you ever put into a task and 10 being the most effort you ever put into a task) how would you rate the amount of effort you put into each task?

Write a paragraph or two describing each of the tasks you rated and why you had trouble getting motivated or staying motivated when completing one or two of your academic tasks earlier this week. What strategies did you use to try to complete your work? Which strategies presented in this chapter may have been even more effective? Why?

Factors That Influence Motivation

Although many factors influence motivation, your goals, your self-efficacy, and your level of effort are perhaps the most important ones for college success. (See Figure 1.3).

Goals

Your goals influence your motivation to complete a task. Without challenging, realistic goals, you may not know where to direct your efforts. You may have noticed that your motivation (or lack of motivation) varies depending on the tasks that you need to complete. Many students find that they are more motivated to work on a task when they have a personal interest in completing it or find it challenging to do so. If you are personally interested in learning how to use a computer program, for example, you may be highly motivated to achieve your goal. Working on a task because you want to learn or do something (even when you don't have to) can be described as **intrinsic motivation.**

On the other hand, you may also be motivated by the promise or expectation of earning rewards, grades, or other types of external gain. Being motivated by external factors can be described as **extrinsic motivation.** If you were told to learn to use a computer program as part of a course assignment but have little personal interest in using it, you may find that you are less motivated. Many times, our efforts are motivated by a combination of intrinsic and extrinsic motivation. You may begin to read a textbook chapter, for example, because you're concerned about your grade in the course (extrinsic motivation). However, as you're reading, you may find that you become interested in the material itself and want to learn more about the topic (intrinsic motivation). Your increased interest in the material may actually increase your motivation to complete the task, perhaps with even more effort.

Self-Efficacy

Your belief in your own ability to successfully complete a task can also affect your level of motivation. If you believe that you can successfully complete a task, you are more likely to be motivated to work on it. This belief in your ability to successfully complete a task is often described as **self-efficacy.** Each time that you are successful in accomplishing one of your goals (completing a task), it increases your self-efficacy (self-confidence) so that you can complete a similar or even more difficult task in the future. Students who have high self-efficacy are also more likely to per-

FIGURE 1.3
Factors That Influence
Motivation

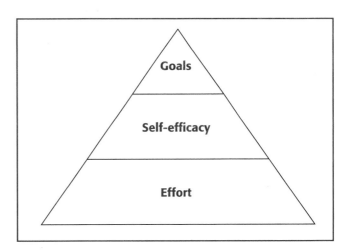

sist on a task when it is difficult. For these reasons, many psychologists believe that past successes lead to future successes.

Effort

Your motivation is also affected by the strength of your belief that the amount of effort you put forth on a task can affect your performance. If you attribute your successes and your failures to your level of effort, you are more likely to be motivated to work hard to complete a task. The amount of effort that you exert when working on a task is something that you can control. Unlike luck, which is out of our control, we can exert a lot of effort, very little effort, or no effort in completing a task. Many study skills experts believe that students need to work hard at the beginning of the semester so that they can see that the amount of effort they put toward their academic tasks does have a positive effect on their performance. Early success (knowing you can learn the material and achieve your grade goals) is very motivating for new college students. This early success can therefore lead to even more success. You may find the following formula will help you put all of this together: $M \rightarrow \uparrow E \rightarrow S$ (Motivation leads to increased effort, which leads to success).

Strategies to Increase Motivation

There are hundreds of strategies that students can use to increase motivation. Just go to a bookstore and check out the reference or self-help shelf. Books on how to get motivated or increase your motivation at home, at school, and at work are plentiful. Many of the chapters in this text in fact contain strategies that will help you increase your motivation. A number of basic strategies can help you get more motivated now.

- **Set challenging but realistic goals.** We are more motivated to complete tasks when we feel that they are challenging and yet attainable, within our reach. You may also find that thinking of each task as a step toward achieving your long-term personal or career goals can also help keep you motivated.

- **Set learning goals.** Decide what facts, concepts, or ideas you want to learn before you begin working on a task. Setting learning goals can help motivate you to put more effort into the task.

- **See the value in the task.** Understanding why you are doing the task—seeing the importance of the task—can help motivate you to complete it. You may also find that you have a personal interest or find enjoyment in completing the task.

- **Have a positive attitude.** As you begin a task, think about similar tasks that you completed in the past. Knowing that you've done it before can increase your motivation. Reminding yourself that you are good at math can help motivate you to study for your upcoming math exam.

- **Use positive self-talk.** When working on a long or difficult task, you may find that telling yourself that you can do it, why it's important, or that you are almost done with the task can keep you going.

- **Work hard.** One of the most important steps in getting motivated is to work hard, exert effort, on a task. Not working on a task or exerting very little effort often results in failure to complete the task successfully. This can lead to reduced motivation the next time you need to complete a similar task if you attribute your failure to some external factor.

- **Use active-study strategies.** Using strategies that work can also help you successfully complete a task. Knowing which strategy to use for a specific task and that it will work can help you be more motivated to work hard as you complete your academic tasks. You may find that you like the strategy (taking notes or predicting questions) more than the material. Using a strategy you like can increase your motivation.

- **Break down tasks.** Some students have trouble getting motivated to start a task that appears to be long and difficult. By breaking down the task into parts (and working on them one at a time), you can increase your motivation. Checking off or crossing off each part of the task as it is completed can give you a sense of accomplishment, which motivates you even more.

- **Monitor your learning.** Answering your own self-test questions, taking end-of-chapter tests, or reciting from memory are just a few ways of monitoring your learning. When you know your time, effort, and study strategies are working to help you learn, you'll be more motivated to continue working. On the other hand, you may find that you get motivated when you find out that you don't know the information for a test, for example. In both cases, finding out whether or not you are learning is the key to staying motivated.

- **Learn from your mistakes.** Learning why you were unable to successfully complete a task or achieve your goals can also help increase your motivation. Knowing what you need to do differently can help you be more motivated to work hard after a "failure."

Getting Your Money's Worth

A college education is your key to the future, but it is also one of the most expensive investments you or your parents will ever make. A college education can cost anywhere from $20,000 to $100,000. If you break down your tuition costs, you may find that you're paying several hundred to several thousand dollars for each course you take. Divide that number by the number of class sessions that you have in each course. You may be astounded by the actual cost of each of your classes. What's the point of all of this math? Well, it's to help you realize that every time you miss a class, you're wasting money. Some students are excited when a professor cancels a class or doesn't show up. But students who are paying the bill or attending college on loans—which they'll have to repay—often feel angry because they believe that they are not getting their money's worth. In the same way, each time you cut a class, sleep through one, or show up unprepared, you aren't getting your money's worth, either. You can get your money's worth and maximize your success by going to class and staying up-to-date with your assignments.

Work Hard to Get Your Money's Worth

Working hard will also help you get your money's worth. In high school, many students did just enough to get by. Did you "cruise" through high school? Did you spend only one hour a day doing homework assignments or studying for tests? If you answered yes to either of these questions, you'll have to change your study patterns in college. To get your money's worth, you need to put school first; you need to spend twenty-five to thirty-five hours or more each week if you're a full-time student reading, doing assignments, and preparing for exams.

Activity 1-9

Are You Getting Your Money's Worth in Class?

Are you getting your money's worth out of every class? Answer the following questions to find out.

	Yes	No
Do you ever cut class?	_____	_____
Do you plan to this semester?	_____	_____
Have you ever fallen asleep in class?	_____	_____
Have you ever daydreamed in class?	_____	_____
Have you ever done an assignment during a class?	_____	_____
Have you ever spent time looking out the window?	_____	_____
Have you ever thought about other plans during class?	_____	_____
Do you find classes to be boring and a waste of time?	_____	_____
Do you just skim the chapter before class?	_____	_____
Do you think you can remember the lecture without taking notes?	_____	_____

Add up all of your *no* answers. If you have a high score, you're most likely getting your money's worth out of every class. If you have a low score, you need to get more actively involved during class to get your money's worth in college.

Increase Your Level of Interaction

You're probably wondering how you could possibly spend so much time studying. Think about how you completed your last reading assignment. Did you just skim it? If so, you probably exerted very little effort and put very little time into the task. Unfortunately, you probably didn't get much out of the chapter, either. During the first week of the semester, I try to get my students to increase their level of interaction with their reading assignments. I developed a hierarchy of tasks that shows increasing levels of involvement with the material. Take a look at Figure 1.4 and put a check mark at your level of involvement.

Some of you may find that your check mark is near the bottom of the staircase, and I'm sure that some of you are working somewhere in the middle. I hope one or two of you are working very hard and your check mark is near the top of the staircase. You probably can't jump from the bottom of the staircase to the top overnight—you may not have a good knowledge of all the skills involved. However, as you move through the text and acquire many of the skills that were listed, I hope you will increase your level of involvement as you complete your assignments. As

FIGURE 1.4

Levels of Interaction When Reading a Text Assignment

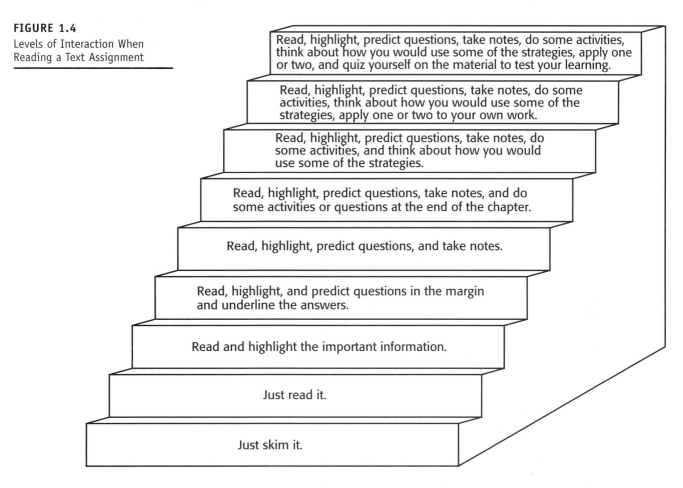

Read, highlight, predict questions, take notes, do some activities, think about how you would use some of the strategies, apply one or two, and quiz yourself on the material to test your learning.

Read, highlight, predict questions, take notes, do some activities, think about how you would use some of the strategies, apply one or two to your own work.

Read, highlight, predict questions, take notes, do some activities, and think about how you would use some of the strategies.

Read, highlight, predict questions, take notes, and do some activities or questions at the end of the chapter.

Read, highlight, predict questions, and take notes.

Read, highlight, and predict questions in the margin and underline the answers.

Read and highlight the important information.

Just read it.

Just skim it.

you can see, increasing your level of involvement is not just about putting in more time and more effort. It's also about using the right strategies for the task. The formula below should help you be more successful in college.

$$T + E + \text{the right strategies} = \text{success}$$

You may find that you're willing to work harder in some classes and put less effort into others. Ideally, you should make the greatest effort in all of your classes, but your prior knowledge, your time constraints, and your goals all are factors that will determine your effort. Remember, the more actively involved you are with the task, the more you'll learn. If you work hard, you'll get your money's worth and a good education, too.

Why Are You in College?

As you're getting ready to learn, maintain a positive attitude toward your progress. Think about why you're in college and what you plan to accomplish during your college career. Take some time to visit the career services office on your campus and explore the job opportunities available in your major field of study. Talk to other students and to your professors about the options available to you. Having a clear set of goals can be very motivating and can help you over some of the hurdles that you will have to face. If you haven't chosen a major yet, that's okay, too. Use your first year or two of college to explore various courses and majors. Make an appointment to discuss your interests with your advisor, the department chairperson, or with someone in the counseling or career services office. Colleges offer courses of study that you never even heard of in high school—one of them may be the right one for you. You may even think about changing your major. Most college students do change their major at least once; many change their major several times. The important thing to remember is that career goals help motivate you to set and achieve your academic goals, which help motivate you to set and achieve your study goals. Why are you in college? Think about it.

Activity 1-10

Describe Why You Are in College

Using your own paper, write an essay describing the reasons you chose to attend college. Did anyone or anything influence your decision?

MAKE THE TRANSITION TO LEARN

Attending college requires a certain amount of adjustment for most students. If you started college immediately after high school graduation, you'll experience many changes in your life. You may be on your own for the first time—you may have to take on many of the responsibilities that your parents or teachers previously handled. If you're a commuter or a nontraditional college student, you'll have to make adjustments, too. Although juggling work, school, and home responsibilities is a challenging task, many students do it every day. College life offers many exciting new experiences, and many new freshmen want to join in on the activities.

Attending college can be very stressful, however. Learning to manage stress and to use good decision-making and problem-solving strategies can help make the transition to college an easy one. New students have to make academic transitions, too. College courses are much more difficult than high school classes. Many resources are available on your college campus to help you deal with both your social and your academic problems. Getting motivated to work hard and learn is critical to your college success. Thinking about why you are in college can motivate you to succeed.

Balancing School, Home, and Work Responsibilities

The U.S. Department of Education has predicted that by 2013, 38.8 percent of all students enrolled in institutions of higher education will be twenty-five years of age or older.[6] If you work and have home responsibilities, you may need to attend on a part-time basis.

Returning adult learners are often described as more motivated, more committed, more organized, more independent, and more self-directed than traditional students. Many of these qualities come from their greater maturity, wealth of life experiences, and strong motivation to succeed in college.

Even so, many returning students have problems adjusting to college. They worry about feeling out of place, competing with traditional students, getting good grades, disappointing their families, finding time to get their schoolwork done, and

---

[6]National Center for Education Statistics, "Projections of Education Statistics to 2013" (October 2003 report).

maintaining their job and home responsibilities. Fortunately, you probably won't have to deal with all of these concerns, but most returning students do have to make adjustments in order to overcome some of these problems.

If you've been out of school for five, ten, or twenty years, you may need to take one or two refresher courses to brush up or upgrade your skills. Most colleges offer programs or specific courses on math, writing, study skills, and computer skills that help bridge the gap for nontraditional students. Enrolling in one or two of these courses when you first return to college can also help you feel more confident about yourself as a student and make the transition to college a little smoother. Taking a reduced course load the first semester or two is an excellent way to ease into the academic and the personal adjustments that you will have to make.

Activity 1-11

Consider the Advantages of Being a Nontraditional Student

Make a list of the advantages and disadvantages of being a nontraditional college student. Select three advantages that you listed and describe how they will help you succeed in college. Select three disadvantages that you listed and describe the reasons that they may interfere with your success. Consider ways that you could overcome these disadvantages and list several possible suggestions for each one. Write a paragraph or two describing what you found.

Accepting New Responsibilities

If you just graduated from high school, you may have spent the summer before college learning how to sort, wash, and iron your clothing. Did you practice scheduling your time, budgeting your money, or setting priorities? These new responsibilities are critical to college success. It's important to set up a schedule for the week so that you can accomplish all of your goals. Chapters 2 and 3 will help you establish realistic goals and learn how to manage your time.

Learning to set priorities is one of the most difficult tasks you will face. Everything seems so interesting, exciting, and new when you begin college. College life offers many opportunities to get involved in social, organizational, and sporting events. All these activities are appealing and interesting to new college students, and all of them take time—some a great deal of time. Although you should get involved in campus life, you need to start out slowly. Join one or two clubs instead of every club that your roommate or next-door neighbor joins. If you become too involved in campus activities, you won't have enough time to complete your academic tasks.

Improving Your Academic Standing

If this is your second or third semester in college, you may be reading this text because you want to improve your academic standing. Many of the strategies presented in this chapter and in the remainder of this text can help you improve your grade point average (GPA). One of the best strategies for getting off probation or achieving your GPA goal is to repeat courses in which you had low grades. If your college allows you to replace a D or F with the grade you get when you repeat a course, you'll see a significant change in your GPA. Another important strategy for improving your GPA is to take a light course load and get good grades in all of your courses. One advantage of a lighter load is that you can put more time and effort into each of the classes. If you work or have other responsibilities, your time for study will be limited. If you take a heavy course load, you may find that you just don't have enough time to do all of your work to the best of your ability. This will lead to getting low grades in some classes, which will continue to drag your GPA down. As you begin this new semester, think about where you want to be and not where you were last semester. If you work hard and use effective strategies, you can achieve your goals.

Avoiding Plagiarism

Many students unintentionally are guilty of plagiarism when they write reports and research papers. **Plagiarism** is a difficult concept, but can be described as taking someone else's ideas or words and using them as if they were your own. The easiest way to avoid plagiarizing is to carefully document all of the information that you take from reference sources. Many students think that as long as they put the information into their own words, they don't have to cite (indicate the source of) the information. In most cases, even paraphrased information must be documented. The only time you really don't have to document reference material is in the case of common knowledge. Information that is included in every source or many sources that you referenced may be considered to be common knowledge. On the other hand, information that is contained in only one of your sources is considered to be the unique idea(s) of the author of that book or article. This information must be documented in order to give credit to the person who developed it.

You can cite a source by including the publication information of the article or book or other work in a footnote, endnote, or reference list. Since many different citation styles are used in college, you should check with your professor to find out which format he or she expects you to use and then use your style manual or handbook to verify the proper form for each reference work you are citing.

Managing Stress

Attending college can be stressful for many students because they are forced to deal with so many new responsibilities, opportunities, challenges, and decisions. **Stress** can be described as feeling tense, overwhelmed, or under pressure. Identifying the causes of stress and learning some strategies for coping with it can help students manage the stress in their lives.

Sources of Stress

Many college students experience stress because they're concerned about their academic performance. Most new college students experience stress when they realize that their courses are much more demanding and fast paced than were their high school classes. Some students experience a great deal of stress about achieving the grade goals that they have set for themselves or that their families may expect them to achieve.

Lifestyle changes are another common source of stress for college students. Balancing work, home, and school responsibilities puts additional stress on students. Some students find that after they complete all of their class assignments, there is little time left for their families or themselves. At times, this leads to conflicts and may result in even more stress. Other students experience stress from living on their own. Besides being responsible for managing their time and setting priorities (perhaps for the first time), they are trying to form new relationships while maintaining connections with their families and friends at home.

Many college students also experience stress due to personal problems. Many students spend a lot of time worrying about money, social relationships, family crises, or health problems, just to name a few concerns. All these personal problems add to the stress of academic and lifestyle changes that most students experience.

Methods of Coping with Stress

Although there are many positive ways to deal with stress, some college students use negative, nonproductive methods of dealing with it, such as ignoring the problem or pretending that it doesn't even exist. Others use escapist techniques like watching television, playing video games, or even use drugs or alcohol. Although these strategies appear to eliminate feelings of stress for the moment, they don't bring about any productive resolution of the problem. There are, however, more positive and productive ways to cope with stress.

Take Action. One of the best ways to deal with stress is to take action to eliminate or reduce the stress itself. This may involve taking control of how you use your time. Making up a daily "To Do" list can reduce stress if you are worried about getting all of your work done on time. You may also find that making out a list of important due dates will help you organize your time and relieve anxiety. Chapter 3 contains many other effective strategies for better time management. If you are stressed out about money problems, go to your campus financial aid office. Getting more information about how you can apply for scholarships, grants, and loans can help you reduce your stress. When students experience conflicts about family, work, and school responsibilities, it may be time to make a few changes. Delegating some of your responsibilities (at home or at work) may reduce your stress dramatically.

Seek Social Support. Another method of dealing with stress is to seek social support. Just talking about your problem with someone else is often a good way to relieve some of the stress you're feeling. A friend or family member also may be able to provide some much needed emotional support or suggest a way of dealing with the problem that you hadn't considered.

Your professor, advisor, or someone in your college learning center may be able to help you deal with your academic concerns. The school counselor is trained to help students with personal problems. Sometimes the most effective method of reducing stress is to seek help from someone who can help.

Activity 1-12

Identify Causes of Stress in College

What is stress? List up to ten reasons that students experience stress in college. Then think about how you would deal with each situation. Talk about your suggestions with your classmates. What would you do to reduce stress in each situation?

Decision Making and Problem Solving

During your first year of college, you'll be making many decisions. Each time you choose to read a textbook chapter or study for an exam, you have made a decision to complete an academic task instead of socializing, sleeping, or cleaning. However, even that decision involves making more decisions. You also need to decide what to study, what strategies to use, where to study, and how long to work on the task.

TEN TIPS FOR MAKING THE TRANSITION TO COLLEGE

BELIEVE THAT COLLEGE IS THE RIGHT DECISION FOR YOU. Many students come to college feeling uncertain of their ability to succeed. Give yourself at least one or two semesters to make the transition; don't give up too soon.

MAKE ACADEMICS YOUR TOP PRIORITY. Some college students get so caught up in social activities that their grades suffer. If you aren't working full time, you should have enough time to get your course work done and still have time for leisure activities. Set a goal to get your course work done before you participate in social activities.

TAKE A LIGHT COURSE LOAD YOUR FIRST SEMESTER. Many college freshmen think that taking five or six classes will be as easy as it was in high school. However, they don't realize how much time they will be expected to spend on each course outside of class. Taking the lightest full-time course load available will help you do well during this transitional semester.

MAKE USE OF THE RESOURCES AT YOUR COLLEGE LEARNING CENTER. If you find that you aren't getting the grades that you expected on papers, quizzes, or exams, go to your college tutoring or learning center immediately. If you wait until after you've gotten two or three low test grades, it may be too late to change your course grade.

TAKE A REFRESHER COURSE TO BUILD YOUR SKILLS. If you haven't used your math, writing, or study skills for ten years or more, you probably have become a bit rusty. Taking a refresher course or two will help you upgrade your skills.

GET TO KNOW YOUR COURSE INSTRUCTORS. Stop by your TA's or professor's office to introduce yourself or chat about the course. Making this initial contact will help you feel more comfortable about asking for help when you have a question or problem.

DEVELOP A SUPPORT NET AT HOME. Talk to your family and friends about why you are in school. By sharing what you're doing, what you're learning, and how you're feeling, you can get their support, too. Plan activities with your family and friends at least one or two hours each week and during semester breaks.

GET INVOLVED IN CAMPUS ACTIVITIES. Early in the semester, you'll have an opportunity to join clubs and organizations on campus. Pick one or two that interest you, but don't join everything. Clubs provide you with opportunities to enjoy extracurricular activities and make new friends.

TAKE CARE OF YOURSELF. It's important to eat well-balanced meals, get enough sleep, and get some exercise. If you don't take care of yourself physically, you may find that you aren't able to concentrate on your work or even stay awake during class. If you don't take care of yourself, you may also lower your resistance to infection and miss class.

LEARN TO USE COMPUTERS. You don't have to be a computer expert, but you do need some basic computer skills to make it in college today. Take an introductory computer course during your first semester or check into tutorials offered through your college learning center, adult reentry center, or the computer labs.

Although most of these decisions can be made without a lot of reflection, other decisions may require more thought and planning. You also need to make good decisions when you set long- and short-term goals. Deciding what grades you can achieve in each of your classes, whether or not to change your major, what to do if you're failing a class, or which courses to schedule for the next semester require serious consideration.

The Problem-Solving Process

Making a decision when the choices are quite obvious, like choosing between chocolate or vanilla ice cream, is fairly easy. However, when some or all choices are unknown, you may need to use a problem-solving process. This five-step approach to problem solving will help you make a more informed decision or find the correct (or best) solution to your problem.

1. **Define the problem.** Identify the problem or the choice that you have to make. If possible, break down the problem into parts. Think about how you would like to change things. Write down what you want to do.

2. **Consider the alternatives.** Think about all the possible choices that you could make or all the possible solutions to the problem. Gather all relevant information on each alternative and consider any obstacles that could prevent you from reaching your goal (the solution). Finally, consider all the possible outcomes that could occur for each alternative.

3. **Make a plan.** List each alternative that appears to be a reasonable solution to the problem. Decide which alternative you want to try first, second, third, or fourth. Be careful not to choose the most familiar or the easiest alternative on your list because these often don't lead to the best solutions to the problem. You may need to try several alternatives before you find the best solution to the problem.

4. **Take action.** Choose the best option from your plan and put it into action. Taking action itself requires that you make a decision. After developing a plan, some students choose not to act on it. They may be concerned about the outcome or afraid that the plan won't work. Deciding not to act is an alternative that must also be carefully thought out.

5. **Evaluate the results.** If you aren't satisfied with the outcome, try another option on your list. Think about what went wrong. Did you consider all the possible alternatives? Did you gather all the relevant information? Did you just use the easiest or most obvious solution to the problem? Did you take the time to implement your plan in a step-by-step manner? Finally, did you have a positive attitude—did you believe you could solve the problem?

Activity 1-13

Making Informed Decisions

 Use the five steps in the problem-solving process to make a decision about a personal or academic problem that you encounter this week. Describe each step of the process that you used. How effective was this process in helping you reach a good decision? What changes would you make the next time you have to make a decision?

MAKE THE MOST OF YOUR COLLEGE RESOURCES

Many resources are available on your college campus, to help you succeed. By familiarizing yourself with the various student support services, the library, and computer labs early in the semester, you can improve your chances for college success. Your professors and your advisor are the first people that you should contact if you have a question or a problem. If they can't help you personally, they'll know who can.

Getting to Know the Turf

One of the most important steps in adjusting to college is feeling comfortable in your new environment. One way that you can speed this process is by getting to know your campus and the resources that are available to you. You may have already taken a tour of the campus during a college visit or during an orientation program, but that tour was probably one of many that you took. During the first week of school, take your own tour. Walk through buildings and check out some of the offices, such as the dean's office, the financial aid office, and the learning center. Make a special point of visiting the computer labs on campus and sign up for a tour of the library. (You'll be expected to use library resources throughout your college career.) The more that you know about your campus, the more comfortable you'll feel and the more easily you'll become a part of the college landscape.

Student Support Services

Some students are reluctant to ask for help; they think that they should be able to solve all their problems on their own. Sometimes, though, asking for help is the right decision. If you have a personal or an academic problem, talk with your advisor, counseler, or professor. Go to your financial aid office for help when you need to apply for scholarships, loans, or grants. If you're having a problem in one of your classes, make an appointment to discuss it with your teaching assistant or professor. Get a tutor if you're having difficulty understanding the course material or doing the homework assignments. Go to your college learning center if you're having difficulty with test preparation, note taking, reading your text, and so on.

Your College Library

Learning to use your college library or library system is another important step in achieving college success. After you take the library tour, go back several times to get acquainted with the resources that you may need to use. You may want to focus on using some of the reference materials. Set up an appointment with one of the reference librarians to learn more about using the various online indexes, abstracts, and databases that you may be required to use when completing assignments for your courses. Knowing how to use these resources will save you a great deal of time when you're ready to do research for a paper or project.

Your Professors

College professors are different from your high school teachers, but they are not inhuman or superhuman. Although some college professors appear to be unapproachable in the classroom, they are often very different in less formal settings. At many colleges, graduate students may teach or may assist the professor in teaching the course. Even though they may not be much older than their students, they should be approached in the same way as other professors. If you have questions about the course content or any of the assignments, schedule an appointment during your professor's office hours. You may also want to stop in to see your professors just to introduce yourself and chat about the course. Making this initial contact will help you feel more comfortable about seeing your professor when you do have a question or problem.

Your College Advisor

Most college students are assigned an advisor during their first year. Your advisor, generally a professor in your major field of study, is the person who will help you

monitor your progress toward your degree. You are still the one responsible, however, for completing all the degree requirements. When you plan your schedule,
your advisor will either approve your selections or make suggestions about alternative courses. Your advisor can also help you find out how to get help, find an in-
ternship, or explore career options.

Activity 1-14

Select Strategies for Success

Select one of the topics: becoming an active learner, becoming a strategic learner, becoming an independent learner, or becoming a motivated learner. Jot down strategies
used by that type of learner in two minutes. Then go find another student in the class
who chose the same topic and compare your lists. Add or delete any items to form a
group list. Go find another group with your topic and compare your lists. Add or
delete items until you have five or six good strategies on which you all agree. Finally,
write your group list on the chalkboard or share it with the class. Choose one or two
strategies to use this week.

Activity 1-15

Where Are You Now?

Now that you have completed Chapter 1, take a few minutes to repeat the "Where Are
You Now?" activity, located on the *College Study Skills* Web site. What changes did you
make as a result of reading this chapter? How are you planning to apply what you've
learned in this chapter?

SUMMARY

Many factors contribute to your college success. One of the most important,
though, is your commitment to the academic demands of your course work. Becoming an active, strategic, and independent learner will help you achieve that success. Determining your learning style, how you learn best, will help you learn to select the appropriate study strategies to use for each of the study tasks you will need
to complete. Getting motivated to work hard and learn is critical to your college
success. Choosing to use some of the strategies to increase your motivation can
make a difference. Attending college involves making many transitions and taking
on new responsibilities. If you're a nontraditional student, balancing your commitments at work, home, and school may be your most challenging task during
your first year in college. If you're a traditional student, you'll have to learn to set
priorities, balance a budget, and accept responsibility for your own learning. Many
new college students experience stress during this transitional period; that's normal. However, too much stress can be harmful. Using effective coping strategies
can help you reduce your stress so you can focus on your education. Learning to
make good decisions using a problem-solving process may help you reduce some
of the stress in your life. During your first week in college, get reacquainted with

your campus; locate the various offices and services that are available to help you succeed. Don't forget to stop in the library and sign up for a tour. Get to know your professors, your advisor, and other support people personally—they are all there to help you succeed in college.

REVIEW QUESTIONS

Terms You Should Know: Make a flash card for each term.

Active learners	Learning style	Skill
Auditory learners	Mapping	Strategic learners
Extrinsic motivation	Motivation	Stress
Independent learners	Plagiarism	Visual learners
Intrinsic motivation	Self-efficacy	Will
Kinesthetic learners	Self-regulated learners	

Completion: Fill in the blank to complete each of the following statements.

1. Reading over your notes is an example of _____ learning.

2. The most common learning style for college professors is _____.

3. Strategic learners are students who view studying and learning as a _____ process that is, to a good degree, under their control.

4. You can get your money's worth in college by _____ all classes.

5. Taking a _____ course load during your first semester or first year can help make the transition to college easier.

Multiple Choice: Circle the letter of the best answer for each of the following questions. Be sure to underline key words and eliminate wrong answers.

6. Learning to set _____ is one of the most difficult tasks you will face.
   A. study goals
   B. time plans
   C. priorities
   D. a budget

7. A kinesthetic learner learns best by:
   A. reading.
   B. listening.
   C. doing.
   D. integrating all three learning modalities.

Short Answer–Essay: On a separate sheet, answer each of the following questions.

8. What are the three factors that influence motivation? Describe each briefly.

9. Describe a self-regulated learner.

10. Describe three ways to deal with stress.

"Setting goals for myself has really had a positive effect on my life. When I set a goal for myself, it makes me want to accomplish it even more so I can be proud of myself. Goal setting has not only boosted my study habits, but, more important, it has boosted my self-confidence."

Heather Mulcahy
Student

Chapter 2

GOAL SETTING

In this chapter you will learn more about:

- **Types and characteristics of goals**
- **Setting goals for the new semester**
- **Writing effective goal statements**

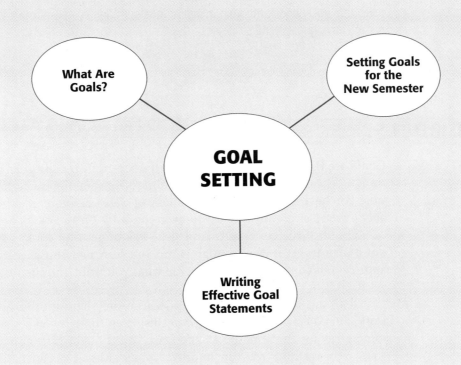

Activity 2-1

Where Are You Now?

Take a few minutes to answer *yes* or *no* to the following questions.

	YES	NO
1. Have you decided what grade point average (GPA) you want to achieve this semester?	____	____
2. Have you decided what grade you want to get in each of your courses this semester?	____	____
3. Have you written down the grade that you want to get in each of your courses this semester?	____	____
4. Are the goals that you set for your courses attainable?	____	____
5. Do you use words like *try* and *hope* when you describe your goals?	____	____
6. Do you set goals for yourself each week?	____	____
7. Do you set daily study goals?	____	____
8. Do you tend to achieve the goals that you set?	____	____
9. Do you tend to give up if you don't achieve your goals?	____	____
10. Do you revise your goals during the semester?	____	____
Total Points		____

Give yourself 1 point for each *yes* answer to all questions except 5 and 9 and 1 point for each *no* answer to questions 5 and 9. Now total up your points. A low score indicates that you need some help in setting goals. A high score indicates that you are using effective goal-setting strategies.

WHAT ARE GOALS?

Goals are the ends toward which we direct our effort. In other words, goals are things we want to achieve, things we aim for as we pursue a certain course of action. You have been setting goals since you were very young, although you probably weren't aware of it. Did you ever climb up on the kitchen counter to get a cookie out of the cupboard? Your goal was to get that cookie, and you worked out a plan to get it even though it was out of reach. You need to take the same approach in college. You must decide what you want and then figure out how to get it.

Goals are important in college because they help motivate you to do your work, attend classes, and study for exams. Even though you already may have set some goals for the semester, chances are you thought little about whether those goals were realistic. You can improve your academic performance in college by learning to set goals that motivate you to do well and that increase your chance for success.

Characteristics of Goals

To be both useful and motivating, the goals you set must have some important characteristics. Your goals should be self-chosen, moderately challenging, realistic, measurable, specific, finite, and positive. (See Figure 2.1.)

1. **Goals should be self-chosen.** Goals that are set by your parents, teachers, or friends may not always work for you. You need to determine or choose your own goals; *you* need to decide what you want to accomplish. If you set your own goals, you will be more motivated to achieve them.

2. **Goals should be moderately challenging.** You probably were told to set high or even exceptionally high goals for yourself in college; you may have been told to "shoot for the stars" or "go for straight As." In fact, this may not be the best advice. If your goal is to achieve all As during your first semester in college, you may be disappointed. As soon as you "lose your A" in one class, you may feel that you failed to achieve your goal, and you may be tempted to give up.

   One way to set moderately challenging goals is to consider what you have done in the past. Of course, everyone is different, but high school grades are fairly good predictors of college success. Why were you successful in some classes yet unsuccessful in others? You may have been more motivated, so you may have worked harder. Of course, if you didn't work very hard in high school, you can do better in college if you choose to apply yourself; increased effort can make a difference. Even so, you should set goals that are moderately challenging—goals that will require you to achieve more than you did before but will not place undue pressure on you. Goals can always be revised if you discover you can achieve more than you originally set out to accomplish.

3. **Goals should be realistic.** Think about whether your goals are attainable. It would be unrealistic to expect to get a B or better in Calculus if your math background is very weak and your high school grades in math were never higher than a C. To set realistic goals, you must carefully evaluate your chances of achieving each goal. Using the Five-Step Approach to setting goals (discussed later in this chapter) can help you make this decision.

4. **Goals should be measurable.** A goal is measurable if you can determine whether you reached it. It would be difficult to determine whether you achieved your goal if you just wanted to "do well in a course." How can you measure that?

FIGURE 2.1
Characteristics of Goals

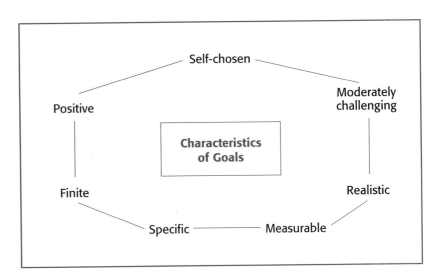

What does "well" really mean? It undoubtedly means different things to different people. It would be much easier to measure your success if you had aimed for an A or a B. At the end of the semester, you should be able to look at your final grade in a course and at the grade you set as your goal and evaluate your efforts.

Goals for specific study sessions need to be measurable, too. Studying chemistry is not a measurable goal. "I will read pages 12 to 22 in my chemistry text and work all the sample problems" is a good example of a measurable goal statement. At the end of your study session, you'll be able to determine whether you did what you planned to do.

5. **Goals should be specific.** The more specific your goals are, the more motivated you'll be to achieve them. If you formulate vague or unclear goals, you'll be less likely to accomplish them. Getting a B+ in College Algebra is a specific goal; getting a "good grade" in College Algebra is not. Study goals should be specific, too. The goal "I'll do my homework at 7:00" is rather vague. It's important to think of your homework as a series of individual assignments. You need to write separate goals for each of these assignments. A more specific goal statement is, "I'll do problems 1 to 20 in my chemistry text (page 54) at 7:00 on Tuesday."

6. **Goals should be finite.** Goals need to have a limited time frame. You just learned that you need to set a specific time to start a study goal. You need to set a specific time to complete your goals, too. Setting deadlines to complete your study goals seems rather obvious. If a paper is due by Friday, you need to have it done by Friday. However, you might decide to have the paper done by Wednesday so that you can prepare for your big Biology exam on Friday. It's important to set deadlines for all of your goals. You might also want to set intermediate deadlines to complete different parts of a task. Without a deadline, many students tend to put off starting, working on, and completing their goals. As you'll see in the next chapter, setting deadlines is also an important time management tool.

7. **Goals should be positive.** Negative goal statements tend to make you feel that you can't really be successful; they aren't motivating. "I don't want to get any lower than a C in any of my classes," "I won't go to dinner until I get this calculus work done," and "I'm not going to fail this test" are all examples of negative goal statements. You'll always do better if you are working *toward* *something*—when you have a positive attitude.

Also avoid using words like *try, think, hope,* and *should* when you describe your goals. What's wrong with including those kinds of words? You're right if you said that they offer "a way out." If you state your goal this way: "I'm going to *try* to write my sociology essay tonight," and later push your paper away unfinished, you may say to yourself, "Well, I did *try.*" Positive goals that emphasize success help motivate you to get your work done.

Activity 2-2

Evaluate Some Written Goals

 Read the following five goal statements. Decide whether the goals seem realistic and attainable. If not, revise the statements to make the goals more appropriate. Remember to consider all seven characteristics of effective goals.

1. I want to get an A or a B in Psychology.

Continued

2. I hope that I can make the Dean's List this semester.

3. I should read pages 15 to 35 before making dinner.

4. I will learn everything that I am taught this semester.

5. I will do problems 1 to 20 in *College Algebra* (page 56).

Long- and Short-Term Goals

Most students have long-term goals in mind when they enter college. Even if you don't know exactly what major you want to pursue, you have probably thought about getting a degree and getting a job. You may even know what field interests you most, whether it be education, engineering, nursing, or politics. Long-term goals are helpful to your success in college because they give you direction. However, there are times when long-term goals can seem awfully far in the future. That's where short-term goals can help. **Long-term goals** are the objectives you set for yourself for the end of the year, for four or five years from now, or even for a lifetime. **Short-term goals,** on the other hand, can be set for an hour from now, for the end of the day, the week, the month, or the semester. Short-term goals include things like completing a reading assignment, writing an essay, getting a B in a course, getting off probation, or making the Dean's List for the semester. Think of your short-term goals as steps toward achieving the long-term goals you've set for yourself. By accomplishing daily, weekly, and semester goals, you move closer to your long-range academic, career, and personal goals.

Activity 2-3

Describe Your Long-Term Goals

Write several paragraphs in which you describe your life five years from now. Include as many details as you can. How will your course work this semester help you achieve your long-term goals?

Activity 2-4

List Your Short-Term Goals

Make a list of ten goals that you would like to accomplish during this semester.

Academic and Personal Goals

In college it's important to balance your academic and personal goals. **Academic goals** relate to your course work. They include things like going to class, completing assignments, and preparing for exams. To achieve your academic goals, you need to learn to set study goals, too. **Study goals** can be defined as the objectives you want to achieve during a particular study session. They may include reading your sociology assignment, reviewing your class notes, conducting research for a term paper, or preparing for an exam. When you write study goals, be specific about exactly what you want to do. Your academic goals should be your highest priority in college. **Personal goals,** like making new friends, participating in clubs or sporting events, exercising, or even doing your laundry, are important, too. Although many students believe their personal goals cannot be changed, they can. Some household tasks can be postponed, eliminated, or delegated to other family members. If each member of your family accepts just one task, you'll be amazed at the time you'll gain. Although it takes some planning and flexibility, balancing academic and personal goals may be necessary. However, if you allow yourself to focus on your personal goals, you may find that you have little time left for study. By learning how to balance your goals, you can have time for both your academic work and your personal life.

Goal Setting Improves Performance

You learned in Chapter 1 that setting goals increases your motivation and that being motivated improves your performance. How does that actually happen, you may be asking? According to Locke and Latham, who do research on goal setting, there are four main reasons to explain the process.[1]

- **Goals direct our attention to the task at hand.** Goals keep you working on an assignment and direct you back to it if you begin to think about something else or are distracted.

- **Goals mobilize effort.** Goals motivate you to work hard (to increase your effort) in order to complete the task.

- **Goals increase persistence.** Goals help you continue to work on the task (persevere) even when the task becomes difficult.

- **Goals promote the development of new strategies when old strategies fall short.** Goals help you monitor (keep track of and evaluate) the effectiveness of the strategy or strategies that you are using to complete the task. Goals can help you determine whether the strategy is working, and, if it isn't, goals can motivate you to select another strategy to use. For example, if you were trying to learn the four reasons that goals help improve performance by reading over the list two times, you might find that you could only remember two of the reasons. Your goal to learn them could motivate you to recite the list of reasons or even to write them out a few times instead.

Activity 2-5

Work as a Group to Set Goals for One Week

During the first five minutes of the class, make a list of five to ten goals that you plan to accomplish for the week. Then share your list with a group of your classmates. As each student's list of goals is reviewed, identify the type of goal (work, personal, or study) and decide how well it is formulated according to the seven characteristics of good goal statements. Make suggestions for changing some of the goal statements to make them more positive, realistic, measurable, and specific.

---

[1]E. A. Locke and G. P. Latham, *A Theory of Goal Setting and Task Performance* (Englewood Cliffs, NJ: Prentice Hall, 1990).

Activity 2-6

Label Your Academic and Personal Goals

Now go back to your lists from Activities 2-4 and 2-5 and label each goal (A) if it is an academic goal or (P) if it is a personal goal. Then answer the following questions.

How many of the goals in each list were academic goals? _____ _____

Were your first three goals in each list academic or personal goals? Why did you list the goals in that order?

Activity 2-7

Set Deadlines For Your Goals

Go back to your list of goals from Activity 2-5 and add a deadline date and time for each of your goals. Talk with your group about how long you think it will take to complete each of the tasks you listed and add a little extra time before you set your deadline. It's better to finish early than to run out of time at the end of the day.

SETTING GOALS FOR THE NEW SEMESTER

The most important time to set your goals and start using specific strategies for achieving them is during the first three weeks of the semester. Setting new goals often involves making changes. You need to be willing to change the way you do some things to achieve your goals. If you make academics your first priority and get off to a good start in each of your classes, you'll find you'll continue to do well throughout the semester. Setting priorities, planning for early success, planning rewards, and revising your goals periodically can all help you achieve the academic goals you set for yourself. It's important to start using these strategies right from the start of the semester.

Be Open to Change

Throughout this text you'll be introduced to a wide variety of new learning and study strategies. Although it's important for you to learn how and when to use these strategies, that's not the most critical part of becoming a successful student. You also need to actually apply the strategies to your own work both in and out of class. Some students see this as an opportunity to learn some new study strategies, but others find the idea of changing the way they study and learn to be somewhat threatening. Some students have a hard time changing the way they do things—they like keeping things the same. A couple of years ago, I had a student in my class who told me that he had failed his first Psychology exam. He asked for some suggestions on how to study for the exam, and I spent some time with him talking about making word (definition) cards and predicting questions and self-testing. A few weeks passed and the student came to class and told me he had failed his second Psychology exam. I was rather surprised and asked him how many of his word cards and questions had appeared on the exam. He replied that he didn't do any.

When I asked him why he hadn't tried out the new strategies, he responded that he liked studying his way—the way he felt comfortable. I tried one more time and said to him, "but your way isn't working is it?" At that point he finally was ready to make a change. I asked him to try my suggestions one time only and promised that if the strategies didn't work, I wouldn't "bug" him ever again. He probably saw that as a way to get me off his back, so he did try the strategies. Several weeks later, Jeff came to class and reported that he got his grade from his third Psychology exam. He was very proud to say that he got an A and with a sheepish grin admitted that my suggested strategies did help. From that point on, Jeff was willing to try new strategies.

Some students have a hard time making changes. Do you? Prochaska and Prochaska suggest four reasons individuals have difficulty changing their behaviors: (1) they believe they can't change, (2) they don't want to change, (3) they don't know what to change, (4) they don't know how to change.[2] If you're having difficulty trying new things, you need to think about what might be stopping you.

Not all of the strategies presented in this text or in your class are going to work for you. That's why you need to try each one—you need to find the ones that do work for you. As you experiment with the various strategies, keep track of how they work for you. If Jeff had earned a C on his exam instead of an A, he may not have felt like the strategies were working, even though a C is two letter grades higher than his previous two Fs. If you don't reach your goal the first time you try a new strategy, don't give up. Look at the progress you have made. If you wanted a 70% (C) but got a 69%, you came very close to your goal, even though you didn't quite achieve it. You may need to practice the strategy a little more or make some modifications in how you used it. Sarah made two hundred question cards but failed her exam. When I asked her how many times she had practiced answering her questions, she told me that she ran out of time and never got to quiz herself at all. By changing her time frame for using this strategy, Sarah was successful on her next exam.

Meet with your course instructor and talk about what you did to prepare for the exam and which questions you got right and which you got wrong. You may find that you can make a small change in the way you prepared and do even better on the next exam. Change takes time, so don't give up if something doesn't work the first time you try it. When you see how the changes you make (over a period of weeks) improve your performance, I think you'll be more open to make other changes.

Many people have written books and articles about making changes. Companies are always changing things to become more profitable, individuals join programs to diet, exercise, stop smoking, find new careers, and learn new skills and hobbies. Joel Garfinkle developed seven steps to becoming a change leader. He developed this list to help people find their dream jobs, but these strategies will work nicely to help you change the way you study and learn. Consider them as you set your goals for this new semester.

Seven Steps to Becoming a Change Leader

1. Create tomorrow, don't maintain yesterday.

2. See your challenges as opportunities.

3. Be willing to risk.

---

[2]J. O. Prochaska and J. M. Prochaska "Why don't continents move? Why don't people change?" *Journal of Psychotherapy Integration*, 9 (1) (1999): 83–102.

4. Focus on successes and opportunities versus problems.

5. Use resources wisely.

6. Imagine new possibilities.

7. Take action today for what you want tomorrow.[3]

Activity 2-8

Monitor the Changes You Make

Use the chart below to keep track of the changes that you make in the next couple of weeks. List up to ten changes that you make in your study techniques, time management, or class participation (or any other change you make). Be sure to record the outcome of these changes as you learn of them.

CHANGE MADE	OUTCOME OF CHANGE	BENEFIT OF CHANGE

---

[3]Joel Garfinkle "Steps to Becoming a Change Leader." Retrieved May 14, 2004, from http://www.dreamjobcoach.com/changeleadersteps.shtml.

Set Priorities for the First Three Weeks

If you make academic goals your priority for the first three weeks, you'll practically ensure your success for the semester. Many students think that the first few weeks of a new semester are a breeze; typically, there are no exams, and often there are few papers, projects, or presentations. What you do during those first few weeks, though, often affects your performance during the rest of the semester. If you start doing your reading and other assignments right from the beginning, getting your work done will become a habit. In the same way, attending classes and meeting with study groups and tutors will also become part of your daily routine. Another real advantage of working hard right from the start is not getting behind in your work. If you don't keep up with your reading and assignments, you'll spend so much time trying to catch up (if you can) before your first round of exams that you won't be properly prepared for them. On the other hand, if you work hard during the first three weeks, you'll be able to find out early if your strategies are working. If you find they aren't, you can make changes before your exams. By working especially hard at the beginning of the semester, you also learn to make your academic goals your top priority.

Activity 2-9

Set Priorities for the First Three Weeks

Take a few minutes to set up a plan for making academics your top priority. At the end of the first three weeks, evaluate the plan that you established.

How do you plan to make academics your top priority for the first three weeks of the semester? Write a list of goals that you plan to use.

Plan for Early Success

Another way to get off to the right start is to plan for early success. Getting an A or a B on the first quiz or first homework assignment should be one of your short-term goals for the semester. Once you get an A on one of your quizzes or assignments, you won't want to lose it. That first A lets you know you can do the work—increasing your self-efficacy. You know that by attending all your classes and by doing your assignments you can be successful. That motivates you to keep working hard in all your classes.

If you try to breeze through the first few weeks of the semester, you may end up with a D or F on your first assignment or quiz, and that low grade can have a negative effect on your future performance. Some students begin to doubt their ability to succeed in a particular course or in college in general. Even though they really may not have applied themselves, the doubts still are there. Some students respond well to a low grade early in the semester; it shakes them up and they "start to hit the books." Others, though, just get depressed about their performance and eventually give up. It's much better to avoid those early low grades by striving hard for early success. The Tip Block on page 39 lists ten tips that should help you get off to the right start this semester.

Plan Rewards

When you think about achieving your goals, a ten- or fifteen-week semester can seem like a long time to wait. Unfortunately, there aren't a lot of "warm fuzzies" or

TEN TIPS TO GET OFF TO THE RIGHT START THIS SEMESTER

BE SELECTIVE IN CHOOSING CLASSES. Choose courses your first semester that will help you build the skills you need to succeed in college or entry-level courses in your major. Taking a class you find interesting is another good way to start out. Your advisor will help you select courses that are appropriate for you.

GO TO ALL CLASSES AND TAKE NOTES. Your goal is to write down as much information as you can. Four weeks from now, you won't remember much of what you heard today. Edit your notes within twenty-four hours to organize and expand the information.

KEEP UP WITH YOUR READING ASSIGNMENTS. Break down long reading assignments into more manageable units of about seven to ten pages. Read the ten pages and then switch to another subject. Take a short break; then go back and read ten more pages. Remember to carefully highlight your text or take notes as you read.

LEARN TO SAY NO. While you're attending college, you don't have time for many outside activities. You may find that working, taking care of yourself and your family, and going to school is all you can handle. When you do say no, explain that when you complete your education, you'll be happy to help out.

CREATE A GOOD STUDY ENVIRONMENT. Find a quiet place to study. If studying in your dorm room or at the kitchen table is too distracting, find another place to do your work.

SET REALISTIC GRADE GOALS. Although many students are very successful in college, they don't all get As their first semester in college. Earning a B or a C your first semester (or any semester) is fine. Consider what *you* can accomplish in each of your courses.

STUDY FOR EXAMS BY WRITING AND RECITING OUT LOUD. You won't learn the information by just reading it over and over. Writing and reciting are active strategies that help you learn the information.

LEARN TO PREDICT EXAM QUESTIONS. This is important for all exams, but it is critical for essay exams. After you predict five to ten possible questions, plan the answers before the exam and then learn the main points.

WHEN TAKING EXAMS, RELAX AND BE SURE TO READ THE DIRECTIONS. Answer the easiest questions first, skipping the ones that you don't know immediately. Then go back and complete the ones that you skipped.

GO TO YOUR COLLEGE LEARNING CENTER WHEN YOU NEED HELP. Don't wait until it's too late. Stop in to talk about any classes in which you're having difficulty. Gathering suggestions on how to study or signing up for tutoring can improve your grades dramatically.

immediate rewards in college. You may not get a grade on an assignment until the fourth or even the seventh week of the semester. You also may find that you miss that pat on the back or verbal recognition that you got in high school. It can be hard to stay motivated when no one is "telling you" that all your hard work is paying off, so you need to begin to reward yourself. Establish a method for rewarding yourself for knowing the answers to the questions that the professor asks in class, for being able to explain the solution to a problem, or even for being up to date on your reading assignments. If no one else is there to give you that pat on the back, you may need to give it to yourself.

Consider Consequences

If you're having difficulty achieving your short-term goals, try using rewards as motivation. If that doesn't work, you may need to consider seriously the consequences of your actions. Think about how not achieving one or two of your short-term goals might affect the successful completion of your long-term goals. You learned earlier in the chapter that each of your goals is really made up of a series of steps or smaller short-term goals. If you leave out one or two of those steps, you may not be able to complete the larger task. Consider the steps to achieving your goal as rungs of a ladder. If you eliminate too many or even one at a critical location, you may never get to the top. Each step is crucial for achieving success.

Learn How to Calculate Your GPA

To achieve your grade goals this semester, you need to consider how the grade you earn in each course contributes to your overall grade point average (GPA). Learning how to calculate your grade point average (GPA) will help you set better goals for the new semester. You may want to decide on the overall GPA that you want for the semester and then work backward in order to set your individual course goals. For example, let's say you decided to aim for a 2.75 for the semester. You could achieve that average in a number of ways. You could have one A (4.0), one B (3.0), and two C's (2.0) and still get a 2.75. You could also earn three B's and one C and still earn a 2.75 for the semester.

In order to calculate your GPA, you need to calculate the grade points that you earn in each of your courses. Grade points are determined by multiplying the grade's numerical value by the number of credits assigned to the course. An A in a one-credit class is worth 4 grade points, whereas a C in a four-credit course is worth 8 grade points. It appears here that the C is worth more, but it's not because you have to divide your total grade points by your total credits in order to determine your GPA. (If your college doesn't use the same numerical values for grades, adjust the table accordingly.) Consider the following example:

John's Grades

Course	Grade	Numerical Value	Credits	Grade Points
Sociology	B	3.0	3	9.0
English	C	2.0	3	6.0
Algebra	A	4.0	3	12.0
Chemistry	B	3.0	4	12.0
Phys. Ed.	A	4.0	1	4.0
			14	43.0 = 3.07 GPA

In order to determine his GPA, John listed each of his courses, the grades he earned, and their numerical values. He then listed the credit value for each course and multiplied that by the numerical value to determine the grade points for each course. After calculating the grade points for each course, he added up his total credits and his total grade points. The final step is dividing the total grade points (43) by the total credits (14). John earned a 3.07 for the semester. If John had used this method at the beginning of the semester to predict his grades, he would have had the opportunity to decide whether a 3.07 was a satisfactory goal for the semester. If he had decided that he wanted to earn a higher GPA, he could have gone back and recalculated his GPA by changing one or more of the grades in order to reach his goal. If John's goal had been a GPA of 3.25, he might have decided that he had to earn a B, instead of a C, in English. This would have improved his grade point total to 46 points, while his credit total would have stayed the same at 14. His new GPA would be 3.285.

Activity 2-10

Calculate Some GPAs

Work in a group to calculate the GPAs for the following students.

Student A

Grade	Value	Credits	Grade Points
A	4.0	3	
B	3.0	3	
B	3.0	3	
C	2.0	3	
A	4.0	1	

Student B

Grade	Value	Credits	Grade Points
C	2.0	3	
A	4.0	3	
B	3.0	4	
B	3.0	3	

Student C

Grade	Value	Credits	Grade Points
A	4.0	4	
D	1.0	3	
C	2.0	1	
C	2.0	3	
F	0.0	3	

Student D

Grade	Value	Credits	Grade Points
B	3.0	4	
A	4.0	3	
B	3.0	3	
A	4.0	3	
B	3.0	1	

Revise Your Goals Periodically

It's important to rethink your goals at some point during the semester. Some students tend to "play it safe" and set unrealistically low goals for themselves at the beginning of the semester. It may seem like a good idea to set safe goals; that way you always are successful at what you set out to do. However, "safe" goals can also hold you back because they don't challenge you to achieve all that you might be able to achieve. Some students have the opposite tendency; they set goals that may be completely unattainable. By doing this, they are setting themselves up for failure and disappointment.

Remember, goals should be moderately challenging; they should be just a little out of reach so that you can work toward them. How can you find just the right level of challenge? You can't, at first. Once you gain some experience in college, however, you'll become much better at knowing what you can achieve. Until then, you need to revise your goals as you gather more information about your skills and your performance. Of course, you could change your goals, raise them or lower them, at almost any time during the semester. However, the best time to review your "grade" goals is after the first exam. If you decided to work for a B in algebra but got a high A on the first exam, you should revise your goal upward. Your first exam demonstrated that you're capable of doing A work and consequently capable of getting an A in algebra.

Many students continue to improve in courses after the first exam, so you need to review your goals again after the second, third, or even fourth exam. In general, you should sit down and really think about where you are and where you want to be after the first round of exams, after midterms, and about two weeks before final exams.

Activity 2-11
Revise Your Goals

Over the course of the semester, you need to monitor your performance in each of your classes and revise your goals as needed. Use the chart below (photocopy it or replicate it on your computer) to revise your goals after your first round of exams, after midterms, and about two weeks before your finals.

CLASS	ORIGINAL GOAL	GRADES TO DATE	REVISED GOAL

WRITING EFFECTIVE GOAL STATEMENTS

By putting your goals in writing, you increase the chances that you will actually accomplish them. However, another factor that affects your success is how you formulate your goal statements. You can write down the first thing that comes to mind, or you can spend some time and explore each of your goals by using the Five-Step Approach to goal setting. Developing and implementing an action plan for each of your goals can also help you achieve them.

Use the Five-Step Approach

Writing effective goal statements isn't as easy as it sounds. You need to consider what you want to accomplish, any obstacles that could prevent you from achieving your goal, and the resources available to you. You then need to formulate your goal statement and polish it. Because each of your courses has different requirements,

FIGURE 2.2

Tomi's Five-Step Approach to Setting Goals

COURSE: _____ Biology _____

STEP 1: Tentative Goal Statement
   I want at least a B in Biology

STEP 2: List of Obstacles

1. There is a ton of reading, and I usually put it off.

2. I have trouble following the lecture, and I struggle to take notes.

3. Class would be easy to skip because it's in the auditorium and attendance isn't taken.

4. The book is very hard to read and understand.

5. The class is so big that I am easily distracted.

6. The subject matter is very difficult for me.

STEP 3: List of Resources

1. I will set up a schedule to read 15 pages each night.

2. I'll read the chapter before the lecture. I'll rewrite my notes afterward.

3. I can't afford to miss class. I'll go from my 8:00 class directly to Biology at 9:00.

4. I'll highlight and take notes as I read.

5. I'll read Chapter 4 on Concentration early and sit up front.

6. I'll get a tutor in the learning assistance center.

STEP 4: Revised Goal Statement
   I'll try to earn a B in Biology.

STEP 5: Polished Goal Statement
   I will achieve a B in Biology this semester.

---

you must consider each course separately. If you're taking five courses, you must go through this process five times. See Figures 2.2 and 2.3 for two examples of the Five-Step Approach to setting goals.

STEP 1: Write Down What You Want to Accomplish

This initial description can be thought of as a *tentative* goal statement. The easiest way to begin your tentative goal statement is with the words "I want to." Think about what you want to accomplish.

STEP 2: Write Down Any Obstacles

Think about whether there are any course requirements, assignments, tests, or other factors that could jeopardize your success. Make a list of the difficulties you may encounter. Some students, for example, panic when they find out that their exams are going to be essay tests. You might consider this an obstacle if you know that you ordinarily don't do well on essay tests. Others may be concerned about attendance policies or oral presentations.

STEP 3: Write Down Any Resources Available to You

First, consider your *general* resources. You have successfully completed twelve years of school, so you have acquired some of the skills that can help you become a suc-

FIGURE 2.3

Kevin's Five-Step Approach to
Setting Goals

COURSE: _____ History of Western Art _____

STEP 1: Tentative Goal Statement
I would like an A in History of Western Art.

STEP 2: List of Obstacles

1. The class is in the afternoon
   and I usually want to skip.

2. The material is boring and uninteresting because it is a
   general education class.

3. The readings are long and boring.

4. There is a vast amount of
   material covered each day
   in lecture.

5. The notes that I take are
   sloppy and incomplete.

6. There is a great deal of
   detailed information in each of
   the assigned readings.

STEP 3: List of Resources

1. I will go to class right after
   lunch.

2. I will treat this class like any
   required course and devote the
   needed time and effort to succeed.

3. I will break the reading down
   into 15 page sections each night.

4. I will study my notes from
   class on a daily basis for
   30 minutes or more.

5. I will rewrite and edit all of
   my notes after checking with
   several classmates.

6. I will take notes as I read
   to organize the important
   facts and concepts.

STEP 4: Revised Goal Statement
I will try to get an A in History of Western Art.

STEP 5: Polished Goal Statement
I will achieve an A in History of Western Art.

---

cessful student. You have also acquired a background in quite a few subject areas. In addition, you probably earned some As and Bs, so you know that you can be successful in your academic pursuits. If you're a returning adult student, you also have developed skills in meeting deadlines, setting priorities, and managing multiple tasks—all necessary skills for college success. All these things are general resources that will help you achieve your goals. Next, consider each of the obstacles you listed individually. Think about how you might use your resources to overcome each obstacle. Write down *specific* resources you could use to achieve each goal. Specific resources include your friends and family, the faculty and staff members at your college, and you yourself. For instance, if you have difficulty with essay tests, you could go to your professor or to your college learning center to get some help before the exam.

STEP 4: Review and Revise Your Tentative Goal Statement
Now that you have thought about any possible difficulties and have figured out whether they can be resolved, you're ready to write your final goal statement. In some cases you may find that you don't change your tentative goal statement at all; in other cases you may do a lot of revising.

STEP 5: Polish Your Goal Statement
Check to be sure that your final statement is well written and takes into consideration the seven characteristics of effective goals.[4]

Activity 2-12

Set Your Goals for This Semester

Use the Five-Step Approach to set goals for each of your courses this semester. Photocopy or replicate the chart in Figure 2.4 or use the form on the *College Study Skills* Web site. Look at the examples in Figures 2.2 and 2.3 if you need some more ideas.

Activity 2-13

Overcoming Obstacles as a Student

Make a list of the obstacles that you as a student have encountered in college (or think you may encounter). Then make a list of the resources that are available to you at your college or through your work and home life. Match each resource to at least one obstacle on your list. Choose one obstacle (and list of resources) and describe how you could use the resources to overcome that obstacle.

Develop an Action Plan

When you were younger, did you ever try to find the presents that your parents had hidden from you? Did you actually plan how you were going to search the house? Have you ever tried to find a job, lose weight, or start a weight-lifting program? Each of these activities involved formulating a step-by-step plan that led to the ultimate goal.

To achieve your long- and short-term goals, you need to develop an action plan. An **action plan** is a carefully thought-out method of implementing a strategy to achieve your goal—one that will help you get from where you are to where you want to be. Writing an action plan for a long-term assignment (such as a term paper, semester project, or portfolio) can help motivate you to work on the task throughout the semester because you have to identify each step of the process in advance. You can develop an action plan on notebook paper, on an index card, or by using the form shown in Figure 2.5, which can be found on the *College Study Skills* Web site. By breaking down your goal into a series of smaller, more specific goals, you can develop a set of action tasks for your plan. **Action tasks** are the specific tasks that you need to complete to achieve your original goal. To write a term paper, you might include action tasks such as choosing a topic, writing a tentative thesis statement, using a database to identify three to six good sources of information, taking notes on the source materials, developing an outline, and so on. Next, think about any materials you may need to complete your action tasks. For example, to take notes on your sources, you would need to have your laptop or index cards, copies of your articles or books (or if you can't check them out, a list of

---

[4]Based on some ideas from Walter Pauk, *How to Study in College,* 4th ed. (Boston: Houghton Mifflin, 1989).

FIGURE 2.4
The Five-Step Approach to
Setting Goals Form

COURSE: _____

STEP 1: Tentative Goal Statement

_____

STEP 2: List of Obstacles   **STEP 3: List of Resources**

1. _____   1. _____

2. _____   2. _____

3. _____   3. _____

4. _____   4. _____

5. _____   5. _____

6. _____   6. _____

STEP 4: Revised Goal Statement

_____

STEP 5: Polished Goal Statement

_____

FIGURE 2.5
An Action Plan Sheet

Goal:

Target Date	Action Tasks	Materials Needed	To Do Date	Evaluation

Outcome:

Adapted from *Motivation and Goal-Setting*, 2d ed. (Hawthorne, NJ: Career Press, 1993), p. 38.

where each is located in the reference area of the library), and a pen or pencil. Next, set a target date for the completion of each of your action tasks. Giving yourself one week to complete each step in the plan is a good guide for completing a term paper, for example. You may find that you can complete some of your action tasks in one day while others (such as taking notes for your paper and writing your rough draft) may take two or three weeks. Be sure to include a To Do date for each step in the plan. Once you establish your target date, it may be useful to set up a specific date and time to work on each of the tasks. Set the To Do date for the next action task when you complete the previous one. Checking off each task as it is completed can help you see the progress you're making in completing your goal. Finally, include an outcome statement at the end of your action plan. After completing your plan (and your goal), you should describe how well your action plan helped you achieve your goal. You could list, for example, the date that you actually finished your term paper, any problems that you encountered using the plan, and the grade that you received.

Figure 2.6 contains the list of action tasks that DaShawn developed to complete a history paper. DaShawn also included target dates and To Do dates for each step. By scheduling the dates for each step, she was able to complete the task ahead of time.

FIGURE 2.6
DaShawn's Action Plan

Goal: Prepare my history paper on family heritage

Target Date	Action Tasks	Materials Needed	To Do Date	Evaluation
January 17	Prepare outline	Directions for assignment	January 14	✓
January 17	Prepare interview questions	List of possible questions	January 14	✓
January 17	Call my grandmother to schedule a time to visit and talk to her about my family	Planning calendar, phone #	January 15	✓
January 20	Ask my grandmother specific questions and jot down her responses below each of my questions	Typed questions, clipboard	January 16	✓
January 20	Tape record the interview just in case I miss something important	Tape recorder, extra batteries, extra tape	January 16	✓
January 24	Write the rough draft	Notes, questions, tape, assignment directions	January 19	✓
January 25	Have my grandmother review the paper to check to be sure my facts are correct	Questions and responses, rough draft	January 22	✓
January 26	Type my paper on the computer. Do the cover sheet and introduction, too	Rough draft, directions for cover sheet and introduction	January 23	✓
January 27	Proofread and make any necessary corrections	Handbook, rough draft	January 25	✓
January 28	Turn in the paper	Paper and question sheet with answers	January 28	✓

Outcome: I completed my paper on family heritage ahead of schedule

Activity 2-14

Develop Action Plans

Look back at the list of short-term goals that you wrote in Activity 2-4 or 2-5. Choose one personal goal and one academic goal and develop action plans for each goal. Exchange one of your plans with one of your classmates. What suggestions would you make to make your partner's action plan more effective?

Activity 2-15

Where Are You Now?

Now that you have completed Chapter 2, take a few minutes to repeat the "Where Are You Now?" activity, located on the *College Study Skills* Web site. What changes did you make as a result of reading this chapter? How are you planning to apply what you've learned in this chapter?

SUMMARY

Setting goals helps motivate you to attend class regularly, keep up with your day-to-day assignments, and complete long-term projects on time. Writing goal statements that are self-chosen, moderately challenging, realistic, measurable, specific, finite, and positive will help you accomplish the goals that you set this semester. Setting priorities is also important to your success because you'll need to find the right balance between your academic and personal goals. To achieve your goals this semester, you must be open to change—you must be willing to try new strategies. Monitoring your progress, calculating your GPA, and revising your goals periodically will help you be more successful. Use the Five-Step Approach to setting goals in order to realistically set grade goals for each of your courses this semester. Developing action plans and making academics your top priority, especially for the first three weeks of the semester, will get you off to a good start. Setting and writing down goals lets you know where you're going, gives you the motivation to get there, and allows you to look back to see what you accomplished.

REVIEW QUESTIONS

Terms You Should Know: Make a flash card for each term.

Academic goals	Goals	Short-term goals
Action plans	Long-term goals	Study goals
Action tasks	Personal goals	

Completion: Fill in the blank to complete each of the following statements.

1. Goals should be _____ challenging.

2. You should avoid words like _____ and _____ in your goal statements.

3. The third step in setting goals is to list your _____.

4. _____ _____ help students break long-term goals down into individual steps.

5. When you have clear, _____ goals, you are more likely to persevere when a task becomes difficult.

Multiple Choice: Circle the letter of the best answer for each of the following questions. Be sure to underline key words and eliminate wrong answers.

6. The goal statement, "I will earn an A or B in Biology" should be revised because it is not:
   A. specific.
   B. measurable.
   C. realistic.
   D. positive.

7. Why should you revise your goals?
   A. You may have set your goals too low.
   B. You may have set your goals too high.
   C. After the first exam, you'll have a more accurate picture of your performance.
   D. All of the above are good reasons.

Short Answer-Essay: On a separate sheet, answer each of the following questions.

8. What are four main reasons that setting goals improves performance?

9. Why should students make academics their top priority for the first three weeks of the semester?

10. Why should students use the Five-Step Approach to setting goals?

"After my first week of school I honestly thought I'd never be able to juggle all of my responsibilities both at work and at home—not to mention keeping up with the homework. However, after actually doing the fixed commitment calendar and identifying just when I had to do what, it didn't seem so overwhelming. I was able to see that I had time for it all. . . . I like the organization this brings to my somewhat chaotic life."

Dawn Davis
Student

TIME MANAGEMENT

In this chapter you will learn more about:

- **How to evaluate how you use your time now**
- **How to organize your study time**
- **How to manage multiple tasks**
- **Time management strategies that will help you stay motivated**
- **How to reduce your procrastination**

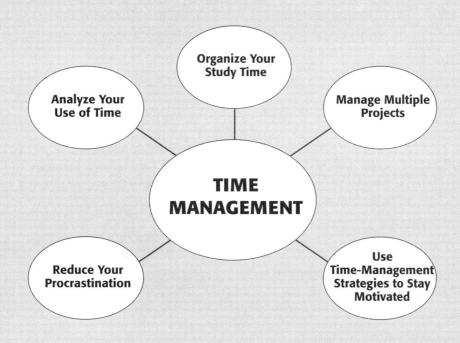

Activity 3-1

Where Are You Now?

Take a few minutes to answer *yes* or *no* to the following questions.

	YES	NO
1. Have you estimated how many hours you need to study this semester?	_____	_____
2. Do you tend to complete your assignments on time?	_____	_____
3. Have you estimated how long it takes you to read ten pages in each of your textbooks?	_____	_____
4. Do you begin working on long-term assignments early in the semester?	_____	_____
5. Do you make lists of things to do in your head rather than on paper?	_____	_____
6. Do you find that you go out even when you know you should be studying?	_____	_____
7. Do you schedule time to study for exams?	_____	_____
8. Are you working at a job more than twenty hours a week?	_____	_____
9. Do you know exactly what you are going to work on when you sit down to study?	_____	_____
10. Do you do the assignments from your favorite class first?	_____	_____
Total Points	_____	

Give yourself 1 point for each *yes* answer to all questions except 5, 6, 8 and 10, and 1 point for each *no* answer to questions 5, 6, 8, and 10. Now total up your points. A low score indicates that you need some help in managing your time now. A high score indicates that you are already using many good time-management techniques.

ANALYZE YOUR USE OF TIME

You can establish a good time plan once you know how you actually spend your time. Identifying how much time you have available for study and how much time you need for study can help you decide whether or not you should make any changes in your current time plan.

Why Is Time Management Important?

Time management is the way you regulate or schedule your time. You can make more efficient use of your study time and complete your work in less time by using good time-management skills. The key to successful time management is allowing enough time to complete your work while still finding time to complete all of your other responsibilities. If you have additional time, you can take advantage of the other opportunities for growth and development that occur in college. Attending concerts, getting together with friends and family, and going to conferences or rallies are important parts of the college experience. However, these activities can be enjoyed more fully when you know that you have your course work done. Learning good time-management techniques can help keep you motivated to accomplish the goals that you set for yourself in Chapter 2.

In high school, your study time was fairly well defined or structured. In college, though, you won't find that kind of structure. You may need to use time-management strategies to balance school and work responsibilities.

Unlike high school students who are in class for almost thirty-five hours a week, most college students are in class for only twelve to fifteen hours a week. To a college freshman, this seems like a breeze. However, in college, *most of your work must be completed outside of class.* And, even though you may not want to admit it, you can't get all that work done in just a few hours every evening. To achieve your goals, you also need to make use of your available daytime hours for study.

Learning to schedule your time is a complicated task. As you have just seen, you have many hours of time that need to be scheduled. Instead of sixty hours of structured class and study time, you may have only about fifteen structured hours. You are the one who is responsible for structuring the remaining hours. If you are in class on Mondays, Wednesdays, and Fridays, you can't consider Tuesdays and Thursdays as free days. You need to use these days for out-of-class study time. Also, you'll need to adjust your schedule as your workload changes during the semester. You may find that your plan to sleep until noon each day must be revised as exams, projects, and paper deadlines approach.

Good time-management skills can actually save you time. A few minutes each week spent on planning can make a real difference in how your study time is organized and spent. Once you learn good time-management skills, you may be surprised to find that you can do all the things you want to do. You may find that for the first time, you are in control of your life. The first rule of good time management is: *Don't let time manage you; you must learn, instead, to manage your time.*

How Do You Manage Your Time Now?

The first step in learning better time management is to evaluate how you actually use your time now. The score you received in Activity 3-1 gave you an indication of your ability to manage your time. However, you also can find out a lot about your own time use by comparing how you think you will use your time to how you actually use it.

Activity 3-2

Consider Your Use of Time

How do you think you will use your time this semester? As a group, talk about how much time you think students should spend in various activities during a typical week in college. Then record your results in column A. You may add a couple more categories or substitute the titles of a few if you need to. Remember the column should total 168 hours. Next, think about how you as an individual will spend your time. Complete column B individually. Finally, after completing your time log (in Activity 3-4)

Continued

Activity 3-2

Consider Your Use of Time (continued)

record your totals for column C and then compare your time estimates to how you actually spent your time.

	A How many hours **should** you	B How many hours **will** you	C How many hours **did** you
Sleep			
Attend class			
Study			
Eat			
Get ready			
Commute			
Work			
Watch TV			
Socialize			
Surf the Net			
Exercise/workout			
Attend sports practice			
Talk on the phone			
Chat/e-mail/instant message			
Play video games			
Total hours			

Keep a Time Log

Although most students think that they spend enough time on academic tasks, many of them don't. By keeping a time log, you'll be able to see how much or how little time you are actually spending on various activities. A **time log** is a record of what you do each hour of the day for one week (Figure 3.1). To create your own time log, just write down what you did in the morning at lunchtime, what you did in the afternoon at dinnertime, and what you did in the evening at bedtime. Some students prefer to carry an index card to record their activities and then copy them on to the log at a later time. If you wait until the end of the day, you may have trouble remembering what you did. Split hours by drawing a diagonal line, but don't worry about five- or ten-minute activities.

FIGURE 3.1
Time log

	Monday	Tuesday	Wednesday	Thursday	Friday	Saturday	Sunday
6:00 A.M.							
7:00 A.M.							
8:00 A.M.							
9:00 A.M.							
10:00 A.M.							
11:00 A.M.							
12:00 P.M.							
1:00 P.M.							
2:00 P.M.							
3:00 P.M.							
4:00 P.M.							
5:00 P.M.							
6:00 P.M.							

Continued

FIGURE 3.1 (continued)
Time Log

	Monday	Tuesday	Wednesday	Thursday	Friday	Saturday	Sunday
7:00 P.M.							
8:00 P.M.							
9:00 P.M.							
10:00 P.M.							
11:00 P.M.							
12:00 A.M.							
1:00 A.M.							
2:00 A.M.							
3:00 A.M.							
4:00 A.M.							
5:00 A.M.							

You may find it helpful to color code your time log. Highlight all of your academic tasks (classes, meetings with professors or tutors, and study time) in one color, your sleep hours in another, and the rest of your life (work, social time, meals, and so on) in a third. A quick glance can tell you a lot about how effectively you are using your time now. To get a more accurate picture, complete a time-use chart (Figure 3.2) to count the number of hours you used for each of the various activities. You'll need to add or modify the categories depending on your own activities. Limit your total miscellaneous hours to ten for the week. If you include many more, you won't have a very accurate picture of your time use.

If you're a full-time student, you should divide your total hours into three overall categories. You should spend about 56 hours a week sleeping (one-third of your time), about 56 hours for academics (classes, study time, tutoring, review sessions, and meetings with your professors or advisor), and 56 hours for the rest of your life. If you're working full-time and attending college on a full-time basis, you won't have much time left over for social activities or home responsibilities. You may find that your time use is unbalanced.

Many students sleep too much (or too little), spend seventy to ninety hours on "the rest of their lives" and very little time on their academic tasks. After completing his time-use chart, Kevin (a student in my class) found that he was spending almost two-thirds of his time on social activities. He was shocked by this and included the following statement in his time use analysis, "I realize that I have the rest of my life for 'the rest of my life' but I only have now to get a good education." Finding out how he really spent his time led Kevin to make dramatic changes in his use of time.

After completing this activity, many students are surprised to find that they have time-management problems. When Lisa discovered that she had spent ten hours listening to music during the week, she decided to use music as a reward for completing her work and set a goal to reduce her total listening time by 50 percent. After completing his time log, Mike realized that he was spending over twenty hours a week playing pool and Ping-Pong in the student union. He decided that he could return to his part-time job if he reduced the time he spent "hanging out" in the union. Looking realistically at how you're using your time *now* can help you make some necessary changes to be more successful in college.

Activity 3-3
Keep a Time Log

Keep a time log for one week using the calendar in Figure 3.1 or print one from the Web site. Write down how you spent each hour of the day, being as specific as possible. Complete the time-use chart in Figure 3.2 or use the chart available on the *College Study Skills* Web site, indicating how many hours you spent in various activities (attending class, working, sleeping, eating, studying, commuting, completing personal tasks, watching television, playing video games, socializing, exercising, and so on) each day and then for the entire week. Then write several paragraphs describing any patterns that you noted in your use of time. Consider the amount of time that you spent on various activities as well as whether you did the things that you planned (or needed) to do. Discuss the changes that you plan to make in your time plan as a result of monitoring your use of time.

FIGURE 3.2
Time-Use Chart

	Sleep	Get Ready	Meals	Class	Study	TV	Work	Internet/E-Mail	Commute	Social Time	Computer Games	Phone	Misc.	Total Hours
Mon.														
Tue.														
Wed.														
Thur.														
Fri.														
Sat.														
Sun.														
Total Hours														

SLEEP ☐   **ACADEMICS** ☐   **THE REST OF MY LIFE** ☐

Complete a Prospective-Retrospective Calendar

Learning to manage your time effectively also depends on how well you can stick to a schedule. A Prospective-Retrospective Calendar allows you to compare what you *plan* to do on a given day (**prospective**) with what you *actually* do (**retrospective**). What you do during each hour of the day is not important here. Instead, the key is how well you stick to your plan.

Just setting up a plan for each hour of the day often provides sufficient motivation for completing it. Some students who try this activity are surprised to find that they faithfully follow their time plans. They are motivated to do everything that they planned to do. Many report that this was the first time they ever got all of their work done. Because this calendar worked so well for them, they decided to use it every day. Other students find that they have a great deal of difficulty staying on a schedule. Their most common problem involves getting study assignments done as planned. Do you?

Michelle's calendar in Figure 3.3 is fairly typical. She planned six hours for study on Monday but didn't complete any class assignments at all. Did you notice that all of Michelle's study goals were rather vague? Do you think she would have completed more study tasks if she had planned *exactly* what she had to do? Michelle also had trouble following her time plan during the evening hours. If you had been in Michelle's place, what would you have done differently?

Activity 3-4

Create a Prospective-Retrospective Calendar

Take a piece of notebook paper and fold it vertically down the middle. In the left margin, from top to bottom, write in the hours of the day. Then write "Prospective" or "What I Plan to Do" above the left column and "Retrospective" or "What I Did" above the right

Continued

FIGURE 3.3
Michelle's Prospective-Retrospective Calendar for Monday

Time	Prospective	Retrospective	Evaluation
7:00	sleep	slept	+
8:00	sleep	slept	+
9:00	shower/dress/eat	showered/dressed/ate	+
10:00	history class	history class	+
11:00	do history	washed hair	–
12:00	go to lunch	ate lunch	+
1:00	homework for Tues. classes	watched soaps	–
2:00	homework for Tues. classes	watched soaps	–
3:00	soccer practice	soccer practice	+
4:00	soccer practice	soccer practice	+
5:00	soccer practice	soccer practice	+
6:00	eat supper	ate supper	+
7:00	finish Tues. assignments	went to mall	–
8:00	read	ate at mall	–
9:00	shower	watched a movie	–
10:00	read	watched a movie	–
11:00	watch news	watched news	+
12:00	sleep	slept	+

Activity 3-4

Create a Prospective-Retrospective Calendar (continued)

column. On the left side, write down exactly what you plan to do during each hour of the next day (tomorrow). Plan carefully and realistically. The next day, write down on the right side of the paper what you actually did. Because days do get very busy, you may want to jot down your morning activities at lunch, your afternoon activities at dinner, and your evening activities before bed. After you've completed your chart, check to see how many times you did what you planned to do and what types of activities you were unable to complete. Did you complete all your tasks? What problems did you notice?

Identify Time Available for Study

Identifying how much time you have available for study is the next step in setting up a good time plan. This involves looking at how much of your time is committed to other activities and also how much time you, as an individual, need to complete your work.

To establish how much of your time is committed to other activities, you should complete a **Fixed Commitment Calendar.**[1] What are fixed commitments? If you said classes, work hours, or even mealtimes, you were right. **Fixed commitments** are things you do the same time every day or every week. When completing your calendar, you should first write in your classes. You also should write in hours when you are asleep (normal sleep hours, not naps), mealtimes (setting regular times for meals helps you stay on a schedule), and work hours. If your work hours vary, don't write them in yet; we'll talk more about study and work later in this section. If you're involved in clubs, organizations, or sports, you may need to include additional hours for regularly scheduled meetings (same time each week) or practices and games. If you have family responsibilities such as dropping off or picking up your children at school or day care (or other regularly scheduled tasks), write them in, too. If you know that you'll be socializing on most Friday and Saturday evenings, you should write in those times even though your plans aren't definite. If you plan to sleep in or attend religious services on Saturday or Sunday morning, include those hours as well.

After you have written in all the regularly committed hours, you should begin to see some patterns in your uncommitted time. You may have some very short blocks of time between classes, some two- or three-hour blocks in the morning or afternoon, and some longer blocks in the evenings and on weekends. Think of these time blocks as time *available* for study rather than free time. You also may notice that you have a lot of time to study on certain days but very little on others. All this information will be useful as you begin to schedule your study time.

After determining your available study time, trace around the perimeter of each time block (see the sample in Figure 3.4). Use a brightly colored marker to outline each time block. Being able to see at a glance the hours when you have time to study can be very helpful when scheduling study time.

---

[1]Adapted from Time Analysis Worksheet in Nancy V. Wood, *Reading and Study Skills,* 3d ed. (New York: Holt, Rinehart & Winston, 1986), pp. 18–20.

FIGURE 3.4
Greg's Fixed Commitment
Calendar

	Monday	Tuesday	Wednesday	Thursday	Friday	Saturday	Sunday
7:00 A.M.	sleep	sleep	sleep	sleep	sleep	sleep	sleep
8:00 A.M.	shower/dress/eat	shower/dress/eat	shower/dress/eat	shower/dress/eat	shower/dress/eat	sleep	sleep
9:00 A.M.	Algebra class	lift weights	Algebra class	lift weights	Algebra class	sleep	sleep
10:00 A.M.	lift weights	lift weights		lift weights	lift weights	shower/dress	shower/dress
11:00 A.M.	English class	History class	English class	History class	English class	eat	eat
12:00 P.M.		eat		eat		work	watch football
1:00 P.M.	eat		eat		eat	work	watch football
2:00 P.M.	Sociology class		Sociology class		Sociology class	work	watch football
3:00 P.M.						work	watch football
4:00 P.M.	practice	practice	practice	practice	practice	work	watch football
5:00 P.M.	practice	practice	practice	practice	practice		work
6:00 P.M.	eat	eat	eat	eat	eat	eat	work
7:00 P.M.							work
8:00 P.M.					out	out	work
9:00 P.M.					out	out	work
10:00 P.M.					out	out	
11:00 P.M.	TV	TV	TV	TV	out	out	
12:00 A.M.	sleep	sleep	sleep	sleep	out	out	sleep
1:00 A.M.	sleep	sleep	sleep	sleep	out	out	sleep
2:00 A.M.	sleep	sleep	sleep	sleep	sleep	sleep	sleep
Hours Available for Study __34__				Hours Needed for Study __32__			

If your work schedule changes each week, this calendar is even more important for you. Before you put your work hours on the schedule, make a photocopy of the calendar for each week of the semester. As you get your work schedule each week, go through and write in your hours. This will save you a lot of time because you won't have to start from scratch each week.

As a final step in preparing your Fixed Commitment Calendar, count the number of hours you have available for study. If you're not working, you may find that you have fifty to seventy hours available for study. Don't panic—you won't need all of them for study. If you are working, however, this number may be substantially smaller, depending on the number of hours that you work each week.

FIGURE 3.5
Rayna's Fixed Commitment
Calendar

	Monday	Tuesday	Wednesday	Thursday	Friday	Saturday	Sunday
5:00 A.M.	shower/dress	shower/dress	shower/dress	shower/dress	shower/dress	sleep	sleep
6:00 A.M.	breakfast/drive	breakfast/drive	breakfast/drive	breakfast/drive	breakfast/drive	sleep	sleep
7:00 A.M.	work	work	work	work	work	sleep	sleep
8:00 A.M.	work	work	work	work	work	sleep	sleep
9:00 A.M.	work	work break	work break	work break	work break	shower/dress	sleep
10:00 A.M.	break work	work	work	work	work	breakfast	shower/dress
11:00 A.M.	work	work	work	work	work	clean apartment	breakfast
12:00 P.M.	work lunch	work lunch	work lunch	work lunch	work lunch		
1:00 P.M.	work	work	work	work	work		
2:00 P.M.	work	work	work	work	work		buy groceries
3:00 P.M.	work	work	work	work	work	lunch	lunch
4:00 P.M.	drive home	drive home	drive home	drive home	drive home		
5:00 P.M.	drive	drive	drive				
6:00 P.M.	Biology	Anthropology	Study Skills				
7:00 P.M.	Biology	Anthropology	Study Skills	go to laundromat			
8:00 P.M.	Biology	Anthropology	Study Skills	go to laundromat	out to dinner		dinner
9:00 P.M.	drive home/dinner	drive home/dinner	drive home/dinner	dinner	out to dinner	dinner	
10:00 P.M.					out to dinner	dancing	sleep
11:00 P.M.	sleep	sleep	sleep	sleep	sleep	dancing	sleep
12:00 A.M.	sleep	sleep	sleep	sleep	sleep	dancing	sleep
1:00 A.M.	sleep	sleep	sleep	sleep	sleep	dancing	sleep
2:00 A.M.	sleep	sleep	sleep	sleep	sleep	sleep	sleep

Hours Available for Study 28½   Hours Needed for Study 21

Greg (see Figure 3.4) has only thirty-four hours available for study. He is working ten hours a week and is participating in sports. He spends one or two hours a day lifting weights and another two hours a day practicing. To complete his assignments, Greg will have to make efficient use of his time.

Rayna's schedule (see Figure 3.5) is even tighter because she works full time and attends college three evenings a week. She has very little study time available during the week and spends most of the weekend completing her study tasks. Do you think that Rayna could handle a full-credit load this semester?

Activity 3-5

Complete a Fixed Commitment Calendar

Now fill out the Fixed Commitment Calendar in Figure 3.6 (or use the form on the Web site). Write in your activities that are regularly scheduled for class, work, meals, and other obligations. Then box in the times that are available for study. Indicate the total number of available study hours at the bottom of the page. You'll be able to determine the hours that you need for study soon. Leave that space blank for now.

Identify Time Needed for Study

Knowing how much time you have available for study is useless until you identify how much time you need for study. Formulas, such as those that allot two hours of outside study time for every hour in class, are designed to simplify the task of determining how much time you need for study. So, a student who is taking fifteen credits would need thirty hours of study time per week. Many students find that this simple formula just doesn't work. To find out how many hours you need for study, you need to consider a number of other factors.

Consider Your Credit Load

The first indicator of how much time you really need for study is your credit load. If you're taking fifteen credits, you should begin with a 2 to 1 ratio (two hours of study time for every hour in class). Remember that this is a *minimum* and probably will change when you consider the other factors—the goals you have set, how quickly or slowly you work, and the difficulty of your courses. If you're taking more than fifteen credits this semester, you need to think of yourself as someone who is working overtime (12 to 15 credits is generally considered a full-time credit load). You'll need to work extra hours to successfully complete your work and earn good grades.

Consider the Difficulty Level of Your Classes

You'll need to increase your study hours if you're taking very difficult classes. Certain classes at every school seem to have a reputation for being "killer" classes. If you're enrolled in a "killer" class, you may have to increase your study ratio to 3 to 1 (three hours of outside work for every hour in class) or even 4 to 1. Even if you're not taking a "killer" course this semester, you may find that one particular class is especially difficult for you. College algebra can be a tough course if you haven't used your math skills for a few years. A Chemistry class can be difficult for a student who is an English major. If you're taking a course that is especially demanding, you should allow three or four hours of outside work for every hour that you're in class.

Consider Your Grade Goals

You may also need to increase your study time if you want to get As or Bs in one or more of your courses. The formula of spending two hours outside of class for every hour in class was the average time that students spent on study. Remember the average grade students earn in college is a C. You'll have to spend more time on your course work to earn high grades. This may involve editing your lecture notes (see Chapter 5), annotating your text or taking notes as you read your text assignments (see Chapter 9), and studying more actively for quizzes and exams (see Chapter 10). You may need to spend more time on your assignments to ensure that they reflect your best effort. Some students also work with tutors or form a study

FIGURE 3.6
Fixed Commitment Calendar

	Monday	Tuesday	Wednesday	Thursday	Friday	Saturday	Sunday
5:00							
6:00							
7:00							
8:00							
9:00							
10:00							
11:00							
12:00							
1:00							
2:00							
3:00							
4:00							
5:00							
6:00							
7:00							
8:00							
9:00							
10:00							
11:00							
12:00							
1:00							
2:00							
3:00							
4:00							

Hours Available for Study _____   Hours Needed for Study _____ group to maximize their grades. Many students think that they can get a good grade on a paper by simply writing a first draft and running the spell checker. However, to get an A or B, you may need to spend additional time planning your paper, outlining it, revising it, and editing it for grammatical, spelling, and mechanics errors. All these activities take additional time.

Learn How Long It Takes to Do Your Assignments

You also can learn to judge how much time you need for study by estimating how long it takes you to do individual assignments. Not everyone reads, writes, or works problems at the same speed. Time yourself the next time you read ten pages in each of your textbooks. You may have noticed that it didn't take you the same amount of time to read the ten-page selections in all of your texts. Why do you think the times were different? If you said it's because you like some of the subjects better than others, you're correct. Your interest in the material makes a difference in how fast you read. Other factors that can affect your reading rate are the difficulty of the text material, your prior knowledge of the subject, the size of the page, the size of the print, the number of pictures or charts on a page, and whether you highlight or take notes. You may find it useful to make a note in the front cover of each text, such as 10 pages = 20 minutes. When you have a thirty-page reading assignment, you'll know that you need one hour to complete it. On the other hand, if it takes you one hour to read ten pages of physics, then you need three hours to complete that same thirty-page assignment. Finding out how long it takes to read ten pages in each of your texts will help you plan more accurately. You can also time yourself as you complete math assignments and writing assignments or as you review your notes. When you know how long it takes to do the routine work, you'll be able to accurately determine how much time you need for study.

Consider Long-Term Assignments

Many students forget to build in study time for long-term assignments. You need to allow time to study for exams, prepare term papers, and complete semester projects. Some students expect the regular assignment load to disappear when test or paper deadlines roll around. Unfortunately, this doesn't happen. If you don't adjust your study schedule for these long-range assignments, you may find that you have to "steal" time from your regular work in order to prepare for them. As a result, you may fall behind in everything else.

Activity 3-6

Determine Time Needed for Study

Use the chart in Figure 3.7 (or the form on the Web site) to calculate the time you need for study. Go back to your Fixed Commitment Calendar in Figure 3.6 and write in the number of hours that you need this semester for study. Remember that this number will change each semester, depending on your schedule of classes and your goals. Now compare the time available for study to the time that you need. Do you have enough time to complete all your work?

Monitor Your Current Study Time

One way to get a better estimate of how much time you actually need for study is by monitoring your current study time. By keeping track of how many hours you actually study (read, take notes, edit lecture notes, do math or writing assignments, and

FIGURE 3.7

Time Needed for Study Chart

Course Name	Credits	Grade Goal	Difficulty Level	Long-term Assignments	Study Ratio	Hours per Week
					Total Hours	

Note: A full-size version of this chart is available on the *College Study Skills* book-specific Web site.

so on) during a typical week, you can evaluate the accuracy of your estimate of study time needed. You can also repeat the experiment during a week that is not so typical. Choose a week in which you have one or more exams and a paper or project due.

You may also find it helpful to keep a study log. A **study log** is a calendar where you write in the number of hours you spend doing assignments and studying for each of your courses. Use the chart in Figure 3.8 or a full-size copy available on the Web site. By keeping track of exactly how many hours you spend each day (and each week) on each of your courses, you can monitor your time use. You may find that you don't spend enough total time over the course of a week or that you don't spend enough time on one class. You may find that you're getting lower grades in the classes you're spending less time working on. You may also notice that on some days you spend a lot of time on academic tasks and very little time on other days. Look for patterns that will help you correct any problems early in the semester. Compare the total hours for each of your classes to the time goals that you set when you completed the study ratio chart. Like some of my students, you may find that keeping a study log will help motivate you to put more time into your work.

Activity 3-7

Keep a Study Log

Use the study log in Figure 3.8 (or the form on the Web site) to keep track of how much time you spend studying every day for the next week. (Be sure to include weekends.) List each of your classes. How closely does this total match your estimated time needed for study? What patterns did you notice? Did you complete all of your work? Did you put in enough time and effort on each assignment?

Establish a New Time Plan

If you found that you need more time to complete your work than you actually have, you need to modify your time plan. Basically, you have two options. One is

FIGURE 3.8
Study Log
_____

Course	Sunday	Monday	Tuesday	Wednesday	Thursday	Friday	Saturday	**Total**
Total								

Note: A full-size version of this calendar is available on the *College Study Skills* book-specific Web site.

to make more time for study, and the other is to reduce the amount of time that you need for study.

One way to reduce the amount of time that you need for study is to consider reducing your credit load. If this is your first semester in college, you should take twelve to fourteen credits only. If you're a returning adult student, you may find that taking only one or two classes (three to six credits) is a good way to begin. Earning good grades the first semester is much more important than earning a lot of credits. If you're working full time, you may have to take a lighter load as well. After all, what's the point of working so hard to pay for a college education if you can't find enough time to do your best?

If you absolutely can't reduce your credit load, then you need to reduce some of your fixed commitments and make more time for study. In many cases that means reducing work hours. If you're attending school full time, you may find it difficult to work more than twenty hours a week. Certainly, some people can go to school full time and work full time, but many of them report that they don't have time for *anything* else (even meals or sleep).

Some extracurricular activities can take as much time as a part-time or full-time job. Although it's important for students to be involved in college experiences outside the classroom, some students go too far. If you're always running off to some meeting, practice, or activity and don't have enough time to study, you need to rethink your level of involvement in extracurricular activities. You don't have to eliminate all activities; instead, be selective and choose one or two that you really enjoy. Let the others go for another semester.

Reevaluate Your Time Plan

After you've used your time plan for a while, you may find that it's not working. You may need more time for long-range assignments, or you may discover you need more time available for study than you thought. It's important to take a look periodically at how you're using your time during the semester.

A good time to reevaluate your time plan is after the fourth week of the semester; that's when the first round of exams usually occurs. One good way to determine whether you're putting in enough time studying is to consider the grades you received on your first set of exams. If your grades are in line with the goals you set, then your time plan is probably working effectively for you. You also can judge whether you're using your time efficiently by looking back at some of your calendars and "To Do" lists. Have you been accomplishing the study goals that you set each day? Are you moving many tasks to the next day? Are you leaving work undone? Did you have time to prepare adequately for your exams? By answering these questions, you can determine whether you need to change your time plan. Go back and change your plan whenever you need to. If your workload changes during the semester, you may need to make changes in your time plan, too.

The second point at which you should evaluate your time plan is after midterm exams. By this time in the semester, you should be able to determine quite accurately which parts of your time plan work and which don't. This is the best time to make some changes that will help you improve your grades. Finally, you also should rethink your time plan about two weeks before final exams. We'll talk more about this in chapter 14.

ORGANIZE YOUR STUDY TIME

Once you've set up a time plan that allows you enough time to complete all your work, you need to learn how to organize your time so that it can be used efficiently. By learning to plan and schedule your study time, you can begin to take control of your time.

Create a Semester Assignment Calendar

One of the best ways to organize your study time is to make a semester calendar. A **semester assignment calendar** includes all of your assignments, quizzes, and exams. Seeing what you have to do for each day of the semester is the first step in planning your study time.

The easiest way to prepare a semester assignment calendar is to use a blank block calendar similar to the one in Figure 3.9. Write in the name of the month, and number the days of the month. Next, pull out your course syllabi. Write all your assignments on your calendar. (You may have reading assignments, math exercises, and an English paper all due on the same day.) If some of your professors don't give you a day-to-day syllabus, you'll need to add assignments to your calendar as you learn of them. You may find it helpful to put the assignments for each separate course in a different color or list them all in black ink and then use colored markers to differentiate each subject. By color coding your assignments, you can quickly identify the work that you have to do each day. Make exams stand out on your calendar by writing them in large capital letters and putting a box around them.

After you've completed your calendars for each month of the semester, post them where you can see them easily—for example, on your refrigerator or bulletin

FIGURE 3.9
Blank Semester Assignment
Calendar

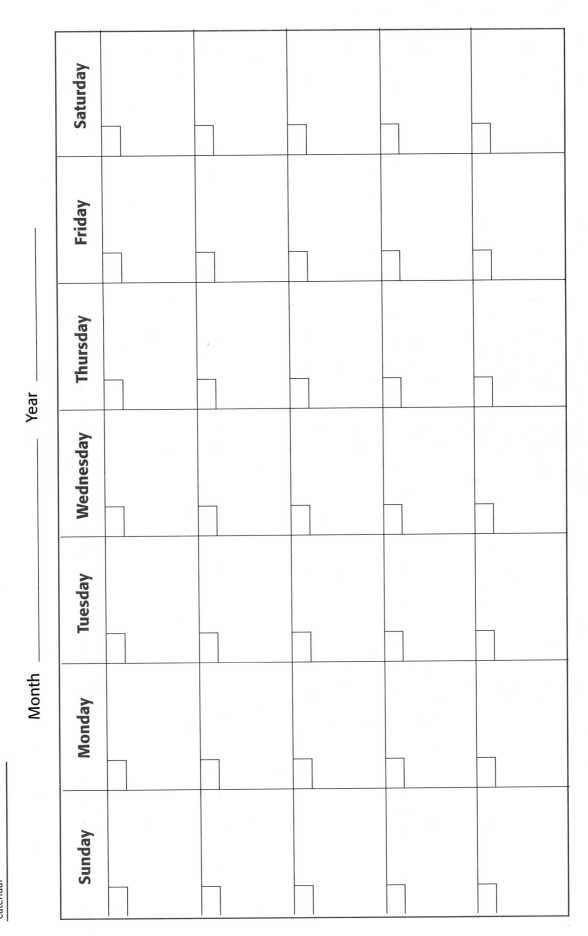

board—and make sure that you're able to see two months at any one time. There is nothing more frustrating than turning the page on your calendar too late and realizing that you missed an important event. This is true for assignments and exams, too. Look at the sample calendars in Figures 3.10 and 3.11. The last week of September looks like a pretty easy week—after the Sociology exam on Monday. There is a little reading to do, but the workload definitely seems to be on the light side. If this were your calendar, you might think that you could take it easy for a week. Now look at the first week of October. You have exams in History, Algebra, and Study Skills, three papers due for English, and two chapters of reading. If you had waited until the beginning of October to turn the page of your calendar, it would have been too late to prepare for your exams and complete your papers.

Activity 3-8

Fill In Your Semester Assignment Calendar

Photocopy the calendar in Figure 3.9, print the blank calendars available on the Web site, or purchase blank calendars in your college bookstore or a local office supply store. Begin filling in your calendar by writing in the months and the dates for the entire semester. Then use your syllabi to list all your assignments on the calendar. Remember to color code your assignments. Don't forget to write exams in capital letters and to box them in so that they really stand out.

Prepare Weekly Task Lists

After you've completed your semester assignment calendar, you should begin to think about identifying your study tasks and planning when to do them. Each assignment that you put on your calendar represents a study task that must be completed. One way to plan your study time is to prepare **weekly task lists.** Just list all of the assignments (reading, math, writing, exams, and so on) due for the following week. It's a good idea to set aside one hour a week to use for planning. Remember to look ahead for exams or long-range assignments and to include these tasks in your plan. You can list your assignments for the week in the order that they're due or by the course; either way is fine. You may also find it helpful to keep a running list of study tasks and projects. Anytime your professor gives you an assignment or you think of one you need to do, add it to the list. Each day review the list and select the ones you need to do tomorrow. The important thing is to learn to plan ahead.

Use Daily "To Do" Lists

After you decide what you need to do for the week, you need to begin to plan what you're going to do each day. A **"To Do" list** is a list of the tasks that you want to complete each day. Break down some of the tasks from your weekly task list. You might decide to read your History assignment over the next two days or work on writing your English essay for one hour every day during the week. (Refer to the section in Chapter 2 on how to write good study goals.)

Putting your personal goals on the list is important, too. This further reinforces your commitment to put all your plans in writing. In addition, writing your personal goals on your "To Do" list will help you stay more organized. The more organized you are in completing your personal goals, the more time you'll have to complete your academic goals.

FIGURE 3.10
Sample Semester Calendar
for September

Month _____September_____

Sunday	Monday	Tuesday	Wednesday	Thursday	Friday	Saturday
2	**3**	**4** H - Ch 1 SS - Ch 1	**5** A - 1.1 & 1.2 E - 1-35 Journal	**6** H - Ch 2 SS - Ch 2	**7** A - 1.3 & 1.4 E - 38-52 Journal Soc - Ch 1 (2-24)	**8**
9	**10** A - 1.5 & 1.6 E - Experience essay-draft	**11** H - Ch 3	**12** A - 2.1 & 2.2 Soc - Ch 2 (26-48)	**13** SS - Goal statements	**14** A - 2.3 & 2.4 E - Experience essay	**15**
16	**17** A - 2.5 & 2.6 E - 53-56 Soc - Ch 3 (52-74)	**18** H - Ch 4 SS - Ch 3 To Do lists	**19** A - 3.1 & 3.2 E - Observation essay-draft	**20** SS - Ch 4 & H.O. Calendars due	**21** A - 3.3 & 3.4 E - Observation essay due	**22**
23	**24** A - 3.5 & 3.6 SOC-EXAM 1	**25** H - Ch 5 SS - Ch 5 notes due	**26** A - 4.1 & 4.2 Soc - Ch 4 (75-103)	**27**	**28** A - 4.3 & 4.4 E - 65-81	**29**
30						

A = College Algebra H = Western Civilization SS = Study Skills
E = English Composition Soc = Sociology

FIGURE 3.11
Sample Semester Calendar for
October

Month _____October_____

Sunday	Monday	Tuesday	Wednesday	Thursday	Friday	Saturday
	1 A - 4.5 & 4.6.6 E - Exposition essay-draft	**2** H - EXAM 1 SS - Text marking due	**3** A - EXAM 1 E - Revision Soc - Ch 5 (105-130)	**4** H - Ch 6 SS - EXAM 1	**5** A - 5.1 & 5.2 E - Exposition essay due	**6**
7	**8** A - 5.3 & 5.4 E - 82-111 Soc - Ch 7 (162-189)	**9** H - Ch 7 SS - Ch 9 text notes	**10** A - 5.5 & 5.6 E - Revision due	**11** SS - Predicted questions	**12** A - 6.1 & 6.2	**13**
14	**15** A - 6.3 & 6.4 E - Portfolio due	**16** H - Ch 8 SS - Ch 6 & H.O.	**17** A - 6.5 & 6.6 Soc - Ch 8 (191-240)	**18** SS - Ch 7	**19** A - 7.1 & 7.2 E - 112-125	**20**
21	**22** A - 7.3 & 7.4 E - Definition essay-draft SOC - EXAM II	**23** H - Ch 9 SS - Ch 10	**24** A - 7.5 & 7.6 E - 127-140	**25** H - Ch 10 SS - Study plan due	**26** A - EXAM II E - Definition essay due Soc - Ch 11 (278-310)	**27**
28	**29** A - 8.1 & 8.2 E - Argument essay due	**30** H - EXAM II SS - EXAM II	**31** A - 8.3 & 8.4 E - 141-162			

A = College Algebra H = Western Civilization SS = Study Skills
E = English Composition Soc = Sociology

FIGURE 3.12
Sample "To Do" Lists

JEAN'S "TO DO" LIST	ROBIN'S "TO DO" LIST

JEAN'S "TO DO" LIST

DAY _____ Wednesday _____

Study Goals:

- √1   Go to student aid office
- √2   Do laundry
- 7   Final draft Engl paper
- √6   Go copy Fr tape Ch 3
- √3   Get card for Grandma B-day
- 11   Make to do list for tomorrow
- 5   Study Ch 2 Fr
- √8   Read Art pp 53-63
- 9   Do Alg Ch 2-5
- √4   Dentist Appt. 2:30
- √10   Meet Tom 5:30

Personal Goals:

- ☐ _____
- ☐ _____
- ☐ _____
- ☐ _____

ROBIN'S "TO DO" LIST

DAY _____ THURSDAY _____

Study Goals:

- √2   MAKE COPY OF SPEECH OUTLINE
- √3   PRACTICE SPEECH
- √4   READ PP. 135-145 IN BLACK LIT
- √1   READ ESSAY 2 IN POL SCI
- √8   DO FEB. CALENDAR
- √6   READ PP. 146-156 IN BLACK LIT
- √5   READ 10 PPS. OF CH. 1 POL SCI
- √7   READ PP. 163-173 IN SS
- √9   DO "THINGS TO DO" FOR TOMORROW
- ☐ _____
- ☐ _____

Personal Goals:

- √10   WRITE LETTER HOME
- √11   CHECK MAIL
- √12   GO TO BASKETBALL GAME
- 13   CLEAN ROOM

Making "To Do" lists can become habit forming, so by all means get started immediately. Don't worry if you don't accomplish everything on your list; few people do everything they set out to do every day. Just move the one or two tasks that were left uncompleted to the top of the list for the next day. Remember, though: It's important that you plan realistically. A pattern of planning too much to do and then moving half of your tasks to the next day can lead to procrastination.

Establishing priorities will help you complete your most important (or pressing) tasks first. Use numbers, a star, or another symbol to indicate that certain tasks need to be done first. Look at the "To Do" lists in Figure 3.12. In the first example, Jean mixed study goals and personal goals together. As you might expect, the personal goals were completed, and the study goals were left undone. Put your academic goals at the top of the page and your personal goals at the bottom. By putting your study goals first, you're reinforcing your commitment to academics. By setting priorities, Robin was able to complete all of her study tasks before beginning her personal goals (Figure 3.12).

Many students use professional planners (available in college bookstores or office supply stores) to keep track of assignments and personal goals. Many planners are designed with space for hour-by-hour planning, blocks for listing tasks due each week, and monthly calendars. Using a professional planner can help you organize all your study, work, and personal goals in one place. Remember: It doesn't matter what kind of planner you use; the important thing is to plan ahead and write down what you plan to accomplish each day.

Activity 3-9

Complete Your "To Do" Lists

Write "To Do" lists every day for the next week. Photocopy the form in Figure 3.13 or print copies from the Web site. Be sure that you break tasks down, number them to show their priority, and check off completed tasks. Were you able to complete all your assignments? Did using the "To Do" lists help?

Set Up Your Study Schedule

To make the best use of your study time, you should begin to plan weekly or daily what you're going to do and when. Now that you know how long it takes to read ten pages in each of your textbooks, you can easily schedule all your reading assignments. You also should have a pretty good estimate of how long it will take to complete your writing, math, and study assignments. All these factors affect how efficiently you use your study time and how effectively you complete your assignments.

Assign Tasks to Available Study Time

To set up your study schedule, you need to refer to your Fixed Commitment Calendar to assign specific tasks to your available study time (see Figure 3.14). Use your "To Do" list to slot assignments into one-hour time blocks, two-hour time blocks, or longer time blocks. If you look back at Greg's Fixed Commitment Calendar in Figure 3.4, you'll notice that Greg has three one-hour time blocks and a four-hour time block on Wednesdays. Greg prefers to do his Algebra homework right after class when the information is still fresh. If he has a thirty-page chapter of History to read, for example, he could read the first ten pages before lunch, the next ten pages right after class, and the last ten pages from 7:00 to 8:00. Of course, Greg could have begun reading his History on Tuesday, too. Greg could then use his longer time block in the evening to work on an upcoming English paper. Assigning specific tasks to specific blocks of study time can help you complete your work on time.

Use One-Hour Time Blocks

Many students ignore one-hour blocks of time because they think that one hour is not long enough to really accomplish anything. In fact, one-hour blocks are the most important study blocks that you have. During a one-hour block of time, you can get a good start on a math assignment, complete a "chunk" of a reading assignment, complete a short writing assignment, or even review or expand on your lecture notes. If you've planned ahead, you'll find you can get a lot done in these short periods of time.

Schedule Time to Complete Each Task

There are a number of ways to indicate when you're going to do your assignments. One method is to write down the time you're going to complete each task right on your "To Do" list. Just jot down the time next to each of your tasks. You may also use a calendar similar to the one you used to keep your time log or a copy of your Fixed Commitment Calendar to jot down what you want to do during your available study times. In this case, you can write the specific tasks that you want to accomplish in each time block. If you're accustomed to using a daily planner, write your assignment down in your calendar as if it were a dentist appointment.

FIGURE 3.13
"To Do" List Form

"TO DO" LIST

DAY _____   **DAY** _____

Study Goals: **Study Goals:**

☐ _____   ☐ _____

☐ _____   ☐ _____

☐ _____   ☐ _____

☐ _____   ☐ _____

☐ _____   ☐ _____

☐ _____   ☐ _____

☐ _____   ☐ _____

☐ _____   ☐ _____

☐ _____   ☐ _____

☐ _____   ☐ _____

☐ _____   ☐ _____

☐ _____   ☐ _____

☐ _____   ☐ _____

Personal Goals: **Personal Goals:**

☐ _____   ☐ _____

☐ _____   ☐ _____

☐ _____   ☐ _____

☐ _____   ☐ _____

☐ _____   ☐ _____

☐ _____   ☐ _____

☐ _____   ☐ _____

FIGURE 3.14
Steps to Organizing Your Study
Time

Semester Assignment Calendar

Weekly Task List

Daily "To Do" List

Consult Your Fixed Commitment Calendar

Schedule Your Study Task

Use Your Daytime Study Hours

When you're planning your study schedule, don't forget to use your daytime study hours. In high school you may have been able to get all your homework done during the evening, but there aren't enough evening hours to complete all your study assignments in college. Look back at Greg's Fixed Commitment Calendar in Figure 3.4. Greg needed a minimum of thirty-two hours of study time per week to complete his assignments. If he used only his evening hours, he would be twelve hours short of his minimum. The fourteen hours that Greg has available during the day are necessary for him to do his work. By starting your study tasks early in the day, you increase your chances of completing them.

Use Time Between Classes

You can also accomplish a lot by using the hours that you have between classes. Instead of going back to your room to drop off your books, find an empty classroom or sit in the hall and begin your next reading assignment. By getting a good solid start on the assignment, you increase your probability of completing it. You may also find that right after a class is the best time to edit your lecture notes (see Chapter 5). If you have a quiz scheduled or suspect that one will be given, you should use the time between classes to review your lecture notes and your highlighting or text notes before the quiz. Take a few minutes now to count how many hours you have between classes this semester. Using this time to accomplish some of your study goals is an important step in achieving good time management.

Activity 3-10

Schedule Your Assignments

Choose one of the formats described earlier and make a list of your study goals for tomorrow. Don't forget to break long assignments down into manageable units. Then refer to your Fixed Commitment Calendar and schedule your assignments into appropriate time blocks. Take your plan to class and discuss it with a group of your classmates. Did anyone have suggestions to improve your schedule?

MANAGING MULTIPLE PROJECTS

Many students have difficulty managing **multiple projects**—two or more quizzes, exams, papers, or projects due during the same or overlapping time frame. For the purpose of this section, think of a project as a quiz, an exam, a paper, a speech, or a project. Basically, a project is a major task you need to do usually requiring more time and counting for a higher percentage of your grade than your regular assignments. What happens when you have two exams on the same day or an exam, a quiz in a different class, and a paper due all in the same week? Have you ever worked hard to prepare for one exam, but "sacrificed" the other? Did you spend two or three hours preparing for a quiz only to realize later that you should have spent that time on the exam instead? Did you let a paper go until after your exams were over? If you answered *yes* to any of these questions, you may have a problem managing multiple projects.

Activity 3-11

How Well Do You Manage Multiple Projects?

Think back to the last time you had two exams or a quiz and an exam on the same day or more than one paper or project due at the same time. Did you feel overwhelmed? Did you have trouble keeping all of your materials organized? Did you ever earn a low grade on one because you spent more time on the other? Describe your past experiences with managing multiple projects, citing specific examples, if possible, and discuss the strategies you used.

Why Multiple Projects Cause Problems

Many students are used to preparing for one paper, project, or exam at a time; in fact, many students feel most comfortable finishing one task before beginning another. It's not easy to work on two or three or more projects at a time. Some students have difficulty setting priorities, staying on task, and keeping track of their materials. If you don't learn to manage multiple projects, you may find that you fall into the trap of sacrificing your grade on one exam to do well on another or earn a low grade on one paper because you must do well on another.

How to Manage Multiple Projects

To successfully complete all of your work, you need to develop some new strategies for managing your time and organizing your materials. You need to develop a plan, learn to set priorities, set up a system, and monitor your progress (see Figure 3.15).

Make a Plan

The first step in dealing with multiple projects is to make a plan for each. You may find it helpful to create a project sheet. Put the name of the project on the top and put the due date right underneath or in the top corner. Then jot down what you have to do. Next, break the project down into smaller pieces by listing each step on your sheet. Then create an Action Plan for your project. Finally, set target dates for each step and write them on your action plan. If it's a semester-long project, you may want to create a time line like the one in Figure 3.16. If you're preparing for

FIGURE 3.15
Steps to Managing Multiple Projects

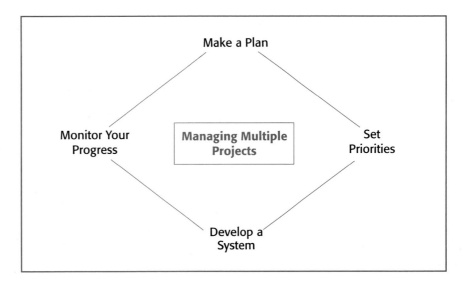

exams, look ahead to Chapter 10 and you'll see that the Five-Day Study Plan incorporates many of these steps for preparing for an exam. Once you've developed your plan and your target dates for each of the steps, mark them on your Semester Assignment Calendar. Think of them as due dates just like any of your other assignments.

Once you know what you need to do and when you expect to complete each part of your project, you need to think about when you're going to do it. One strategy for managing multiple projects is to separate them by the time you work on them. You could decide to work on one project in the mornings, another every afternoon, and a third in the evening. Dividing the projects by time frames can help you keep them separate in your mind and keep you on task. Some students prefer to work on one proejct one day a week (perhaps every Sunday afternoon) or work on one on Mondays, Wednesdays, and Fridays and the other on Tuesdays and Thursdays. Choosing to work on different tasks on different days of the week or during different times of the day can help you get them done and keep you more focused as you complete each task.

Set Priorities

Although you may be surprised to read this, sometimes it's smart to sacrifice one project to do well on another. For example, I give quizzes in my class that count for 20 points out of 600, or about three percent of the course grade. At the beginning of the semester, I always have a student or two who complain to me that they have one or two big exams (counting for 20 to 25 percent of their course grade) on the same day as one of my quizzes. When they ask me what to

FIGURE 3.16
Time Line for Research Paper

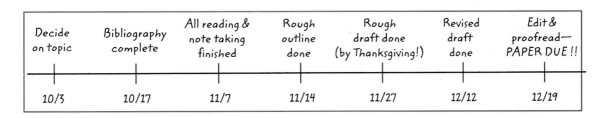

do, I usually reply that if they are pressed for time, they should spend a much smaller amount of time or not even study for the quiz and use that time instead to prepare for their exams. On the other hand, if you have two exams on the same day, don't sacrifice the one to do well in the other. Exams almost always have a major impact on your course grade. One of the biggest mistakes some of my students make is studying for one exam and letting the other go (and hoping for the best).

Unfortunately, three or four weeks later, the same two exams occur on the same day again. This time the students study hard for the second exam (after all, they have a low grade on the first exam in that class) and let the other go. The overall result of this strategy is that the students end up with two mediocre grades in these courses. When you have two projects due at the same time, you need to look at your priorities (including the percentage of the grade that each project represents) and your goals before deciding how much time to spend on each task.

Develop a System

If you've ever worked on three papers at the same time or tried to prepare for five finals in the same week, you know that you need a system to get things done. One of the things you need to do is create a system to keep track of your materials, what you've done, and what you still need to do. For smaller projects, you may find that using a different color file folder for each project will work well. Then color code all of the materials related to that project the same color. If you decide to color code your Biology project red, choose a red folder, use red index cards for your note cards, and use a red highlighter to color code your project sheet, action plan, and any articles that you photocopy on the topic. Again, use red to write the target dates on your Semester Assignment Calendar or for your time line on your bulletin board. If you're working on three papers or projects all due at or around the end of the semester, you may need a larger space for your materials. You may want to use a file or box to hold all of your materials. Using one area of your desk or table for each project can also help you keep your materials separated and easily accessible. Post each of the project sheets on your wall or bulletin board above your file (or pile) and refer to them often to stay on task.

Monitor Your Progress

Making up a plan and developing a system are good ways to start working on your projects, but they won't guarantee that you'll get your projects done. You need to monitor your progress on each task on a regular basis. Set up a regular time during the week to review each of your projects. Pull out your action plans and check off the tasks you've completed and then add the next step to your weekly or daily task list. It's probably a good idea to meet with your professor every few weeks to discuss your progress (and make sure you're following directions) for semester-long projects. Finally, adjust your action plan and your project plan when necessary to accommodate delays (illness or an unexpected assignment) or if you're accomplishing your tasks more quickly than you anticipated. With a good plan, a system of organization, and some careful monitoring, you can manage multiple projects and achieve all of your goals. A side benefit of developing these new strategies is that they are the same type of strategies you'll find yourself using in the workplace where everyone works on multiple projects.

Activity 3-12

Create a Plan For Managing Multiple Projects

 Look ahead at your syllabi or your Semester Assignment Calendar, if you've already completed it, and identify a week where you have to complete multiple projects. Briefly describe the projects, when each is due, and the percentage of your grade that they represent. Write the information for each project on an index card and take them to class. In class, work with a group to discuss how each member should manage his or her multiple projects. On the back of each card, develop a brief plan, time frame, and prioritization, and suggest a system of organization for success.

USE TIME-MANAGEMENT STRATEGIES TO STAY MOTIVATED

Organizing your work and scheduling your time can make a huge difference in how much time it takes to do your work. However, just planning to read twenty pages at 2:00 P.M. is no guarantee that you'll get it done. Schedules are designed to organize your use of time, but they're not designed to make you do the work. *You have to do that.*

One thing that can make a difference in whether you accomplish your goals is your level of motivation. You can keep your motivation high by using some specific techniques.

Study in One-Hour Blocks

One effective strategy for keeping yourself motivated is to study in sixty-minute time blocks. As you schedule your study tasks, break them down so that they can be accomplished in one-hour blocks of time. Then plan to read, do problems, write, or study for fifty minutes. If you find that you can't concentrate on your work for the entire fifty minutes, work for thirty minutes and then take a five-minute break.

Take Breaks

After each study block of fifty minutes, you should plan a ten-minute break. Be realistic about the kind of activity that you plan for a study break. Taking a ten-minute nap just will not work, and going out to play a quick game of basketball inevitably will lead to a longer game of basketball. What can you do in ten minutes? You can grab a snack, check your mail, check on your kids, throw a load of laundry in the washer, or make a phone call. (Resist the temptation to call a good friend to chat—you won't be able to hang up in ten minutes.) Doing aerobics or just stretching is also a great activity for a break between study periods.

Tackle Difficult Assignments First

Do the assignments for the course you dislike first and get them out of the way. You can easily complete the assignments for your favorite classes late in the day, even when you're feeling tired. Unfortunately, that usually is not true for those more dif-

MORE TIME-MANAGEMENT TIPS

DEVELOP A SCHEDULE. Set up a schedule for both studying and completing your other responsibilities. Put your schedule in writing and stick to it. You may need to explain to your friends or parents (or your children) that you need more time to study now that you're in college and won't be able to spend as much time going out or doing household chores as you did before.

POST YOUR STUDY SCHEDULE. Put your list of study tasks on the bulletin board or on the refrigerator each week so that everyone in your family knows what you need to accomplish that week. This will help keep you more organized and let your family know what you need to do.

MAKE USE OF SMALL BLOCKS OF TIME. Use time between classes to get started on an assignment, edit notes, or review for a quiz. Instead of waiting for large blocks of time to do your work, break down your tasks and work on smaller portions of the assignment during fifteen-, thirty-, or even forty-five-minute time blocks throughout the day.

STUDY DURING BREAKS AT WORK. You'd be surprised at how much school work you can do during breaks over a one-week period. You could read five pages of a chapter during lunch. You could review your word cards (flash cards for technical terminology) during a fifteen-minute break. You could even mentally review or quiz yourself on the material for an exam during a slow time at work.

PLAN TIME WITH YOUR FAMILY. Set aside time to spend with your family or friends each day or each week. Make this a regular part of your time-management schedule. During "slow" weeks or term breaks, plan special activities as a way of saying thank you for their support, patience, and help during the busier weeks.

DELEGATE SOME HOUSEHOLD TASKS. Unless you aren't planning to sleep, eat, or ever relax, you won't have time to do all your household chores when you're going to school. Do what you *have* to do and leave the rest for a slow week, day off, or even until term break. Ask your family to help out by doing some of the cooking, cleaning, or laundry. If each member of the family accepts just one task, you'll be amazed at the time you'll gain.

COOK AHEAD AND FREEZE MAIN COURSES. Instead of making one meat loaf for dinner tonight, make two and freeze one for the next week. You can also cook ahead during "light" weeks of the semester or during term breaks. Having dinner ready to pop in the microwave can be a real time-saver during busy weeks.

LEARN TO SAY NO. Believe it or not, I was a Girl Scout leader my first year in graduate school. As a mother, it was a great decision. As a returning student, it was a disaster. While you're attending college, you won't have time for many outside activities. When you do say no, explain that when you complete your education, you'll be happy to help out.

ficult assignments. If you leave them until the wee hours of the morning, you may find instead that you don't do them at all.

Also, if you do the assignments that you like the most first, you have nothing to look forward to. It's kind of like eating dessert before you eat your meal. The best part is already over, and the rest is somewhat disappointing. You also may find that if you leave the more difficult tasks for the end of the day, you worry about them as you work on other tasks. A difficult assignment can feel like a heavy weight hanging over your head. Doing your least favorite or most difficult assignments first and your easiest or favorite assignments last will help you stay motivated throughout the day.

Switch Subjects

Another good strategy for maintaining your motivation to study is to switch subjects. By alternating between reading psychology and working algebra problems, you can get more done without becoming bored and tired. If you have a long time block available for study (for instance, from 6:00 to 11:00), you should switch subjects every hour. Occasionally, you'll find that you're really progressing on an assignment and, after the ten-minute break, want to continue working on it. In such cases, you should do so. However, most students find that after an hour they're only too willing to work on something else for a while.

Break Tasks Down

You may find that breaking down your tasks into manageable units will help you accomplish your goals. Which would you rather read, a fifty-page chapter or a ten-page chapter? Most people would agree that a ten-page chapter sounds much more appealing. If you have long reading assignments, break them down on your "To Do" list. You could divide that fifty-page chapter into five separate tasks. It may make your list a little longer, but it also will allow you to shorten it more rapidly. Once you complete the first ten-page chunk of reading, you'll feel a sense of accomplishment and be motivated to read the next ten pages. Many of my students find that breaking down tasks reduces their tendency to procrastinate—perhaps you will, too.

Work Ahead

To be in control of your time, learn to work ahead on your assignments. You'll find college much less stressful if you stop doing Tuesday's assignments on Monday. Get into the habit of doing the work due for Tuesday on Sunday or even on Friday. Always being a little ahead of the game will give you a feeling of security. If something comes up (and something always does, at just the wrong time), you'll still be prepared for class the next morning.

You should work ahead on long-range assignments, too. Schedule one to two hours each week to work on a term paper or project. By starting early in the semester, you can easily complete your term paper and still keep up with your regular assignments. To plan ahead for a long-range project, use the same strategies described earlier for managing multiple projects. For a term paper, some of the steps are: select a topic, develop a bibliography, find books and journal articles, read and take notes, develop an outline, do more research if necessary, write the rough draft, and so on. By working ahead, you can avoid the time crunches that often occur at the end of the semester.

Plan Rewards

In many ways, your ten-minute study break is a reward for having completed one block of study tasks. These short breaks, however, aren't always enough of a reward to keep you motivated. It's a good idea to get into the habit of rewarding yourself for completing difficult tasks or for completing all your work on a particular day. **Rewards** are whatever you can plan to do that will help keep you working when you want to stop. Students use many kinds of rewards to stay motivated. Ordering a pizza after finishing a tough assignment works for some students. Others work hard to complete their studying in time to watch a favorite television show. If you know that you want to watch "Monday Night Football," plan your work on Sunday and Monday so that you can be finished in time; then you'll be able to sit back and watch the game without feeling guilty.

REDUCE YOUR PROCRASTINATION

Procrastination, putting things off, is a common behavior pattern for many students. It's often the result of not wanting to start a task that seems difficult or time-consuming. Unfortunately, procrastination can become a habit. The more you avoid the task, the more daunting it becomes; the more you tend to dwell on the negative aspects of the task, the more it's blown all out of proportion. After a while you may feel that you can't ever complete the task because you don't have the time to finish it.

Activity 3-13

Check Your Procrastination Level

Go to the *College Study Skills* book-specific Web site and follow the link in Chapter 3 to the University of Texas Procrastination Quotient online evaluation tool. After answering each of the questions, score your responses.

Main Causes of Procrastination

According to Albert Ellis and William Knaus, the three main causes of procrastination are "self-downing," low frustration tolerance, and hostility.[2] Learning more about each of these causes may help you learn to control your own procrastination problems.

Self-downing
Self-downing refers to putting yourself down—telling yourself you can't do it or you're not smart enough. When you don't complete tasks successfully or on time, you may begin to doubt your ability to succeed. If you set unrealistic goals such as planning to study the entire weekend or getting an A in every class, you may begin to worry about whether you can really achieve them. This can result in procrastination or avoidance caused by self-downing.

Low Frustration Tolerance
A second cause of procrastination is low frustration tolerance. Students who experience **low frustration tolerance** are easily frustrated; they tend to give up or have trouble starting on a task when it appears to be difficult or too time consuming. Instead of getting to work, they are often thinking, "It's too hard." Some students experience a great deal of frustration when they attempt to complete certain assignments or projects. Writing a twenty-page term paper for your Political Science class, for example, may be extremely difficult for you. The task may appear to be too difficult or require too much of your time, and just thinking about it may be-

---

[2]Albert Ellis and William J. Knaus, *Overcoming Procrastination* (New York: Signet, 1977), p. 16.

come a very unpleasant experience. Your low tolerance for frustration may lead you to put off this difficult task and do something else instead. Before you know it, you've fallen into the procrastination trap. The next time you decide that you had better start that paper, you may experience even more feelings of anxiety and panic because by then there is even less time available to complete the paper.

Hostility

Ellis and Knaus's third cause of procrastination is **hostility** toward others. You may put off doing that term paper because of your anger toward your professor. Comments like "He just expects too much of our class" or "She didn't even assign us that paper until two weeks before the end of the semester" or "That assignment is so unfair" are indicative of angry feelings toward your instructors. If you are angry at one of your instructors for giving you a difficult assignment, because you received a poor test grade, or for embarrassing you in class, you may find it unpleasant to work on the assignment for that class. Your angry feelings can in fact increase your feelings of frustration about the task. Together, these feelings lead to procrastination.

Other Reasons Why Students Procrastinate

Some students put off studying for exams until it's almost too late. Have you? You may be procrastinating for another reason—to protect yourself from feelings of inadequacy. By not studying well enough, you can protect your ego because you can blame your failure on your lack of preparation rather than on your lack of ability. For example, you might say, "Well, if I had studied, I would have gotten a B, but I just didn't have time." In this way you tell yourself that you *could* have done a good job if you had chosen to.

Procrastination also can be the result of poor time management. Not planning ahead for long-range assignments leaves some students in a time crunch when they realize that a paper or project deadline is approaching. Instead of having six to eight weeks to prepare a term paper, procrastinators may find themselves with one week or less to complete it. Of course, this often leads to panic and poor performance.

Procrastination can become a habit, a way of life, for some students. Procrastination leads to more procrastination. Once you start to put work off, things pile up. As your workload grows, it becomes even more difficult to get it all done. Knowing you are weeks behind in one class can be so overwhelming that you can't even think about trying to catch up.

Another reason students procrastinate is lack of motivation; they sometimes just can't get motivated to start a particular assignment. This may be the result of poor performance in the course to date or poor performance on similar tasks. A student who has a low grade in a class after midterm may find it difficult to get excited about a group project that's due in two weeks. If you feel that a course or an assignment is irrelevant or has little meaning, you also may find it difficult to become motivated. Some students find that they tend to procrastinate on tasks that are not directly related to courses for their major. Business majors may think that courses in English composition or literature are irrelevant to achieving their career goals. Literature majors may believe that required science courses are a waste of time. This attitude can seriously affect students' motivation to complete their study tasks.

Finally, some students procrastinate because they're waiting for the *perfect* time, place, or mood to do the assignment. Without realizing it, they fall into the procrastination trap.

Activity 3-14

Make a Procrastination Profile

List ten tasks that you have put off in the past month. Be sure to include both academic and personal tasks. Then identify the main reason that you procrastinated on each one. Some of your reasons may be ones discussed above; others may be ones you've identified on your own. What patterns did you identify? What changes do you plan to make?

Strategies for Overcoming Procrastination

Because so many people have problems with procrastination, many books, articles, and Web sites are devoted to the topic. They include hundreds of suggestions for dealing with procrastination. Below, you'll find a number of strategies and techniques that will help you overcome procrastination related to your academic work.

- **Just get started.** The best way to overcome procrastination is simply to get started—to take action. When you decide to work on your term paper or your English assignment, don't think about why you should or shouldn't do it—just start it. Do anything. Take out paper and write anything. Work for five to ten minutes. At the end of that time, you can decide whether you want to work for another ten minutes.

- **Set realistic goals.** If you set reasonable expectations for yourself, you're more likely to accomplish your goals and less likely to have negative feelings about your capabilities.

- **Clarify the directions.** Make sure that you know how to do the assignment before you begin. If you're unsure, check with the professor, a tutor, or another classmate. It's hard to get started when you really aren't sure what it is you're expected to do.

- **Start with the easiest part of the task.** Do the easiest part of the assignment or only a small part of it. Once you start the assignment, you're likely to continue. Remember, getting started is half the battle.

- **Avoid overscheduling.** Estimate how much time it will take to complete your daily tasks. If you plan only what you can accomplish in the time you have available for study, you won't have a long list of tasks to carry over to the next day.

- **Create "To Do" lists.** Putting your tasks in writing helps you see exactly what you must accomplish and strengthens your commitment to complete your work. Adding a specific time to begin each of your tasks will help you organize your study time and avoid procrastination.

- **Set priorities.** If you complete your most important tasks first, you won't feel as though you have failed or let yourself down.

- **Break down large tasks.** Breaking down large tasks makes them appear less difficult and time-consuming. It's always easier to get yourself motivated to do a small task. Remember how much easier it was to read ten pages of the chapter than the fifty pages that were assigned?

- **Recognize that not all assignments are easy.** You will have to do some assignments that you don't like or enjoy. Some of them will be difficult or time-consuming. If you can accept the fact that not all your tasks will be pleasant experiences, that in itself will help you approach them more willingly.

- **Recognize that all courses are relevant.** Learning to see the relevance of your courses and assignments also can motivate you to do your work. Too many students think of college as something to do in order to get a job. A college education will help prepare you for a career, but it is also your opportunity to become an educated person (something that will serve you well in *any* career).

- **Use positive self-talk.** Tell yourself that you can complete the task, that you want to do it, and that you can be successful. Don't tell yourself that it's too hard, too big, or that you probably won't do it right. Making excuses for not working on the task leads to procrastination; using positive self-talk helps you get started now.

- **Identify escapist techniques.** You also can help yourself avoid procrastination by identifying your **escapist techniques**—things you do to keep from doing your work. Do you suddenly decide to clean the house, take a nap, check your email, watch television, or visit a friend when you should be doing assignments? You may find that you aren't even aware that you're trying to avoid doing your work; you may not discover these procrastination patterns until you actually look for them.

- **Plan rewards.** Using some of the reward systems that were described earlier may help you overcome your tendency to procrastinate on certain tasks. Remember: Plan to do something that you really like as a reward for completing something you don't like to do.

Activity 3-15

Identify Your Escapist Techniques

On a separate sheet of paper, create a chart using the following headings. Jot down all of the escapist techniques that you use in a one-week period to keep from doing your work. What can you do to keep from repeating these avoidance patterns?

DATE	ASSIGNMENT OR STUDY TASK	WHAT DID I DO TO ESCAPE?	WHY DID I WANT TO ESCAPE?	WHAT STRATEGIES CAN I USE TO KEEP FROM TRYING TO ESCAPE MY WORK?

Activity 3-16

Describe Possible Strategies to Overcome Procrastination Problems

Refer to the Procrastination Profile that you created in Activity 3-14. Work in a group to suggest strategies that you could have used to overcome your procrastination problems. Select five common procrastination problems to present to the class along with several of the coping strategies your group suggested.

Activity 3-17

Where Are You Now?

Now that you have completed Chapter 3, take a few minutes to repeat the "Where Are You Now?" activity, located on the *College Study Skills* Web site. What changes did you make as a result of reading this chapter? How are you planning to apply what you've learned in this chapter?

SUMMARY

Good time-management strategies are crucial to your college success. Monitoring how you use your time now is the first step to achieving good time management. Keeping a Time Log will help you get a better picture of any time-use problems that you have. Complete a Fixed Commitment Calendar to see how much time you actually have available for study tasks. Then set up a Semester Assignment Calendar so that you get a semester view of your workload and important due dates for each of your courses. Preparing weekly task lists and daily "To Do" lists will keep you organized and up to date with your work. Make academics your number one priority when you decide how to use your *free* time. Learning to manage multiple projects will help you be more successful in college. Taking breaks, switching subjects, and planning rewards are just a few of the strategies that will keep you motivated and on schedule. Many students fall into the procrastination trap. Understanding the real reasons for procrastination will help you learn why you may procrastinate in certain situations. By identifying your escapist techniques and making a decision to use more effective strategies, you can overcome this problem. Breaking down tasks, starting with the easiest part of the assignment, and setting specific goals are all good strategies for breaking the procrastination cycle. If you use good time-management techniques, you can stay up to date on your course assignments, have time for relaxation and other responsibilities, and eliminate the stress and panic that often result from not getting your work done.

REVIEW QUESTIONS

Terms You Should Know: Make a flash card for each term.

Escapist techniques	Procrastination	Study log
Fixed commitment	Prospective	Time log
Fixed commitment calendar	Retrospective	Time management
Hostility	Rewards	"To Do" list
Low frustration tolerance	Self-downing	Weekly task lists
Multiple projects	Semester assignment calendar	

Completion: Fill in the blank to complete each of the following statements.

1. The first step in good time management is _____ how you use your time now.

2. You need to spend almost one- _____ of your time each week on academic tasks if you are a full-time student.

3. The average student spends about _____ hours outside of class for every hour in class to complete assignments.

4. Completing a _____ calendar will help you determine how well you can stick to a schedule.

5. The best way to overcome problems with procrastination is simply to _____ _____ .

Multiple Choice: Circle the letter of the best answer for each of the following questions. Be sure to underline key words and eliminate wrong answers.

6. You can determine your time available for study by completing a:
   A. time log.
   B. fixed commitment calendar.
   C. semester assignment calendar.
   D. prospective-retrospective calendar.

7. Which of the following is *not* one of the main causes of procrastination?
   A. Self-downing
   B. Low frustration tolerance
   C. Feelings of inadequacy
   D. Hostility

Short Answer–Essay: On a separate sheet, answer each of the following questions.

8. Describe the five factors that influence how much time you need for study.

9. How can time-management strategies keep you motivated?

10. What are five strategies that students can use to overcome problems with procrastination?

MEMORY AND LEARNING

In this chapter you will learn more about:

- **How information is processed in memory**
- **Why you need memory strategies**
- **General strategies to improve your memory**
- **Specific strategies to improve your memory**

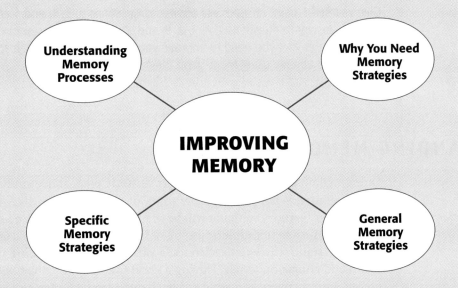

Understanding Memory Processes

Why You Need Memory Strategies

IMPROVING MEMORY

Specific Memory Strategies

General Memory Strategies

Activity 4-1

Where Are You Now?

Take a few minutes to answer *yes* or *no* to the following questions.

		YES	NO
1.	Do you often know the answer to a question but find that you can't think of it?	____	____
2.	Do you organize or group information to help you remember it?	____	____
3.	After you study, do you go back and test yourself to monitor your learning?	____	____
4.	Do you make up rhymes or words to help you remember some information?	____	____
5.	Do you space your practice when reviewing information?	____	____
6.	Do you try to memorize all the information that you need to know for an exam?	____	____
7.	Do you often find that you get confused by closely related information?	____	____
8.	Do you often forget a lot of the information that you studied by the time you take the test?	____	____
9.	Is the TV or stereo on while you study?	____	____
10.	Can you learn and remember information just by making up a rhyme, word, or other memory aid?	____	____
	Total Points		____

Give yourself 1 point for each *yes* answer to questions 2, 3, 4, and 5 and 1 point for each *no* answer to questions 1, 6, 7, 8, 9, and 10. Now total up your points. A low score indicates that you need to improve your memory skills. A high score indicates that you are already using many good memory strategies.

UNDERSTANDING MEMORY PROCESSES

Doing well on exams requires an effective study plan, active study strategies, and a good memory. What you typically think of as learning involves storing information in your memory so that it will be available later when you need it. In this chapter, you'll gain a better understanding of how information is learned. This will help you understand why you need to use a variety of active learning strategies to learn and retain course material. "Having a good memory" involves both putting information into memory and getting it back out—both storage and retrieval. Can you recall a time when you thought you had studied a particular topic well enough that you knew it for the exam, only to find that you couldn't remember the information during the test? Perhaps you never really got the information into your long-term

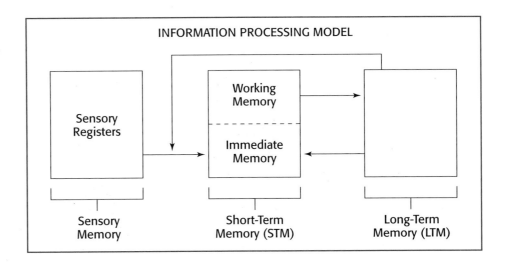

memory, or perhaps you simply were unable to recall it when you needed to. Why do we forget? How do we learn? Many students really don't understand how memory works. Do you? Learning about how we store and retrieve information will help you understand why some study strategies work and others don't. Over the years, psychologists have tried to develop theories to explain how memory works. One of the most useful of these is the Information Processing Model.

Information Processing Model

The **Information Processing Model** suggests that memory is complex and consists of various processes and stages. For example, there are at least three types of memory: sensory memory, short-term memory (STM), and long-term memory (LTM). In addition, there are three important memory processes: encoding, storage, and retrieval. Figure 4.1, which was adapted from a model developed by Bourne, Dominowski, Loftus, and Healy,[1] shows the three types of memory (represented as boxes) and the memory processes (represented as arrows).

To learn and remember, we must encode, store, and retrieve information. The first step in this process is **encoding**—interpreting information in a meaningful way. Suppose you want to remember what a cloud looks like. Clouds are amorphous (without a definite shape) and lack any clear structure. You might find it difficult to remember exactly how a cloud looks after observing it briefly. However, if you notice that the cloud looks somewhat like an elephant, you'll be better able to remember its shape later simply by picturing an elephant. To be remembered, information must be encoded; it must be interpreted in a meaningful way. The second step in the memory process, **storage,** involves working on (for example, repeating and organizing) information so that it can be placed into LTM. Information doesn't automatically move into LTM unless you work to store it there. Much of what you think of as studying involves storage processes. The third step, **retrieval,** involves getting information out of LTM. As you'll see, retrieving a memory is very much like going into your basement to find the badminton set that you know is there, somewhere—you may have to hunt for a while, but eventually you'll find a clue that will lead you to it.

---

[1]L. E. Bourne, R. L. Dominowski, E. F. Loftus, and A. F. Healy, *Cognitive Processes,* 2d. ed. (Englewood Cliffs, NJ: Prentice Hall, 1986).

Sensory Memory

You probably have heard about short-term and long-term memory. However, **sensory memory,** also known as the **sensory registers,** may be new to you. Essentially, our senses (vision, hearing, smell, taste, and touch) are always very busy. We hear, see, smell, taste, and touch hundreds of stimuli each moment. Most of these stimuli are unimportant and are therefore quickly forgotten. However, some stimuli are important to us and worth remembering, but we have to pay attention to them or they are quickly forgotten. Attention is critical to the functioning of the sensory registers. Have you ever found yourself daydreaming in class? When you're daydreaming or thinking of something else, you aren't paying full attention to what the professor is saying. Without attending to the information presented, you can't process that information through the sensory registers. In the same way, if you're trying to read a text chapter and watch television at the same time, you may find that you won't remember much of what you read (or much of the TV show). To complete a new or difficult task, you must pay full attention to it. Anderson found that we can only pay attention to one cognitively demanding (one that requires thinking) task at a time.[2]

Activity 4-2

Conduct an Immediate-Memory Experiment

For this activity you'll be the experimenter. You will need two groups of participants (one or more friends or relatives for each group). Test each group separately and don't allow those in group 2 to observe what you do with group 1. Read the following directions to each group:

> "You're about to participate in a memory experiment. You'll need a pen or pencil and a piece of paper. In a moment I will slowly recite a dozen letters of the alphabet. As I recite the letters, I want you simply to try to remember them in order. When I'm finished, I'll signal with my hand, and you'll try to write down all of the letters in order."

For each group, read the letters as listed below. Read the letters slowly, at the rate of about one per second. Pause for two seconds between groups of letters. For group 1 use the following list:

TVI	BMC	ODN	ATO

For group 2 read the list this way:

TV	IBM	COD	NATO

Now check to see how the members of each group performed. To be counted as correct, each letter must be listed in the correct order. Which group do you think will do better? Write a paragraph describing the results of your experiment.

Short-Term Memory

Once you decide you want to remember something, you immediately have to move it into short-term memory. This process is represented by the arrow in Figure 4.1

---

[2]J. R. Anderson, *Cognitive Psychology and Its Implications,* 4th ed. (New York: Freeman, 1995).

that goes from the sensory registers to the immediate memory. However, to do this, the material must be encoded—you must make it meaningful. Short-term memory has two components: immediate memory and working memory.

Immediate Memory. **Immediate memory** is related to the concept of consciousness. Whatever you currently are thinking about is in your immediate memory. Think of your immediate memory as being similar to a small desk. In a two-hour study session you may work on several tasks at your desk. However, because your desk is very small, you can place only a limited amount of material on it at any one time. If you want to work on something new, you need to move aside the material on which you were just working. Immediate memory is similar to this because you can remember only the material that is "sitting on your desk" at any one time. Because immediate memory is very limited, you typically can retain only about seven (plus or minus two) chunks of information on your "desk." Furthermore, without continual rehearsal, those seven chunks can stay on the "desk" for only twenty to thirty seconds before they slip away.

Think back to your last class lecture. Have you ever found that you couldn't recall some of the information as you were writing it down in your notes? Did you get down the first part of a statement but have trouble remembering the second part? Taking notes in some lecture classes puts a real strain on your immediate memory. You can't hold on to some of the information long enough to get it into your notes. There may be too many words to remember (you may be trying to write down every word the professor says) or it may take you too long to write it down. In the next chapter, you'll learn some new strategies for taking notes that will help you overcome the limitations of your immediate memory.

Now that you understand the limits of immediate memory, let's look at the results of the experiment in Activity 4-2. The members of group 1 probably couldn't remember all twelve letters. After all, we typically can hold only five to nine pieces of information in immediate memory at one time. This list was longer, so some of the letters were lost. Putting more than seven items into immediate memory results in *displacement,* the bumping of earlier items by later ones. Many of the members of group 2 probably remembered all twelve letters. That was because of a process known as *chunking.* A **chunk** is a group of familiar stimuli stored as a single unit.[3] Although the letters for group 2 were in the same order as they were for group 1, they were grouped differently. For group 2 the letters were grouped into four chunks that were actually four familiar acronyms (TV, IBM, COD, and NATO). If the participants recognized the acronyms, then they had only four pieces (or chunks) of information to remember, instead of twelve. Because we can easily hold four chunks of information in our immediate memory, people in that group were much more likely to remember the letters. Chunking allows you to stretch the capacity of your immediate memory.

Working Memory. To hold on to information and get it into your long-term memory, you must first move the material into the other part of your short-term memory, the **working memory.** This part of the memory system is aptly named because you really have to "work" on the material to make it meaningful, memorable, and easy to retrieve. You can use a variety of strategies to move information into your working memory, but all have one thing in common. The harder you

[3]From W. Weiten, *Psychology: Themes and Variations,* 6th ed. (Belmont, CA: Wadsworth, 2004).

work on the material, the greater the probability that you'll put the material into LTM in a place where you can find it again.

You need to use active learning strategies to move information into long-term memory. Just reading over material a few times may have worked in high school, but it won't work as well in college. One of the big differences you'll face is a longer time frame between exams. Another major difference is the large amount of information you need to know for an exam in college. The strategies presented in the second half of this chapter and those in Chapter 10 will help you process your course information into long-term memory in a way that you'll be able to recall it during your exam.

Long-Term Memory

Once material has been processed in working memory, it can be moved into long-term memory (represented by the arrow going from working memory to long-term memory). Long-term memory has an almost unlimited capacity. We have not yet discovered anyone who has completely filled his or her LTM. In fact, the more we learn, the more capacity for learning we appear to have. Building long-term memories appears to provide a structure for adding new memories. LTM also is remarkable because we appear to hold on to most of our memories indefinitely. We also rely on our LTM to encode new information. You couldn't identify a cloud shaped like an elephant if you didn't already have prior knowledge of an elephant in your LTM. This process is represented by the arrow that starts at long-term memory and points to the encoding arrow.

Long-term memory can be compared to a warehouse full of filing cabinets. The cabinets in the warehouse and the material within the cabinets are arranged in a logical order; each cabinet drawer is labeled, and there are dividers within each drawer. Materials (memories) are placed in specific folders, in specific sections, in specific drawers, in specific file cabinets, in specific sections of the warehouse. However, the warehouse (your LTM) is enormous. Unless the material is carefully classified, labeled, and placed in the correct file, it can easily be lost. Once material is misfiled, or just poorly labeled, classified, and filed, it's much more difficult to retrieve. Only when you really work to appropriately classify and label it are you able to retrieve it easily. When material isn't well classified, you must resort to searching through all of the various files where you might have stored the material. In that case you would be very lucky to find it quickly, and it's just as likely that it could take a considerable amount of searching before you find it. If you need to remember important information for an exam, you'll be much better off if the information has been carefully "filed" in your LTM for easy retrieval.

Activity 4-3

Take Two Memory Tests

Go the *College Study Skills* book-specific Web site and follow the link in Chapter 4 to the QueenDom.com Web site to take a visual memory test. Then take the Short-Term Memory Test by clicking on the University of Washington link. Be prepared to discuss the results.

WHY YOU NEED MEMORY STRATEGIES

Now that you understand how information is encoded, stored, and retrieved, you may wonder why you need to learn specific strategies to aid your memory. According to Kenneth Higbee, ". . . remembering is hard work, and memory techniques do not necessarily make it easy, they just make it more effective."[4] To perform well in college courses, you need to use strategies that aid the acquisition, retention, and retrieval of the information that you want to learn. In college, learning to get information out of memory is just as important as learning to put that information into memory. Let's try an experiment to find out what kinds of strategies you already use. Be sure to complete Activity 4-4 before you continue reading.

Activity 4-4

Test Your Memory

Can you name all fifty states? Write down the first ten that you can remember in the margin of your text, then read the remainder of this page.

How did you remember the states that you wrote down in Activity 4-4? What method did you use to remember them? Look at the first couple of states that you wrote down. Do they follow some type of order? Some students use alphabetical order to list the states. Is that what you did? Others use a geographic order like Maine, New Hampshire, Vermont or Washington, Oregon, California. Although these are the two most common ways that students tend to remember the states, many students use other strategies. What strategies did you use? How you remembered the states for Activity 4-4 really isn't important. The important thing is that most of you used some strategy to recall information that you probably learned many years ago.

If you learned the states in alphabetical order, it's easier for you to retrieve that information alphabetically than geographically. On the other hand, if you learned the information geographically, by doing maps or by travel, you may find it difficult to list the states alphabetically. From this exercise, you should have learned that the method you use to organize information during study will in some way determine how effectively you can retrieve that information. In addition, the more associations you develop for particular information, the easier it'll be to retrieve. In the next two sections, you'll learn some general and specific strategies that will help improve your ability to learn and retrieve information.

Retrieval and Forgetting

Even when you work hard to remember information, you still forget things. As you might guess, there are a number of reasons for forgetting, some of which are related to retrieval. At times, you think that you've forgotten information, but in fact you never really got it into LTM at all. Either you never really paid attention to it, worked

---

[4]Kenneth L. Higbee, *Your Memory: How It Works and How to Improve It* (New York, Marlowe & Company, 1996), p. 5.

on it too little to store it, or did such a poor job of organizing it that, although it's in LTM, it's in a form that is unrecognizable and unusable—it's not accessible.

If you learn something, it's available to you in your LTM; however, it may not be accessible. To access a memory, you need to know how to find it. Many times you need a key term, or what psychologists call a **cue,** a label, a hook, or link to the information, to unlock the memory. Memories that you use frequently typically are stored with a number of cues, thus making them easier to remember. However, at times you store memories with only one or two cues. Unless you use those cues, you can't retrieve those memories. Clearly, the more ways you devise for material to be remembered, the more cues you develop that make the material more accessible. For example, creating study sheets with a specific topic and a series of specific headings (see Chapter 10) helps integrate the material better than just learning lists of facts, details, and definitions in isolation because more associations (more cues) are formed with the material.

Other processes also affect retrieval. For example, organization affects retrieval. Material that is well organized is easier to retrieve than material that is not well organized. Anxiety also affects retrieval. When you're anxious, it's more difficult to recall cues and retrieve important information because anxiety affects your ability to focus and concentrate. Many of us have had the experience of being unable to recall an answer during an examination and then remembering the material once the exam is over and our anxiety is reduced.

Interference theory also is important to the concept of forgetting. Interference theory states that memories can interfere with one another during the retrieval process. Over the years we tend to learn many things that are similar to one another. Unless you make each of these memories distinctive, there's a strong likelihood that one memory will interfere with another. It's well worth the effort to develop some unique cues that will help make each memory distinctive.

Due to a combination of failing to store information properly in LTM, using too few cues, and interference, you may forget newly learned material rapidly if you don't continue to rehearse it. The remainder of this chapter will discuss strategies you can use to improve your memory.

GENERAL MEMORY STRATEGIES

The following general strategies can help you acquire, retain, and retrieve course information.

Spaced Practice

There are many benefits to using spaced practice instead of massed practice. Research studies have shown that you'll retain more information if you study for eight hours over four days (spaced practice) instead of eight hours at one time (massed practice). **Massed practice,** like cramming, involves studying all the material at one time. **Spaced practice,** on the other hand, involves spacing your study time over a longer period, with breaks between practice sessions.

Studying for short periods of time, such as one- or two-hour time blocks, prevents boredom, helps avoid fatigue, and improves concentration and motivation. If you space out your study over a period of days (see the Five-Day Study Plan in Chapter 10 for more information on how to space your study), you gain additional benefits. First of all, you delay forgetting. As pointed out earlier, even when you think you've learned the information, some information usually is forgotten. By reviewing the same material the next day, you have a chance to find out what you've forgotten and work on it again. In addition, you benefit by reviewing and reinforcing the information that you previously studied.

Spaced practice, or distributed practice—as it is also known—allows time for the information to consolidate or jell in long-term memory. During **consolidation,** information is organized and stored in LTM. If you try to shove too much information into memory at one time, you won't be able to retrieve very much of it. One explanation for this is that the longer you study, the more inhibitions you develop (feeling tired, bored, and so on) that decrease your efficiency for storing the material in LTM. With massed practice, you may get to the point where you're just reading over the material rather than "working on it" to learn it.

Another problem that may occur with massed practice is that you don't organize the information well enough to store it in a way that allows you to find it again in your LTM. Allowing breaks between learning sessions gives you time to think about what you've been studying and to structure or organize it according to what you already know about the topic.

Break Tasks Down

Instead of trying to learn all of the material for your exam at one time (cramming), study only one or two chapters (and the accompanying lecture material) each day. When you study small chunks of material at one time, you can do a better job of getting it into LTM. It's easier to stay focused and actively involved in your learning when you don't feel as if you have to learn all of the information at one time. You'll be more willing to take the time to use active learning strategies such as creating study sheets, predicting questions, making word cards, reciting the information in your notes, or testing yourself on the material. By breaking down study tasks and organizing and storing small units of material, you increase the likelihood that you'll efficiently and effectively store the material in your LTM.

Repetition

Do you play a musical instrument? Have you ever? Did you ever play in a recital or a concert? How many times did you practice a new piece of music before that recital? Most of my students, when I ask that question, indicate that they practiced a lot (some 40 or more times). Many indicate that they practiced everyday for weeks and often several times a day. When I ask them why they didn't just practice it once, they reply that they wouldn't know it well enough to play it perfectly. Do you feel the same way? If you don't play a musical instrument, think of a similar experience. Maybe you participated in sports or debating, or were in the school play. I'm sure you practiced a new play, answers to possible questions, or your part many times. You need to think of learning material for a college exam in much the same way.

Unfortunately, you can't learn information by repeating it only one time. If you only had a few things to remember for an exam and they were very simple things, you might be able to look over them once before the exam and remember them. However, there is so much information to learn for college exams and so much complex material to master, that you need a great deal of repetition to learn it all. Each time you write, recite, or even think about a particular concept, you practice opening one of those drawers in your LTM filing cabinet and putting that information in the correct folder. The more times you open that same drawer and pull out that same folder, the easier it is to do it the next time; you know just where to go in the LTM warehouse and exactly where in the filing cabinet to look. If you continue to practice that same material over a period of days, you'll be able to strengthen and maintain your memory of it.

Overlearning

Overlearning is an important strategy for test preparation. **Overlearning** involves continuing to work on material even after it's learned—after it's stored in LTM. This practice is very helpful in improving your memory. Each time you review the material, you reduce forgetting and strengthen the path to your LTM. Overlearning may lead you to review the material in other ways, so you may form different cues for, or associations with, the material. You may even find that as you continue to work on the material, you gain a better understanding of it. Overlearning information will also help you retrieve the information more quickly, especially if you practice retrieval through self-testing.

Overlearning also can help you cope with test anxiety, which interferes with your ability to retrieve information from LTM. If you're worrying about an exam, you may have difficulty identifying or remembering the cues that you need to locate the information that you stored. Overlearned material is less susceptible to the debilitating effects of anxiety because it's so firmly embedded in LTM. You can count on overlearned information to help you get started during the exam. Answering questions that cover overlearned information is a good way to use your test time efficiently until you calm down.

SPECIFIC MEMORY STRATEGIES

Besides the general strategies described earlier, many specific learning strategies are effective in helping you learn and remember. Weinstein and Mayer describe five groups of learning strategies: rehearsal strategies, elaboration strategies, organizational strategies, comprehension monitoring strategies, and affective and motivational strategies.[5] Each category includes a variety of learning strategies that can be

FIGURE 4.2
Five Groups of Learning
Strategies

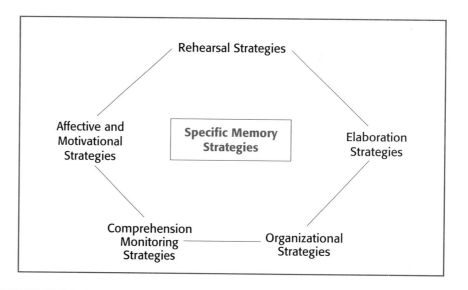

---

[5]C. F. Weinstein and R. F. Mayer, "The Teaching of Learning Strategies," In M. C. Wittrock, ed., *Handbook of Research on Teaching* (New York: Macmillan, 1986).

used to improve the various memory processes (Figure 4.2). Let's look at some of them.

Rehearsal Strategies

Rehearsal strategies involve repeating the material until it is learned. How did you study your spelling and vocabulary word lists in elementary school and junior high? If you wrote them ten times or recited them over and over again, you were using low-level rehearsal strategies. You may have studied for many of your high school exams by simply reading over the material two or three times until you felt that you knew it. Here again, you were using low-level rehearsal strategies. Although these rehearsal strategies are quite effective for learning simple lists or remembering easy-to-recall information, they're not as well suited to some of the more complex learning tasks that you need to use for college classes.

However, simply repeating information doesn't always mean that you'll learn it. Take a minute and read the following lines a few times.

Le matin le train est toujours bondé. Quand le train arrive à sa gare il en descend et it monte l'escalier.

Now look away from the text and try to repeat the lines. Can you? If you're fairly fluent in French, you may have been able to do so. However, if you don't understand French, you couldn't understand what you just read, so you won't be able to remember it. By the way, the translation is "In the morning the train is always crowded. When the train arrives at his station, he gets out and goes up the stairs." Have you ever read over material for an exam that you really didn't understand? I recall doing exactly that when I took Physics in college. No matter how often I reread the material, I just couldn't remember it because I didn't understand it. To prepare for exams, you need to use **elaborative rehearsal** (repetition that involves making the information meaningful). I had to get someone to help me understand what I was reading and then I had to practice the material by writing it in my own words and generating examples that made sense to me.

High-level rehearsal strategies such as outlining, predicting questions, and creating charts and concept maps all help you rehearse the information (you're still going over it) as you make it more meaningful, organize it, and condense it for later review. When you use higher-level rehearsal strategies, you're operating on the material—you may be adding information that you already know, organizing the material in a way that's more memorable to you, or creating additional cues to help you locate and recall the material in LTM. In the next chapter you'll learn how to generate questions in the margin of your notes. To make up even one question, you have to reread, write, or think about the material several times—providing you with a significant amount of rehearsal. You're also using high-level rehearsal strategies when you recite information from the recall columns or your word and question cards, explain information in your own words, answer review questions, or take self-tests.

In Chapter 10, you'll learn other high-level rehearsal strategies, such as creating study sheets and making self-tests. Just about any strategy that you use to prepare for a quiz or test involves rehearsal. The key, though, to effective rehearsal is combining your review of the material with one or more of the organizational, elaboration, comprehension monitoring, or motivational strategies that are presented in the remainder of this chapter.

Elaboration Strategies

Elaboration strategies involve expanding on the information, forming associations, or connecting new information to what you already know. Paraphrasing, summarizing, explaining, answering questions, forming mental images, and using mnemonics ("ni-mon-iks") are all elaboration strategies. Effective note taking requires you to embellish or refine what the professor or the author has said. When you take notes in your own words and add comments or make connections, you're using an elaboration strategy. One of the chief advantages of elaboration strategies is that they help you create more associations with the material to be learned, thereby providing you with more routes for getting to the information during retrieval. Explaining the material out loud, creating questions in the margin, and making maps also are examples of elaboration strategies that you may already be using. You'll learn more about how to use those strategies in Chapters 9 and 10. In this section we'll discuss some other elaboration techniques, including the use of mnemonics.

Mnemonic devices or techniques often are referred to as memory tricks. However, many of these techniques aren't tricks at all. They are, instead, techniques that can help you remember things when you can't seem to remember them any other way. The advantage of mnemonic devices is that they form an *association* with the material, so if you remember the mnemonic, you remember the material. Mnemonics provide an organizational framework or structure for remembering information that may not appear to have a structure of its own.

This brings up a very important point. Mnemonic devices are aids to retrieval, but they do not guarantee that you'll learn the material. You can't just decide that you're going to remember Weinstein and Mayer's five categories of learning strategies by remembering the word REOCA (Rehearsal, Elaboration, Organizational, Comprehension monitoring, Affective and Motivational). Before you can use "REOCA" to help you list or discuss these strategies, you have to practice the connection between the mnemonic and the information to be learned. Although this section focuses on the use of mnemonics, it's important to remember that you must use the other high-level rehearsal strategies to learn the information in the first place. You can then use mnemonics to help you retrieve what you've learned.

According to Kenneth Higbee, "A mnemonic system may help you in at least three ways when you're trying to find items in your memory: (1) It will give you a place to start your search, a way to locate the first item. (2) It will give you a way of proceeding systematically from one item to the next. (3) It will let you know when your recall is finished, when you have reached the last item."[6] You'll learn more about how to make those connections and use mnemonics as retrieval aids as you examine the use of associations, acronyms, acrostics, and imagery.

Associations

Forming associations is always important when you're trying to remember something. We use this technique every day.

When I was in eighth grade, we were studying longitude and latitude in geography class. Every day for a week, we had a quiz, and I kept getting longitude and latitude confused. I went home and almost cried because I was so frustrated and embarrassed that I couldn't keep them straight in my mind. I stared and stared at

---

[6]K. Higbee, *Your Memory: How It Works and How to Improve It* (Englewood Cliffs, NJ: Prentice Hall, 1977), p. 78.

those words until suddenly I figured out what to do. I told myself, when you see that *n* in longitude it will remind you of the word *north*. Therefore, it will be easy to remember that longitude lines go from north to south. It worked; I got them all right on the next quiz, and the next, and on the exam.

When I tell this story in class, some of my students laugh because it seems silly to them that anyone could get longitude and latitude confused. However, some of us do get confused about things that may seem simple to others. It's very easy to become confused by closely related information. Mnemonics helps you *know* for sure which choice is the correct one.

Did you ever get confused about how to spell *dessert?* You'll never goof on that one again if you remember that dessert has lots of sugar, so it has two *s*'s. Taby remembers it a different way. She noticed that *desserts* spelled backward is *stressed*, and the first thing she goes for when she's stressed is dessert. No one taught her that system, but when you can't remember something that you need to remember, you learn to create your own system.

Activity 4-5

List the Associations You Use

During the next week, make a list of at least ten associations that you use to help you remember information both in and out of the classroom. Which of the associations were helpful? Why? Discuss your responses with other members of your group. Did you get any good memory ideas from the other members of your group?

Acronyms, or Catchwords

Acronyms are "words" that are made up of the first letters of other words. Acronyms are so commonly used today that most of us don't even realize that some aren't real words. SCUBA, NASA, FBI, and COD are all quite familiar. We don't even think of them as standing for self-contained underwater breathing apparatus, National Aeronautics and Space Administration, Federal Bureau of Investigation, and cash on delivery; they all are well understood in their abbreviated form.

John Langan used the term *catchword* to describe an acronym.[7] In a sense, acronyms do help us catch or hold on to the information that we have learned. Catchwords, or acronyms, can be real words or nonsense words designed to aid recall. You probably can name all of the colors in the spectrum because someone taught you to use the catchword "ROY G. BIV" (red, orange, yellow, green, blue, indigo, violet). "REOCA" also is an example of a catchword; each letter stands for the first letter in a list of other words. Can you say them now? Try it.

How to Create Catchwords. Catchwords are useful for remembering lists of information. You can use catchwords to remember the following four kinds of fossils:

1. <u>A</u>ctual remains

2. <u>P</u>etrified

---

[7]J. Langan, *Reading and Study Skills,* 4th ed. (New York: McGraw-Hill, 1989), p. 207.

3. <u>I</u>mprint

4. <u>M</u>olds and Casts

You might create a catchword like "PAIM" (sounds like *pain* but with an M instead; it would be painful to become a fossil) or "IMAP" (fossils are my maps of the past). In both cases your catchword also provides an *association* with the material that you learned. You also can use catchwords to remember longer lists of information. Five of the general principles of nonverbal communication are listed below. Try to create a catchword to remember them.

1. Nonverbal communication is multichanneled.

2. Nonverbal communication conveys emotions.

3. Nonverbal communication is ambiguous.

4. Nonverbal communication may contradict verbal messages.

5. Nonverbal communication is culture-bound.[8]

To make an acronym or catchword, you first have to identify a key word in each statement. Go back and underline the following words: *multichanneled, emotions, ambiguous, contradict,* and *culture-bound.* These words should work well as hooks or tags to help you remember the entire list of principles. Next, list (or underline) the first letter of each word: M, E, A, C, C. "MEACC" doesn't sound as though it will be very memorable, but by simply rearranging the letters you could form the catchword "MECCA" or "CAMEC." Both of these are fairly easy to recall.

Your work isn't done, though. Can you list the five general principles of nonverbal communication? Just creating the catchwords doesn't mean that you've learned the material. To strengthen the associations and learn the material, you need to practice connecting the catchword to the key word and then the key word to the entire phrase. Reciting or writing will help you form the connections. If I were going to use the catchword "MECCA," I would rehearse the information this way: "M" stands for "multichanneled," and "multichanneled" stands for "nonverbal communication is multichanneled." "E" stands for "emotions," and "emotions" stands for "nonverbal communication conveys emotions" (and so on). You may need to practice this connection several times. Of course, you still have to be sure that you understand what the terms *multichanneled* and *emotions* mean in this context. Students who say that mnemonics don't work for them often think that simply constructing the mnemonic should firmly embed the information in long-term memory. Unfortunately, the mere construction of a word or phrase doesn't replace learning the information. Your catchword will help you retrieve the information from memory *only after the information is learned.*

Student Examples. Let's take a look at how some students used catchwords to remember course material (Figure 4.3). Kwan made up two catchwords to help her prepare for a Philosophy test about Swinburne's and Aquinas's views on God's relationship to time and His knowledge of the future. After classifying and listing the important information that she wanted to learn, she identified a key word in each statement and then used the first letter of each key word to form a catchword. Of

[8]From W. Weiten and M. A. Lloyd, *Psychology Applied to Modern Life,* 7th ed. (Belmont, CA: Wadsworth, 2003), p. 183. Used with permission.

Swinburne's and Aquinas's Views

Swinburne—SWOMP

S   simultaneously
W   within time
O   own actions
M   mutable
P   personable

Aquinas—ICON

I   immutable
C   continuum
O   omniscient
N   not in time

Kwan's Catchwords

FASCISM

1. Authoritarian governments
2. Masses are incapable of governing themselves (democratically)
3. State terrorism is used
4. Hierarchically structured organic society
5. Elites govern

A M S H E = SHAME

Heather's Catchword

Four Stages of Food Processing

1. Ingestion—eating
2. Digestion—breaking down food
3. Absorption—cells absorb nutrients
4. Elimination—undigested wastes removed

I D A E = IDEA (extra association: Eating is a good IDEA)

Cheri's Catchword

course, to prepare properly for the exam, Kwan had to practice the connections between the words "SWOMP" and "ICON" and the material that each represented.

Heather listed the main characteristics of fascism, conservatism, liberalism, socialism, and communism in order to prepare for her Sociology exam. After identifying key words for each of the ideologies, she created either a catchword or a catchphrase to help her remember the specific characteristics of each. Figure 4.3 includes only one of Heather's lists. She created the catchword "SHAME" to help her recall each of the key words she identified for fascism.

Cheri's professor indicated that she needed to know the four stages of food processing for her biology exam. After listing the information, she created the catchword "IDEA" to remember the four stages. You may have noticed that she did have to remember to reverse the last two letters to put the stages in order, but since she was using the catchword only to recall the steps (not learn their order, which she had already practiced), that was no problem.

Activity 4-6

Create Catchwords

Make up a catchword that will help you remember each of the following lists of information. Put your catchword on an index card and exchange your card with another classmate. Could your classmate retrieve the information using your catchword? Compare the catchwords you made to those of others in your group.

1. The five great lakes: Superior, Michigan, Huron, Erie, Ontario.

2. Freud's five stages of psychosexual development: oral, anal, phallic, latency, and genital.

3. Refer back to Chapter 1 and create a catchword to remember the five steps in the problem-solving process.

Acrostics, or Catchphrases

Acrostics, or catchphrases as Langan called them, are phrases or sentences that are made up of words beginning with the first letters of other words. Just as the catchword "FACE" helped most of us remember the names of the spaces in music class, the catchphrase "Every Good Boy Does Fine" worked to recall the names of the lines. Did you remember learning "My Very Educated Mother Just Served Us Nine Pies" to remember the nine planets in order? If you did, you used an acrostic, or catchphrase, to remember the information. Catchphrases worked in junior high, and they can work in college, too. The difference, though, is that you need to create your own catchphrases in college to help you remember the information that you want to remember for your exams.

When to Use Catchphrases. Catchphrases are especially useful if you have to remember the information in a special order or if you can't form an easy-to-remember word from the letters available to you (for instance, you may have all consonants but no vowels). You can create catchphrases to recall all kinds of course material. Remembering lists of names, steps in a process, causes and effects, and key points for essay answers are just a few ways that students use catchphrases.

How to Create Catchphrases. You can create catchphrases in much the same way you created catchwords. If you had to learn the five principles of nonverbal behavior in order, you might find that "Mary Ellen Answered Conrad Curtly," is more memorable than "MEACC." This example can provide us with some additional tips for creating acrostics, or catchphrases. You may have noticed that in the example ("Mary Ellen Answered Conrad Curtly"), the two *c* words have the same second letters (the vowels *o* and *u*) as the original key words (*contradict* and *culture-bound*). When you have two key words that start with the same letter, it's helpful to use the second letter to show which one comes first. You may also find that making your mnemonic sentences outrageous, silly, or humorous help you remember them. We tend to remember funny or outrageous catchphrases better than dull and boring ones.

Whenever you're using catchphrases to help you remember text material, consider the following six rules:

1. Make a list of the information you need to learn.

TEN TIPS FOR IMPROVING YOUR MEMORY

DON'T ASSUME THAT YOU'LL REMEMBER. Many students think that they'll remember everything that they read in their textbooks and hear in their class lectures. However, even if it worked for you in high school, it won't in college because college tests are spaced further apart, allowing us to forget much of the information. Take good class notes and highlight or take notes as you read and then work hard to learn the information.

REVIEW REGULARLY. Review your text and lecture information on a daily or weekly basis to keep the information fresh in your memory. Doing an end-of-week review also allows you to integrate text and lecture material and organize it in long-term memory.

ORGANIZE THE INFORMATION LOGICALLY. The more logically you organize the information that you need to remember, the easier it will be to learn it and retrieve it from memory. Restructuring the information so that it's more meaningful to you aids your memory of it.

WRITE AND RECITE TO MOVE INFORMATION INTO LONG-TERM MEMORY. You won't even get information into long-term memory (or at least not very much of it) by just reading over your course material. You have to get actively involved with the material to make it meaningful so that you can learn and remember it.

FORM ASSOCIATIONS TO INCREASE MEMORY CUES. Don't study information in isolation. It's very difficult to recall information when you learn it as an isolated piece of information. By developing study sheets, explaining the material, or making maps, you form associations with and among the material that add a variety of cues that will help you remember it for an exam.

ORGANIZE THE INFORMATION IN YOUR STUDY SHEETS. The more organized the information is when you put it into long-term memory, the more easily you'll be able to find it when you're taking an exam. Creating titles, headings, and main points in your study sheets helps you organize the information and provides you with cues to aid retrieval.

USE YOUR OWN EXPERTISE TO AID MEMORY. When information is meaningful, it's easier to remember. Think of how what you're learning connects with your own life and work experiences. Create examples from your own experiences to help you remember the information you're learning in your college classes.

USE MNEMONICS TO AID MEMORY. Mnemonics can be used very effectively to aid retrieval. However, unless you learn the information to begin with, mnemonics won't work. You also need to practice the connection between the mnemonic device you create and the actual material you want to remember.

USE RHYMES, STORIES, OR SONGS TO HELP YOU REMEMBER. If you're good at writing or remembering songs, rhymes, or stories, use those methods to help improve your memory. Words that rhyme, the details of a story, or even the melody of a song add additional cues that may help you remember information for your exam.

MONITOR YOUR MEMORY. Many students are frustrated when they can't remember information during an exam. If this has happened to you, you may not have *learned* the information (at least not at the recall level). Check your memory of the information before the exam by self-testing on paper or by reciting. If you can't say the answer out loud without peeking, you don't really know it.

2. Select a key word to represent each piece of information.

3. Underline or write down the first letter of each key word.

4. Form a catchphrase from words beginning with the first letter of each word.

5. Practice associating the new word to the key word and then the key word to the actual information that you need to know.

6. Use the mnemonic to test your memory—to retrieve the original information.

Student Examples. After a little practice, you'll find that you can use catchphrases to help you recall information for many of your college courses. Figure 4.4 includes several examples of acrostics, or catchphrases, that students used when preparing for essay exams.

Terri devised the catchphrase "Can Henry Omit Dents" to remember the four classes of heterotrophic organisms. She also created some associations to help her remember what each one ate:

"A" in "c<u>a</u>rnivores" is like the "a" in "animals."

<u>H</u>erb reminds me of plants—plant eaters.

"O" for b<u>o</u>th plant and animal eaters.

<u>De</u>composers means <u>de</u>cay—decaying organisms.

Todd developed the catchphrase "<u>J</u>eff is <u>dep</u>ressed about <u>c</u>oming to <u>s</u>ee <u>D</u>avid" to remember the five building blocks of structure for his management course. Did you notice how Todd distinguished between the two terms that began with the same letter?

FIGURE 4.4
Student Examples of
Catchphrases

> ### Four Classes of Heterotrophic Organisms
>
> <u>C</u>arnivores—animal eaters
> <u>H</u>erbivores—plant eaters
> <u>O</u>mnivores—animal and plant eaters
> <u>D</u>ecomposers—eat decaying organisms
>
> "<u>C</u>an <u>H</u>enry <u>O</u>mit <u>D</u>ents"
>
> Terri's Catchphrase
>
>
> ### Five Building Blocks of Structure
>
> 1. <u>J</u>ob design
> 2. <u>D</u>epartmentalization
> 3. <u>C</u>oordinating mechanisms
> 4. <u>S</u>pan of management
> 5. <u>D</u>elegation
>
> "<u>J</u>eff is <u>dep</u>ressed about <u>c</u>oming to <u>s</u>ee <u>D</u>avid"
>
> Todd's Catchphrase
>
>
> ### FOUR KINDS OF LOVE
>
> 1. <u>P</u>assionate love   3. <u>F</u>atuous love
> 2. <u>C</u>ompassionate love   4. <u>C</u>onsummate love
>
> <u>P</u>eggy <u>c</u>ounted <u>f</u>our <u>c</u>hickens   Peggy's Catchphrase
> <u>P</u>laying <u>c</u>ards <u>f</u>or <u>c</u>ash   Mathew's Catchphrase

Peggy and Mathew, who were taking the same Psychology course, each devised a different mnemonic sentence to remember the four kinds of love. Which do you think would be the most effective in helping you recall the information? Can you think of a better one?

Activity 4-7

Create and Use Catchphrases

Work as a group to create a catchphrase to help you recall the following information. Then test your memory of the material by writing or reciting the key points from memory. The key words are already underlined for you. Then create a list of information from your own course material and repeat the activity.

IMPROVING CONCENTRATION

1. Set specific <u>goals</u>.

2. Create a good study <u>environment</u>.

3. Form <u>associations</u> that say "study mode."

4. Monitor <u>distractions.</u>

5. Use your <u>preferred</u> learning style.

6. Stay <u>focused</u> on the material.

7. Take <u>breaks.</u>

8. <u>Switch</u> subjects.

9. <u>Deal</u> with personal problems.

Catchphrase: _____

_____

Imagery

You've already seen how effective visual imagery can be in helping you remember catchphrases. However, you can create visual images to remember course material without writing catchwords or catchphrases. Concept maps can be used to present a visual display of material that you need to remember (see Chapter 9). After developing and practicing a map, you'll be able to recall much of the information by visualizing the map itself.

You also can paint visual pictures in your mind to remember main points and supporting information. If you were studying the Boston Tea Party, for example, you could remember many of the details about this historic event just by visualizing what happened. Picture Boston Harbor with three of the British ships (you can see the flag on each) carrying the tea shipments. Can you see the chests (340 of them) full of tea? What is that written on the side of one? It says "Property of the East India Company" and lists the date as "December 16, 1773." Of course, these words were not printed on the real chests, but you can imagine they were in order to create a more helpful mental picture. Can you see the colonists, many disguised as Indians, throwing the chests overboard? By incorporating names, places, dates, and so on in your visual image, you can recall a great deal of information about your topic.

Another mnemonic device that uses imagery is known as the method of place or the **method of loci** ("lo-sigh," meaning locations). Here you form an association between something you want to remember and a particular location on a familiar walk. Let's say that you have to present a speech about healthy eating habits in one of your classes and that your speech consists of seven main ideas. You simply imagine yourself taking a very familiar walk. As you pass the first familiar landmark on that walk, you develop an image that somehow connects that familiar landmark to the first point in your speech. (For example, the image of a tree with a nest of baby birds could help you remember that you have to begin providing healthy foods when children are young.) You continue in this manner until you have developed an image connecting each point in your speech to a landmark. Then, when it's time to present the speech, you simply imagine that you're taking that familiar walk. As you pass each landmark, you should be able to recall the next point in your speech.

Activity 4-8

Create Mnemonics from Your Own Life Experiences

As you prepare for your next exam, use work or home experiences to help you remember some of the information that you need to know. List at least three things that you need to know for your exam and describe the "life experience" mnemonic that you developed. Try creating a story about the information, a catchphrase about someone from work, an association with something you already know, or all three. After your exam, write a paragraph or two to describe how you created your mnemonics and how they worked.

Organizational Strategies

Organizational strategies allow you to organize the information to make it easier to learn and recall. Tasks such as listing, ordering, grouping, outlining, mapping, charting, and diagramming are all examples of organizational strategies. In each of these activities, you act on the material that is to be mastered. With outlining, charting, or mapping, for example, you organize the material in a way that shows how each component is related to the others. One of the advantages of organizational strategies is that by structuring the material, you provide yourself with new ways to remember many of the details. If you can remember the structure—the main headings of the outline, the categories in your chart, or the web strands of your map, for example—you'll be able to remember many of the details. Before you continue reading, complete Activity 4-9.

Activity 4-9

Try Some Organizational Strategies

Look at the following list of words for sixty seconds; then cover it with your hand or a piece of paper and try to write the words in the margin.

Newspaper, pencil, bus, automobile, book, pen, boat, magazine, comic book, chalk, crayon, train

Continued

You may have found that it was difficult to remember all twelve of the items. Do you know why? Earlier you learned about the capacity of short-term memory. If you recall, you can remember only about seven pieces of information at one time. You can, however, increase this capacity by chunking (grouping) the information. You probably will be able to remember all twelve items if you group them as follows:

THINGS YOU READ	THINGS YOU WRITE WITH	THINGS YOU RIDE IN
newspaper	pencil	bus
book	pen	automobile
magazine	chalk	boat
comic book	crayon	train

With this grouping, you have three pieces or chunks of information to remember instead of twelve. It's easy to remember three things, right? You also can remember the four items in each category quite easily because the headings help trigger your memory. Now look at the three groups for sixty seconds and try to write down as many of the items as you can in the margin.

Did you find that grouping made it easier to remember the words in Activity 4-9? Did you use any other strategies for remembering? You may have used some rehearsal and elaboration strategies. You may have used a catchword such as "BABT" to help you remember *bus, auto, boat,* and *train.* Did you notice that the second column contains two words that start with *p* and two words that start with *c*? Can you think of a catchphrase that would help you remember the four "things you read"? You might find that you could learn and recall the fifty states more easily if you classified or grouped them into categories such as New England, Mid-Atlantic, Southern, Midwestern, Western, and so on.

Organize Material by Grouping
You can improve your ability to learn and recall a large amount of material by grouping or chunking it. However, you should follow some basic guidelines when setting up your groups. First, never set up more than seven groups. Why? If you make up ten or fifteen groups, you won't be able to remember all the group headings. For the same reason, limit the number of items in each group to seven. Second, be sure you use a simple system. If your plan for remembering the information is extremely complex, you won't be able to remember it (the plan), and then you won't be able to remember the information itself. Third, you can't learn the information just by looking at it. You need to write or recite the lists and then test yourself. Finally, there's a tendency to forget the items in the middle of the list more quickly than those that are first or last. Did you have that problem earlier? You can avoid this problem by practicing the items in different orders or by using some of the elaboration strategies previously described. Remember, the more organized the information is when you put it into LTM, the more easily you'll be able to retrieve it later.

Before her exam in Computer Literacy, Heather organized the information on the five different programming languages by using the informal outline and mnemonic sentences in Figure 4.5. She pulled the important information out of her text and notes and structured it in such a way that she could learn and remember it. Then she created catchphrases to prompt her memory. Her first sen-

FIGURE 4.5

Heather's Informal Outline (with Mnemonic Sentences)

Computer Programming Languages

Corey	1. COBOL	Corey
	– widely accepted	wins
	– English statements, business applications	every
	– processes, records, produces	program
Finds	2. FORTRAN	Fanny
	– solve science, math, engineer problems	Smith
	– programming	plays
	– widespread use, science – engineer	walleyball
	communities	Saturdays
	– solve problems	
Bobby	3. BASIC	Bobby
	– teaching tool	tells
	– easiest	everyone
	– programming language	Pat
	– Apple, IBM	ate
	– data structure – FORTRAN	dirt.
Playing	4. PASCAL	Pat
	– preferred teaching language	prefers
	– teaching tool	tulips
Alone	5. ADA language	All
	– general purpose	girls
	– most advantages	must
	– structures – PASCAL	stay
	– strong type	strong.

tence, "Corey Finds Bobby Playing Alone," provides hooks for the five programming languages. The other five sentences are designed to help her remember the details about each language. By organizing the information and practicing the connections between the catchphrases and the material she wanted to learn, Heather ensured her ability to recall the information.

Activity 4-10

Organize Information

After you read and mark the text selection "Political Theories and The Media" in Figure 4.6, organize the information that you need to learn. Group, outline, or map the information to make it more meaningful. Then devise a strategy for remembering the main points that you included. Compare your organizational structure and any mnemonics you create with those of your group.

FIGURE 4.6
Political Theories and the Media

▶ Political Theories and the Media

No institution as sizable and influential as the mass media can escape involvement with government and politics. The media are not only channels for the transmission of political information and debate, but also significant players with a direct stake in government's attitude toward free speech and dissent. Remember that *the way a country's political system is organized affects the way the media within that country operate.* Media systems can be divided broadly into those systems that allow dissent and those that do not.

To categorize the political organization of media systems, scholars often begin with the 1956 book *Four Theories of the Press*, by Fred S. Siebert, Theodore Peterson and Wilbur Schramm. These four theories, which originally were used to describe the political systems under which media operated in different countries, were (1) the Soviet theory, (2) the authoritarian theory, (3) the libertarian theory and (4) the social responsibility theory. A fifth description, the more modern *developmental theory*, updates the original categories.

The Soviet Theory Historically in the Soviet Union (which dissolved in 1991 into several independent nations and states), the government owned and operated the mass media. All media employees were government employees, expected to serve the government's interests.

Top media executives also served as leaders in the Communist party. Even when the press controls loosened in the 1980s, the mass media were part of the government's policy. Government control came *before* the media published or broadcast; people who controlled the media could exercise *prior restraint.* They could review copy and look at programs before they appeared.

This description of the Soviet press system was conceived before the events of the 1990s challenged the basic assumptions of Soviet government. Many Eastern bloc countries, such as Romania, Slovakia and the Czech Republic that once operated under Soviet influence, based their media systems on the communist model. Today, the media systems in these countries are in transition.

The Authoritarian Theory Media that operate under the authoritarian theory can be either publicly or privately owned. This concept of the press developed in Europe after Gutenberg. Until the 1850s, presses in Europe were privately owned, and the aristocracy (which governed the countries) wanted some sort of control over what was printed about them. The aristocracy had the financial and political power necessary to make the rules about what would be printed.

Their first idea was to license everyone who owned a press so the license could be revoked if someone published something unfavorable about the government. The British crown licensed the first colonial newspapers in America. Licensing wasn't very successful in the United States, however, because many people who owned presses didn't apply for licenses.

The next authoritarian attempt to control the press was to review material after it was published. A printer who was discovered publishing material that strongly challenged the government could be heavily fined or even put to death.

Today, many governments still maintain this type of rigid control over the media. Most monarchies, for example, operate in an authoritarian tradition, which tolerates very little dissent. Media systems that serve at the government's pleasure and with the government's approval are common.

The Libertarian Theory The concept of a libertarian press evolved from the idea that people who are given all the information on an issue will be able to discern what is true and what is false and will make good choices. This is an idea embraced by the writers of the U.S. Constitution and by other democratic governments.

This theory assumes, of course, that the media's main goal is to convey the truth and that the media will not cave in to outside pressures, such as from advertisers or corporate owners. This theory also assumes that people with opposing viewpoints will be heard—that the media will present all points of view, in what is commonly called the free marketplace of ideas.

The First Amendment to the U.S. Constitution concisely advocates the idea of freedom of the press. Theoretically, America today operates under the libertarian theory, although this ideal has been challenged often by changes in the media industries since the Constitution was adopted.

The Social Responsibility Theory This theory accepts the concept of a libertarian press but prescribes what the media should do. Someone who believes in the social responsibility theory believes that members of the press will do their jobs well only if periodically reminded about their duties.

This theory grew out of the 1947 Hutchins Commission Report on the Free and Responsible Press. The commission listed five goals for the press, including the need for truthful and complete reporting of all sides of an issue. The commission concluded that the American press' privileged position in the Constitution means that the press must always work to be responsible to society.

If the media fail to meet their responsibilities to society, the social responsibility theory holds that the government should encourage the media to comply. In this way the libertarian and the social responsibility theories differ. The libertarian theory assumes the media will work well without government interference; the social responsibility theory advocates government oversight for media that don't act in society's best interest.

The Developmental Theory A fifth description for media systems that can be added to describe today's media has been called the developmental or Third World theory. Under this system, named for the developing nations where it is most often found, the media *can* be privately owned, but usually are owned by the government.

The media are used to promote the country' social and economic goals and to direct a sense of national purpose. For example, a developmental media system might be used to promote birth control or to encourage children to attend school. The media become an outlet for some types of government propaganda, then, but in the name of economic and social progress for the country.

Although the theory that best describes the American media is the libertarian theory, throughout their history the American media have struggled with both authoritarian and social responsibility debates: Should the press be free to print secret government documents, for example? What responsibility do the networks have to provide worthwhile programming to their audiences? The media, the government and the public continually modify and adjust their interpretations of how the media should operate.

Text material from S. Biagi, *Media/Impact: An Introduction to Mass Media,* 7th ed. (Belmont, CA: Wadsworth, 2005), pp. 348–351. Used with permission.

Comprehension Monitoring Strategies

Comprehension monitoring strategies allow us to monitor or keep tabs on our learning. They help us monitor our progress in mastering the material and allow us to evaluate the effectiveness of the strategies that we use to gain that mastery. Setting goals and then assessing your progress, reciting from recall columns or question cards, taking self-tests, replicating study sheets, and even just asking yourself whether you understand something are all examples of comprehension monitoring strategies.

All these activities involve **metacognition**—the ability to think about and control one's learning.[9] Metacognition involves three types of awareness on the part of the learner. First, students must learn *task awareness*—they must learn to identify what information they have to study and learn in a particular situation. Second, students must learn *strategy awareness*—they need to determine which strategy will be most effective for learning specific information, for preparing for different types of exams, and for using with different types of course material. Finally, students must learn *performance awareness*—they must learn to determine whether they have mastered the material that they previously identified as important, and how well it has been learned.[10]

When to Use Comprehension Monitoring Strategies

Comprehension monitoring strategies help us determine when learning or understanding breaks down. For example, you may find, as you read and take notes on one of your textbooks, that you can't figure out how to formulate questions about the information under one of the headings. At that point, you should realize that you didn't comprehend or understand that section of the text.

When you use self-testing activities, you're also monitoring your learning. If you find that you don't really know the information as well as you thought you did, you can review it again. Self-testing also allows you to practice retrieving the information from LTM in a testlike situation. Some students become frustrated when they take exams because they spend hours and hours studying but can't seem to recall the information during the exam. Although they may have worked on acquisition and retention, they probably didn't spend much time practicing retrieval of the information. Each time you self-test, you practice getting the information back out of memory. This provides you with an opportunity to practice the cues and strategies that you intend to use during the exam and to monitor their effectiveness.

Comprehension monitoring strategies also help you examine and evaluate the strategies that you're using to acquire, retain, and retrieve information. By taking a self-test, for example, you may discover that you don't really know as much as you thought you did about a particular section of the text and lecture material. Again, your discovery that you haven't learned that material provides you with some feedback on your progress in preparing for an exam. However, it also may allow you to evaluate the strategy that you originally used to "learn" that material. You may realize, for example, that just reading over the material was not very effective for getting it into LTM or that just reciting the information from your notes didn't prepare you to write an essay about it. Once you determine that your study strategies

[9] L. Baker and A. L. Brown, "Metacognitive Skills and Reading," in P. D. Pearson, ed., *Handbook of Reading Research*, 2d ed. (New York: Lawrence Erlbaum, 2002).

[10] S. E. Wade and R. E. Reynolds, "Developing Metacognitive Awareness," *Journal of Reading*, 33 (1989): 6–14.

aren't effective, you can modify the way you learn and select more effective strategies to use.

Activity 4-11

Monitor Your Learning

Which of the memory strategies did you find most effective for helping you learn and retrieve information? Describe how you used each one and explain why it worked for you.

Affective and Motivational Strategies

Affective and motivational strategies are strategies that relate to your attitude, interest, and motivation toward learning. They can influence how effectively you learn and remember information. Many of the strategies that you use for setting goals, managing time, and improving concentration are examples of affective and motivational strategies. These strategies help prepare you mentally for studying and create a positive learning environment. Setting realistic, moderately challenging goals helps get you motivated to study and learn. Using "To Do" lists, planning rewards, and taking breaks are just a few of the motivational strategies that you probably are using on a regular basis. They help you keep up with your daily assignments and give you a sense of accomplishment at the end of the day.

Your attitude about learning the material can influence how well you'll attend to it, organize it, and store it. If you're trying to prepare for an exam, it's important that you feel interested in the material and motivated to learn and remember. Establishing a purpose for studying, seeing the relevance of the course, and using active learning strategies can all help increase your motivation. If you think studying won't help, you won't be very motivated to study. In Chapter 10, you'll learn a number of active learning strategies that will help you learn and remember course material. Using strategies that are both effective and interesting can make learning fun. Many students actually enjoy studying for a test using these strategies because they end each study session feeling good about what they've accomplished.

Monitoring your learning also can be an effective motivational device. If you test your learning by covering the material and trying to recite the information, you'll be able to evaluate your storage and retrieval processes. You also can accomplish this by reciting from the headings in your notes, taking self-tests, reproducing maps or charts, and so on. One advantage of reciting is that it allows you to test your memory. If you're able to remember the information that you're reviewing, you feel good—you know you're learning. Successful recitations motivate you to continue to study and to continue to use that learning strategy because it worked. Changing to a different learning strategy or studying for a longer period of time may be necessary to store the information you couldn't recall from memory. When you know that you know the important information for a test, you develop more confidence in yourself as a student, and this can affect your performance on the exam.

In Chapter 10, you'll also learn to use the Five-Day Study Plan. This plan helps you select, organize, and schedule your exam preparation tasks. The Five-Day Study Plan includes many affective and motivational strategies. You'll know each day exactly what you need to accomplish and can check off your completion of each task. The Five-Day Study Plan also incorporates active learning strategies that make studying effective and interesting and provides you with numerous opportunities to monitor your learning. If you're still having difficulty recalling information during an exam, you may need to change the way you're studying. Try using the Five-Day Study Plan—you may find that using it significantly improves your exam performance.

Your state of mind during the exam also affects how well you're able to retrieve the information. If you experience test anxiety, you may not be able to concentrate on the exam questions. You may find that you're so upset that you can't think of the answers. Knowing you are well prepared for an exam reduces and, in some cases, eliminates feelings of test anxiety. Not knowing the material well enough or not being sure that you know the material well enough can actually lead to more test anxiety. Spacing your study, using active learning strategies, and practicing retrieval all help you prepare well for the exam. If you begin the exam with a positive attitude about your preparation and expect to do well, you can increase your probability for success.

When you get your test back, use it to evaluate how well your study plan and strategies worked for you. Go over all of the test items, both the correct and incorrect ones, to examine your preparation and test-taking skills. Instead of being discouraged by a poor test grade, find out why you made the mistakes that you made. Plan ways to avoid making the same mistakes again. Think of a good test grade as a reward for the hard work that you did. High scores on exams don't just happen; they're the result of effective preparation.

Activity 4-12

Compare Affective and Motivational Strategies That You Use

List in the margin five affective and motivational strategies that you used during the past week. Get together with a group of your classmates and compare the strategies you used. Describe how effective they were in improving your learning and memory? What other strategies do you plan to use in the future?

Activity 4-13

Monitor How You Learn and Remember

Choose a chapter or part of a chapter in one of your textbooks, select the material that you think you need to learn for an exam, and organize it on a separate sheet of paper. Then determine how you could learn the material. Then work on it until you think you know it. Finally, test yourself to monitor your learning. Write a paragraph or two describing the process that you used to learn the material and how you decided to monitor your learning. Describe your results.

Activity 4-14

Where Are You Now?

Now that you have completed Chapter 4, take a few minutes to repeat the "Where Are You Now?" activity, located on the *College Study Skills* Web site. What changes did you make as a result of reading this chapter? How are you planning to apply what you've learned in this chapter?

SUMMARY

Learning how information is stored and retrieved in the human brain—learning how memory works—may help you better understand why you need to be actively involved with your course material as you complete day-to-day assignments and prepare for exams. To learn anything, we must encode it—make it meaningful. At that point, we must rehearse the material to move it from short-term to long-term memory. The more organized the information is as we store it, the more easily we'll be able to locate it later—retrieve it. By working on the material in different ways, we can form many associations or cues to help us retrieve the information when we need it. However, interference, anxiety, improper encoding, and passive study can all lead to poor retrieval and what we call forgetting.

Learning to use general and specific memory strategies can help you improve your ability to encode, store, and retrieve information. Strategies such as spaced practice, breaking down tasks, repetition, and overlearning are the cornerstones of improving your memory. Specific memory strategies can also be used effectively to increase your ability to store and retrieve information. Rehearsal strategies help you store course information in long-term memory. Elaboration strategies such as taking notes in your own words, adding recall questions, and creating study sheets build cues to aid retrieval. Forming associations, creating acronyms and acrostics, and using visual imagery are mnemonic devices that can help you more easily retrieve the information that you've already learned. You can also improve your memory by using organizational strategies like grouping, outlining, mapping, and charting. Through comprehension monitoring strategies such as recitation, self-testing, and evaluating your progress in learning, you can keep tabs on how well you're learning the material and how effective your strategies are. As you've probably discovered, many of these strategies work best when you use them together. Affective and motivational strategies help keep you on task, encourage you to work hard, and reward you when your efforts pay off. A good memory is not something most people are born with, but anyone can develop a good memory by working hard and becoming an active, strategic learner.

REVIEW QUESTIONS

Terms You Should Know: Make a flash card for each term.

Acronyms	Massed practice
Acrostics	Metacognition
Affective and motivational strategies	Method of Loci
Chunk	Mnemonic devices
Comprehension monitoring strategies	Organizational strategies
Consolidation	Overlearning
Cue	Rehearsal strategies
Displacement	Retrieval
Elaboration strategies	Sensory memory
Elaborative rehearsal	Sensory registers
Encoding	Spaced practice
Immediate memory	Storage
Information Processing Model	Working memory

Completion: Fill in the blank to complete each of the following statements.

1. _____ memory is very susceptible to interference.

2. If information is well _____, it is easier to learn and recall.

3. Another term for spaced practice is _____ practice.

4. Mnemonic devices are designed to aid _____, not _____.

5. _____-level rehearsal strategies are more effective in getting information into long-term memory.

Multiple Choice: Circle the letter of the best answer for each of the following questions. Be sure to underline key words and eliminate wrong answers.

6. _____ occurs when we make things meaningful.
   A. Encoding
   B. Storage
   C. Retrieval
   D. Memory

7. Which of the following is not an advantage of overlearning?
   A. It helps you organize the information you need to learn.
   B. It reduces test anxiety.
   C. It prevents forgetting.
   D. It helps you understand the material better.

Short Answer–Essay: On a separate sheet, answer each of the following questions.

8. Compare and contrast short-term and long-term memory.

9. Why do some students have difficulty retrieving information? What should they do differently?

10. Describe Weinstein and Mayer's Five Groups of Learning Strategies.

"I edited my notes from today's classes using the tips given in class. I skimmed through the text to see what mistakes I might have made and corrected them in my notebook. I added headings to make my notes more organized. I also added a recall column. I like using the recall column because it points out quickly the information that I'm looking for."

Keesha Johnson
Student

TAKING LECTURE NOTES

In this chapter you will learn more about:

- **Why to take lecture notes**
- **How to take lecture notes**
- **Effective note-taking systems**
- **How to edit your notes**
- **How to review your notes**

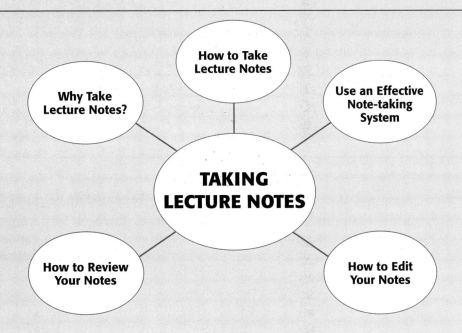

Activity 5-1

Where Are You Now?

Take a few minutes to answer *yes* or *no* to the following questions.

	YES	NO
1. Do you review and edit your notes within twenty-four hours after each of your classes?	_____	_____
2. Do you try to write down exactly what your professor says in class?	_____	_____
3. Do you separate the main points from supporting information in your notes?	_____	_____
4. Are you able to read and understand your notes when you study for your exam?	_____	_____
5. Do you sometimes find that your notes don't make sense when you review them before an exam?	_____	_____
6. Do you tend to write down only key words when you take notes?	_____	_____
7. Do you review your notes by reciting them out loud?	_____	_____
8. Do you tend to miss a lot of information when you take notes?	_____	_____
9. Are you actively involved in the lecture?	_____	_____
10. Do you read your textbook assignment before you go to your lecture class?	_____	_____
Total Points	_____	

Give yourself 1 point for each *yes* answer to questions 1, 3, 4, 7, 9, and 10 and 1 point for each *no* answer to questions 2, 5, 6, and 8. Now total up your points. A low score indicates that you need some help in note taking. A high score indicates that you are already using many good note-taking strategies.

WHY TAKE LECTURE NOTES?

Other than attending class every day, taking good lecture notes is probably the single most important activity for college students. Taking notes during college lectures is a difficult task for most entering college students because little or no real practice in note taking occurred when they were in high school. There, note taking involved copying the information off the chalkboard as the teacher talked and wrote. In college, however, most professors don't do the job of note taking for you. Instead, you must listen, select the appropriate information, paraphrase it, condense it, and then write it down with few (if any) clues from the professor. Developing good note-taking skills takes both time and practice. Taking lecture notes promotes active listening, provides an accurate record of information, provides an opportunity to interpret, condense, and organize the information, and provides an opportunity for repetition of the material. Learning and practicing effective strategies for how to take lecture notes will help you become a more successful student.

Promotes Active Listening

Taking notes in class promotes active listening by helping you concentrate on the lecture. Have you ever sat in class and realized that you had no idea what the professor just said? This is a very common experience for many students. Even though everyone gets distracted once in a while, it becomes a real problem if you daydream so much that you miss what your professor is saying. By taking notes, you can improve your concentration because you're focusing your attention on what's being said; you have a purpose—listening for the next point that the professor will make so that you can write it down.

Some students find sitting in lecture classes very boring; they prefer classes where they're more actively involved in the learning experience. Taking notes, however, is a very active process. You can generate a high level of involvement in your own learning by taking notes. Note taking involves more than just writing down what the instructor is saying. It includes thinking about what's been said, determining what's important, recognizing how different points relate to others, anticipating what will be said next, putting the information into your own words, and organizing the information in your notes. Condensing and interpreting the information helps make it more meaningful to you, which helps you learn it. The process of taking good lecture notes can help you become both an active listener and an active participant in your classes.

Provides an Accurate Record of Information

The most important reason for taking notes in college is to get an accurate record of the information that was presented in class. Taking notes can actually help you learn and remember the information. Even if you learn some of the information during the lecture class, you probably won't remember it by the time you take your exam. In college, exams are given after four, seven, or even fifteen weeks; you won't remember all the lecture material by the time you take a test. Research studies indicate that without rehearsal, you may forget 50 percent of what you hear in a lecture within twenty-four hours and 80 percent in just two weeks.[1] In fact, you may forget 95 percent within one month. This comes as a big shock to most college students; however, it explains why some students have difficulty on exams. If you don't leave a lecture class with a good set of notes, an accurate record of information, you won't have the opportunity to review that material again before the exam. You can't just rely on your memory of the lecture; you need your notes, too! Why? In many classes the majority of the exam questions come from the lecture material. Without a good set of notes, you won't be able to prepare for the exam.

Helps You Organize the Information

Taking lecture notes forces you to interpret, condense, and organize the information that's presented. You've probably already discovered that you can't write as fast as your professor speaks. If you were able to do so, you could simply jot down the lecture word for word with little thought, and as a result, you wouldn't really learn

---

[1]H. Spitzer, "Studies in Retention," *Journal of Educational Psychology* 30 (1939): 641–656.

very much. In many ways it's probably better that you can't. Because you have to condense the information, you have to think about each sentence and interpret it—often putting the information into your own words. As you write down the information in a condensed form, you also are forced to create a system of organization that separates the main and supporting points. You can structure the information your own way—the way that makes sense to you. These processes make note taking very active and help you understand and learn the information during the lecture. They also provide you with a record of the important information in a format that's more useful for later study. Remember, the more organized the information is, the easier it is to learn and remember.

Provides Additional Repetition

Taking lecture notes also provides you with repetition on the material. By writing down the important information, you are, in fact, reviewing it several times. To take notes, you must actually work on the material (think about it). You need to listen to each sentence the professor states, evaluate its importance, interpret its meaning, condense it into a meaningful phrase, organize it under a heading or subheading, and finally write it down. You may find that you think about the material again as you go through the same process for the next sentence, too, because it may connect to the previous notes you took. In this way, you get a great deal of repetition on each point—something that may not occur were you simply listening to the lecture. Of course, as you edit (discussed later in the chapter) and review your notes, you'll get even more repetition.

HOW TO TAKE LECTURE NOTES

Learning to take notes effectively and efficiently takes time. You can begin to improve your note-taking skills rapidly, however, if you learn to use some basic strategies. One of the first things you need to do is learn to become an active listener. Although there's no one correct way to take notes, some methods or systems work better than others. In this section, you'll learn a number of basic strategies to help improve your note taking, as well as several options for form and format. Instead of just selecting one method to use, you may find it beneficial to try all the techniques and then decide which ones work best for you. First, you may want to evaluate your own note-taking skills.

Evaluate Your Note-Taking Skills

Now that you know how important it is to take notes, you're probably thinking about the quality of the notes you usually take. Although Activity 5-1 gave you a general indication of how well you take notes, an even better way to evaluate your note-taking skills is to compare the content (the information) of your notes to that of other students. In Activity 5-2 you have the opportunity to do that.

Activity 5-2

Practice Taking Notes

As your instructor plays the video, *Piaget–Intellectual Development,* which presents the first ten minutes of an actual lecture from an Introductory Psychology class, take notes. This video is available to instructors (see the Instructor's Manual for contact informa-

Continued

tion). As you listen to the lecture, take notes as you usually do. It is a real lecture, so take the best notes you can. Save your notes because you'll need them for a later activity. After you complete this activity, evaluate the quality of your notes.

Consider the Content
Evaluate your notes from Activity 5-2 according to two main criteria: content and organization. First, consider the **content** that you recorded in your notes. Did you get an accurate record of the information? The best way to figure out if you're taking good notes is to find out whether you're getting down the information that you'll need to master the material and to review for the exam. This is not easily determined in one attempt. Throughout the chapter, you'll be given opportunities to evaluate the content in your notes.

One way to judge the content of your notes is to compare them with those of other students in your class. If you're fairly new at taking notes, you may want to get together with a classmate and compare notes. By reading your notes and following along in your classmate's notes, you may be able to determine whether or not you're getting all the information that you need.

Another way to evaluate the content of your notes is to compare the information in your notes with the information in your textbook (assuming your instructor follows the text). You also can evaluate the completeness and accuracy of your notes after you take a quiz or exam on the material. Look back at your notes to see if you were missing or had inaccurate information that contributed to the errors on your test.

Consider the Organization
The way you **organize** your notes is the second criterion for how "good" they are. If you try to write down everything without organizing the information, you may find yourself with a jumble of unrelated facts and ideas. It's important to separate main points and details and to show the relationships between clusters of information in your notes. You'll learn more about how to organize your notes later in this chapter. Remember, the more organized your notes are, the more easily you'll be able to study from them.

Activity 5-3
Compare Student Notes

 How would you evaluate the content and organization in the notes of a group of your classmates? Look at each student's set of notes as a group and compare the information for the first headed section. Did everyone have the same information? What was missing, if anything? Then look at the next section and repeat the process.

Prepare Before Taking Notes

Before you ever walk into a lecture class, you need to prepare to take notes. The best way to prepare for your note-taking activity is to read the text assignment before class. Much of the material that's presented in college lectures will be new to you. By reading the text assignment before the lecture, you build up some background about the topic. If you have some idea what the lecture is about, it will be easier for you to understand the presentation and take good notes. Reading before the lecture also will give you the opportunity to become familiar with the main topics or ideas that will be presented. You'll find it easier to identify main ideas and organize your notes as the professor delivers the lecture. Finally, you'll be somewhat familiar with key terms and names after reading the text. This will help you keep up with the lecturer and avoid making content errors in your notes. If you've been having difficulty understanding the lecture or taking notes, try reading your text assignment before the next lecture. Remember, you only get one chance to listen to the lecture, but you can read the text as many times as you want.

As you walk into the lecture classroom, get ready to take notes. If you sit near the front, you'll be able to see and hear better. You'll probably find that other interested and motivated students also tend to sit in the first few rows of the class. By avoiding the back of the room, you'll avoid those students who tend to chat and walk in late. While you're waiting for class to begin, review the notes that you took during the last class meeting. Many professors pick up where they left off in the last lecture. Your review will remind you of the main topics and the general organization of the lecture and will prepare you for the next point that will be made.

Become an Active Listener

Although reading your text assignment helps you build some background for understanding the lecture, it doesn't guarantee that you'll take good notes. Researchers have discovered that we ignore, misunderstand, or forget about 75 percent of what we hear.[2] As you may have discovered earlier, note taking is an active process that involves a number of steps (also shown in Figure 5.1).

- deciding you want to listen

- paying attention to the lecture

- selecting relevant information and ignoring the distractions around you

- interpreting the information to make it meaningful

- condensing the information before writing it down

- organizing the information under the appropriate headings or subheadings

- taking notes

Activity 5-4

Test Your Listening Skills

Go to the *College Study Skills* book-specific Web site and click on the link for the listening test under Chapter 5. As you check your listening skills, respond to the questions as you think of yourself in a classroom situation.

---

[2]Diane Bone, *The Business of Listening* (Los Altos, CA: Crisp Publications, 1988), p. 5.

FIGURE 5.1
Steps in the Listening/
Note-taking Process

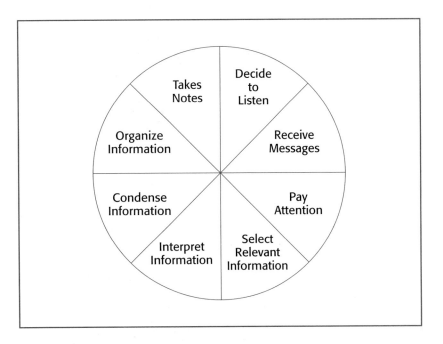

Active Versus Passive Listening

Many students confuse hearing and listening. Your ears may receive sounds during a lecture, or you may listen by watching a sign language interpreter or real-time reporter, but that doesn't mean that you're listening—paying attention to and interpreting what you're hearing. As you learned in Chapter 4, you only remember a small proportion of all sounds that you hear because you don't attend to (pay attention to) most of them. **Hearing** is a passive process; it is *nonselective* and *involuntary.* **Listening,** on the other hand, is an active "process that involves receiving, attending to, and assigning meaning to aural [verbal] and visual [nonverbal] stimuli"[3] (material in brackets not in the original definition).

Characteristics of Active Listeners

Active listeners are physically and mentally focused on the lecture. They sit up straight, lean forward slightly (indicating interest), and make the lecturer the center of their attention by making eye contact or sitting directly in the lecturer's line of vision. Active listeners often sit near the front of the classroom to avoid external distractions. They eliminate internal distractions, too, by pushing other thoughts out and focusing all their attention on the information being presented. They're open minded and willing to listen to the lecture, putting aside their own biases. Students who are actively involved in the lecture ask questions, answer questions, and take notes. They evaluate what they're hearing and often consider how this information connects to their prior knowledge of the subject. Professors often can identify students who are actively involved in the lecture by their body language, too. They may nod or smile in agreement, look amazed or confused at times, and pull back or frown when they disagree with what's being said. Active listeners are physically, intellectually, and emotionally involved in the lecture.

Factors that Interfere with Effective Listening

Without realizing it, even the most dedicated students may at times be thwarted in their efforts to be active listeners. Both internal and external distractions can interfere

---

[3]A. D. Wolvin and C. G. Coakley, *Listening,* 5th ed. (Dubuque, IA: Brown and Benchmark, 1996), p. 69.

with a student's ability to concentrate during a lecture. Not attending to the lecture can lead to uncertainty about what was said, difficulty understanding the information, or missed information. Many students also either stop listening or become less involved in the presentation when they're angry or offended by the speaker or the message. They react emotionally to the situation and blame the speaker and often stop paying attention to what he or she is saying as a way of retaliating. Some students become angry or closed minded when the lecturer discusses controversial material that's in direct opposition to their own personal point of view. Similarly, some students are "turned off" by language or gestures that they consider inappropriate. They allow their personal sense of propriety to interfere with their listening.

Strategies to Improve Your Listening Skills

Although there are many strategies for becoming an active listener, the following should help you increase your skills:

- Read the text assignment before the lecture to build background on the topic.

- Review your last set of notes before the lecture begins.

- Sit in the professor's line of vision (first row across or middle row from the front to the back of the room).

- Decide that you want to listen.

- Focus your attention physically by sitting up and making eye contact with the speaker.

- Focus your attention mentally by eliminating or avoiding distractions.

- Listen with an open mind, setting aside your own biases.

- Control your emotional responses.

- Listen for the main points and related details and take notes.

- Ask and answer questions.

- Monitor your listening. Check with the lecturer or a classmate (at the end of the lecture) if you're unsure of some of the information.

- Hold yourself accountable for the material presented.

USE AN EFFECTIVE NOTE-TAKING SYSTEM

Dozens of systems have been developed to help students become effective note takers. Some of them are quite complex and provide explicit details on every step of the process. Unfortunately, a number of these systems involve so many steps and so much work that many students resort to their old methods or just don't take notes at all. Other systems are rather simple and provide only a few basic guidelines. For the new college student, they may not provide enough structure about how to get the information on paper.

The Cornell note-taking system (developed at Cornell University) includes an excellent format for setting up your notes. Use an 8½- by 11-inch notebook (I recommend a separate notebook for each class), so that you have enough space to take notes, create a recall column, and write a summary at the end of each page. A sample note page using the **Cornell system** is shown in Figure 5.2. To set up your page,

FIGURE 5.2
Cornell Note Page

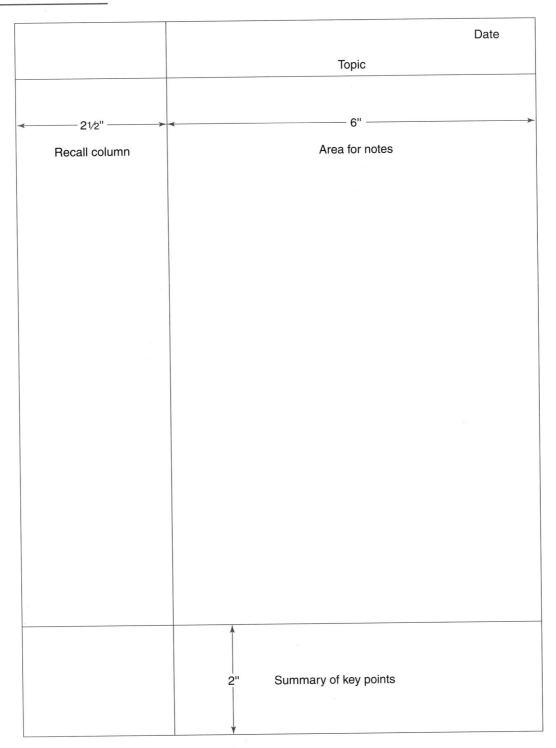

use a ruler to create a new margin line that's 2½ to 3½ inches from the edge or purchase a summary margin notebook available in some college bookstores. Most notebooks have only a one-inch margin, which doesn't allow enough space to write recall questions (you'll learn more about this later in the chapter). At the end of each page, leave a two-inch margin so that you can write a summary of the important points as you review your notes. In the large six-inch space to the right of the margin, write down as much information about the lecture as you can. You can use a variety of methods to take your notes, but the outline, block, and modified-block styles have proven to be effective for most college lectures.

Three Note-Taking Systems

Although there are many note-taking systems, the informal outline, the block, and the modified-block styles work well for college lectures. Try them all and see which one(s) work best for you.

The Informal Outline

Many students use outlining to take notes in lecture classes. **Outlining** involves indenting each level of supporting details under the preceding heading, subheading, or detail. One of the reasons this style is so popular is that it's familiar to many students. Is this the style that you're using now? You probably learned formal outlining in school and feel comfortable putting information into outline form. Some students use outlines because their professors provide them with some form of outline at the beginning of the lecture. Even the four- or five-point outline written on the board can set the pattern that you use for taking notes. Outlines work, however, only when the lecturer is well organized and proceeds in an orderly manner from main points to supporting points.

You can effectively use an outline style of note taking as long as you are careful not to fall into several traps. Don't get distracted by the "rules" of formal outlining. You could spend so much time thinking about how you should label or designate the next point in your notes that you miss some of the content. You may find yourself thinking about whether you should write a "B" or a "2" in your notes instead of concentrating on the content of the lecture.

Too often, students equate outlining with just writing down key words. One-word outlines (Figure 5.3) contain too little of the content of the lecture to provide an accurate record of information. As you can see, there's no real information here to answer test questions on any of the topics. Sometimes students don't realize how little information they have in their notes until they look at another student's notes. Look at the sample notes in Figure 5.4, which were taken by two students in the same Economics class. Gary simply wrote down key words. His notes look well

FIGURE 5.3
Example of One-Word Notes

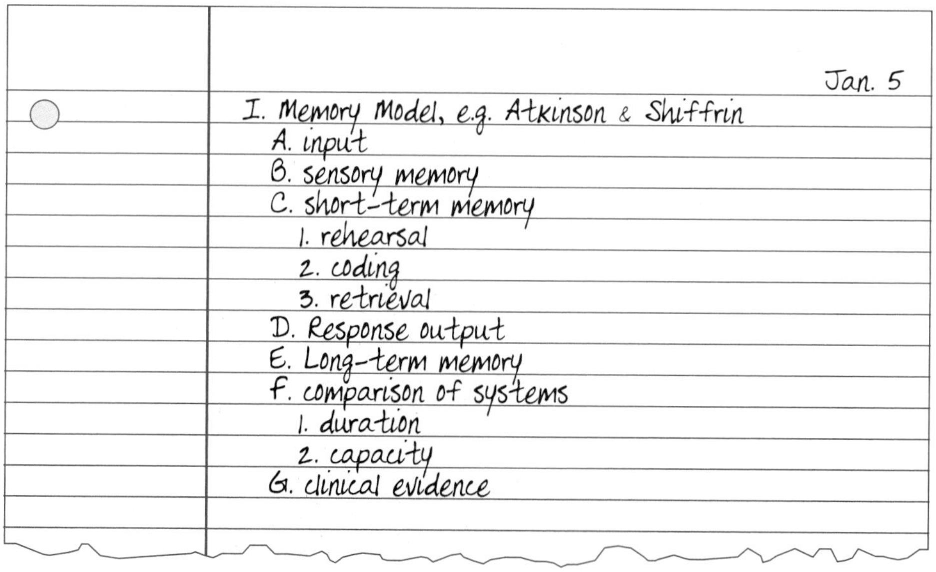

Jan. 5

I. Memory Model, e.g. Atkinson & Shiffrin
  A. input
  B. sensory memory
  C. short-term memory
    1. rehearsal
    2. coding
    3. retrieval
  D. Response output
  E. Long-term memory
  F. comparison of systems
    1. duration
    2. capacity
  G. clinical evidence

FIGURE 5.4

Two Examples from the Same Economics Lecture

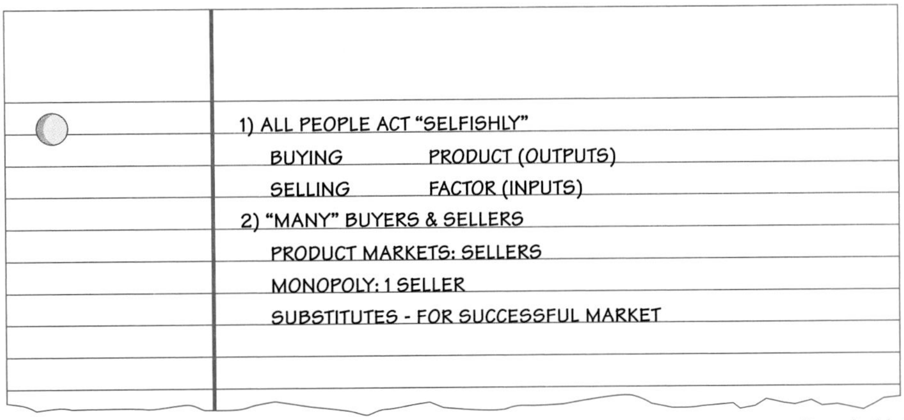

1) ALL PEOPLE ACT "SELFISHLY"
    BUYING   PRODUCT (OUTPUTS)
    SELLING   FACTOR (INPUTS)
2) "MANY" BUYERS & SELLERS
    PRODUCT MARKETS: SELLERS
    MONOPOLY: 1 SELLER
    SUBSTITUTES - FOR SUCCESSFUL MARKET

Gary's Notes

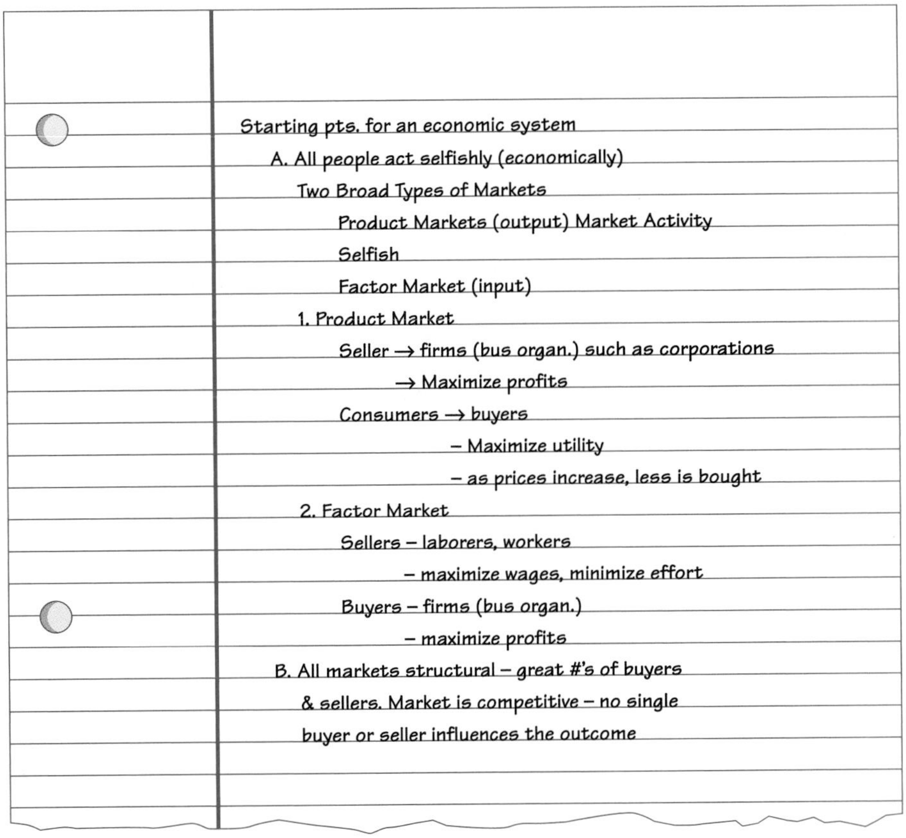

Starting pts. for an economic system
    A. All people act selfishly (economically)
        Two Broad Types of Markets
            Product Markets (output) Market Activity
            Selfish
            Factor Market (input)
      1. Product Market
          Seller → firms (bus organ.) such as corporations
             → Maximize profits
          Consumers → buyers
              – Maximize utility
               – as prices increase, less is bought
      2. Factor Market
          Sellers – laborers, workers
             – maximize wages, minimize effort
          Buyers – firms (bus organ.)
             – maximize profits
    B. All markets structural – great #'s of buyers
      & sellers. Market is competitive – no single
      buyer or seller influences the outcome

Bryan's Notes

organized and effective until you compare them with the notes taken by Bryan. Bryan's notes contain much more information about the topics presented in the lecture. Bryan included **meaningful phrases,** condensed versions of the statements made by the professor that still contain the critical concepts that were presented. When it's time to prepare for exams, students with "one-word notes" simply don't have enough information from which to study. Which set of notes would you rather have before the exam?

If you do plan to outline as you take notes, use an informal outlining style (see Figure 5.5). After designating the main points next to the margin line, just use indentation to show that the next points are subordinate. (Instead of aligning the next point with the sentence above, move it in a little from the lefthand side.) If the

FIGURE 5.5
Informal Outlining

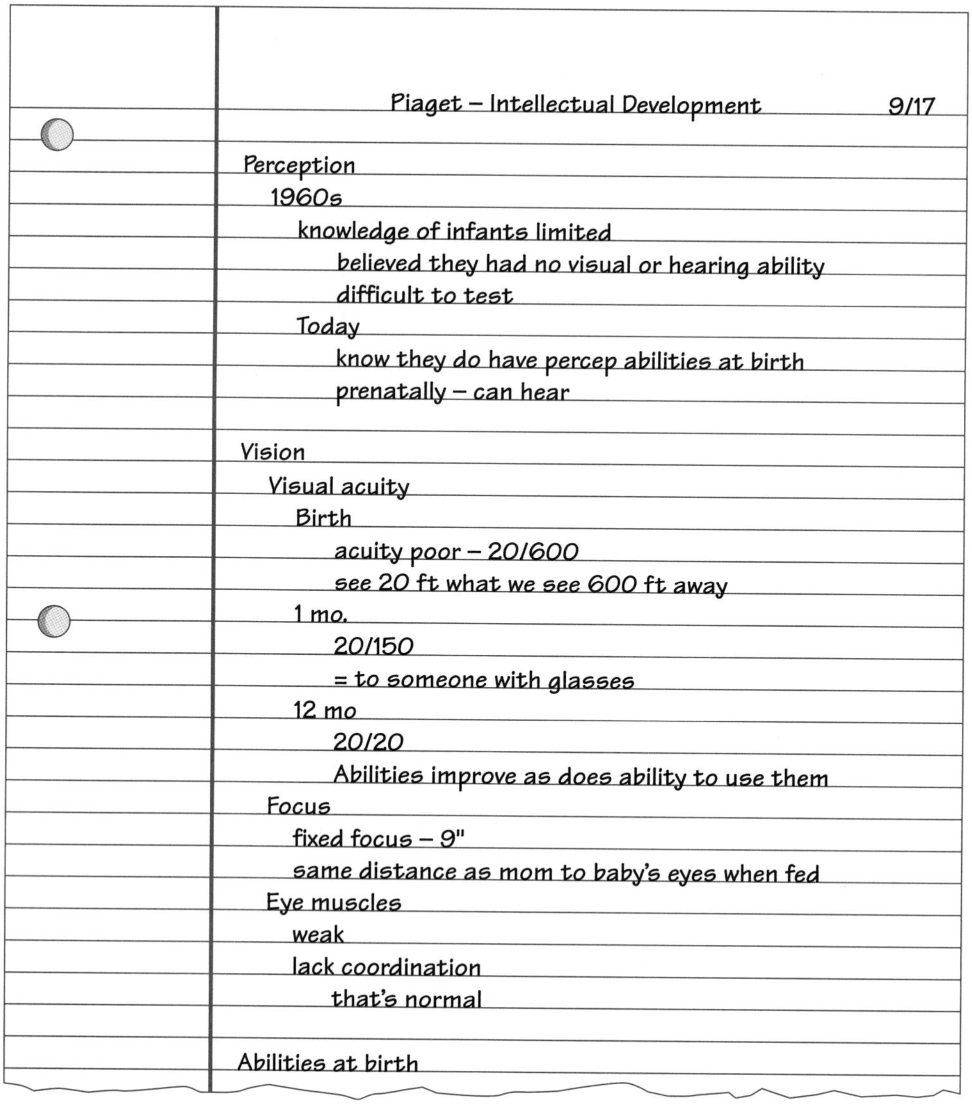

```
                Piaget – Intellectual Development        9/17

     Perception
       1960s
         knowledge of infants limited
           believed they had no visual or hearing ability
           difficult to test
       Today
           know they do have percep abilities at birth
           prenatally – can hear

     Vision
       Visual acuity
         Birth
           acuity poor – 20/600
           see 20 ft what we see 600 ft away
         1 mo.
           20/150
           = to someone with glasses
         12 mo
           20/20
           Abilities improve as does ability to use them
       Focus
         fixed focus – 9"
         same distance as mom to baby's eyes when fed
       Eye muscles
         weak
         lack coordination
           that's normal

     Abilities at birth
```

lecturer numbers points as he or she is speaking, by all means, include the numbers. But don't try to make your professor's lecture or your notes adhere to a formal outline style.

The Block Method

The block style of note taking is another very simple system to learn. Block notes are especially useful if you need to record a great deal of information very quickly. Do you have a professor who talks so fast you can't keep up? Who never goes back over information? Who never seems to pause to catch his or her breath? When taking block notes you need only to write down the heading and then focus on writing as many details as you can. **Block notes** are written continuously across the page, separating the details by dashes (—) or slashes (/). Demonstrating the block form, Figure 5.6 contains a set of notes from the lecture on Intellectual Development. The headings from the lecture stand out because they're next to the margin, whereas the details are clustered together in a block indented slightly under each heading. Remember, you don't have to write complete sentences just because your notes are shaped like a paragraph; you still

FIGURE 5.6
Block Notes

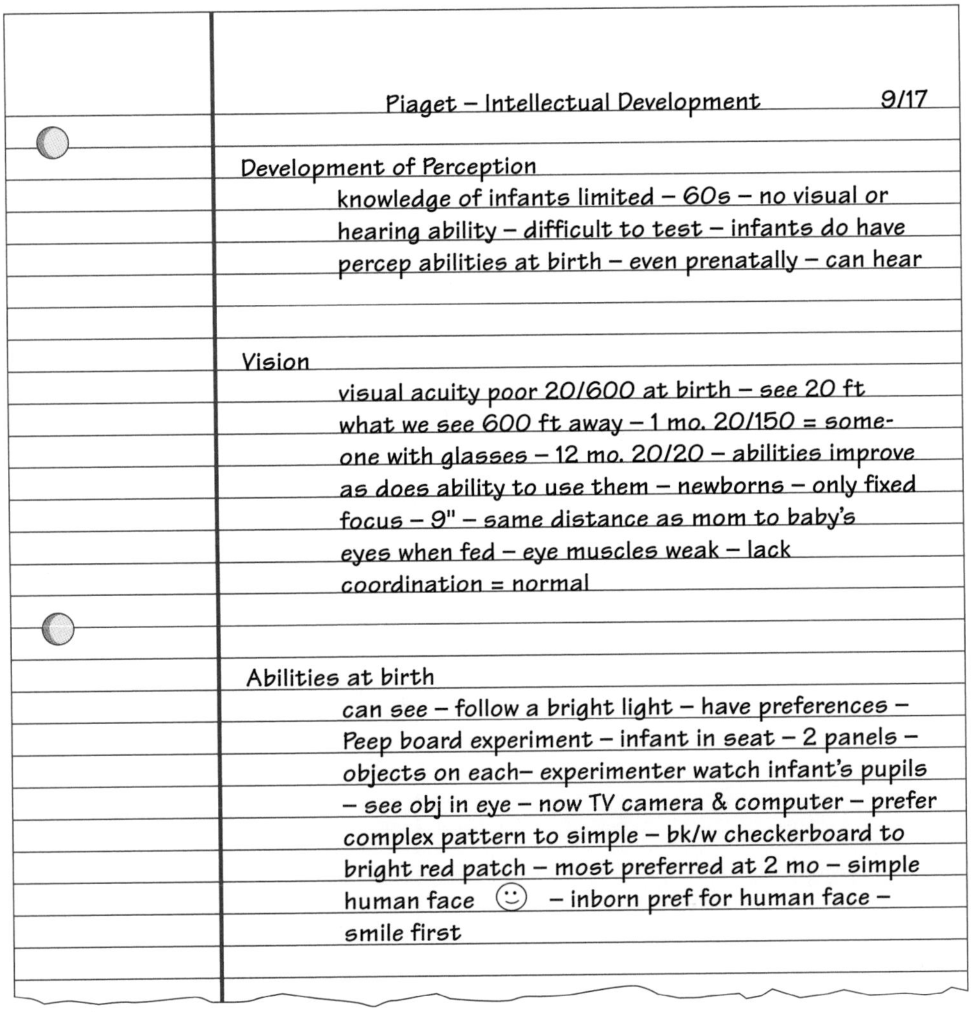

Piaget – Intellectual Development   9/17

Development of Perception
        knowledge of infants limited – 60s – no visual or
        hearing ability – difficult to test – infants do have
        percep abilities at birth – even prenatally – can hear

Vision
        visual acuity poor 20/600 at birth – see 20 ft
        what we see 600 ft away – 1 mo. 20/150 = some-
        one with glasses – 12 mo. 20/20 – abilities improve
        as does ability to use them – newborns – only fixed
        focus – 9" – same distance as mom to baby's
        eyes when fed – eye muscles weak – lack
        coordination = normal

Abilities at birth
        can see – follow a bright light – have preferences –
        Peep board experiment – infant in seat – 2 panels –
        objects on each– experimenter watch infant's pupils
        – see obj in eye – now TV camera & computer – prefer
        complex pattern to simple – bk/w checkerboard to
        bright red patch – most preferred at 2 mo – simple
        human face ☺   – inborn pref for human face –
        smile first

---

want to concentrate on using meaningful phrases. By skipping a line or two between each main heading, you can organize your notes and leave room to add something later in the lecture.

The Modified-Block Method

Some students are uncomfortable putting all their notes in block form. If you like the idea of having all of the information grouped under a heading without showing various levels of support as in an outline, you may prefer to use a modified-block format. To use **modified block notes,** you would simply indent about one-half inch and list all related details straight down the page under each heading. You would take each of the details clustered under the heading, "Development of Perception" and list them individually, one statement per line (Figure 5.7). Having each detail on a separate line makes it easy to take notes, organize them, and review for the exam.

The block and modified-block methods allow you to take notes efficiently and effectively because you have to concentrate on only two things: (1) writing down the main points (headings) and (2) writing down any details about them. You don't have to spend a lot of time trying to figure out where to place or how to label each new piece of information.

FIGURE 5.7

Modified-Block Notes

> Piaget – Intellectual Development   9/17
>
> Development of Perception
>   knowledge of infants limited 1960s
>   believed no visual or hearing ability
>   difficult to test
>   now know infants do have percep abilities at birth
>   prenatally can hear
>
> Vision
>   visual acuity poor at birth 20/600
>   see at 20 ft what we see 600 ft away
>   1 mo   20/150 = someone w glasses
>   12 mo   20/20
>   abilities improve as does ability to use them
>   newborns have a fixed focus – 9"
>   same distance as mom to baby's eyes when
>   being fed
>   eye muscles weak
>   lack coordination = normal
>
> Abilities at birth
>   can see
>   follow a bright light
>   have preferences
>   peep board experiment
>   exper infant in seat
>   2 panels w objects on each
>   watch infant's pupils
>   see preferred obj in infant's eye
>   computer experiment
>   now use TV camera connected to computer

Activity 5-5

Turn Statements into Phrases

Condense the following statements into phrases you would use if you heard them in a lecture. The first one is done for you. Compare your responses to those of your classmates.

1. Early in the seventeenth century, a scholar by the name of Galileo Galilei put two glass lenses in a cylinder.

   _____ early 17C—Galileo put 2 lenses in cylinder _____

2. With this instrument he happened to look at an insect, and later he described the stunning geometric patterns of its tiny eyes.

   _____

Continued

3. Thus Galileo, who wasn't a biologist, was one of the first to record a biological observation made through a microscope.

_____

4. The study of the cellular basis of life was about to begin.

_____

5. First in Italy, and then in France and England, scholars set out to explore a world whose existence had not even been suspected.

_____

6. At mid-century, Robert Hooke, Curator of Instruments for the Royal Society of England, was at the forefront of these studies.

_____

7. When Hooke first turned a microscope to thinly sliced cork from a mature tree, he observed tiny compartments.

_____

8. He gave them the Latin name *cellulae*, meaning small rooms—hence, the origin of the biological term "*cell*."

_____

9. They actually were the interconnecting walls of dead plant cells, which is what cork is made of, but Hooke didn't think of them as being dead because neither he nor anyone else knew cells could be alive.

_____

10. In other plant tissues, he observed cells "fill'd with juices" but didn't have a clue to what they represented.[4]

_____

Activity 5-6

Practice Different Note-Taking Methods

Develop a set of notes from the following material on cells, using the block, modified block, or outline method. Exchange notes with a classmate and compare your content and organization.

Today we are going to discuss the basic aspects of cell structure and function. Cells differ hugely in size, shape, and activities, as you might gather by comparing a tiny bacterium with one of your relatively giant liver cells. Yet they are alike in three respects. All cells start out life with a plasma membrane, a region of DNA, and a region of cytoplasm.

Continued

---

[4]Adapted from C. Starr and R. Taggart, *Biology: The Unity and Diversity of Life*, 10th ed. (Belmont, CA: Brooks/Cole, 2004), p. 54.

Activity 5-6

Practice Different Note-Taking Methods (continued)

The plasma membrane, the cell's outermost membrane, maintains the cell as a distinct entity, apart from the environment, and allows metabolic events to proceed in organized, controlled ways. The plasma membrane does not *isolate* the cell interior; substances and signals continually move across it.

Depending on the species, the DNA occupies a membrane-bound sac (nucleus) in the cell or simply a region of the cell interior (nucleoid).

The cytoplasm is everything between the plasma membrane and the region of DNA. It consists of a semifluid matrix and other components, such as ribosomes (structures on which proteins are built).[5]

What to Include in Your Notes

Although some general rules will help you figure out what to include in your notes, there's no simple answer to the question "What should I write down?" Some students are so afraid that they'll miss even one point during the lecture that they try to write down every word the professor says. This is both impractical and ineffective. You can't write as fast as your professor can talk. A good general rule is to treat a lecture class like a lab class. You should be an active participant during the entire period. The best thing to do is to take as many notes as you can in a well-organized format. As soon as you pick out the heading, listen carefully for any information that explains or expands upon it, and add that information to your notes. Have you ever caught yourself thinking, "I wonder if I should write that down?" Anytime you think about whether to write something down, go ahead and write it down. You may even find that your hand hurts at the end of the period; that's fine. *Remember: When in doubt, write it out.*

Headings

Always note all **headings**—the main points—that are made during a lecture. You may find that sometimes you have no trouble at all identifying the main points, and other times you have a lot of trouble. Main points appear to be obvious during some lectures because the lecturer states them in an easily recognizable manner. Introductions such as: "The next thing we're going to talk about is . . . ," "Another reason is . . . ," "What about vision?" and "First of all, . . ." make main points easy to pick out. Listen during your next lecture and see how your professor introduces each main topic. If your professor puts an outline on the board, you may want to copy it into your notebook right away. However, as each main topic comes up during the actual lecture, write it down again in your notes.

Nonverbal clues may help you decide what is important in a lecture. Some lecturers unconsciously stress certain points by altering their voice level, changing their position in the classroom, or gesturing. If your professor raises his or her voice, you may be getting a signal that a main point or test answer is being presented. Some professors move away from the podium and toward students when they present key points during a lecture. Others point to specific information that

---

[5]Adapted from C. Starr and R. Taggart, *Biology: The Unity and Diversity of Life,* 10th ed. (Belmont, CA: Brooks/Cole, 2004), p. 56.

ADDITIONAL STRATEGIES FOR TAKING LECTURE NOTES

DON'T RELY ON YOUR MEMORY ALONE. Many students think they should be able to remember the information presented in a lecture if they pay careful attention. Unfortunately, we tend to forget rapidly. With four to seven weeks between exams, taking notes is critical.

USE A FULL-SIZE NOTEBOOK. Use a separate 8½ by 11-inch notebook for each of your classes. Using smaller notebooks can unconsciously lead to writing fewer notes.

INCLUDE THE TOPIC IN YOUR NOTES. By including the topic, you're helping to organize your mind for listening and your notes for later review.

LEAVE SOME SPACE IN YOUR NOTES. By leaving a 2½-inch margin on the left side of the page, you'll be able to add recall questions when you edit your notes. Also, leave a line or two before you write each of your headings in case the professor adds information later in the lecture.

USE COMMON ABBREVIATIONS IN YOUR NOTES. By using some familiar abbreviations, you can get the information down more quickly. Don't use too many abbreviations, though, or you won't know what they mean. See the list of common abbreviations on the Web site.

SKIP A FEW SPACES IF YOU MISS INFORMATION. Skip a line or two and go on to the next point. If you miss a keyword, draw a line and keep going. Ask a classmate or the professor about the missing information after the lecture.

USE A TAPE RECORDER WITH A COUNTER. If you need to use a tape recorder at the beginning of the semester, get one with a counter on it. When you can't keep up with the lecturer and miss information, make a note of the location where the information occurred on the tape (the number on the counter) in the margin of your notebook and leave some space in your notes. Later, fast forward using the counter numbers to fill in the material you need.

PLAY TAPED LECTURES WHILE YOU COMMUTE. If you have a long commute to and from school, you may want to tape your lectures for your most difficult classes. Then you can play them while you drive or ride the bus or train. The additional review may help you improve your understanding of the material.

FIND A NOTE-TAKING "BUDDY." Many students have to miss class due to illness or emergencies. Set up a plan with one of your classmates to let you copy his or her notes in case you're absent. Exchange phone numbers or e-mail addresses to check on any upcoming assignments or scheduled exams.

DON'T LET OPPOSING OPINIONS TURN YOU OFF. Part of a professor's job is to present various viewpoints about a topic and generate class discussion. Sometimes that's done by purposely taking an opposing view. Discuss your own views in class if open discussion is provided. If not, share your views after class or during the professor's office hours. In any event, continue taking notes on the discussion.

is written on the board, clear their throats, or look at their notes before presenting key information. Do any of your professors use these methods to signal important information during a lecture?

Details

After you write the heading in your notes, listen for all of the **details,** the points that support each heading the professor presents about that topic. Until you develop more sophisticated note-taking skills, you may want to rely on some of the following tips in deciding which details to include.

1. Details, facts, or explanations that expand or explain the main points that are mentioned.

2. Definitions, word for word, especially if your professor repeats them several times.

3. Enumerations or lists of things that are discussed.

4. Examples; you don't need to note all of the details for each example, but you do need to know to which general topic (heading) each example relates.

5. Anything that is written on the chalkboard, powerpoint slide, or on a transparency (on an overhead projector).

6. Anything that is repeated or spelled out.

7. Drawings, charts, or problems that are written on the board.

Discussion Classes

Most students don't take notes during discussion classes or during those portions of a lecture class that are devoted to discussion. This is a big mistake. Many professors prefer the discussion format when teaching. They could very easily just "tell" students the information, but they prefer to allow the information to emerge through a guided discussion. Even though the material is presented in a different format, the information often will still appear on tests.

You can easily take notes on a discussion. Instead of writing down the main heading, write down the question that's posed. Then jot down the various points that are made during the discussion. Remember, it's very important to indicate who made which point in the discussion. The easiest method is to simply write "P" in front of any statement made by the professor and "S" in front of any statement made by a student.

Math and Science Classes

Taking notes in math and science classes requires special strategies. The modified-block method probably will be more effective than the outline method because you'll need to include many problems and drawings that are written on the board. You may not think that you need to write down all problems that the professor puts on the board, but you should. Even more important, however, you need to write down what the professor says *about* the problems. Get into the habit of writing the name or type of problem first. Then copy down the problem and take notes on steps to follow, tricky areas, what to do first, and even why you should do it. Think of the explanations about a particular problem or model as minilectures. You may find it helpful to write the problem on the left side of the note page and anything the professor says about it directly across from each step. Listen carefully for the main points and the important details and put them in your notes.

PowerPoint Presentations

Many professors are now using PowerPoint presentations (which incorporate a series of "slides" containing main points, details, diagrams, and examples) to enhance their lectures. In addition to showing each "slide" on a large screen, many of them pass out a paper copy with space for notes to their students (Figure 5.8). As you can see from Rhonette's notes, there isn't much space to write down all of the information. Rhonette only wrote down two of the definitions during the lecture. She didn't have room for the five other details she listed in her notes. Instead of taking notes on the handout sheet, use it to organize your notes by copying the headings and subheadings into your notes as the professor refers to them. Then lis-

FIGURE 5.8
Rhonette's Notes from One
"Slide" of a PowerPoint
Presentation

Cell Reactions

• Activation energy—energy hump
reactants must climb over before
reactions

• enzymes—biological catalysts they are
the push that gets the reaction going

ten to what the professor says about the "slide" and take notes. Leave space in your notes to tape in the "slides" showing diagrams or problems (make a note with the name for each).

Activity 5-7

Practice Taking Notes in Real-Life Situations

Practice taking lecture notes as you talk with a friend on the phone, watch the news, or attend a meeting. Select one new strategy to incorporate into your practice notes each time until it becomes routine. Each week look back at your old notes and compare them with the newest set you took. What changes have you made? How would you evaluate your progress?

Activity 5-8

Test Your Notes

A good set of notes should stand up to the test of time. Try the following exercise several times during the semester. Be sure to test the notes from each of your classes. Go back to the notes that you took yesterday in one of your classes and read them. Do they make sense to you? Do you feel as though you are sitting in the lecture and hearing your professor talk about the topic? Now go back to the notes that you took at the beginning of the semester. Do they still make sense? Do you feel as though you understand and recall all the information from the lecture? Write several paragraphs describing what you found in each situation.

HOW TO EDIT YOUR NOTES

Taking good lecture notes is only the first step in the note-taking process. After you leave the classroom, you need to **edit,** revise your notes to correct errors, clarify meaning, make additions, and improve organization. Editing is a fairly easy process once you know how to do it. Early in the semester you may spend a lot of time making corrections or additions to your notes. You may need to reorganize your notes or rewrite them to make them useful. You'll soon benefit from these editing experiences, however, and your ability to take good notes will improve. You'll probably find that by the second half of the semester, you won't need to spend nearly as much time editing, and you can instead devote that time to more active review of your notes.

Editing your notes helps you become a better note taker because you get feedback on the quality of your notes. As you go through your notes to check for accuracy, fill in gaps in information, and improve the organization, you can see where you made mistakes. This feedback can help you become a better note taker. Without knowing what types of errors you tend to make, you may not make changes in your preparation, attention, or note-taking style. Editing also helps you hold yourself accountable. If you know you're going to check your notes after the lecture, you'll take better notes during the lecture. Editing also helps you be better prepared for exams; because most test questions tend to come from lecture notes, it's important that you have a complete, accurate, and well-organized set of notes. Finally, editing provides you with an active review of all of the important information in both your text and notes. This additional repetition (which requires both critical thinking and an active restructuring of the material) helps you reinforce what you read and heard, leading to a better understanding of the material.

Edit your lecture notes within twenty-four hours after the lecture. If you wait much longer, you won't remember the lecture well enough to make any necessary additions or corrections in your notes. Look back at your Fixed Commitment Calendar and set aside a certain time each day to edit and review your lecture notes. In as little as half an hour, you can turn "so-so" notes into excellent notes.

Fill in the Gaps

The first thing you should do is read through your notes and fill in any missing information that you can recall from memory. As you read your notes, the lecture will "come back" to you. You may be able to add a few words to further clarify a point, fill in additional details, or even add information that you didn't have time to record during the lecture. Look at Nikki's edited Life Science notes and Todd's edited Accounting notes in Figures 5.9 and 5.10. Both Nikki and Todd added some additional information (shown in blue) after the lecture. Nikki also added a brief summary of the key information in the bottom margin of her notes.

You also can refer to your textbook to help fill in gaps in your notes. If you still feel your notes are incomplete, you may need to use a friend's notes to expand on the ones you took in class. If you taped the lecture, listen to the recording and fill in the information you weren't able to write down during the lecture.

Check for Accuracy

As you go through your notes, you also need to check for accuracy. If you notice some incorrect information in your notes or if you're unsure of the accuracy of

FIGURE 5.9
Nikki's Revised Notes for Life Science

	1/22
What are decomposers?	*(3) Decomposers* *– heterotrophs* *– get nourishment from other organisms* *– do not have digestive tracts*
What are scavengers?	*(4) Scavengers* *– let something else kill organism* *– bacteria that break down dead tissue*
What are waste feeders? *What do they feed on?*	*(5) Waste feeders* *– type of scavenger* *– feed on dung, feces, undigested food* *– have digestive systems* *– eat food* 　　*Ex: Egyptian scarab beetles*
What is detritus? *Give two examples.*	*detritus – miscellaneous organic material passing by* *– mixture of decaying organisms + dung w/partially* 　　*digested food* 　　*Land – mixes w/soil – earthworms/soil insects eat* *– May float or settle on bottom*
How do filter feeders eat?	*(6) Filter feeders* *– pass water thru comb-like feeders* *– take things floating in water* *– may use mouth parts, gills, special limbs*
	Four types of consumers are decomposers/scavengers, *waste feeders, and filter feeders. Detritus is a mixture of* *decaying organisms + dung along with partially digested* *food.*

some points, check with the professor or a friend or use your textbook to verify whether the information is correct. If you find that some of your information is incorrect, change it. Some students lose points on exams because they have incorrect information in their notes. Even though they study for the exam, they still get questions wrong because they've been rehearsing inaccurate information.

Clarify Meaning

You may find that some of your notes are cryptic or hard to understand. To make your notes more readable and understandable, you may need to expand some abbreviations, finish some words, or correct spelling errors. If you use a lot of abbreviations or shortcuts in note taking, you should try to clarify some of them while you still know what words they represent. For example, if you wrote "priv" in your notes, you may want to add on "ileged" after class, because "priv" is not a common abbreviation and you may become confused about what you meant when you re-

What are corporations?	Corporations- legal entity having an existence separate and distinct from that of its owners
What rights does an artificial person have?	- Artificial person - same legal rights as a person - can be such, can sue
Who owns the assets of a corporation?	- assets of corporation belong to a corporation itself, not to stockholders.
What are 5 advantages of a corporation?	Why have a corporation? (Advantages) 1. No personal liability for stockholders 2. Ease of accumulating capital 3. Ownership shares are readily transferable 4. Continuous existence - lives on forever 5. Professional management
What are the limits of risk for stockholders?	- amount of money stockholders risk is limited to the amount of their investment
What are the 3 disadvantages of a corporation?	Disadvantages of having a corporation 1. Heavy taxation - tax twice, when they earn and pay income- double taxation
What is the role of the owner of a corp.?	2. Greater regulation 3. Separation of ownership and control -guy who owns corporation doesn't run it
What is double taxation?	Double taxation - First taxing corporate income and then taxing distributions of that income to stockholders

view your notes at a later time. It's not necessary, however, to go back and add on the tail ends of all words that you shortened or abbreviated. For example, the abbreviations "w" and "w/" are commonly used to stand for "with," so there would be no need to write out the word.

Rewrite to Improve Organization

You may need to rewrite your notes in order to improve the organization of the information. If you took notes on a lecture that was poorly organized, your notes may be disorganized, too. Even though you may have an accurate record of the information, you may find it difficult to study. By reorganizing the information in your notes, you can clarify the relationship between the main points and the supporting details. You may need to add headings or make the headings that you have in your notes stand out. You can do that by writing the headings next to the margin and then indenting the subordinate points. You also may need to reorganize your notes in order to group together related information. If your professor tends to jump from point to point during the lecture, you may find that information on the same topic is scattered over several pages in your notes. As you rewrite your notes, group these points together under the appropriate heading. Reorganizing

FIGURE 5.11
Amy's Original Geography notes

	2/21
	Canada

Boreal Forest
    Coniferous/extends to Russia, China,
    Scandinavia
Permafrost on a lot of country
2nd largest country in world
Part of livable country is permafrost 10% of year
Most of population in southern Quebec &
    Ontario/Along Great Lakes
Population
    30½ million about
1999 Nunavut
    Became a new province/Aboriginal
    Canadians
English is mother tongue/many speak French
Didn't become self government until 1901
Capital became Ottawa in 1960s
Under the constitution, Quebec has the right to
    break away from Canada/Cree said . . . . ?
60% of population lives on 2.2% of land
85% live w/in 185 miles of U.S. border
59% speak English/24% French/16% other/
    1%Aboriginal

and editing your notes will make your notes more useful when you're ready to study for the exam.

Compare Amy's original Geography notes (Figure 5.11) to her revised notes (Figure 5.12). All the information in blue was added after the lecture. What changes do you see that improved the overall organization of the information? What other changes did Amy make as she edited her notes? Which set of notes would you rather study from?

Another way to organize your notes is by using concept maps, diagrams, charts, and matrixes to show the relationships between main points and supporting details. You may find that you can restructure some or all of the information from the lecture into a visual display that's easy to picture and recall for exams. Creating maps, diagrams, and charts is an active-editing process. You'll learn more about these strategies in later chapters, but if you think this is something you would like to try now, refer to Chapter 9 for some tips.

Activity 5-9

Work Together to Edit Lecture Notes

Make a copy of the lecture notes that you took earlier this week. Exchange your notes with another member of your group. Ask your classmate to explain the course information to you. How similar was this explanation to the original lecture? What information in your notes needs to be expanded or clarified? Edit a set of your notes. What changes will you make the next time you take notes?

FIGURE 5.12
Amy's Revised Geography notes

2/21

Canada

Recall Questions	Notes
What rank (in order of land size) is Canada?	General Information
	2nd largest country in world
When did Canada become self-governed?	Became self-governed in 1901 after French & Indian War
In the 1960s which city became the capital?	Constitution recognized Ottowa as capitol in 1960's
? % of population lives on ? % of the land?	Population
	60% of population lives on 2.2% of land
How many people occupy Canada?	30.6 million people
	ex: less than state of Calif (33 million)
What % of pop. lives w/in 155 mi of U.S.?	85% lives w/in 185 mi of U.S.
What bodies of water do most Canadians live by?	Most of pop. in S. Quebec & Ontario/ Middle Manitoba/Saskatchewan, & Alberta/S. British Columbia/All along Great Lakes & St. Lawrence River
The province Nunavut was created for what purpose?	1999 – New province – Nunavut/created for Aboriginal Canadians (Eskimos)/called "First Peoples"
	Language
	English as Mother Tongue/many French
What % of Canadians speak English? French?	59% speak English/24% French/16% other (primarily Chinese)/1% speak First Peoples
	Land
How much of Canada is permafrost?	⅓ land is permafrost
	part of inhabited land is permafrost 10%/yr
What forest extends the whole way to Asia?	Boreal Forest – coniferous trees/extends to Russia, China, Scandnavia

Develop Recall Questions

Adding recall questions in the margin helps increase the value of your notes. **Recall questions** are questions you write that can be answered by the important information in your notes. The process of making up these questions forces you to identify the most important aspect of each statement and condense the information down to its essence. These questions then serve as cues to prompt your memory as you study for quizzes and exams.

Writing recall questions is also an effective strategy for editing. After you identify a key point that you want to remember for your exam, develop a question to which that point is the answer. Be sure to write the question directly across from the "answer." You may find it helpful to highlight the answers. Developing both broad and specific questions will help you learn the information in different ways. Of course, the more questions you write, the more effectively you can use them to study the information in your lecture notes. Questions have been added to the recall column for the notes in Figure 5.13. Notice the wide variety of questions that Carrie used and how she shaded each of the answers. Refer also to Todd's, Nikki's,

FIGURE 5.13
Carrie's recall questions

	Learning
	Learning def.
What is learning?	change in behavior resulting from exper
	Habituation
	Simplest form of learning
What is habituation?	no response to a stimulus after repeated
	exposure
Give an ex. of habituation	ex: bird no longer afraid of scarecrow
	highly adaptive
What does habituation allow animals to focus on?	allows animals to focus on relevant things
	Imprinting
What does imprinting involve?	involves both innate behavior & experience
What type of learning is imprinting?	learning that is irreversible
What is the result of imprinting?	results in a strong bond between new
	offspring and parents
	occurs at a specific period in an animal's
	life
What is the name of the period when certain learning behaviors can occur?	Sensitive Period
	phase in an animal's life when the learning
	of certain behaviors occur.
Who studied imprinting in geese?	Konrad Lorenz
What kind of geese were used?	used greylag goose to demonstrate
	imprinting
How did he conduct the experiment?	divided batch of eggs, some to mothers
	some in incubator
What was the control group?	control group: ones with mother
How did the geese in the control group act?	showed normal behavior and interacted with
	other geese

and Amy's notes (Figures 5.9, 5.10, and 5.12), which include recall questions in the margin.

Activity 5-10

Develop Recall Questions

Download and print the enlarged copy of the lecture notes from the lecture on Intellectual Development from the *College Study Skills* Web site. After you review the notes, write as many recall questions for the important information as space permits. Compare your questions with those of the other members of your group. Did you write questions on the same information?

HOW TO REVIEW YOUR NOTES

Reviewing your notes is the final step in the note-taking process. Even though editing your notes provides you with a review of the lecture material, reviewing daily, weekly, and before an exam all help you master the information in your notes and prepare for exams. After you edit your notes and complete the recall column, you're ready to review. You can't learn all the information in your notes just by editing or reading over them. You also need to study the information in your notes using more active methods. How you review your notes often determines how much of the information you learn.

When and Why You Should Review

As you learned in Chapter 4, you need to review your lecture notes on a regular basis in order to store the information in your long-term memory. Even though you may have an accurate record of the information presented, you still need to learn it. The best time to review and edit your notes is immediately after the lecture, when the material is still fresh in your mind. You also can review your notes when you're waiting for your next class to begin. You may want to set aside an hour or two each weekend to review the notes that you took in all of your classes during the week. If you've been reviewing daily, you'll need only to test your memory (using the recall questions) during your weekly review. Reviewing your notes frequently during the semester will keep you actively involved in the learning process and will reduce the amount of time you need to study before exams.

Three Ways to Review

The best way to review your notes is to recite the information—to say it out loud. Just reading over your notes is a very passive activity. Reciting also helps because you may learn more by *hearing* information than just by seeing it. Use the recall questions that you created or the headings in your notes to test your memory of the information. This self-testing will let you know whether you really do know the information in your notes.

Recite from the Recall Column

When you think that you know the information in your notes, use the recall questions to test your memory of the main points and supporting details. Put your hand or a piece of paper over your notes so that you can see only the recall questions. Then recite the answers. If you can't say them out loud, you don't really know the material. Use this technique to review the information in your notes on a regular basis. You should perform this kind of active review immediately following the lecture, at the end of the week, and again before the exam.

Recite from the Headings

You also can review your notes by using the headings or topics to prompt your memory. After you review your notes by reciting them aloud, cover the information under each heading and try to recall all points relating to that topic. Try to explain or recite aloud all details you can remember about each of the main topics in your notes. Then check your notes to see whether you missed anything. If you study in a place where you can't recite out loud, you can accomplish the same thing by mumbling quietly to yourself or by writing out the information from memory. Repeat this process until you know all the information in your notes.

Talk About the Information with Others

Another way to study the information in your notes is simply to talk about it. Putting the information in your own words and explaining it to others is an excellent way to move it into long-term memory. Get together with your note-taking buddy or a study group to edit and review your notes. You can take turns discussing the information (be sure you do some of the explaining), predicting test questions, and quizzing each other on the information. More strategies to review your lecture notes can be found in Chapter 10.

Activity 5-11

Recite to Review Your Notes

Select a set of your notes for review. Recite the information in your notes in order to learn it. Then cover the supporting points with your hand and try to recite them using only the headings as cues. Work on one section until you know it; then go on to the next. Halfway through your notes, switch and use the recall questions to review. Which strategy worked best for you? Why?

Activity 5-12

Edit and Review Your Notes

Choose a set of lecture notes that you took within the last twenty-four hours. Edit them, making any necessary changes or corrections. Also, write down any additional information that you remember. If you know that you're missing specific information, refer to your text or to someone else's notes in order to complete your notes. Finally, add recall questions in the margin and then review your notes. Write a paragraph describing the changes that you made, the type of recall cues that you used, and the method of review that you found most effective. Attach a copy of your original and your edited notes.

Activity 5-13

Where Are You Now?

Now that you have completed Chapter 5, take a few minutes to repeat the "Where Are You Now?" activity, located on the *College Study Skills* Web site. What changes did you make as a result of reading this chapter? How are you planning to apply what you've learned in this chapter?

SUMMARY

Taking good lecture notes in college is critical to your success because the primary mode of instruction for most college professors is the formal lecture. Without an accurate record of information from the lecture, you won't have good information to review before the exam. However, just taking notes doesn't mean that you took good notes. The two most important criteria in evaluating the quality of your notes are the content and the organization. You can improve your note-taking skills by reading the text chapter prior to the lecture. Not only will you pick up background information about the topic but you'll also get a sense of how the information is organized. To take good notes, you have to be actively involved in the lecture; you need to be an active listener. Unless you focus your attention on the professor and get actively involved in the lecture, you may miss a great deal of information. Many students get caught up in fancy note-taking systems. Using a simple system such as the informal outline, block, or modified-block will help you focus on the lecture material. These systems involve writing down the main topic (the heading) and then jotting down any information the professor provides about that topic (the details).

After the lecture, edit your notes within twenty-four hours. Recopying your notes to clean them up or make them look nicer is often a waste of time. Unless you're actively involved in evaluating and restructuring your notes, you won't benefit from the editing process. Checking the accuracy of your notes, filling in gaps, creating recall questions, and improving the organization of your notes are all active editing processes. Then review your notes daily, weekly, and before the exam in order to learn the information. Passive studying, like reading over your notes, doesn't help much. Instead, study your notes by reciting out loud from the recall column or from the headings. Talk about the material, explain key points to a friend, or try to reconstruct the lecture from your headings or recall questions.

REVIEW QUESTIONS

Terms You Should Know: Make a flash card for each term.

Active listener	Edit	Modified-block notes
Block notes	Headings	Organization
Content	Hearing	Outlining
Cornell system	Listening	Recall questions
Details	Meaningful phrase	

Completion: Fill in the blank to complete each of the following statements.

1. The most important reason to take lecture notes is to get a(n) _____ record of information.

2. _____ is an active, selective process.

3. Take notes in _____ _____; don't write whole sentences.

4. Writing questions in the _____ provides you with an opportunity to test your memory of your notes.

5. You should edit your notes within _____ _____ of the lecture.

Multiple Choice: Circle the letter of the best answer for each of the following questions. Be sure to underline key words and eliminate wrong answers.

6. You can improve your listening skills in all of the following ways except:

   A. reading along in the text as the professor gives the lecture.
   B. deciding that you want to listen.

C. controlling your emotional response.
D. holding yourself accountable for the material presented.

7. Which of the following is not a way to edit your notes?

   A. Recopy your notes to improve the appearance.
   B. Rewrite your notes to fill in missing information.
   C. Rewrite your notes to improve the organization.
   D. Add a recall column to your notes.

Short Answer–Essay: On a separate sheet, answer each of the following questions.

8. What are the key features of the outline, block, and modified-block methods of taking notes?

9. How do students benefit from taking notes?

10. How should students review their lecture notes?

"I think I have the ability to concentrate better now than I used to. Before, I used to always drift off while studying, but now when I start to, I catch myself. I can stay focused, and I am able to maintain my concentration much better. I have learned many new techniques for improving concentration, which I have put to use. I believe that when I am able to concentrate on my work, I also study much better."

Martin Ng
Student

IMPROVING CONCENTRATION

In this chapter you will learn more about:

- **Different levels and types of concentration**
- **Causes of concentration problems**
- **Strategies for improving concentration**
- **Benefits of improved concentration**

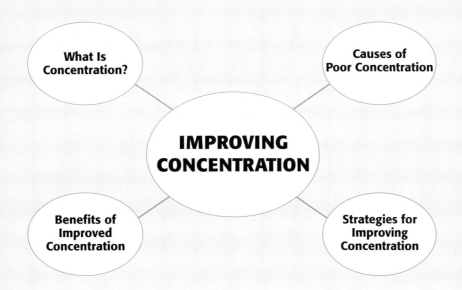

Activity 6-1

Where Are You Now?

Take a few minutes to answer *yes* or *no* to the following questions.

	YES	NO
1. Do you have trouble getting back into your work after you've been interrupted?	_____	_____
2. Do you read and study in a noisy, cluttered room?	_____	_____
3. Do you find that even though you schedule study time, you don't actually accomplish very much?	_____	_____
4. Do you use any strategies to help increase your ability to concentrate?	_____	_____
5. Can you concentrate on your work even if the subject doesn't interest you?	_____	_____
6. Do you use your preferred learning style when completing assignments?	_____	_____
7. Do you tend to think about personal plans or problems when you are reading and studying?	_____	_____
8. Do you find that when you finish reading your textbook assignment, you don't really remember what you read?	_____	_____
9. Do you get totally engrossed in the material when you read and study?	_____	_____
10. Do you daydream a lot when you are listening to lectures?	_____	_____
Total Points		_____

Give yourself 1 point for each *yes* answer to questions 4, 5, 6, and 9, and 1 point for each *no* answer to questions 1, 2, 3, 7, 8, and 10. Now total up your points. A low score indicates that you need some help improving your concentration. A high score indicates that you are already using many good concentration strategies.

WHAT IS CONCENTRATION?

Concentration is focusing your attention on what you're doing. Concentration is important in just about anything you do, but in this chapter we'll focus on improving concentration during reading, listening, and studying. It's hard to describe what concentration is, but it's easy to explain what it isn't. Consider the following example. If you're reading a chapter in your sociology text, you're concentrating on it only as long as you're thinking of nothing else. As soon as you think about how many pages you have left to read, what time you're going to eat dinner, or what the professor will discuss in class, you're experiencing a lack of concentration. If you think about the fact that you *should* be concentrating on the assignment, that

FIGURE 6.1
The Concentration Cycle

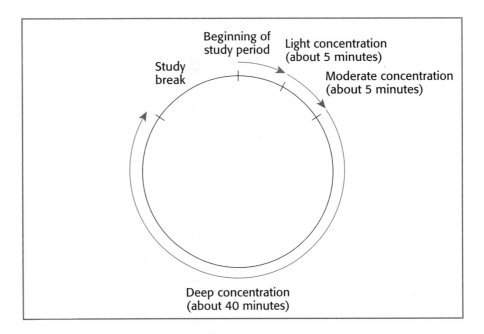

means you've in fact lost your concentration. Let's look at another example. If, during a lecture class, you become interested in the conversation going on in the row behind you, you've lost your concentration. You may even find that you've missed several new points that your professor just introduced.

Being distracted interferes with your ability to attend to or focus on the task at hand. In each of the above examples, you were actually concentrating on something. The problem is that you were concentrating on something other than the lecture or the reading material—you were concentrating on the distractions.

Difficulty with concentration is a common problem for college students. Every semester, I ask students to look over the syllabus and mark the three topics that they think will help them the most. Improving concentration is one of the most common choices.

The Three Levels of Concentration

As you read one of your text assignments, ask someone to time you for about twenty minutes. Each time you think of something else or even look up from your reading, put a check mark in the margin of your book. You may have found that you weren't always concentrating at the same level. At some points during the twenty-minute period, you may have noticed that you were more focused on the material than at other times. Look back at the check marks you made in your book. Were more of them located in the early pages of the assignment? Why does this happen?

To understand why students are less distracted toward the end of a twenty-minute reading period, let's take a better look at how concentration works. Anne Bradley has divided concentration into three levels: light, moderate, and deep.[1] Look at the diagram in Figure 6.1.

Light Concentration

When you first sit down to read or study, you're in a state of **light concentration.** This stage of concentration continues for about the first five minutes of study. At

[1]Adapted from Anne Bradley, *Take Note of College Study Skills* (Glenview, IL: Scott, Foresman, 1983), pp. 41–42.

this point, you're just getting settled into your reading, listening, or studying. Students in light concentration can be seen wiggling around in their chairs, twisting their hair, or pulling out study supplies. When you're in light concentration, you're easily distracted. You may hear people talking down the hall, notice other students walking into the room, be annoyed by any noise occurring around you, or find yourself thinking about other things. You don't accomplish much during this stage, and very little learning actually occurs.

Moderate Concentration

During the next five minutes or so, you move into **moderate concentration.** At this point you begin to pay attention to the material that you're reading, hearing, or studying. You may find that you're actually getting interested in the lecture or text material. In this stage you'll probably find that you are not as easily distracted. Although you may lose your concentration if someone talks directly to you, you may not notice the voices of people talking down the hall or even someone coughing in the same room. Some learning occurs in this stage.

Deep Concentration

Once you move into **deep concentration,** you aren't thinking about anything except what you are hearing, writing, or reading. At this point, you are totally engrossed in the material. Have you ever jumped when someone came up behind you and touched your arm? Because you were in deep concentration, you may not have even noticed that person enter the room or call your name. When you're in deep concentration, you're not aware of the clock ticking, the door opening, or the things that you normally would find rather distracting. It's at this stage in the concentration cycle that you're working most effectively. You learn the most and can complete more work in less time in deep concentration.

The Concentration Cycle

You may be thinking that it sounds fairly easy to reach a high level of concentration—that after an initial ten minutes or so, you can expect to remain at a level of deep concentration. Unfortunately, this isn't the way it really works for many students. Instead, they move in and out of the three stages of concentration.

Look at the diagram of the ideal study session in Figure 6.2A. In this situation, you would be able to work in deep concentration for forty minutes during a fifty-minute study session. You can learn the most during this type of study session because when you're in deep concentration, you're working at your highest level of comprehension and learning.

Unfortunately, some students never get into deep concentration. They move back and forth between light and moderate concentration because they are distracted constantly (Figure 6.2B). Every time you're distracted, you move back to the stage of light concentration. If your roommate asks if she can borrow your navy sweater and you respond, you've experienced a distraction. If you stop to check how many more pages you still have to read, you've been distracted. If you look up when someone walks past you in the library, you've been distracted. If a family member asks you a question, you've been distracted. Each time you're interrupted while you're listening to a lecture, working on a homework assignment, or studying for a test, you move out of deep concentration.

You may find it doesn't take you quite as long to get interested in the material on your second or third try. However, you will still have to move through the "warming up" stages again before you can reach a state of deep concentration. If

FIGURE 6.2

Study Sessions and Levels of Concentration

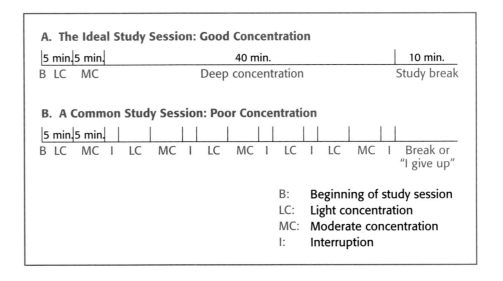

you tend to study in places where you're interrupted a lot, your study session may more closely resemble the concentration cycle in Figure 6.2B. Without strategies that will improve your ability to concentrate, you may have difficulty concentrating on a lecture, or you may spend a lot of time reading or studying yet accomplish very little.

You may also find that your ability to concentrate varies from text to text (what you study), place to place (where you study), and time to time (when you study). You may have to use more active strategies or different strategies in order to increase your ability to concentrate when you're working on material that doesn't interest you, in noisy or distracting study areas, or even at different times of the day.

Activity 6-2

Evaluate Your Last Study Session

Use the following time line to evaluate your last fifty-minute study session. Plot the interruptions that you experienced and how much time you spent in each of the three levels of concentration. What did you discover?

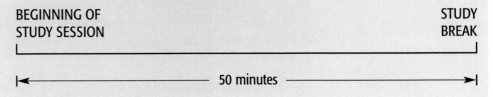

Types of Concentration

Most students have concentration problems, but not all students actually have the same problems concentrating. There are three types of concentration: the ability to focus at will, the ability to sustain focus over a period of time, and the ability to limit focus to one task at a time.[2]

---

[2]Becky Patterson, *Concentration: Strategies for Attaining Focus* (Dubuque, IA: Kendall Hunt, 1993).

The Ability to Focus at Will

Have you ever noticed that you have difficulty concentrating when the professor begins to lecture? You may find yourself looking around the room, pulling out your notebook and pen, or even thinking about whether you'll get out of class early. If you have trouble focusing your attention on the lecture, you may have difficulty **focusing at will**—being able to turn your attention to the task of listening to a lecture at the moment the professor begins to speak.

Why can some students concentrate immediately while others find it difficult to focus their attention? Many students have developed techniques to focus their attention on the task. Have you ever competed in a sporting event? Picture yourself at that critical moment when you're about to "make your move." Do you go through a ritual designed to calm yourself, to focus your attention, to remove all other distractions? Ball players, bowlers, tennis players, and runners (just to name a few) all have strategies for focusing their attention just as they shoot a foul shot, attempt a difficult split, serve, or begin a race. Of course, listening to a lecture, writing a paper, and reading a text chapter aren't exactly the same as sporting events, but you can use the same techniques to focus your attention.

Many students use self-talk to focus at will. You may say things like: pay attention; okay, I need to do this; let's get going now! However, creating a verbal prompt is only one way to help you focus at will. Other students find that creating physical prompts are just as effective. Sitting down in your seat and pulling out your notebook and pen may be enough to focus your attention. Some students can instantly begin to concentrate when they sit down at a table or desk, pick up a special pen or highlighter, or put on a special hat or study slippers. Anything that you associate with concentrating on your work can help you learn to focus at will.

Sustaining Your Focus Over a Period of Time

Although learning to focus your concentration immediately is important, **sustaining your focus** is also important. As you learned in the previous section, the concentration cycle, this is not always as easy as it sounds. Some students have difficulty maintaining their concentration no matter what the task. Other students, however, can concentrate for long periods of time when reading their text assignments, but are constantly distracted when doing their math and vice versa. What makes the difference? The difficulty level of the task, the student's interest in the material, and the student's level of motivation all could be factors. In the next two sections, you'll learn more about the causes of poor concentration and some suggestions for improving concentration. Many of the strategies described will help you sustain your concentration for a longer period of time.

Limiting Your Focus to One Task at a Time

The final type of concentration is **limiting your focus** to one task at a time. You may find this to be especially difficult during high-pressure weeks. You need to learn to focus your attention on one page in your text (without looking over at the English paper you must do for tomorrow), one math problem (without thinking about how many others are on the page), or studying for one exam (without thinking about the other two you have this week). Many of the strategies that involve creating a good study environment can help you avoid distractions around you. The strategies that you learned for setting goals, managing your time, and establishing priorities will also help you focus on one task at a time.

FIGURE 6.3
Causes of Concentration
Problems

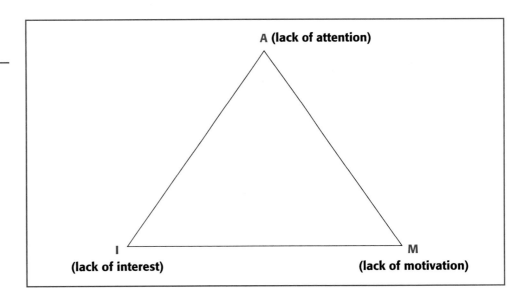

A **(lack of attention)**

I
(lack of interest)

M
(lack of motivation)

CAUSES OF POOR CONCENTRATION

When you find yourself thinking of other things, staring out the window, or being distracted by noises around you, you may not be focusing your attention. You may be having difficulty focusing at will, sustaining your focus, or limiting your focus to only one task.

The real causes of most concentration problems are lack of attention, lack of interest, and lack of motivation. (See Figure 6.3.) By identifying the real reason for your concentration problems, you'll be able to select the appropriate strategy to overcome each of your concentration problems.[3]

The two main signs of poor concentration are external and internal distractions. A **distraction** is anything that diverts your focus (attention) from the task at hand. **External distractions** include things like noise, an uncomfortable study area, and, of course, other people. If you try to study in a noisy place, you may find that you're constantly distracted and interrupted. Dorm rooms and the kitchen table at home are not always good places to do your work. The phone rings, people stop by, and TVs and stereos are on all the time.

Although you can walk away from noisy study areas, you can't escape internal distractions; they go with you wherever you go. **Internal distractions** are things that you think about or worry about. Common internal distractions are anxiety caused by a certain course, the feeling that study won't help, worry over personal problems, indecision about what to do next, and so on. Many students even worry about the fact that they can't concentrate, and *that* worry interferes further with their ability to concentrate on their work.

You've probably already found that it's easy to concentrate when you're interested in what you're doing. Do you find that you can concentrate well in some lecture classes but not in others? Is it easy to stay involved in your reading in some texts but not in others? If you answered yes to either of these questions, your level of interest in the course or in the material may be the reason for your concentration success in one course and difficulty in the other. Without a high level of in-

---

[3]Based on ideas from "AIM to Listen," from *The Secretary* magazine, reprinted in *Communication Briefings*, 1991.

terest, it's easy to lose concentration, especially when you're surrounded by distractions.

Lack of motivation is another cause of poor concentration. If you really don't care about getting a college degree, it's hard to go to class, read your text assignments, take lecture notes, and prepare for exams. If you don't see the relevance of the course or the assignment, it's hard to exert the effort to do it well. If you don't really care about making the grade, it's going to be very difficult to concentrate on your work. If you ever find yourself asking, "Why am I even trying to do this assignment?" "Why am I sitting in this class?" or "Why am I in college?" you may have a motivation problem. To improve your ability to concentrate, you need to be motivated to succeed. We can refer to these three causes of concentration problems as AIM (attention, interest, and motivation). They are often the real reasons that internal and external distractions are able to disrupt your concentration.

Activity 6-3

Identify Concentration Problems

List ten concentration problems that you've had during the last week. Try to focus on academic tasks like taking lecture notes, reading text assignments, writing papers, or preparing for exams as you develop your list. Next, list the distraction that interfered with your concentration. Consider the underlying cause of your concentration problem and label it as A (attention), I (interest), or M (motivation). What was the most common cause of your concentration problems?

	Task	Distraction	Cause (AIM)
1.			
2.			
3.			
4.			
5.			
6.			
7.			
8.			
9.			
10.			

Concentration Problems During Lecture Classes

Many students experience problems with concentration when they're trying to listen and learn in class. Do you ever have trouble concentrating on the lecture your professor is presenting? What gets in your way? One of the more common problems is distractions caused by other students. It's hard to concentrate on what your professor is saying when the person sitting next to you is constantly talking to you or to someone near you. Even a conversation two or three rows behind you can interfere with your ability to stay focused on the lecture. Noises outside the lecture room also can be distracting and can interfere with your ability to stay focused.

Internal distractions are another cause of difficulty during lecture classes. Worrying about personal problems and thinking about what you have to do after class are common internal distractions. Feeling hungry or tired is another common internal distraction.

A number of students indicate that they can't concentrate on a lecture if they're not actively involved in the class; they have difficulty playing the role of a passive observer. Other students complain that it's impossible to stay involved and focused on a lecture when the professor always mumbles or speaks in a quiet voice. Still others have problems when the professor doesn't ask questions or interact with them during the lecture.

Finally, some students have concentration problems during lecture classes because of their attitude toward the class or the material. Many students have more trouble concentrating when they place a low value on the material or the course. Moreover, they experience more difficulty paying attention to the lecture when the topic is uninteresting or difficult to understand. In situations like this, some students begin to daydream, think about more interesting things, or even doze off.

Activity 6-4

Evaluate Your Concentration During Lecture Classes

Make a list of the problems or difficulties that you experience in at least two of your lecture classes. What differences did you notice in your ability to concentrate in each class? What were the causes of your concentration problems?

Concentration Problems When You Read Your Text

Many students have difficulty concentrating when they read textbook assignments. Unlike lecture classes, where the professor may help keep you focused by varying his or her tone of voice or by asking questions, you alone are responsible for concentrating on your reading assignments. Do you have trouble concentrating when you read some or all of your text assignments? If you think that you're the only student with this problem, you're wrong. Many students indicate that they have more trouble concentrating when they read than at any other time.

External distractions such as a cluttered or uncomfortable study environment, noise, and other people are common causes of poor concentration when reading. How many times this week were you interrupted as you tried to read a text assignment? Many students need complete silence in order to concentrate on reading assignments. If you live in a dormitory, finding a quiet study place can be quite a problem. However, students who live at home find that a family can be just as distracting.

The time of day that you tackle your reading assignments also can affect your ability to concentrate. If you try to do your reading late at night, you may experience more difficulty staying focused because you're tired. Concentration requires effort, and it's harder to make that effort when you're tired. Have you noticed that it's more difficult to concentrate on the road when you're driving late at night and feel tired? For the same reason, many students have more difficulty maintaining their concentration when they try to read for long periods of time without a break.

Although most students indicate that their problems with concentration stem from external distractions or from internal distractions such as the interest they have in the material or the value they place on the course, other internal distractions can also be a factor. Personal problems, concerns about grades or progress in the course, and fear of not knowing the answer or how to do the problems in class can all interfere with a student's ability to focus on the material. Many students find that when they have difficulty concentrating (for any of the above reasons), they tend to think about other things. Sometimes they worry about both academic and personal problems. At other times, they tend to use escapist techniques and daydream about something that they would rather be doing—something that would be a lot more interesting or a lot more fun than reading a textbook.

Activity 6-5

List Your Distractions as You Read

 Choose one of your texts and read a section that you haven't already read. After you finish reading, make a list of the distractions you experienced. Repeat the task using another text or at a different time of day. What differences do you notice in your lists or in your ability to concentrate on the two reading assignments? What was the main cause of your concentration problems?

Concentration Problems When You Study for Exams

Some students have a lot of trouble concentrating when they're preparing for exams. Aside from the usual external distractions, they often experience special problems. Some students may not be as motivated to focus on the task of test preparation early in the semester because they don't put as much value on the first exam. It's more difficult to concentrate when you're studying for a test on which you place little value. Other students get distracted when they study because the material is difficult or uninteresting. Some students have concentration problems because studying is not a specific assignment like "reading pages 186 to 201." Any time your goals are vague or you're not sure what to do, it's more difficult to stay focused.

A common complaint from students is that they get tired of studying and begin to think of other things. Some think about things they would rather be doing or things that their friends, who don't have exams, are doing. Worrying about what the test will be like, what questions will be on it, and how well you will do are all common internal distractions.

Another problem that leads to poor concentration when preparing for exams is passive study techniques. Most students still study for college exams by simply reading over the text and lecture material. If you use passive strategies, you'll be more susceptible to both internal and external distractions.

Procrastination can also lead to poor concentration. When you leave your test preparation to the last minute, you may feel overwhelmed by having too much to learn in too little time. In situations like this, students generally try to cram for the exam, which often results in passive study and increased worry about the results.

Activity 6-6

Evaluate Your Concentration While You Study

 Make a list of the problems or difficulties you experience the next time you prepare for an exam. If you have several exams in the next few weeks, evaluate your preparation for one class that you are very interested in or place a high value on and one that you don't. What differences do you notice in your lists or in your ability to concentrate as you prepared for different exams? Share your findings with a group of your class-mates. What were the most common problems faced by your group?

STRATEGIES FOR IMPROVING CONCENTRATION

By now you probably realize that problems with concentration are fairly common for college students. Although it may make you feel better to know you aren't the only person in the world who can't concentrate, it doesn't help you correct the problem. Many students indicate that they have few, if any, strategies for improving their concentration; they have a problem concentrating, but they don't know how to correct it. You can improve your ability to concentrate by using motivational and organizational strategies, by creating a good learning environment, by dealing promptly with internal distractions, by using active learning strategies, by matching your learning style to the task, and by monitoring your concentration.

Use Motivational and Organizational Strategies

You can improve your concentration by using many of the motivational and organizational strategies that you learned in Chapters 1, 2, and 3. Several of the most helpful strategies are having a positive attitude, setting goals, and scheduling your assignments.

Develop a Positive Attitude Toward Your Work

Having a positive attitude toward your assignments is critical to focusing at will—concentrating on the task the minute you begin to work. First, you must *want* to do the assignment. You need to see the relevance, value, and importance of the task. Second, you must believe that you *can* do the assignment. You need to have confidence in your ability to successfully complete the task. If you have self doubts or feelings of anger or frustration about the task, they will interfere with your concentration. Having a positive attitude will help you focus as you begin to study and will help sustain your focus as you work.

Create Interest in the Task

If you aren't interested in completing the task, you'll have more difficulty concentrating. It's much easier to concentrate when you're interested in what you're doing. If you're getting ready to read a chapter for your Western Civilization class, for example, and you really aren't very interested in what happened in Egypt 5,000 years ago, you might have difficulty sustaining your focus. You need to find ways to make the material more interesting—you can generate interest in the task. One way you might be able to generate more interest in the assignment is to preview the chapter before reading. You may find as you look through the chapter (see Chapter 7 for how to do a preview), you notice topics that are interesting to you. I've always been fascinated by the great pyramids, have you? If you find even one section in the chapter that sounds interesting, you'll increase your motivation to read and may find that you can concentrate more on the chapter. Another method of generating interest in the task is to change the task itself. If you find reading chapters to be boring, don't just read them. Do something interesting while you read. If you like taking notes, take notes as you read. If you like writing questions in the margin of your lecture notes, write questions in the margin of your text as you read the chapter. If you find that you like using a particular study strategy, if you find it interesting, challenging, or fun, you'll like completing the original task more—you'll find that it's more interesting.

If you work on the assignment in sections, you may also find that it will be easier to maintain your concentration. You'll probably find that you can stay focused on the material better when you read 10 pages of the chapter at a time, instead of trying to read the entire chapter. If you aren't particularly interested in your math assignment, you may find that doing one-third of your math homework is less boring than trying to do it all at one time. Switch to a different subject for a while and come back later and do some more. When you find that you can't maintain your interest in the task, you'll also probably notice that you aren't concentrating very well on it either.

Use Goal-Setting Strategies

Setting clear goals can also help you achieve better concentration. If you know exactly what you want to accomplish when you begin an assignment, you'll be able to limit your focus to the task at hand. Setting learning goals can help you determine what you need to learn or accomplish during a specific study session. It's equally important to know exactly what you need to do to complete the assignment—you need to understand what the professor expects from you and what the grading criteria will be. If you aren't sure about how to do the assignment, check with a classmate or the professor. If you don't, you may find that you'll have problems concentrating on the task because you'll be worrying about whether you're doing it correctly. Having a clear purpose in mind can help you limit distractions as you complete your work.

Use Time-Management Strategies

Almost any of the time-management strategies that you learned in Chapter 3 will help you improve your concentration. Using "To Do" lists and planning calendars are critical to good concentration. One of the most common internal distractions among college students is the worry that they won't get their work done. Many students report that they're constantly thinking of other assignments when they try to concentrate on their work. Do you? If you develop a study schedule each day and assign each of your study tasks to a specific study time, you won't have to worry about getting your work done. You'll be able to focus completely on each task as you work on it, knowing that you have already scheduled all of the others. By organizing your study time, you can better focus your attention on one task at a time.

Create a Positive Learning Environment

You can dramatically improve your ability to concentrate by creating a positive learning environment. The first step is to control external distractions, and the best way to control external distractions is simply to eliminate them. If you can't eliminate all of your distractions, it's important to minimize them as much as possible—to reduce the length of each distraction to the smallest possible time frame. For example, if your phone rings and you answer it, you'll probably spend a few minutes (or many minutes) responding to the caller. If, on the other hand, you set your answering machine or voice mail to pick up your call, you'll spend a much shorter time frame dealing with the call. When you hear the phone ring, you might say to yourself, "I'll get that later," and go right back to work. If you only spend a few seconds on the distraction, you should be able to move back into deep concentration very quickly. If you spend five or ten minutes (or longer) away from your work, you'll find it takes a lot longer to get back into deep concentration.

Strategies for Lecture Classes

In lecture classes, you can avoid most external distractions by moving to the front of the room. Fortunately, most students who chat during class tend to sit in the back. However, you still occasionally may find yourself sitting near some noisy students. If the students sitting near you keep you from concentrating on the lecture, get up and move! You also can be distracted by things going on around you. If you find yourself looking out the window or watching what goes on in the hall, find a seat where you can't see out the window or the door. Make the professor the center of your line of vision.

Strategies for Your Study Environment

Although it's fairly easy to find a new seat during lecture classes, it's not so easy to find a new place to study when you can't concentrate. If you live in a dormitory or if you live at home, you are surrounded by noise. Some students stay in their rooms or work at the kitchen table even when they can't concentrate, almost out of stubbornness. "It's my room and I should be able to work there" is a commonly heard statement. But if you have tried unsuccessfully to eliminate the distractions in your study area and you still can't concentrate on your work, you have only one other option. You need to find somewhere else to study. It may not seem fair that you have to gather up all your materials and go somewhere else, but if you can't change your study environment, you have to find a new one. If you force yourself to continue working in a noisy study area, you probably won't be able to accomplish very much and you may become even more frustrated.

Finding a good place to read and study may require some experimentation. Try working in different places at different times of the day to see which study area works best for you. The library, study rooms, and empty classrooms are usually good study areas. If you're living at home, you may find that setting up a table or desk in the basement or the attic is the only way you can avoid constant interruptions. Once you find a good place to work, establish a regular routine. Studying in the same place at the same time each day helps you get down to work. It may even help to use special objects that you associate with study. By sitting in a special chair, wearing your "study" slippers, or even using a special pen or clipboard, you'll help yourself get into a study mode, and this will help you improve your concentration. The Tip Block includes some additional suggestions for creating a better study environment.

Deal with Internal Distractions

Once you set up a quiet study environment, you should see a big difference in your ability to concentrate. However, just eliminating external distractions doesn't guar-

TEN TIPS FOR SETTING UP A GOOD STUDY ENVIRONMENT

FIND A QUIET STUDY SPACE. Find a place to study that is away from the "center" of household activities. It's almost impossible to concentrate if you're surrounded by distractions. A card table in the basement may not look pretty, but the quiet will make up for it. If you can't study at home, try the library or a quiet study room.

LIMIT YOUR DISTRACTIONS. Put your desk against the wall and remove all photos, mementos, and decorations. When you look up from your work, you won't be distracted by reminders of your friends or family or other responsibilities.

USE YOUR DESK FOR STUDYING ONLY. If you use your desk only for studying, you will automatically think about studying when you sit down.

STUDY IN A NOT TOO COMFORTABLE CHAIR. Sitting in a chair that is *too* comfortable may lead to passive reading. Completing assignments is hard work, so you need to study in a semitense position.

NEVER STUDY LYING DOWN IN BED. You'll have trouble concentrating and may get so comfortable that you fall asleep.

SCREEN YOUR PHONE CALLS. If you're constantly interrupted by phone calls, let an answering machine or voicemail pick up your calls.

TURN OFF THE TELEVISION, STEREO, AND RADIO. If you need some sound to serve as a "white noise" to block out the other noises around you, use soft, familiar music. Save that new CD as a reward for completing your work.

DO YOUR WORK WHEN YOUR HOUSE IS QUIET. Study when family members are asleep or out. Schedule study hours before your children get up and after they go to bed. If you get home from work or school an hour before they do, use that time to do course work.

CONSIDER STUDYING AT SCHOOL. If you can't concentrate at home, you may have to do your work at school, before or after class. You can often find an empty classroom, quiet corner in the library, or study area in the student union. Compare your distractions when studying on campus and at home.

GET HELP WHEN YOU NEED IT. Ask a family member or friend to stay with your children when you are trying to study for exams or complete major assignments. If necessary, hire a sitter or a mother's helper to entertain or care for your children.

antee that you'll be able to focus on your work. Many students find that after they eliminate the external noises around them, they notice the internal "noises" even more. Although you can't really eliminate internal distractions, you can take steps to keep them from interfering with your work.

Activity 6-7

Describe Your Study Environment

Write a short essay describing your current study environment. Where do you read and study? What types of distractions surround you? How often are you distracted? How do you feel at the end of your study sessions? What strategies have you tried to create an environment more conducive to deep concentration? What changes could you make that would help you work more effectively? What plans are you making (or have you made) to create a more positive learning environment?

Deal with Competing Activities

No matter how focused you are when studying, it's not unusual to think about other things. If you think of something that you want or need to do or if you come up with an idea for another assignment, jot it down or plan a time to do it, and then continue with your work. The key is to minimize the distraction—to keep it as short as possible. Then you can move back to deep concentration more quickly. If you don't write it down, you'll probably continue thinking about it or even begin to worry that you may forget it. In either case, you'll be concentrating more on the internal distraction than on your assignment.

Deal with Academic Problems

Worrying about academic problems is a common internal distraction. Instead of worrying, do something! Go see your professor and share your concerns about the course. Get a tutor or have a talk with yourself about what you need to do to meet your goals. Remind yourself that getting down to work and doing your best are steps in the right direction. Then, if you still don't understand the material or can't do the problems, ask for help. Remember, it's easier to block out internal distractions when you have confidence in yourself as a student. You'll gain this confidence by learning that you can be successful in college, not by worrying about it.

Deal with Personal Problems

Personal worries and concerns are common internal distractions. Many students allow an argument with a boyfriend or girlfriend or family problems to interfere with their concentration. Make a decision to do something about your problem as soon as you complete your work. Write down exactly what you plan to do and return immediately to your study tasks. Calling a friend and talking honestly about your problem, or scheduling an appointment at your campus counseling center are good strategies for dealing with personal problems. Some students find that writing about whatever is bothering them in a journal or talking it out with friends helps them experience a feeling of closure about the problem.

Use Active Learning Strategies

One of the best ways to keep external and internal distractions from interfering with your concentration is to become more involved in the lecture, the text, or your test preparation. You can generate this high level of involvement by using active learning strategies. Many students allow internal and external distractions to interrupt their study because they use passive learning strategies that just don't work.

You may have noticed that you concentrate better when you do math problems and grammar exercises or complete a study guide for your Psychology textbook. Why does this happen? One possible reason is that you like those classes or assignments more than some of your other classes. However, another reason may be that you need to use active learning strategies to complete those tasks. Solving problems, correcting grammatical errors in sentences, and looking for answers to study guide questions are all active strategies that get you involved in and help you focus your attention on each of the tasks. Because you are actively involved in working on the material, you can concentrate more on your assignments. When you're attending lectures, reading course assignments, and preparing for exams, you can dramatically improve your concentration by using active study strategies.

Strategies for Lecture Classes

Taking notes during lecture classes helps you focus on what the professor is saying. If you know that you're going to have to write something, you'll be more motivated to pay attention. Many students are bored and begin to daydream or look out the window during lecture classes because they don't have anything to do. The class seems to drag on and on, and they begin looking for other things to pass the time. Does that ever happen to you? If you limit yourself to the role of the passive observer, you can expect to be distracted in all but the most exciting classes. Although it would be great if all classes were that interesting, not all of them are to all students. However, many students actually find that lecture classes become more interesting and go much faster when they take notes. Because they are actively involved, they have reached a state of deep concentration.

Many students have trouble concentrating during lecture classes simply because they're not actively involved in what's going on in the class. Asking and answering questions, predicting what the professor will say next, and taking notes are all ways of becoming more involved during lecture classes. Becoming a more active participant in class is one of the keys to eliminating internal and external distractions and increasing concentration.

You may also find that you can increase your concentration in lecture classes by sitting directly in your professor's line of vision. You're more likely to pay attention if you feel as if you're on the spot. It's pretty hard to fall asleep or look out the window when your professor is standing right in front of you. If you focus your attention on the professor and keep him or her directly in your line of vision, you'll be able to block out distractions more easily, too.

Strategies for Reading Text Assignments

Becoming an active reader will significantly improve your ability to concentrate when you read your textbook assignments. Reading with your eyes but not your brain leads to daydreaming and other concentration problems. Have you ever read a paragraph or even an entire page of text and then realized that you had no idea what you had just read? Even though your eyes did "look at the words," your mind was somewhere else. Using a reading/study system, previewing, highlighting, and taking notes are all active strategies that can improve your concentration. You can also increase your concentration by creating word cards as you read your assignment. Becoming familiar with the technical terminology can help you understand your reading assignment more easily. Predicting questions in the margin also helps you focus on the important information in the text. We'll talk more about all of these strategies in Chapters 7, 8, and 9.

Strategies for Test Preparation

How can you maintain your concentration as you prepare for exams? Jennifer sums it up pretty well: "When studying for a test, I'm active. I don't just reread my notes and the chapter. I write down what I need to know from the text and then I rewrite my notes." Just reading over the textbook and your lecture notes isn't a very effective way to improve your concentration when you study. You need to increase your involvement with the material. When you prepare for an exam, dig through the material, looking for important information. Taking notes, developing study sheets, and creating graphic displays will help you become totally engrossed in the material. Reciting the key information out loud and self-testing are just two of many rehearsal strategies that also can help you learn. Remember that the more actively involved you are in studying the material, the easier it will be to maintain your concentration.

You can also increase your concentration by using motivational strategies. Jennifer motivates herself to study by thinking about getting a good grade. She says, "You just need to make the decision that you want to succeed." Taking breaks, switching subjects, and planning rewards are helpful in increasing your motivation, and they also can help increase your concentration. It's much harder to stay focused on your work when you become tired or bored. When you just can't concentrate anymore, stop and take a break. Then switch to a different subject to eliminate feelings of boredom and frustration. Setting deadlines and limiting the amount of time that you allow for each of your study tasks also can motivate you to use your time more effectively. Deadlines make you feel rushed, so you actually force yourself to concentrate better (unless you've left yourself too little time—in that case, your level of anxiety and the number of your internal distractions may increase).

Match Your Learning Style to the Task

You learned in Chapter 1 that you can maximize your time and effort by working in your preferred learning style or using the learning style that best suits the task you need to complete. You may have also discovered that matching your learning style to the task helps you improve your concentration, too. If you learn best in the morning, you'll also find it easier to concentrate in the morning. If you tend to work best with quiet music playing in the background, you may discover that music helps you concentrate by blocking out other noises that might actually distract you. Approaching a task from your preferred style results in a better fit or match—studying feels right. However, using a style that is inappropriate to the task or to the material you want to learn (even if it is the style you prefer) can itself become distracting and interfere with your ability to concentrate. When you use the appropriate learning style for each task during a study session, you'll probably be less distracted and move into deep concentration more easily.

Activity 6-8

Suggest Strategies to Improve Concentration

What type of concentration problem is shown in each example? What should each of the following students do to improve his or her ability to concentrate? Share your responses with other members of your group.

1. Just as Manuel begins to study for his Psychology exam, his roommate stomps into the room and starts to complain about the grade he got on his Calculus exam.

2. Sasha has trouble concentrating when the material is uninteresting and not in her major. Instead, she thinks about things that she needs to do or how many more pages she has left to read.

3. Lawrence can't concentrate when he tries to study for his Biology exam because he is so worried about his grade in the course. He didn't do as well as he had hoped on the first exam, and he is afraid the same thing will happen again.

4. Meira has trouble concentrating when the lecture is uninteresting and not well organized. She gets confused and frustrated with the professor and the class and stops listening.

Activity 6-9

Work Together to Solve Concentration Problems

Write three concentration problems that you experienced during the past week on each of three index cards. Put the last four digits of your identification number at the top right corner of the back of the card (do not use your name). After the cards are shuffled and distributed to various groups within the class, discuss each of the problems assigned to your group. Discuss possible solutions to the problem and write several of the best on the back of the card. Select one or two of the most common (or most interesting) to describe to the class. At the end of the class period, each student can claim his or her card (by identification number) and make use of the suggestions that were offered.

Monitor Your Concentration

Monitoring how often you lose your concentration can be very helpful in learning how to improve your concentration. Put a check mark or write the time in the margin of your book or your lecture notes every time you're distracted. At the end of your class or study session, count the number of interruptions. Make a commitment to reduce that number the next time you read or go to your lecture. In a few weeks, you may find that your ability to concentrate improves dramatically.

When you notice that you are daydreaming or thinking about other things, try to figure out what actually triggered your loss in concentration. If you can pinpoint the cause of your distraction, you're only one step away from the solution. Hold yourself accountable for your lapses in concentration—find a way to overcome them. Remember, you can improve your ability to concentrate, but it is you who must take the responsibility for doing so.

Activity 6-10

Critique a Distraction Profile

Review Emily's list of distractions from a one-hour study session, available on the *College Study Skills* Web site. Label each distraction as external or internal and personal or academic. Then jot down a suggestion for how Emily should have dealt with the distraction. Discuss your responses in a group or with the other members of your class. What would you have done if this were your study session? Note: Emily read four pages of her Biology text in one hour during this study session.

Activity 6-11

Monitor Your Concentration

Use the chart in Figure 6.4 to record up to ten of the concentration problems that you encounter over a one-week period. Include one or more strategies that you used or should have used to improve your concentration. At the bottom, indicate how well your strategies worked.

FIGURE 6.4
Monitor Your Concentration Chart

Date	Study Task	Concentration Problem	Cause	Strategy

BENEFITS OF IMPROVED CONCENTRATION

There are many benefits to improved concentration. One of the most obvious is that you'll be able to make better use of your time. You'll find that when you spend the majority of your time in deep concentration, you get more done during a study session. In addition, because you're operating in deep concentration for a longer period of time, you'll gain a better understanding of what you have read. It stands to reason that if you spend most of your time focused on the course material, you'll understand it better than if you're constantly distracted.

Improved concentration during lecture classes can help you take better lecture notes. If you're focused on the information your professor is presenting rather than on other people, negative thoughts about the course, or personal plans, you'll be able to take better notes. In addition, you may find that you become more involved in the lecture and gain a better understanding of the material. You'll be able to form connections between the material being presented and the material you already know. This helps you learn and understand what you're hearing.

You may also notice that once you set up a better study environment, you're better able to prepare for quizzes and exams. Working in a quiet, nondistracting study area can have a positive effect on what you study and learn. Setting goals and using active study strategies will not only improve your concentration but also your mastery of the material. After concentrating on your studies for one or two hours, you'll be pleased by what you were able to accomplish. You may even experience increased self-confidence and higher self-esteem.

Activity 6-12

Where Are You Now?

Now that you have completed Chapter 6, take a few minutes to repeat the "Where Are You Now?" activity, located on the *College Study Skills* Web site. What changes did you make as a result of reading this chapter? How are you planning to apply what you've learned in this chapter?

SUMMARY

Most college students have problems with concentration, often defined as focused attention. Unfortunately, if you're focusing on the conversations going on out in the hall, instead of on your professor's lecture, you're concentrating on the wrong thing. During an ideal study session, students move from light, to moderate, to deep concentration—the level where most learning occurs. During a typical study session, however, students move in and out of these stages of concentration because of interruptions or distractions. Some students never even reach deep concentration.

The most common indicators of concentration problems are external and internal distractions. By monitoring your distractions, you can hold yourself more accountable during lecture classes, as you do your day-to-day assignments, and when you prepare for exams. Avoiding common distractions and using active study strategies can help you increase your concentration. Creating a positive learning environment is critical to good concentration. It's easy to blame all concentration problems on a noisy room or a cluttered desk, but the real culprits are lack of attention, lack of interest, and lack of motivation. By analyzing the real cause of your external and internal distractions, you may be able to identify the real cause of your concentration problems. If you set goals, focus your attention, increase your interest, and improve your motivation, your ability to concentrate will improve. Working outside your preferred learning style makes it more difficult to concentrate in certain situations. If you find that you're putting a lot of time into your studies but not getting much accomplished, you may have a concentration problem.

REVIEW QUESTIONS

Terms You Should Know: Make a flash card for each term.

Concentration	Focusing at will	Moderate concentration
Deep concentration	Internal distraction	Sustaining your focus
Distraction	Light concentration	
External distraction	Limiting your focus	

Completion: Fill in the blank to complete each of the following statements.

1. _____ college freshmen experience concentration problems.

2. Some students never get into _____ concentration.

3. Use _____ study strategies to improve your concentration when studying for exams.

4. Both _____ and _____ distractions affect your ability to concentrate during lectures.

5. Having difficulty concentrating at the beginning of a task is referred to as a problem focusing at _____.

Multiple Choice: Circle the letter of the best answer for each of the following questions. Be sure to underline key words and eliminate wrong answers.

6. Which of the following is *not* one of the real causes of poor concentration?
   A. Lack of interest
   B. Lack of attention
   C. Lack of motivation
   D. Lack of self-efficacy

7. You can reduce your distractions by:
   A. studying in an empty classroom.
   B. using your desk only for study.

    C. screening your phone calls.

    D. all of the above are good strategies.

Short Answer–Essay: On a separate sheet, answer each of the following questions.

8. Describe the characteristics of each of the three stages of the concentration cycle.

9. How should students overcome problems with internal and external distractions?

10. How will improving your concentration benefit you in college?

"Using textbook-reading strategies is helping me improve my comprehension when I read material for all of my courses. I think I am reading a lot faster than I used to, and I don't dread reading assignments anymore. I feel more involved as I read because I am highlighting and taking notes now."

Heather Erdley
Student

READING YOUR TEXTBOOK

In this chapter you will learn more about:
- General strategies for reading college textbooks
- How to become a critical reader
- Using a text reading/study system

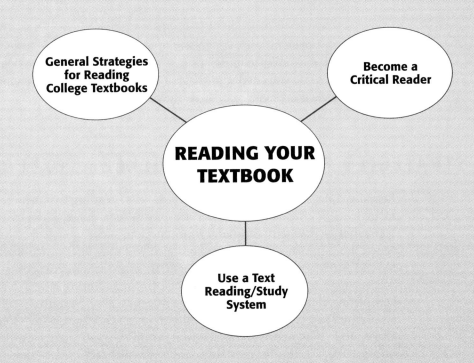

Activity 7-1

Where Are You Now?

Take a few minutes to answer *yes* or *no* to the following questions.

	YES	NO
1. Do you highlight or mark your textbook as you read?	_____	_____
2. Do you use a reading/study system when you read text material?	_____	_____
3. Do you preview a chapter before you begin to read it?	_____	_____
4. Do you usually try to read an entire chapter once you start?	_____	_____
5. Do you think about the quality of the evidence as you read your textbook?	_____	_____
6. Do you tend to read your text chapters again before the exam?	_____	_____
7. Do you generally pause at the end of each paragraph or page to think about what you have read?	_____	_____
8. Do you use different strategies to read more difficult text assignments?	_____	_____
9. Do you often forget what you have read when you complete a reading assignment?	_____	_____
10. Do you "talk to" (interact with) the author of the text as you are reading your assignment?	_____	_____
Total Points		_____

Give yourself 1 point for each *yes* answer to questions 1, 2, 3, 5, 7, 8, and 10 and 1 point for each *no* answer to questions 4, 6, and 9. Now total up your points. A low score indicates that you need some help in text reading. A high score indicates that you are already using many good text-reading strategies.

GENERAL STRATEGIES FOR READING COLLEGE TEXTBOOKS

Reading college textbooks is a different kind of reading from the reading you did in high school. College textbooks are more "idea dense" than most high school texts; that is, they contain many more facts and ideas per page. Not only is there much more information to learn, but also you may have much less time in which to read and learn it. You probably spent an entire school year covering only a part of your high school textbook; in college you may find that you're responsible for completing an entire text in only ten to fifteen weeks. In addition, college textbooks are written at a higher reading level than high school texts are. College textbooks also contain new, specialized, technical terminology. Unlike your high school textbooks, college texts also contain many more abstract ideas. They don't just seem harder—they are. This may be one of the reasons many students find that even though they read their textbooks, they don't understand what they read.

FIGURE 7.1

Factors That Make College Texts
More Difficult to Read

- Many new technical terms
- More abstract concepts
- More idea dense
- More words per page
- Longer chapters
- Higher reading level
- Lower interest level
- Lack of background about the topics

Are you reading about topics that are new to you—things you've never heard about before? Your lack of background knowledge on the topic can also negatively affect your comprehension. As you learned in Chapter 4, we rely on our long-term memory (our prior knowledge) to make new information meaningful. When you lack that prior knowledge, it's harder to understand what you're reading and, therefore, more difficult to learn the new information. You also may have discovered that most of your college textbooks contain longer chapters (one student told me he had a text with 90-page chapters) and smaller print (that means more words per page). That means it will take you longer to read each page and to read the chapter. Is it taking you two or three hours to read a chapter? If it is, you may have discovered that you get bored, tired, or simply can't remember what you've read. You may also have noticed that the writing style tends to be a bit dry and the topics less interesting than some of your other reading materials. All of these factors (see Figure 7.1) make it harder for you to concentrate on, understand, and be motivated to read your assignments.

You can use a number of general strategies to improve your ability to read and comprehend college textbooks. Buying your textbooks early, previewing your texts, reading the chapter before the lecture, dividing the chapter into smaller portions, and monitoring your comprehension are just a few of the strategies that will help you get the most out of reading your texts. If you're already using some of these strategies, you know that they do help. If some of the strategies are new to you, experiment to see whether they're effective, too. The tips in the tip block will help you get off to the right start. Remember, you need a much more strategic approach to read and understand your college textbooks.

Buy Your Textbooks Early

You can get a head start on your reading for the next semester if you buy your textbooks during the current semester—before you leave campus for break. Even if you purchase only one or two of your texts, you can read the first two or three chapters during break. While other students are madly trying to get all their reading done during the first week or two of the new term, you'll be able to devote time to some of your other classes. Reading ahead also will give you additional time to study for quizzes and nail down some As and Bs during those first few weeks.

TIPS FOR READING COLLEGE TEXTBOOKS

READ TEXTBOOKS DIFFERENTLY. You can't read a college textbook the same way you read a novel or magazine article. You won't remember everything you read or even understand all of it after one quick reading. You may need to slow down or reread some portions of the chapter.

READ THE CHAPTER BEFORE THE LECTURE. As you learned in Chapter 5, reading the text chapter before the lecture will help you build background on the topic, learn the basic organizational structure of the material, and take better lecture notes.

BUILD ON PRIOR KNOWLEDGE. Relate what you're reading to what you already know. By connecting the information in your textbook chapter to your own experiences and previous knowledge, you can improve your comprehension and memory of the material.

DIVIDE THE CHAPTER INTO READABLE CHUNKS. A forty-page chapter is probably best read in four chunks of ten pages each. A twenty-page chapter may be read in two chunks of ten or in three chunks of seven, seven, and six pages. Dividing the chapter into smaller reading segments increases your comprehension and actually decreases the time you spend reading the chapter.

PREVIEW THE CHAPTER BEFORE YOU READ. Read the title, introduction, headings, glance at charts and pictures, and read the summary. A two- to five-minute preview reduces the total time you spend reading and increases your comprehension.

USE A READING/STUDY SYSTEM. Use a reading/study system such as P2R, SQ3R, or S-RUN-R, or develop your own system. Be sure you use one or more active strategies before you read the chapter, as you read the chapter, and after you read the chapter.

MARK THE TEXT OR TAKE NOTES AS YOU READ. Highlight, underline, or take notes at the end of each section. Wait until you finish reading the paragraph or a "headed" section before you begin to mark your text.

MONITOR YOUR COMPREHENSION. Stop to check your understanding of the material at regular intervals. Look for connections between topics and how the new information relates to your prior knowledge. Pause at the end of each paragraph or page and ask yourself if you understand what you're reading.

REVIEW WHAT YOU READ. After you complete your reading assignment, take five to ten minutes (or more) to review what you just read. Think about the main points that the author made in the chapter. Develop a recall column or summarize the key information in the margin of the text.

READ OR REVIEW AS YOU COMMUTE. Just thinking about what you read as you drive to class will help you improve your comprehension of the material. If you commute by bus or train, use that time to complete one or two chunks of your text chapter.

PROMPT YOUR MEMORY. Use the headings of your textbook or your notes or use questions in the margin to prompt your memory. Recite the information out loud or write it down.

Preview Your Textbooks

As soon as you buy your textbooks, take a good look at them. You can learn a lot about your course and your textbook just by thumbing through the text. A quick look at the table of contents will give you a good idea of the topics you'll be discussing in the course. By looking at the headings in each chapter, you'll get a general idea of how each chapter is organized. By reading the preface or the "notes to the student," you may learn a little about how the author designed the text and how some topics relate to others. The end of your text may also include important study aids. Check to see whether there's an index, glossary, or answer key.

You also should look through one of the chapters to see how the information is presented. Does the author provide an outline or introduction for each chapter? Look to see whether there are any study aids in the text; they're designed to help you comprehend the material. Check to see whether the chapter includes lists of key terms that you should master, questions or problems, or even a sample test to check your understanding of key concepts. These study aids will help you monitor your comprehension of the text material and your mastery of the main and supporting points.

Activity 7-2

Describe Your Textbook

Choose one of your textbooks. After previewing it in the ways we have just discussed, write a paragraph describing how the text is organized and all the study aids that are available in the text.

Read the Chapter Before the Lecture

Reading the textbook chapter before going to class is a good idea. It gives you some background for the lecture. You will be able to understand more of the lecture and recognize many of the main ideas as they are presented. As a result, you should be able to take better lecture notes during class. If you find that listening to the lecture helps you understand the textbook better, *skim* the chapter before the lecture and then read it more carefully afterward. **Skimming** involves reading the introduction, the headings, the first sentence of each paragraph, and the conclusion in order to get some idea of what the main ideas are and how they are organized.

Read Ten Pages at a Time

Which would you rather read, a fifty-page chapter or a ten-page chapter? Most students say they'd much rather read a ten-page chapter. Did you? Take a look at the chapters in some of your textbooks. You may be surprised by how long they are. Fifty-page chapters are standard for many texts. Reading fifty pages at one time may not seem like a difficult task, but it is. One page of a college textbook may contain as many words as three pages of a novel. Have you ever sat and read 150 pages of a novel at one time? Not only are there more words on the page, but also the text may be difficult to read and understand. If you find that your attention begins to wander or you just aren't grasping the information anymore, you should stop reading and continue later.

Some students find that it takes them much longer to read the second half of the chapter than the first because, as they get tired or lose interest, their reading speed starts to slow. Time yourself as you read one of your chapters. Note the time at the end of each ten-page section. Did you read the earlier sections more quickly?

Using good time-management strategies can help you improve your textbook reading. Reading a chapter in chunks of ten pages or even five pages at one sitting may help you maintain a faster reading speed and still have excellent comprehension. You also may find that when you're working on only ten pages of text at one time, you feel more motivated to highlight or take notes as you read.

Monitor Your Comprehension

As you read your textbook, you should be aware not only of what you're reading but also of whether you understand what you're reading. You should pause frequently to reflect on what's being said. Too many students read their textbooks in a mechanical way. Their eyes see the words, but their minds are a million miles away. Comprehension monitoring will help you keep your mind on what you're reading. **Comprehension monitoring** refers to your own evaluation of whether or not you comprehend (understand) what you read. You can monitor your comprehension of the text material by stopping every so often (at the end of a paragraph, section, or page) and asking yourself what you just read and whether you understood it. When you realize that you don't understand what you've just read—when comprehension breaks down—you may find that you can correct the problem. The easiest thing to do is to read the sentence or the paragraph again (perhaps out loud if you're an auditory learner). Sometimes reading ahead or rereading the previous paragraph can provide more clarification. Looking up the definitions of unfamiliar vocabulary words can also help you gain a better understanding of the material. When you aren't able to correct a comprehension problem on your own, you should mark it and then continue reading. The reading/study systems discussed later in the chapter will also help you monitor your comprehension and get more out of your reading.

Activity 7-3

Monitor Your Comprehension

As you read your next text assignment, put a check mark in the margin every time you stop to think about what you have read and whether you understood it. After you complete the reading assignment, look at the placement of your check marks. Do they occur within paragraphs, mainly at the end of paragraphs, at the end of the page, or even less frequently? What types of comprehension problems did you experience? What strategies did you use to correct your comprehension problems? Did you notice any improvement in your comprehension of the material?

BECOME A CRITICAL READER

What was the single most important thing that you learned in Chapter 6? To answer that question you need to determine the author's purpose for writing the chapter, identify the main and supporting points in the chapter, consider your purpose for reading the chapter, and evaluate the information that was presented. To choose the single most important point the author is making, you need to understand and think critically about each of the points in the chapter. After all, you must judge the value of each statement based on its own merits, your prior knowledge, and your purpose for reading.

What Is Critical Reading?

Actually, it's difficult to define critical reading (perhaps because it's difficult to accurately describe what really happens when we read). However, most reading researchers agree that critical reading involves thinking critically as we read and after we read. This doesn't mean that you're expected to look for what's wrong with everything you read—you're not being critical in terms of finding fault. Instead, **critical reading** involves questioning, analyzing, and evaluating what you read. You use critical reading skills all the time. If you read labels of competing products when you go to the grocery store, you're using critical reading skills. If you read the course description guide before choosing your class schedule, you're using critical reading skills. When you skim several journal articles before choosing the one or two to use for a term paper or speech, you are using critical reading skills. In each case, you're thinking critically about the information as you read it and after you read it.

Understanding Critical Reading Skills

To think critically about what you read, you must be able to comprehend, analyze, synthesize, apply, and evaluate the material. It's a process that requires you to be actively involved as you read each of your text assignments. You need to question as you read, monitor your comprehension, make connections and comparisons to other material or your own prior knowledge, and finally evaluate what you've read. To do all of these things, you must become an active participant in the reading process.

Comprehension

Because many college texts are so difficult, students don't always understand what they read. You need to **comprehend**—understand—what the individual words mean and how each group of words works together to create meaning within a sentence, paragraph, and headed section. The use of new, specialized, technical terminology is one of the most common causes of comprehension problems. You may be dealing with words you've never even seen before—you may not recognize some of the words, know how to pronounce them, or know what some words mean. Some words take on new or specialized meanings because of the way they're used in particular subject areas. Without understanding the words in the text, you can't understand the ideas and concepts that are presented. For this reason, it's important to look up words that you don't understand and gain some familiarity with the new terminology within the text. Making out word cards (see Chapter 10) or jotting a brief definition or synonym above a difficult word will help improve your comprehension. Without a clear understanding of the text material, you can't make judgments about its quality.

Application

You can gain a better understanding of your text material if you **apply** what you're reading to your own prior knowledge of the material or to your own life experiences. Many reading researchers agree that you can't think critically about written material if you don't have some prior knowledge or experiences with which to compare it. Many college texts are difficult because they contain abstract theories and concepts. Thinking about how the information can be applied to real-life situations can make it easier to understand. You may find that you can build prior knowledge by previewing your text material and by reading other books or articles on the same topic. Finally, you can increase your knowledge of the material by talking to others who have expertise in the area.

Analysis

To be a critical reader, you also must learn to analyze the information presented in the text. Learning to break the information into its component parts—**analysis**—

will help you look more critically at the points made within your reading assignment. You need to identify the main points and their supporting details to better understand the relationships among and within the material. To understand the main points within the headed section, you have to consider how each of the reasons, facts, details, or examples supports the topic or main point being discussed. By identifying each component within the paragraph, you also can better evaluate the quality of the arguments the author is making. If you're currently marking your text, you're thinking about what's important as you read. In Chapter 8, you'll learn more about how to identify the main points and supporting points in your text material.

Synthesis

Your ability to organize and **synthesize**—pull information together from individual statements made in the paragraph (or headed section) into more general ideas or concepts—is critical to understanding what you read. You need to think about how each supporting point adds to the meaning of the main points in each paragraph and how the main points in each paragraph connect to form the key ideas presented in the text. By combining the smaller components within the text, you can gain a better understanding of the information or reach conclusions that aren't directly stated. This may involve adding to the prior knowledge you already have about the topic, modifying what you previously thought about the topic, or learning new information about the topic. Chapter 9 contains a number of strategies that help you learn to pull information together, using your own organizational system.

Evaluation

Critical reading also involves **evaluation**—judging the value of the information in the text. You need to think critically about what you read because not all material that you will read is accurate or presented in an objective way. Most textbooks are for the most part reliable sources of information, written and published by reputable authors and publishers. However, you'll also be expected to read many other types of material in many of your classes. You may read journal articles, research studies, critiques, essays, letters, and other original documents. As you begin to use the Internet to locate information, you need to be even more cautious in your acceptance of everything you read as factual and accurate. Anyone can put anything on the Internet. There are few, if any, regulatory agencies to monitor the accuracy or integrity of the information.

Considering the source of the information and the credibility of the author is only one part of critical reading, however. You must also judge the quality of the main and supporting points made in your reading material. Ask yourself if the facts, reasons, details, and examples really do support the author's conclusions. Think about whether there's enough evidence given to prove the point. Consider whether the evidence is **factual** (statements that can be verified as true or false) or only the **opinion** (statements that express feelings, attitudes, or beliefs) of the author. Watch for **biased language** (words used to sway you to believe one side of the argument) or bias in presenting only the evidence that supports one side of the issue. You may find that it's helpful to annotate your text as you read. Janet Maker recommends noting the author's point of view (position or stance on the topic) in the margin of the text and then listing each of the arguments or supporting points under it (across from its location in the text).[1] Jotting the supporting points in the margin helps you identify and evaluate the quality of the evidence.

---

[1]Janet Maker, "The ACT (Active Critical Thinking) Method of Teaching Critical and Study Reading," *Journal of College Reading and Learning* 27(2) (1996): 40–44.

To be a critical reader, you must also think about how the new information fits with what you learned in the lecture, another reading assignment, or your own prior knowledge. You should also consider how well the information that you read accomplishes the author's purpose for writing and your purpose for reading.

Activity 7-4

Use Critical Reading Skills

As you read an assignment for one of your other classes, use the following questions to help you read and think critically about the material. Then describe what you found in a paragraph or two. What were the main points that author made in the selection? What type of supporting evidence was included? How effective was the supporting evidence in defending the main points or any conclusions that the author reached? Did the author include any loaded language (biased words), or was the evidence slanted in such a way to make you agree with the author's points even though they were one sided? How effective was the selection in accomplishing the author's purpose for writing it and your purpose for reading it?

USE A TEXT READING/STUDY SYSTEM

Dozens of reading/study systems have been developed to help students better understand what they read. Because they're all very similar, we'll discuss only three of them in this chapter. After you learn how to use each system, try it out, and then choose the one that works best for you. You may find that you like some parts of one and other parts of another. Mix and match as you see fit. You also may find that one reading/study system works well with one of your texts, but a different one is more helpful for another text. Using the appropriate reading/study system will help you get more out of the time you spend reading your textbooks.

The P2R Reading/Study System

Many study skills instructors no longer teach students to use long, complicated reading/study systems. Although these systems do work, too many of their students don't use them because they simply take too much time. You can get more out of the time you spend reading your textbook by using an easy, three-step approach.

The **P2R** reading/study system is designed for textbooks that are from easy to average level in difficulty. Use P2R on the entire chapter or on ten-page chunks. First, preview the entire chapter. Next, read actively by highlighting or taking notes as you read. Finally, review using an active strategy such as reciting, answering review questions, or writing questions in the margin. If you're still just sitting back and just reading over your text chapters, why not give P2R a try. Many of my students have found that it really increases their comprehension of the text material without adding much time to their reading.

Advantages of P2R

The P2R reading/study system is a very efficient system for dealing with text material. By previewing, reading actively, and reviewing your text, you should be able to significantly increase your comprehension of the material. You may also find that the P2R system helps motivate you to do your reading because it helps you feel more actively involved in the learning process. Finally, using the P2R system will help you be more prepared for class discussions, quizzes, and exams.

Previewing the chapter provides you with some background about topics in the chapter that may be new to you. Even a brief overview of the chapter can help you pick up some general information about the material. You may also gain some understanding of how the information is organized and presented. Both of these kinds of information can help you understand the text material better. Research studies have shown that previewing before reading can increase your comprehension of the textbook chapter by 10 to 20 percent.

Marking your text or taking notes will aid your comprehension even more and prepare your text for later review. In recent years, there has been a great deal of discussion about the value of marking your textbook as you read. One view suggests that marking your textbook is a way to avoid learning the material as you read it. In some ways this is true. However, if you've already started college, you probably realize that you just don't have time to learn all of the material *well* the first time you read. The main reason for marking your text is to identify the important information and condense the text material so that you never have to read the entire chapter again. It is not unusual to have 300 pages of text to review for just one exam. Think about how long it would take to reread all of it. And, remember, rereading the text takes a lot of time and doesn't really help you learn the information for the exam. Highlighting or note taking allows you to keep up with your class assignments, identify and mark the material that you will need to study further, and improve your ability to concentrate, which increases your comprehension.

Reviewing after you read each ten-page chunk helps you reinforce the important information. Without reviewing, you really can't be sure that you did understand the text material or that you can recall it for a quiz or class discussion. Reviewing provides you with an opportunity to move the information into long-term memory and test your learning. As you'll see in later chapters, there are many ways to review text material. A few of the most common ones are described in the next section. Even a five-minute review can increase your comprehension of the material.

The Three Steps in P2R

Preview. You should always preview a chapter before you read it. A **preview** is a brief overview of a chapter done before reading it. Previewing takes very little time and effort—most students can do it in two to five minutes. The first thing to do is read the title of the chapter. Then read the introduction, outline, or structured overview (a visual display of key information) at the beginning of the chapter. If your text doesn't begin with an introduction, outline, or structured overview, read the first two paragraphs. As you turn the pages of the chapter, read the headings in bold print and glance at any pictures, tables, or graphs. Don't stop to read any of the text along the way. At the end of the chapter, read the summary or the last two paragraphs. If your text contains an extensive summary (a page or more in length), you may want to read only the first and last sentence of each of the paragraphs in the summary. If the chapter is extremely short or if you're reading a journal article or other short selection, you may find it helpful to read the first sentence of each paragraph.

Even though previewing appears to add a few additional minutes to your reading time, it probably will reduce the total time that it takes you to read the chapter. You can test this yourself. Select a chapter in one of your textbooks and time yourself as you read the chapter. Then select another chapter. This time, preview the chapter and then read it. Which chapter took more total reading time? Did you notice any difference in your level of comprehension?

Many students also report that they get interested in a chapter because of their preview of it. This is especially true when students are reading texts that they find boring. As you preview, you may notice a particular topic in the middle or at the end of the chapter that seems quite interesting. Getting to that "good stuff" can motivate you to read the less interesting material.

Activity 7-5

Preview Your Textbook Chapter

Select a chapter in one of your textbooks to preview. After you preview, write down any information that you picked up about the chapter. Don't refer back to the text. After you've read the entire chapter, add a few sentences describing how the preview affected your ability to read the chapter.

Read Actively. The second step of the P2R system is to **read actively**—to do something while you read. One way you can become an active reader is by marking your text. After you have read a paragraph or headed section of text, pause to think about what you've read. Go back and use a highlighter to mark any material that you think you'll want to review again before the exam. By highlighting the text, you're actively involved in thinking about the material, and you're condensing what you'll need to review at a later time. Chapter 8 includes much more information on how to highlight.

Another way to read actively is to take notes. Taking notes on a text is a lot like taking notes on lectures. Write the heading in your notebook and then jot down the important details. You could also write recall questions or summary statements in the margin of the text. More information on how to take text notes is given in Chapter 9.

Review. After you complete a ten-page chunk of reading and at the end of the chapter, you need to **review**—do something to reinforce the important information. There are a number of ways that you can review the text material, but here are four of the most common ones. First, if you highlighted or took notes to read actively, write questions in the margin of your text or notes at the end of each ten-page chunk of the chapter. Then when you finish reading the entire chapter, recite the answers to your questions. Second, use the headings to recite the key information. Cover the details with your hand and recite using the headings as cues. Third, do the exercises or do the questions at the end of the chapter. Finally, you can take the end-of-chapter tests or on-line tests to review and monitor your learning. Don't use all of these strategies, but try them as you complete your reading assignments and find the ones that work best for you.

Activity 7-6

Use the P2R Reading/Study System

Use the three steps in the P2R system to read the text selection in Figure 7.2 from an environmental science text or use one of the text chapters available on the *College Study Skills* Web site. Use one of the active reading methods discussed or try a combi-

Continued

Activity 7-6

Use the P2R Reading/Study System (continued)

nation of them. Then choose one of the review methods that was suggested or use one of your own. Compare your marking, notes, and questions in the margin with those of others in your group. Did you find the P2R system helpful in reading and understanding the text material?

Activity 7-7

Do a Text-Reading Experiment at Home

Read the first half of one of your textbook chapters and then talk about the information with one of your friends or family—explain the key points that were made. Then read the second half of the chapter and write out the key points instead. Which strategy helped you understand the text material more? Would you use either of these strategies again? Why, or why not?

The SQ3R Reading/Study System

SQ3R, developed by Francis Robinson in 1941, is one of the most widely taught reading/study systems.[2] Many students learn how to use SQ3R in junior high school, in senior high school, or even in college. Have you ever been taught how to use SQ3R? Did you ever use it? **SQ3R** is an acronym for **S**urvey, **Q**uestion, **R**ead, **R**ecite, and **R**eview. By using these five steps when you read your college textbooks, you can overcome many of the difficulties you may encounter when dealing with hard-to-read and hard-to-understand material.

Some of the steps in the SQ3R system are similar to those in P2R. The main difference, however, is that the steps are performed on each "headed" section rather than on ten-page chunks or on whole chapters. As you will see, this difference makes SQ3R a more time-consuming system. Because of this, you may want to save SQ3R for your more difficult textbooks. Although it takes a lot of time, many students find that it is very effective.

Advantages of SQ3R

One advantage of the SQ3R reading/study system is that it sets the stage for a great deal of interaction with the text material. As you go through the five steps, you are surveying the chapter to gain information about the topics presented, formulating questions about the material, reading to find the answers, reciting important information aloud, and, finally, reviewing again what you've read. By focusing on each "headed" section and going through all of the steps, you're breaking the task of reading an entire textbook chapter down into smaller units. If you have difficulty reading even ten pages of text at one time, you may find SQ3R to be very helpful. Most students who use the five steps in the SQ3R system do report a greater understanding of the text material than they had before.

One of the greatest advantages of using the SQ3R system is that it allows for a great deal of repetition of the important information in the chapter. As you learned

---

[2]The discussion of the five steps in the SQ3R process that follows was adapted from F. Robinson, *Effective Study,* 4th ed. (New York: Harper & Row, 1970), pp. 32–36.

FIGURE 7.2

Excerpt from an Environmental
Science Textbook

2-1 CULTURAL CHANGES AND THE ENVIRONMENT

What Major Human Cultural Changes Have Taken Place? Evidence from fossils and studies of ancient cultures suggests that the current form of our species, *Homo sapiens sapiens*, has walked the earth for only about 60,000 years (some recent evidence suggests 90,000–176,000 years), an instant in the planet's estimated 4.6-billion-year existence.

Until about 12,000 years ago, we were mostly hunter–gatherers who typically moved as needed to find enough food for survival. Since then, three major cultural changes have occurred: (1) the *agricultural revolution* (which began 10,000–12,000 years ago), (2) the *industrial revolution* (which began about 275 years ago), and (3) the *information and globalization revolution* (which began about 50 years ago).

These major cultural revolutions have
■ Given us much more energy and new technologies with which to alter and control more of the planet to meet our basic needs and increasing desires.
■ Allowed expansion of the human population, mostly because of increased food supplies and longer life spans.
■ Increased our environmental impact because of increased resource use, pollution, and environmental degradation.

How Did Ancient Hunting-and-Gathering Societies Affect the Environment During most of our 60,000-year existence, we were **hunter–gatherers** who survived by collecting edible wild plant parts, hunting, fishing, and scavenging meat from animals killed by other predators. Our hunter–gatherer ancestors typically lived in small bands (of fewer than 50 people) who worked together to get enough food to survive. Many groups were nomadic, picking up their few possessions and moving seasonally from place to place to find enough food.

The earliest hunter-gatherers (and those still living this way today) survived through expert knowledge and understanding of their natural surroundings. They discovered (1) which plants and animals could be eaten and used as medicines, (2) where to find water, (3) how plant availability changed throughout the year, and (4) how some game animals migrated to get enough food. Because of a high infant mortality and an estimated average life span of 30–40 years, hunter-gatherer populations grew very slowly.

Advanced hunter-gatherers had a greater impact on their environment than did early hunter-gatherers. They (1) used more advanced tools and fire to convert forests into grasslands, (2) contributed

to the extinction of some large animals (including the mastodon, saber-toothed tiger, giant sloth, cave bear, mammoth, and giant bison), and (3) altered the distribution of plants (and animals feeding on such plants) as they carried seeds and plants to new areas.

Early and advanced hunter–gatherers exploited their environment to survive. But their environmental impact usually was limited and local because of (1) their small population sizes, (2) low resource use per person, (3) migration, which allowed natural processes to repair most of the damage they caused, and (4) lack of technology that could have expanded their impact.

How Has the Agricultural Revolution Affected the Environment? Some 10,000-12,000 years ago, a cultural shift known as the **agricultural revolution** began in several regions of the world. It involved a gradual move from usually nomadic hunting-and-gathering groups to settled agricultural communities in which people domesticated wild animals and cultivated wild plants.

Plant cultivation probably developed in many areas, especially in the tropical forests of Southeast Asia, northeast Africa, and Mexico. People discovered how to grow various wild food plants from roots or tubers (fleshy underground stems). To prepare the land for planting, they cleared small patches of tropical forests by cutting down trees and other vegetation and then burning the underbrush (Figure 2-2). The ashes fertilized the often nutrient-poor soils in this **slash-and-burn cultivation**.

Early growers also used various forms of **shifting cultivation** (Figure 2-2), primarily in tropical regions. After a plot had been used for several years, the soil became depleted of nutrients or reinvaded by the forest. Then the growers cleared a new plot. They learned that each abandoned patch normally had to be left fallow (unplanted) for 10–30 years before the soil became fertile enough to grow crops again. While patches were regenerating, growers used them for tree crops, medicines, fuelwood, and other purposes. in this manner, most early growers practiced *sustainable cultivation*.

These early farmers had fairly little impact on the environment because (1) their dependence mostly on human muscle power and crude stone or stick tools meant they could cultivate only small plots, (2) their population size and density were low, and (3) normally enough land was available so they could move to other areas and leave abandoned plots unplanted for the several decades needed to restore soil fertility. The gradual shift from hunting and gathering to farming had several significant effects.

Source: Text material from G. T. Miller, *Living in the Environment: Principles, Connections, and Solutions*, 13th ed. (Pacific Grove, CA: Brooks/Cole, 2004), pp. 22–23.

in Chapter 4, repetition is one of the key ingredients in learning. By going through all of the steps in the SQ3R system, you're repeating the key information in the chapter at least three or four times.

Another advantage of SQ3R is that it has a built-in comprehension-monitoring system. When you stop to recite the answer to the question that you formulated, you're testing your understanding of the material that you read. This step in the SQ3R process keeps you on track as you read. Knowing that you must be accountable for what you have read can prevent the passive reading that so often characterizes text reading.

The Five Steps in SQ3R

Survey. Survey the chapter before you read it. Go through the chapter quickly, glance at the headings, and then read the final paragraph of the chapter in order to get a general idea of what the chapter is about and the main points that the author is making.

Question. Before you begin to read the first section in your chapter, turn the heading of the first section into a question. Then read to answer the question that you generated. How would you change the heading "Sensory Adaptation" into a question? Actually, you could generate a number of different questions. One of the most typical (though not necessarily the best) is "What is sensory adaptation?" Formulating questions forces you to think about what you're about to read; it makes you try to predict what the author's main point will be.

Read. Read the text material under the heading in order to find the answer to the question that you generated. Turning the heading into a question helps you focus your reading. Reading the section to locate the answer to your question helps you get actively involved in the text material. Read the text selection in Figure 7.3 to find the answer to the question "What is sensory adaptation?" (or whatever question you formulated in step 2, "Question"). As you read the selection, check to see if you can find the answer to your question.

Recite. At the end of the first headed section, answer the question that you formulated. Recite the answer in your own words, without looking at the text. If you find that you're unable to recall a part or all of the answer, glance over the section again. Then jot down a brief answer in outline form on a piece of paper. Don't make any notes until you've read the entire section.

Review. After you've finished reading the entire chapter, look over the notes that you made to again familiarize yourself with the important information in the chapter. Check your memory by covering your notes and reciting the main points out loud. Then cover each main point in your notes and try to recite the subordinate points that you noted until you have reviewed each headed section. This review should take only about five minutes.

Activity 7-8

Practice the SQ3R Reading/Study System

Read the text selection in Figure 7.4 using the SQ3R reading/study method. Did you find the SQ3R system helpful in reading and understanding the text material? Why, or why not? Describe the process you used and your results in several paragraphs.

FIGURE 7.3
Excerpt from a Psychology
Textbook

Sensory Adaptation

The process of sensory adaptation is yet another factor that influences registration of sensory input. *Sensory adaptation* **is a gradual decline in sensitivity to prolonged stimulation.** For example, let's say you find that the garbage in your kitchen has started to smell. If you stay in the kitchen without removing the garbage, the stench will soon start to fade. In reality, the stimulus intensity of the odor is stable, but with continued exposure, your *sensitivity* to it decreases. Sensory adaptation is a pervasive aspect of everyday life. When you put on your clothes in the morning, you feel them initially, but the sensation quickly fades. Similarly, if you jump reluctantly into a pool of cold water, you'll probably find that the water temperature feels fine in a few moments after you *adapt* to it.

Sensory adaptation is an automatic, built-in process that keeps people tuned in to the *changes* rather than the *constants* in their sensory input. It allows people to ignore the obvious. After all, you don't need constant confirmation that your clothes are still on. But, like most organisms, people are interested in changes in their environment that may signal threats to safety. Thus, as its name suggests, sensory adaptation probably is a behavioral adaptation that has been sculpted by natural selection. Sensory adaptation also shows once again that there is no one-to-one correspondence between sensory input and sensory experience.

The general points we've reviewed so far begin to suggest the complexity of the relationships between the world outside and people's perceived experience of it. As we review each of the principal sensory systems in detail, we'll see repeatedly that people's experience of the world depends on both the physical stimuli they encounter and their active processing of stimulus inputs. We begin our exploration of the senses with vision—the sense that most people think of as nearly synonymous with a direct perception of reality. The case is actually quite different, as you'll see.

Source: Text material from W. Weiten, *Psychology: Themes and Variations,* 6th ed. (Belmont, CA: Wadsworth, 2004), p. 128.

Activity 7-9

Use SQ3R for Text Reading

Use the SQ3R system to read the first five or ten pages of two of your text assignments. Choose one textbook that you find rather easy to read and another that you find the most difficult. Write a paragraph or two describing how effective this method was in helping you read and understand your text chapters. Did you notice any difference between using SQ3R on the easy text and the difficult text?

Adapting SQ3R

There are a number of ways that you can adapt or modify SQ3R to make it more effective and easy to use. First of all, you don't have to use SQ3R for all your reading assignments. Many students use SQ3R or a variation of it only for reading their most difficult textbooks. In Activity 7-9, you were asked to use SQ3R with an easy text and with a difficult-to-understand text. You probably discovered that you really didn't need to use SQ3R with your easy textbook, but you also may have discovered that it did help improve your comprehension with your hard-to-understand text.

Because college texts contain so much information in each headed section, you need to modify the way you generate questions for each heading. If you simply ask "What is the . . ." type of questions, you may be ignoring a great deal of important information. For example, the question, "What is sensory adaptation?" would have

FIGURE 7.4
Excerpt from a Biology Textbook

4.5 THE ENDOMEMBRANE SYSTEM

The **endomembrane system** is a series of functionally connected organelles in which lipids are assembled and new polypeptide chains are modified. Its products are sorted and shipped to different destinations. Figure 4.13 shows how its organelles—the ER, Golgi bodies, and vesicles—interconnect with one another.

Endoplasmic Reticulum

The functions of the endomembrane system begin with **endoplasmic reticulum**, or **ER**. In animal cells, the ER is continuous with the nuclear envelope, and it extends through the cytoplasm. Its membranes appear rough or smooth, depending on whether ribosomes are attached to the membrane facing the cytoplasm.

We typically observe *rough* ER arranged into stacks of flattened sacs with many ribosomes attached. Every new polypeptide chain is synthesized on ribosomes. But only the newly forming chains having a built-in signal can enter the space within rough ER or become incorporated into ER membranes. (The signal is a sequence of fifteen to twenty specific amino acids.) Once the chains are in rough ER, enzymes may attach oligosaccharides and other side chains to them. Many specialized cells secrete the final proteins. Rough ER is abundant in such cells. For example, in your pancreas, ER-rich gland cells make and secrete enzymes that end up in the small intestine and help digest your meals.

Smooth ER is free of ribosomes and curves through cytoplasm like connecting pipes. Many cells assemble most lipids inside the pipes. Smooth ER is well developed in seeds. In liver cells, certain drugs as well as toxic metabolic wastes are inactivated in it. Sarcoplasmic reticulum, a type of smooth ER in skeletal muscle cells, functions in muscle contraction.

Golgi Bodies

In **Golgi bodies**, enzymes put the finishing touches on proteins and lipids, sort them out, then package them inside vesicles for shipment to specific locations. For example, an enzyme in one Golgi region might attach a phosphate group to a new protein, thereby giving it a mailing tag to its proper destination.

Commonly, a Golgi body looks vaguely like a stack of pancakes; it is composed of a series of flattened membrane-bound sacs (Figure 4.14). In functional terms, the last portion of a Golgi body corresponds to the top pancake. Here, vesicles form as patches of the membrane bulge out, then break away into the cytoplasm.

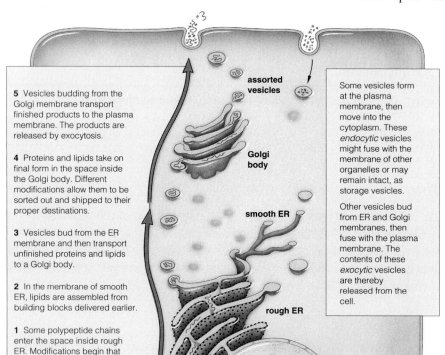

5 Vesicles budding from the Golgi membrane transport finished products to the plasma membrane. The products are released by exocytosis.

4 Proteins and lipids take on final form in the space inside the Golgi body. Different modifications allow them to be sorted out and shipped to their proper destinations.

3 Vesicles bud from the ER membrane and then transport unfinished proteins and lipids to a Golgi body.

2 In the membrane of smooth ER, lipids are assembled from building blocks delivered earlier.

1 Some polypeptide chains enter the space inside rough ER. Modifications begin that will shape them into the final protein form.

SECRETORY PATHWAY

assorted vesicles

Golgi body

smooth ER

rough ER

Some vesicles form at the plasma membrane, then move into the cytoplasm. These *endocytic* vesicles might fuse with the membrane of other organelles or may remain intact, as storage vesicles.

Other vesicles bud from ER and Golgi membranes, then fuse with the plasma membrane. The contents of these *exocytic* vesicles are thereby released from the cell.

DNA instructions for building polypeptide chains leave the nucleus and enter the cytoplasm.

The chains (*green*) are assembled on ribosomes in the cytoplasm.

Figure 4.13 Endomembrane system, a membrane system in the cytoplasm that synthesizes, modifies, packages, and ships proteins and lipids. *Green* arrows highlight a secretory pathway by which some proteins and lipids are packaged and released from many types of cells, including gland cells that secrete mucus, sweat, and digestive enzymes.

FIGURE 7.4 (continued)

Excerpt from a Biology Textbook

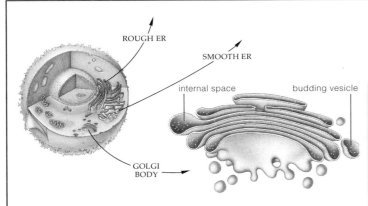

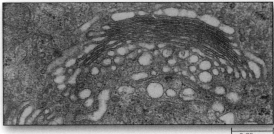

Figure 4.14 Sketch and micrograph of a Golgi body from an animal cell.

A Variety of Vesicles

Vesicles are tiny, membranous sacs that move through the cytoplasm or take up positions in it. The lysosome, a common type, buds from Golgi membranes of animal cells and some fungal cells. **Lysosomes** are organelles of intracellular digestion. They hold enzymes that digest complex carbohydrates, proteins, nucleic acids, and some lipids. Often, they fuse with vesicles formed earlier from patches of plasma membrane that surrounded bacteria, molecules, and other items that docked at the membrane receptors. Lysosomes also digest entire cells and cell parts. For example, as a tadpole is developing into an adult frog, its tail slowly disappears. Lysosomal enzymes are responding to developmental signals and are helping to destroy cells that make up the tail.

Peroxisomes, another type, are sacs of enzymes that break down fatty acids and amino acids. A product of the reactions, hydrogen peroxide, is toxic, as the Chapter 5 introduction describes. But enzyme action converts it to water and oxygen or uses it to break down alcohol and other toxins. Drink alcohol, and the peroxisomes of liver and kidney cells will degrade nearly half of it.

In the ER and Golgi bodies of the endomembrane system, many proteins take on final form and lipids are assembled.

Lipids, proteins (such as enzymes), and other items become packaged in vesicles destined for export, storage, membrane building, intracellular digestion, and other cell activities.

Source: Text material adapted from C. Starr and R. Taggart, *Biology: The Unity and Diversity of Life*, 10th ed. (Pacific Grove, CA: Brooks/Cole, 2004), pp. 64–65.

led only to the review of the definition: "Sensory adaptation is a gradual decline in sensitivity to prolonged stimulation." Other important points would have been overlooked. You may find it more useful to generate broad questions such as "What do I need to know about sensory adaptation?" or "What's important about sensory adaptation?" Broad questions will lead you to read for all of the important information within the headed section.

Writing your question in the margin across from the heading and then noting the "answer" below it in the margin is also an effective modification. By **annotating** (adding explanatory notes) your text, you'll increase your level of involvement with the material and prepare your text for later review. More information on how to annotate your text is presented in Chapters 8 and 9.

Rather than just reciting the answer to the question that you formulated from the heading, highlight the information and then cover the section of text and try to recite all the important information that it contained. Look back at the section entitled "Sensory Adaptation." Which information would you recite from the selection? By modifying the way you use SQ3R, you can still make it an effective and an efficient study tool, especially for reading very difficult textbooks.

The S-RUN-R Reading/Study System

The SQ3R system has been adapted by many reading and study skills educators. Because of its simplicity, one variation that may be very useful for college students is the *S-RUN* (Survey, Read, Underline, Notetaking) reading method designed by Nancy Bailey.[3] Bailey's students were reluctant to use SQ3R because it seemed like too much work; however, they used S-RUN with great success.

The **S-RUN-R** reading/study system combines Bailey's system with a review step to better meet the needs of college students. Because you focus on the text one headed section at a time, S-RUN-R should be used with more difficult text material.

Advantages of S-RUN-R

The S-RUN-R reading/study system contains many of the strengths of SQ3R but also has been adapted so that it's more suitable for college text material. First, like SQ3R, S-RUN-R provides you with a great deal of repetition. You survey, read, mark, take notes on, and review all of the important information in the chapter. You get at least four repetitions on the important points in each headed section. This helps you better understand the information and learn it. Second, S-RUN-R also allows you to focus on one headed section at a time. This helps increase your comprehension because you don't move on to another section until you thoroughly understand the previous one. The S-RUN-R reading/study system also helps you focus on all of the important information in the headed section rather than on only one question and its answer. Finally, S-RUN-R provides you with a system that uses active strategies, which help increase your comprehension and at the same time condenses the material for later review. Many students have found that S-RUN-R is a very effective reading/study system. Try it and see if it works for you, too.

The Five Steps in S-RUN-R

Survey. The first step in the S-RUN-R reading/study system is to survey the entire chapter. Read the title, introduction, headings, subheadings, and summary (and glance at pictures, charts, and graphs). Like P2R and SQ3R, this survey provides a quick overview of the chapter, building background and interest. You should spend only about two (for short chapters) to five minutes (for longer chapters) completing the survey. If it's taking you longer, you're probably reading too much or stopping too long to look at the illustrations.

Read. Instead of formulating a question before reading a headed section, write the heading on a piece of notebook paper next to the left margin. Just copying the heading helps you pay more attention to it and may help focus your reading. Then read the section as you would any other text material, thinking critically about the material.

Underline. After you finish reading each paragraph, think about what was important in the paragraph and underline or highlight the important information. As you'll see in Chapter 8, highlighting takes much less time than underlining, so feel free to make the change. In the next chapter, you'll learn more about how to choose what to mark. For now, highlight the information that you think you would like to review for an exam.

[3]Nancy Bailey, "S-RUN: Beyond SQ3R," *Journal of Reading* 32 (1988): 170.

Note Take. As soon as you complete all of the highlighting for the entire headed section, stop and turn back to your notebook page. Now take notes on the key information. Briefly summarize the underlined or highlighted information under the previously written heading. Skip to the next line in your notebook, indenting slightly, and write the notes using meaningful phrases as you do when taking lecture notes. Don't just copy what you highlighted; try to put the information into your own words. Taking text notes helps you get a better understanding of the information and helps you condense it even more. By putting the information in your own words, you'll increase your comprehension even more. Continue jotting down each heading, reading, underlining (or highlighting), and taking notes for each remaining headed section.

Review. When you've completed the entire chapter, review to reinforce the important information. You can recite the key information that you wrote under each heading. Doing the end-of-chapter questions (if there are any) may also help you review the key information in the chapter. Some students find that predicting questions and creating self-tests helps them identify and practice the key information in the chapter. You may also create a recall column in your textbook or for your text notes. Writing questions in the margin can help you prompt your memory of the key points you underlined (or highlighted) or included in your text notes. You can use the review step to simply get more repetition on the material or to actually check your understanding or memory of it. Writing questions in the margin of your textbook or notebook provides you with repetition on the material, but actually reciting the answers, self-testing, will let you know whether or not you really have learned the material.

Adapting S-RUN-R

As with any of the reading/study systems, S-RUN-R can be adapted or modified to better fit your needs or those of the text you're using. You may find that you still want to read your chapter in ten-page chunks. If that is the case, you should do a quick review after you complete each chunk of the chapter and then choose a different strategy to review when you complete the entire chapter. The more interaction you have with the material, the better you will understand and remember what you read. You can also modify S-RUN-R by taking your notes in the margin of your textbook (if it's large enough) or by writing your notes on a narrow strip of paper (similar to the size of a bookmark) that you can insert in each page to take the place of the wide margin. A number of office supply stores sell note pads that are about this size. It's not important where you complete the note-taking step; rather, the important thing is to complete it. Putting the information in your own words and organizing it in a manner that makes sense to you significantly increases your comprehension of the information.

Activity 7-10

Use the S-RUN-R Reading/Study System

Figure 7.5 contains excerpted material from a history text. Read the selection using the S-RUN-R reading/study system. Don't forget to work on one headed section at a time. Compare your marking and notes with those of other students in your group. Did you find the S-RUN-R system helpful in reading and understanding the text material?

FIGURE 7.5

Excerpt from a History Text book

THE RENAISSANCE

People who lived in Italy between 1350 and 1550 or so believed that they had witnessed a rebirth of classical antiquity—the world of the Greeks and Romans. To them, this marked a new age, which historians later called the Renaissance (French for "rebirth") and viewed as a distinct period of European history, which began in Italy and then spread to the rest of Europe.

Renaissance Italy was largely an urban society. The city-states became the centers of Italian political, economic, and social life. Within this new urban society, a secular spirit emerged as increasing wealth created new possibilities for the enjoyment of worldly things.

The Renaissance was also an age of recovery from the disasters of the fourteenth century, including the Black Death, political disorder, and economic recession. In pursuing that recovery, Italian intellectuals became intensely interested in the glories of their own past, the Greco-Roman culture of antiquity.

A new view of human beings emerged as people in the Italian Renaissance began to emphasize individual ability. The fifteenth-century Florentine architect Leon Battista Alberti expressed the new philosophy succinctly: "Men can do all things if they will."[1] This high regard for human worth and for individual potentiality gave rise to a new social ideal of the well-rounded personality or "universal person" (*l'uomo universale*) who was capable of achievements in many areas of life.

RENAISSANCE SOCIETY

After the severe economic reversals and social upheavals of the fourteenth century, the European economy gradually recovered as manufacturing and trade increased in volume. The Italians and especially the Venetians expanded their wealthy commercial empire, rivaled only by the increasingly powerful Hanseatic League, a commercial and military alliance of north German coastal towns. Not until the sixteenth century, when overseas discoveries gave new importance to the states facing the Atlantic, did the Italian city-states begin to suffer from the competitive advantages of the more powerful national territorial states.

In the Middle Ages, society was divided into three estates: the clergy, or first estate, whose preeminence was grounded in the belief that people should be guided to spiritual ends; the nobility, or second estate, whose privileges rested on the principle that nobles provided security and justice for society; and the peasants and inhabitants of the towns and cities, the third estate. Although this social order continued into the Renaissance, some changes also became evident.

The Nobility

Throughout much of Europe, the landholding nobles faced declining real incomes during most of the fourteenth and fifteenth centuries. Many members of the old nobility survived, however, and new blood also infused its ranks. By 1500, the nobles, old and new, who constituted between 2 and 3 percent of the population in most countries, managed to dominate society, as they had done in the Middle Ages, holding important political posts and serving as advisers to the king.

By 1500, certain ideals came to be expected of the noble, or aristocrat. These were best expressed in *The Book of the Courtier*, by the Italian Baldassare Castiglione (1478–1529). Castiglione described the three fundamental attributes of the perfect courtier. First, nobles are born, not made, and they should exhibit impeccable character, grace, and talents. Second, the perfect noble must participate in military and bodily exercises, because the principal profession of a courtier was arms; however, unlike the medieval knight, who was primarily concerned with military skill, the Renaissance noble must also seek a classical education and adorn his life with the arts. Third, the noble was expected to follow a certain standard of conduct. Nobles should not hide their accomplishments but show them with grace. The aim of the perfect noble was to serve his prince in an effective and honest way.

Peasants and Townspeople

Except in the heavily urban areas of northern Italy and Flanders, peasants made up the overwhelming mass of the third estate—they constituted 85 to 90 percent of the total European population. Serfdom decreased as the manorial system continued its decline. Increasingly, the labor dues owed by a peasant to his lord were converted into rents paid in money. By 1500, especially in western Europe, more and more peasants were becoming legally free.

The remainder of the third estate were inhabitants of towns and cities, originally merchants and artisans. But by the fifteenth century, the Renaissance town or city had become more complex. At the top of urban society were the patricians, whose wealth from capitalistic enterprises in trade, industry, and banking enabled them to dominate their urban communities economically, socially, and politically. Below them were the petty burghers—the shop-keepers, artisans, guild masters, and guildsmen—who were largely concerned with providing goods and services for local consumption. Below these two groups were the propertyless workers earning pitiful wages and the unemployed, living squalid and miserable lives. These poor city-dwellers constituted 30 to 40 percent of the urban population.

Family and Marriage in Renaissance Italy

The family bond was a source of great security in the urban world of Renaissance Italy. To maintain the family, parents carefully arranged marriages, often to strengthen business or family ties. Details were worked out well in advance, sometimes when children were only two or three, and reinforced by a legally binding marriage contract. The important aspect of the contract was the size of the dowry, a sum of money presented by the wife's family to the husband upon marriage.

The father-husband was the center of the Italian family. He gave it his name, managed all finances (his wife had no share in his wealth), and made the crucial decisions that determined his children's lives. A father's authority over his children was absolute until he died or formally freed his children. In Renaissance Italy, children did not become adults on reaching a certain age; adulthood came only when the father went before a judge and formally emancipated them. The age of emancipation varied from early teens to late twenties.

The wife managed the household, a position that gave women a certain degree of autonomy in their daily lives. Most wives, however, also knew that their primary function was to bear children. Upper-class wives were frequently pregnant; Alessandra Strozzi of Florence, for example, who had been married at the age of sixteen, bore eight children in ten years. For women in the Renaissance, childbirth was a fearful occasion. Not only was it painful, but it could be deadly; possibly as many as one woman in ten died in childbirth.

Source: Text material from William J. Duiker and Jackson J. Spielvogel, *World History*, 4th ed. (Belmont, CA: Wadsworth, 2004), pp. 353–354.

Activity 7-11

Discuss Your Use of the Reading/Study Systems

As you read your text assignments during the next week, experiment with the various reading/study systems that were described in this chapter. Begin each assignment with the easiest system (P2R) and proceed to use more complex systems (S-RUN-R and SQ3R) if you find that you're not able to understand and remember the material. You will probably find that you didn't use the same system for all your texts. List the name of each of your texts and describe the system that you found to be most effective. Discuss your reasons with the members of your group.

Activity 7-12

Where Are You Now?

Now that you have completed Chapter 7, take a few minutes to repeat the "Where Are You Now?" activity, located on the *College Study Skills* Web site. What changes did you make as a result of reading this chapter? How are you planning to apply what you've learned in this chapter?

SUMMARY

College textbooks are different from high school textbooks. They're generally written at a higher reading level and are longer and more idea dense. They don't just seem harder—they are! Using good time-management strategies can help you keep up with your reading assignments, which may total 200 or 300 pages per week. To understand what you're reading, you need to use some type of text-reading strategy before you read, as you read, and after you read. It's also important to monitor your comprehension while you're reading your textbooks. Learning to be a critical reader will help you think about and evaluate the information in your textbooks and other reading assignments. Many students use a text reading/study system such as P2R, SQ3R, or S-RUN-R to increase and monitor their comprehension. The strategies suggested in these systems get you more actively involved in your reading. You may find that you need to use only a simple system like P2R when reading your easier textbooks. However, a more complex system like SQ3R or S-RUN-R may be necessary to ensure good comprehension when you're reading your more difficult textbooks. Experiment with all the reading/study systems to find out which one works best for you. You may also choose to adapt one of these systems or design your own text reading/study system. If you find that you often get to the end of the page or the end of the chapter and don't remember or understand what you read, you need to get more actively involved in your reading assignments.

REVIEW QUESTIONS

Terms You Should Know: Make a flash card for each term.

Analysis	Critical reading	Read actively
Annotating	Evaluation	Review
Application	Facts	Skimming
Biased language	Opinion	SQ3R
Comprehension	P2R	S-RUN-R
Comprehension monitoring	Preview	Synthesis

Completion: Fill in the blank to complete each of the following statements.

1. By connecting what you're reading to your _____ _____, you can improve your reading comprehension.

2. You can prevent boredom and increase your comprehension if you read your textbook chapter in _____-page chunks.

3. You need to turn the _____ into a question in the SQ3R reading/study system.

4. You should use the _____ reading/study system with your easy-to-read textbooks.

5. One of the disadvantages of using S-RUN-R is that it is very _____ _____.

Multiple Choice: Circle the letter of the best answer for each of the following questions. Be sure to underline key words and eliminate wrong answers.

6. _____ refers to your evaluation of whether or not you understand what you read.
   A. Critical reading
   B. Previewing
   C. Comprehension monitoring
   D. Analysis

7. Previewing before reading a chapter can increase your comprehension by:
   A. 5 to 10 percent
   B. 10 to 20 percent
   C. 20 to 30 percent
   D. Previewing increases speed but not comprehension

Short Answer–Essay: On a separate sheet, answer each of the following questions.

8. List and define each of the five critical reading skills.

9. Why do some students have difficulty reading their textbooks? What should they do differently?

10. Compare and contrast the P2R, SQ3R, and S-RUN-R reading/study systems.

"Highlighting has always helped me study or read a chapter, but I never really knew what to highlight. This time when I read my algebra book, it seemed like I was concentrating on my work more. I was trying to find answers to my questions in the reading. I formed more questions, looked for key words, jotted down phrases and such. It helped me understand polynomial expressions! It did help improve my comprehension of the material. I wish I could have learned how to highlight the right way a little earlier."

Karen Altschaffl
Student

MARKING YOUR TEXTBOOK

In this chapter you will learn more about:
- **Why you should mark your text**
- **How you should mark your text**
- **What you should mark**
- **How much you should mark**
- **How to review your text marking**
- **How to evaluate your text marking**

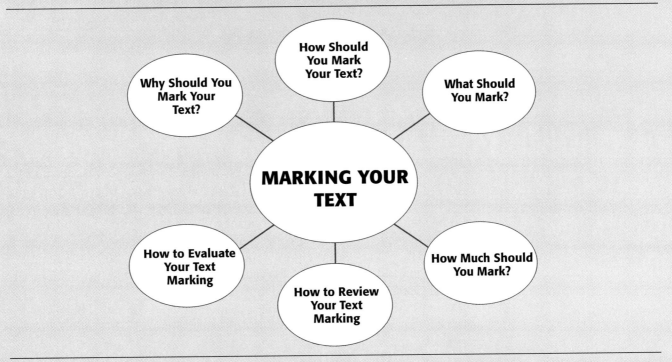

Activity 8-1

Where Are You Now?

Take a few minutes to answer *yes* or *no* to the following questions.

	YES	NO
1. Do you highlight or mark your textbook as you read?	_____	_____
2. Do you find that you often get to the end of a page and have no idea what you just read?	_____	_____
3. Do you begin to highlight or underline an important point before you finish the sentence?	_____	_____
4. Do you evaluate your text marking after an exam?	_____	_____
5. Does your marking make sense when you read it again before the exam?	_____	_____
6. Do you rehighlight or re-mark your text when you review for an exam?	_____	_____
7 Do you mark the headings and subheadings in your text?	_____	_____
8. Do you make notes in the margin when you read your text?	_____	_____
9. Do you tend to mark key words rather than phrases or entire sentences?	_____	_____
10. Do you ever reread the unmarked sections of your text before an exam?	_____	_____
Total Points		_____

Give yourself 1 point for each *yes* answer to questions 1, 4, 5, 6, 7, and 8 and 1 point for each *no* answer to questions 2, 3, 9, and 10. Now total up your points. A low score indicates that you need some help in text marking. A high score indicates that you are already using many good text-marking strategies.

WHY SHOULD YOU MARK YOUR TEXT?

You probably know some students whose textbooks look as new at the end of a course as they did at the beginning. Have you ever wondered why? One explanation is that those students believe text marking is a waste of time. They've heard that if you mark your text, you're just putting off learning the information. (Sometimes this reasoning provides a convenient excuse not to mark.) Other students don't mark their texts because they want to sell them at the end of the semester; they think marked textbooks are less valuable at the resale table. Textbook buyers don't really care if books are marked. But you should!

When done correctly, text marking promotes active reading, condenses the material for later review, increases your comprehension, and serves as a mini comprehension monitoring system.

Promotes Active Reading

Marking your textbook is a useful activity because it promotes active reading. By now you probably have noticed that you're more actively involved in lecture classes because you're taking notes. By marking your textbooks as you read, you can achieve that same level of concentration and activity. Knowing that you should mark specific sections as you read helps keep you alert. It gives you a purpose for reading. Instead of daydreaming or thinking about something else you have to do, you're forced to concentrate on what you're reading. To mark your text effectively, you have to think about the content of the chapter. You constantly need to make decisions about what's important and what isn't. You may find that your reading takes on a whole new dimension when you mark your text.

Condenses the Material

Text marking is also important because it condenses the text material for later review. If you don't mark your textbooks, you may not go back and study the material before an exam. You would have to reread everything before you even could start to study. You would have to rely on only your lecture notes. Because most professors also test on text material, you would be at a decided disadvantage at exam time. By marking, you can reduce the amount of text material you need to review.

Increases Comprehension

Text marking also improves your comprehension of the text material. Identifying and marking the main points and then looking for supporting details help you understand the text. If you highlight these same points after you have read the paragraph, you get a chance to read the information a second time. Have you noticed that your eyes follow your marker as you move it across the text? This second reading helps reinforce the key information. As you make notes or write questions in the margin, you get even more repetition on the important information.

Serves as a Comprehension Monitoring System

Text marking also provides you with feedback on whether you are paying attention as you read a particular section of your text. If everything is marked, you know you really weren't making decisions about the importance of the material. You may not have been able to determine what was important and what wasn't. If nothing is marked, you may not have understood the material well enough to pick out the important information or you may have been distracted. Text marking allows you to monitor your comprehension of the text material.

HOW SHOULD YOU MARK YOUR TEXT?

There are many methods for marking a textbook, but the two most common ones are underlining and highlighting. The first step in effective marking is to read and think about the text material. Text marking is a lot like taking lecture notes. You need to get actively involved in the material—read, think, decide, and then mark.

It's important to read an entire paragraph or headed section before you begin to mark your textbook. After you read a section, you need to decide what's important; then you can begin to mark. Many students really don't know how to mark a textbook, so as soon as they read something that looks as though it might be important, they start to mark. If you mark part of a sentence before you even finish reading it, you're actually interfering with your comprehension of the material. Until you get used to marking, try to read at least to the end of the sentence before you begin to mark. Work up to two sentences, then to the end of the paragraph, and finally to the entire headed section.

Activity 8-2

Mark Important Information

Read the following selection on the ocean. Be sure to read to the end of the paragraph or read the entire selection, and then mark the important information. Remember to read, think, decide, and then mark. Compare your marking to that of others in your group.

WHY ARE THE OCEANS IMPORTANT?

As landlubbers, we tend to think of Earth in terms of land, but Earth is largely a water planet. A more accurate name for the planet would be Ocean, because saltwater oceans cover more than 71 percent of its surface.

The oceans play key roles in the survival of virtually all life on Earth. Because of their size and currents, the oceans mix and dilute many human-produced wastes flowing or dumped into them to less harmful or even harmless levels, as long as they are not overloaded. Oceans also play a major role in regulating Earth's climate by distributing solar heat through ocean currents and by evaporation as part of the global hydrologic cycle. They also participate in other important nutrient cycles.

By serving as a gigantic reservoir for carbon dioxide, oceans help regulate the temperature of the troposphere. Oceans provide habitats for about 250,000 species of marine plants and animals, which are food for many organisms, including human beings. They also supply us with iron, sand, gravel, phosphates, magnesium, oil, natural gas, and many other valuable resources.[1]

Highlight

Highlighting the text as you read is probably the most efficient method of text marking. Because it takes so little extra time, more students are willing to do it. Highlighting does promote active reading, condense the information, and help improve your level of comprehension of the text material. It's a very practical method to use.

As you **highlight** the text, drag your highlighter across the printed words from left to right; in this way you'll be able to reread the sentence or phrase as you mark it. This second reading helps improve your comprehension and memory of the material. If you sweep backward across the line, you won't benefit from a second reading. If you decide to use highlighting to mark your textbooks, use a very soft shade

---

[1] Text material adapted from G. T. Miller, *Living in the Environment: Principles, Connections, and Solutions,* 13th ed. (Pacific Grove, CA: Brooks/Cole, 2004), p. 147.

like yellow or pastel pink. Although fluorescent markers do make the text material stand out, they also cause eye strain when you go back to reread your marking.

When you identify information that you think is important, you should mark **meaningful phrases** rather than just key words. You can either mark a portion of the sentence, a phrase, or clause, or you can create your own meaningful phrase by **linking,** connecting key words together. Marking only the buzzwords really doesn't provide you with enough information from which to study. Mark enough of the sentence so that one month later it will still make sense. Fortunately, it's even easier to mark meaningful phrases in your textbook than it is to write them during a lecture because you have plenty of time to decide what you want to highlight. Look at this example of highlighting. Read only the shaded information. Does it make sense? Now go back and read the entire selection. Does the highlighted text effectively show the important information?

Why Are the Oceans Important?

As landlubbers, we tend to think of Earth in terms of land, but Earth is largely a water planet. A more accurate name for the planet would be Ocean, because saltwater oceans cover more than 71 percent of its surface.

The oceans play key roles in the survival of virtually all life on Earth. Because of their size and currents, the oceans mix and dilute many human-produced wastes flowing or dumped into them to less harmful or even harmless levels, as long as they are not overloaded. Oceans also play a major role in regulating Earth's climate by distributing solar heat through ocean currents and by evaporation as part of the global hydrologic cycle. They also participate in other important nutrient cycles.

By serving as a gigantic reservoir for carbon dioxide, oceans help regulate the temperature of the troposphere. Oceans provide habitats for about 250,000 species of marine plants and animals, which are food for many organisms, including human beings. They also supply us with iron, sand, gravel phosphates, magnesium, oil, natural gas, and many other valuable resources.

Underline

Some students use a highlighter, pen, or pencil to **underline** (draw a line under words to be marked) important text material rather than dragging the highlighter across the words. Underlining has several disadvantages. First it may not increase your comprehension as much as highlighting does because you don't get that second reading when you underline. Try this experiment. Underline a sentence in this section. What did you see? Some students report seeing the line, others see the tip of their pens or pencils, some see blank space. When I did this experiment, I saw the bottoms of the letters—I was trying to make the line go under the words and not through them. What did you see? Most students agree that they don't actually pay attention to the text material when they underline. If you do decide to underline your text, don't use a ruler or straight edge to keep your lines straight—it will really slow you down. Although underlining does promote active reading and it does condense the material, it isn't as efficient or effective as highlighting your text.

Make Marginal Notes

As you mark, you also may want to add **marginal notes,** summary statements in the margin of the text. You can also make notes to indicate that you agree or disagree with a point that the author made. You can put a question mark in the margin to indicate that you don't understand something or would like to ask about it in class, or use a star to indicate that the professor hinted that something would be on the test. Making brief notes in the margin will help increase your level of interaction with the text. However, don't overdo it. If you try to copy all the important information in the margin, you're defeating the purpose of marking. The marginal notes in Figure 8.1 summarize the main points made in the selection.

Avoid Complex Marking Systems

Learning to mark your textbook is not that difficult; however, some students make text marking more complicated than it needs to be. They use **complex marking systems** that lead to ineffective and inefficient marking. Have you ever seen a beautifully marked textbook? If this question made you think of one with three or four different colors of highlighting, you know exactly what I mean. During a workshop several years ago, I asked students to mark a text selection. One student immediately pulled out five different colored markers and began to read and mark the selection. It took this student four times as long as everyone else in the room to mark the selection. At the end of the session, I asked the student about her marking system. She explained that she used one color for main ideas, one color for key words, another for definitions, a fourth shade for examples, and a fifth for supporting details.

Although a multicolored highlighting system does force you to think about how you are marking the text material, it actually can interfere with comprehension. If you spend too much time thinking about whether something is a main idea, a supporting detail, a definition, an example, or a key word, you may not be

FIGURE 8.1
Example of Highlighted Text with Marginal Notes

WHY ARE THE OCEANS IMPORTANT?

Earth ≈ "Ocean"

As landlubbers, we tend to think of Earth in terms of land, but Earth is largely a water planet. A more accurate name for the planet would be Ocean, because salt-water oceans cover more than 71 percent of its surface.

"O" → survival of all life

1. dilute waste
2. regulate climate

The oceans play key roles in the survival of virtually all life on Earth. Because of their size and currents, the oceans mix and dilute many human-produced wastes flowing or dumped into them to less harmful or even harmless levels, as long as they are not overloaded. Oceans also play a major role in regulating Earth's climate by distributing solar heat through ocean currents and by evaporation as part of the global hydrologic cycle. They also participate in other important nutrient cycles.

3. regulate temp
4. habitat ≈ 250,000 species
5. source nat. resources

By serving as a gigantic reservoir for carbon dioxide, oceans help regulate the temperature of the troposphere. Oceans provide habitats for about 250,000 species of marine plants and animals, which are food for many organisms, including human beings. They also supply us with iron, sand, gravel, phosphates, magnesium, oil, natural gas, and many other valuable resources.

FIGURE 8.2
Example of Overly Complex
Marking

> ## WHY ARE THE OCEANS IMPORTANT?
>
> As landlubbers, we tend to think of Earth in terms of land, but Earth is largely a water planet. A more accurate name for the planet would be Ocean, because salt-water oceans cover more than 71 percent of its surface.
>
> The oceans play key roles in the survival of virtually all life on Earth. Because of their size and currents, the oceans mix and dilute many human-produced wastes flowing or dumped into them to less harmful or even harmless levels, as long as they are not overloaded. Oceans also play a major role in regulating Earth's climate by ①distributing solar heat through ocean currents ②and by evaporation as part of the global hydrologic cycle. They also ③participate in other important nutrient cycles.
>
> ①By serving as a gigantic reservoir for carbon dioxide, oceans help regulate the temperature of the troposphere. ②Oceans provide habitats for about 250,000 species of marine plants and animals, which are food for many organisms, including human beings. ③They also supply us with iron, sand, gravel, phosphates, magnesium, oil, natural gas, and many other valuable resources.

thinking much about the content of the selection. In some ways, this is like using your highlighter to mark the nouns, pronouns, verbs, adjectives, and adverbs in each sentence. Although you would be marking various components of the material, you wouldn't really be focusing on the meaning but instead on the function of that component. You would be thinking more about the system instead of the content.

Some students do find that using two colors helps them see better how some of the information is connected. Some students find it useful to use an extra color to identify related details when two or more topics (and their subordinate details) are discussed within the same headed section. You'll have an opportunity to see how helpful this can be in organizing text material in Chapter 9. For almost all of your text marking, it's better to use just one color. However, if you find using a second color can help you better understand or organize the material, use it.

Other complex marking systems recommend using single lines, double lines, wavy lines, boxes, circles, curved brackets, square brackets, asterisks, numbers, and other marking symbols. These multisymbol systems, like the multicolored ones, are very time-consuming and often lead to overmarking. Look at the example in Figure 8.2, which incorporates some of these methods. Deciding whether to use a single line or a double line, a box or a circle, or a number or an asterisk can interfere with your comprehension of the material. You spend too much time thinking about the system instead of the content. Take another look at the marking in Figure 8.2. Did you notice that almost everything is marked? Using a simple system will help you focus on the important information, while reading actively and condensing the material for later review.

Activity 8-3

Use the Newspaper to Practice Marking

Practice text marking as you read the newspaper or magazines every day during the next week. Read to the end of the article (for a newspaper) or the end of a paragraph in a magazine before you mark anything. Write a paragraph or two to answer the following questions. What difference did you notice as you marked the material early in the week compared with similar material later in the week? How did this practice affect the marking you did with your text material? What strategies helped you the most?

FIGURE 8.3

Excerpt from a Political Science Textbook

The Electoral College

Most voters who vote for the president and vice president think that they are voting directly for a candidate. In actuality, they are voting for **electors** who will cast their ballots in the electoral college. Article II, Section 1, of the Constitution outlines in detail the number and choice of electors for president and vice president. The framers of the Constitution wanted to avoid the selection of president and vice president by the excitable masses. Rather, they wished the choice to be made by a few supposedly dispassionate, reasonable men (but not women).

The Choice of Electors

Each state's electors are selected during each presidential election year. The selection is governed by state laws and by the applicable party apparatus. After the national party convention, the electors are pledged to the candidates chosen. The total number of electors today is 538, equal to 100 senators, 435 members of the House, plus 3 electors for the District of Columbia (subsequent to the Twenty-third Amendment, ratified in 1961). Each state's number of electors equals that state's number of senators (two) plus its number of representatives. The graphic in Figure 9–2 shows how the electoral votes are apportioned by state.

Elector

A person on the partisan slate that is selected early in the presidential election year according to state laws and the applicable political party apparatus. Electors cast ballots for president and vice president. The number of electors in each state is equal to that state's number of representatives in both chambers of Congress.

FIGURE 9-2

State Electoral Votes

The map of the United States shown here is distorted to show the relative weight of the states in terms of electoral votes in 2000. Considering that a candidate must win 270 electoral votes to be elected, presidential candidates plan their visits around the nation to maximize their exposure in the most important states. As vice president, Al Gore visited California numerous times in anticipation of the 2000 elections.

Source: From S. Schmidt, M. Shelley, and B. Bardes, *American Government and Politics Today*, 2004–2005 ed. (Belmont, CA: Wadsworth, 2004), pp. 295–296.

Activity 8-4

Mark the Text and Add Marginal Notes or Questions

Read the text material in Figure 8.3 and mark all information that you think is important. Remember to mark meaningful phrases. Add a few marginal notes or questions. Compare your marking to that of others in your group.

WHAT SHOULD YOU MARK?

Now that you know how to mark, the next step is figuring out what you should mark. As you read your text assignments, you probably caught yourself thinking, I wonder if I should mark this. Until you become more experienced at marking, it's better to mark a little too much rather than not enough. Remember the rule of thumb from note taking: When in doubt, write it out. The same thing applies to text marking. You also may want to follow a general rule for text marking: *If you think it might be on the test, mark it.* Of course, after the first test, you'll be able to evaluate your marking and make a more accurate decision about what to mark in the next chapter.

There is no real set of rules for what you should mark. Some students mark only what the author puts in bold or italic print. This information is important and should be marked, but it is not the only important information on the page. Headings, subheadings, main ideas, supporting details, definitions, examples, and statistics are also important (see Figure 8.4), even though they're not always identified by bold or italic print.

Mark Headings

As you read your textbook, mark the headings and subheadings. If you're highlighting, highlight them as well. If you're underlining, you may want to draw a box around the headings. Typically, when students review their marked textbooks, they read only what they've marked. It's incredible, but many students never even look at the headings or subheadings as they review. The headings contain the most important information in the text. They present the topics to which all of the other marking refers. You wouldn't think of reviewing your lecture notes without looking at the headings, would you?

FIGURE 8.4
What to Mark

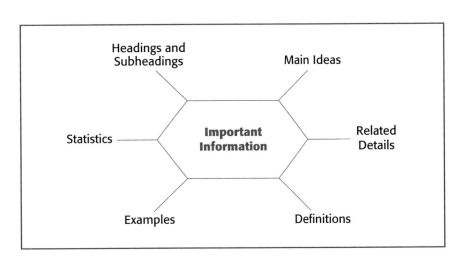

Mark Main Ideas

The second most important information to mark is the main idea statements. **Main ideas** are the general statements that the author makes about the topic. The main idea statement, or topic sentence, is generally found in the first or second sentence of a paragraph. Unfortunately, many students overlook these statements because they don't contain a specific fact or buzzword. Look back at the text selection in Activity 8-2. Which sentence in each of the paragraphs states the main idea? If you said the first sentence, you were right for paragraphs 1 and 2. You may be having a hard time finding the main idea sentence in paragraph 3. That's because paragraph 3 doesn't contain a **stated main idea.** Sometimes authors don't directly state the main ideas; they only imply them. The **implied** (unstated) **main idea** in paragraph 3 is that the oceans provide other important resources to Earth. You'll find that it doesn't take much practice to learn to pick out the main idea statements in most of your textbooks. When they are unstated, you can figure them out from the information given in the paragraph. Ask yourself: What point is the author making here? Rereading your text marking should help you identify the stated main idea or figure out the implied main idea.

Activity 8-5

Mark Main Ideas

Mark the main idea statements in the following two paragraphs from a communication textbook.

> When people withdraw, they physically or psychologically remove themselves from the conflict. People may physically withdraw by leaving the site. For instance, when Justina says, "Eduardo, I thought we agreed that you'd pay my folks back the $60 you owe them this week," Eduardo may withdraw physically by walking downstairs. Eduardo would be withdrawing psychologically if he ignores Justina and continues to read the paper. Withdrawal is an uncooperative and unassertive response to conflict because the withdrawer refuses to talk about the issue.

> Accommodating is resolving conflict by satisfying others' needs or accepting others' ideas while neglecting our own. So this approach is cooperative but unassertive. For instance, Juan has looked forward to vacationing alone with Mariana, his wife of six months. But when she says, "I think it would be fun to have mom and dad come with us, don't you?" Juan gives in and replies, "Sure, whatever you want."[2]

Activity 8-6

Identify Implied Main Ideas

The main idea sentences have been intentionally omitted from the following two paragraphs, which are a continuation of the material in Activity 8-5. After you read and

Continued

---

[2]Text material adapted from R. Verderber and K. Verderber, *Communicate!,* 11th ed. (Belmont, CA: Wadsworth, 2005), pp. 189–190.

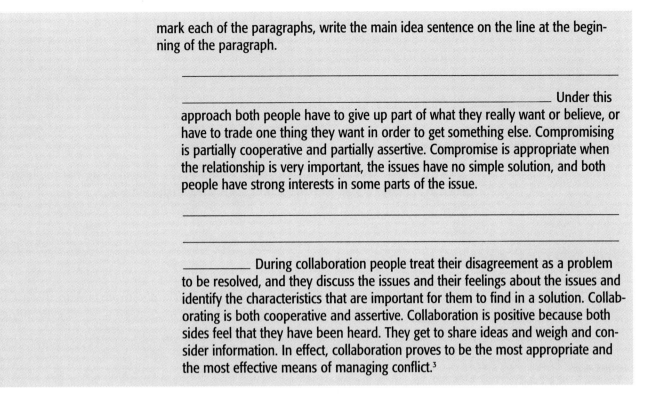

mark each of the paragraphs, write the main idea sentence on the line at the begin-ning of the paragraph.

_____

_____ Under this approach both people have to give up part of what they really want or believe, or have to trade one thing they want in order to get something else. Compromising is partially cooperative and partially assertive. Compromise is appropriate when the relationship is very important, the issues have no simple solution, and both people have strong interests in some parts of the issue.

_____

_____

_____ During collaboration people treat their disagreement as a problem to be resolved, and they discuss the issues and their feelings about the issues and identify the characteristics that are important for them to find in a solution. Collab-orating is both cooperative and assertive. Collaboration is positive because both sides feel that they have been heard. They get to share ideas and weigh and con-sider information. In effect, collaboration proves to be the most appropriate and the most effective means of managing conflict.[3]

Focus on Supporting Details

As you read and mark, you also should focus on definitions, examples, enumera-tions, facts and statistics, and signal words. Definitions are very important, and you'll need to understand what the technical terms in the chapter mean both to comprehend the text material and to answer test questions. You can highlight def-initions as you read, or you may want to copy them onto index cards so that you can begin to learn them. Put the word on the front and the definition on the back, and then practice them out loud as you would with flash cards.

Examples are included in many textbooks because they help you understand abstract theories or concepts by bringing them down to a more concrete level. Ex-amples are sometimes rather long and detailed or are set off in small print or in boxes, so students often view them as extraneous (outside or unrelated) informa-tion. However, examples can be critical to your understanding of the more abstract information in the text. You don't have to mark every word in the example; instead, mark just enough to see the connection between the example and the information to which it refers.

Lists or enumerations should always be marked. They may span several para-graphs or even several pages, but a main idea sentence will let you know what you should look for in a list. For example, the main idea sentence may state that there were three main adaptations that the vertebrates made. As you read, you should look for these adaptations so that you can mark all three.

Facts and statistics also are worth marking because they typically support the main ideas that the author is making and often end up on tests. Finally, it's impor-tant to mark signal words like *however, on the other hand,* and *but.* These **signal**

---

[3]Text material adapted from R. Verderber and K. Verderber, *Communicate!,* 11th ed. (Belmont, CA: Wadsworth, 2005), p. 192.

words or transitions indicate that the author has shifted direction from positive to negative points or vice versa. Leaving them out can result in misinterpretations during later review.

Activity 8-7

Mark Supporting Details

Mark the important information that supports each of the main ideas that you identified in Activities 8-5 and 8-6. Be sure to mark meaningful phrases.

HOW MUCH SHOULD YOU MARK?

Now that you have a good idea of what to mark, it's important to discuss how much you should mark. It may sound as though you'll need to mark everything on

FIGURE 8.5
Samples of Text Marking

Sample 1: Marking Too Little

The largest and most magnificent of all the pyramids was built under King Khufu. Constructed at Giza around 2540 B.C.E., this famous Great Pyramid covers thirteen acres, measures 756 feet at each side of its base, and stands 481 feet high. Its four sides are almost precisely oriented to the four points of the compass. The interior included a grand gallery to the burial chamber, which was built of granite with a lidless sarcophagus for the pharaoh's body. The Great Pyramid still stands as a visible symbol of the power of the Egyptian kings and the spiritual conviction that underlay Egyptian society. No pyramid built later ever matched its size or splendor.

Sample 2: Marking Too Selectively

The largest and most magnificent of all the pyramids was built under King Khufu. Constructed at Giza around 2540 B.C.E., this famous Great Pyramid covers thirteen acres, measures 756 feet at each side of its base, and stands 481 feet high. Its four sides are almost precisely oriented to the four points of the compass. The interior included a grand gallery to the burial chamber, which was built of granite with a lidless sarcophagus for the pharaoh's body. The Great Pyramid still stands as a visible symbol of the power of the Egyptian kings and the spiritual conviction that underlay Egyptian society. No pyramid built later ever matched its size or splendor.

Sample 3: Marking Meaningful Phrases

The largest and most magnificent of all the pyramids was built under King Khufu. Constructed at Giza around 2540 B.C.E., this famous Great Pyramid covers thirteen acres, measures 756 feet at each side of its base, and stands 481 feet high. Its four sides are almost precisely oriented to the four points of the compass. The interior included a grand gallery to the burial chamber, which was built of granite with a lidless sarcophagus for the pharaoh's body. The Great Pyramid still stands as a visible symbol of the power of the Egyptian kings and the spiritual conviction that underlay Egyptian society. No pyramid built later ever matched its size or splendor.

Text material from William J. Duiker and Jackson J. Spielvogel, *World History,* 4th ed. (Belmont, CA: Wadsworth, 2004), p. 19.

the page, but don't panic. Even when you mark all the important information in a section, you'll still be able to condense the material. Learning to mark the right amount of text material is critical to effective marking. You should mark enough information so that you'll be able to review for an exam without ever reading any of the unmarked text again.

Avoid Undermarking

Sometimes students don't really understand how to mark a textbook, and they end up **marking too little** of the information. As you read, it may seem like marking only the important buzzwords in the text is effective marking. However, without marking the related details, the marking lacks meaning during later review (see sample 1 in Figure 8.5). Only the key words have been marked. Read only the highlighted information. Does this marking make sense? Has this student marked all of the important information in the selection?

Another type of undermarking results from **marking too selectively.** Some students do mark meaningful phrases when they mark. However, they miss important information by trying to pick out only one or two important points in each paragraph or headed section. These students may be trying to follow rules for how much to mark; they may have heard or read that you should mark only one main point in each paragraph or that you shouldn't mark more than 20 percent of the words on a page. In sample 2 of Figure 8.5, the student marked only two pieces of information in the paragraph. Are these the only things you would have marked? Many students miss test questions, not because they don't study, but rather because their marking is too selective so they don't study *all* of the important information.

Avoid Overmarking

Overmarking can be just as bad as undermarking. If you mark everything on a page or mark whole sentences you aren't forcing yourself to think about the content of the material. Many times, overmarking is a signal that you're not reading actively. If you mark everything, you aren't actively involved in making decisions about what's important and what isn't. Marking too much also reduces your chances of reviewing the text material before the exam. If you haven't condensed the text, you may be discouraged from reviewing it because there's just too much to reread and study.

Activity 8-8

Identify Effective Marking

Read the marked selections in Figure 8.6. Which selection is well marked? Why? What's wrong with the other two selections? Which selection is most similar to the one you marked?

FIGURE 8.6
Examples of Marked Text
Selections

Sample 1   All such changes in land masses, shorelines, and oceans had a profound effect on the evolution of life. When land masses were widely spread apart, speciation and adaptive radiations proceeded separately, giving rise to diverse arrays of organisms on land and along the shores. When land masses collided, habitats were lost and the overall diversity tended to decline. Thus the mass extinction 240 million years ago at the Paleozoic–Mesozoic boundary reduced the number of species of marine animals by 96 percent. Finally, with each major shift in land masses, the climatic patterns and the direction of warm or cold ocean currents changed, and once again there were evolutionary repercussions for organisms on land and in the seas.

Sample 2   All such changes in land masses, shorelines, and oceans had a profound effect on the evolution of life. When land masses were widely spread apart, speciation and adaptive radiations proceeded separately, giving rise to diverse arrays of organisms on land and along the shores. When land masses collided, habitats were lost and the overall diversity tended to decline. Thus the mass extinction 240 million years ago at the Paleozoic–Mesozoic boundary reduced the number of species of marine animals by 96 percent. Finally, with each major shift in land masses, the climatic patterns and the direction of warm or cold ocean currents changed, and once again there were evolutionary repercussions for organisms on land and in the seas.

Sample 3   All such changes in land masses, shorelines, and oceans had a profound effect on the evolution of life. When land masses were widely spread apart, speciation and adaptive radiations proceeded separately, giving rise to diverse arrays of organisms on land and along the shores. When land masses collided, habitats were lost and the overall diversity tended to decline. Thus the mass extinction 240 million years ago at the Paleozoic–Mesozoic boundary reduced the number of species of marine animals by 96 percent. Finally, with each major shift in land masses, the climatic patterns and the direction of warm or cold ocean currents changed, and once again there were evolutionary repercussions for organisms on land and in the seas.

Activity 8-9

Mark Meaningful Phrases

Mark the following selection from a biology text. Remember to read the entire paragraph before you begin to mark. Then mark meaningful phrases.

FURTHER EVOLUTION ON A SHIFTING GEOLOGIC STAGE

During Paleozoic times, an early continent called **Gondwana** drifted southward from the tropics, across the south polar region, then northward. Other drifting land masses collided to form a tropical continent that is now called **Laurasia.** Then, near the end of the Paleozoic, Gondwana and Laurasia became massed together to form a single world continent, called **Pangea,** that extended from pole to pole. An immense world ocean covered the rest of the earth's surface; to the east of Pangea, it curved around to form the equivalent of a giant tropical bay, called the **Tethys Sea.** Pangea began to break up in the Mesozoic, and the drifting and collisions of the fragmented land masses continue today.

All such changes in land masses, shorelines, and oceans had a profound effect on the evolution of life. When land masses were widely spread apart, speciation and

Continued

adaptive radiations proceeded separately, giving rise to diverse arrays of organisms on land and along the shores. When land masses collided, habitats were lost and the overall diversity tended to decline. Thus the mass extinction 240 million years ago at the Paleozoic–Mesozoic boundary reduced the number of species of marine animals by 96 percent. Finally, with each major shift in land masses, the climatic patterns and the direction of warm or cold ocean currents changed, and once again there were evolutionary repercussions for organisms on land and in the seas.[4]

[4]Text material adapted from C. Starr and R. Taggart, *Biology: The Unity and Diversity of Life*, 9th ed. (Pacific Grove, CA: Brooks/Cole, 2001), p. 329.

MORE TIPS FOR MARKING YOUR TEXT

MARK YOUR TEXT. Many students have difficulty writing in their textbooks. After years of being told not to write in books, it's difficult to actually do it. But it's an important strategy that saves time and improves your comprehension.

AVOID THE USED-BOOK TRAP. If at all possible, buy new texts for your classes. Many students who buy used texts rely on previous highlighting or notes that already exist in the text. It's very tempting, but it leads to passive reading. If you must buy used books, search for texts with little or no marking already in them.

DON'T OVERLOOK "EXTERNAL" TEXT MATERIAL. Some important information is found outside the regular body of the text. You need to read and mark any definitions for technical terms, even if they're in the left-hand margin. Don't omit information included in charts, graphs, and other diagrams. The information under photos, in footnotes, and in boxed features is also important to your understanding of the material.

MONITOR YOUR TEXT MARKING. You need to pause every so often (at the end of a paragraph, headed section, or page) and monitor your marking. If you look back and notice that you didn't mark anything or marked everything on the page, you probably need to go back and read it again. Your marking is a good indicator of whether or not you understood the material and your level of attention to it.

RE-MARK USED TEXTBOOKS. If you're forced to purchase a used textbook, you still should do your own marking. If the text is highlighted in yellow, you could use blue. If it's underlined, you could highlight. What someone else marked may not be what your professor will test on. Would you rely on a stranger's lecture notes?

MARK MATH AND SCIENCE TEXTBOOKS. Box or highlight all formulas, as well as any problems that you want to review. Be sure you also mark the text material that explains or discusses that formula or problem. A lot of students ignore the prose material that's included in math and science texts. This material is as important as or perhaps even more important than the problems themselves.

MARK YOUR LITERATURE BOOKS. You can mark short stories, poetry, novels, and plays as you read. Instead of looking for main ideas and supporting details, look for lines that contain themes, major plot events, key information about the characters, examples of foreshadowing or irony, and so on. Marginal notes are especially effective for literary works.

PHOTOCOPY AND MARK OUTSIDE READINGS. Many professors assign reserved or library readings as part of the course material. Often one or two copies are available on reserve in the library for students to read. You may choose to read the articles and take notes on them. You could also copy them (if time on campus is tight) and highlight them as you read. Whatever you do, be sure to review the material before the exam.

HOW TO REVIEW YOUR TEXT MARKING

The most important reason for marking your textbook is to prepare it for later review. You may think if you read the material carefully and spend lots of time studying it, you shouldn't have to highlight, underline, or even take notes. For most students, however, this is not the case. Even if you were to spend hours reciting and reviewing the information in one chapter of your textbook, you probably wouldn't remember very much of that information by the time you had to take the exam. Although you'll be able to remember "learned" material longer than material you read or hear only once, you still won't remember enough of it by test time. If you mark your text as you read it, the material will be much easier to review before your exam. You can review your text material by remarking, taking notes, predicting questions, and reciting the answers to your questions.

Re-mark Your Text

One of the most common methods of reviewing for exams is to reread highlighted or underlined material. Unfortunately, most students do this in a rather passive manner. They quickly scan the lines of marked text, assuming that the information somehow will be absorbed into their memory. Think about the last time you studied for a test. How did you review the text material?

To conduct an effective review, you need to remain actively involved in your reading. This means you should re-mark your textbook as you review. By holding a marker (or pen or pencil) in your hand, you're defining your reading activity. By planning to re-mark the text material, you're forcing yourself to read actively, to make decisions about the material that you marked before. As you reread the marked selections, you can determine whether or not the information is important enough to review again. Remember, the first time you read the chapter, everything was new to you. At that time, many things may have seemed important. After having completed the chapter, worked through text questions or a study guide, and listened to the professor's lecture, you should be able to reduce the text material even more.

There are a number of ways to re-mark your text. If you used yellow highlighting when you first read the chapter, you can use a different color for re-marking. (If some of the information is already learned, you need not re-mark it.) You might also underline, checkmark, star, or even bracket the information that you want to review again. If you decide to reread your marking a third time, re-mark the text again to remain actively involved and to further condense what you need to review again. Look at the text marking from a political science text (Figure 8.7). The material that's highlighted indicates the first marking, and the underlining indicates the re-marked material. Read only the underlined material. Does it effectively represent the key information in the selection?

Activity 8-10

Re-mark Your Own Text

Choose a selection from one of your textbooks that you read and marked at least a week ago. Re-mark the text material. How did you re-mark? How much more information were you able to condense?

FIGURE 8.7
Excerpt from a Sociology
Textbook

World Poverty

One sad fact of global inequality is the growing presence and persistence of poverty in many parts of the world. There is poverty in the United States, but very few people in the United States live in the extreme levels of deprivation found in some poor countries of the world. In the United States, the poverty level is determined by the yearly income for a family of four that is considered necessary to maintain a suitable standard of living. As mentioned in Chapter 10, the official poverty line in 2000 (for a family of four) was $17,524. By this definition, 31 million Americans, or about 11 percent, were living in poverty in 2000 (Dalaker 2001). This definition of poverty in the United States identifies **relative poverty**. The households in poverty in the United States are poor compared with other Americans, but when one looks at other parts of the world, an income of $17,524 would make a family very well-off.

The United Nations (UN) measures world poverty in two ways. **Absolute poverty** is the situation in which individuals live on less than $365 a year, meaning that people at this level of poverty live on approximately $1 a day.

The UN also identifies a more severe level of poverty, which it calls **extreme poverty**. Extreme poverty is defined as the situation in which people live on less than $275 a year; that is, on less than 75 cents a day. There are 600 million people who live at or below this extreme poverty level. Many of these people are in very dire straits, and many are starving and dying.

Text material from M. L. Anderson and H. F. Taylor, *Sociology: Understanding a Diverse Society,* 3rd ed. (Belmont, CA: Wadsworth, 2004), p. 302.

Take Notes on Your Marking

Taking notes as you review your marking is an excellent way—perhaps the best way—to remain actively involved in your reading. Not only does taking notes force you to decide whether the information is important, but also it requires you to condense the information and write it down. If you put the information in your own words, you also are using higher-level thinking skills to "translate" the text material. In addition, note taking allows you to organize the information so that it's more meaningful to you. You decide what to write down and how to arrange the information so that it makes sense to you. Finally, if you take notes, you can condense the critical information in a lengthy text chapter into a few sheets of notebook paper. In Chapter 9, you'll learn many new strategies and techniques for taking notes from text material. For now though, write the heading next to the margin, skip a space, and indent slightly to list each of the details.

Predict Questions

After you finish reading and marking your text chapter, go back and review the important information by predicting and writing questions in the margin. You can use these same questions to review for exams, of course, but they will provide you with an excellent way to reinforce and learn the information before you even walk into class for the lecture or a quiz.

There are four basic steps involved in predicting questions. First, go back and reread the highlighted material for the first paragraph and identify an important point that you want to remember (see Step 1 in Figure 8.8). Next, turn it into a question and write it directly across from the information, in the margin of the textbook (see Step 2). Be sure you write questions that have stated answers in the text and not *yes* or *no* answers. Next, underline the answer to the question in your text (see Step 3). After you finish reading, go back and quiz yourself by covering the text material and reciting the answers from memory (Step 4).

The more questions that you write, the more repetition you get on the material and the more you can test your learning. It's a good idea to write both broad

FIGURE 8.8
Example of Predicted Questions

STEP 2: Write question → What are the seven characteristics of goals?

STEP 3: Underline answer →

Why should goals be self chosen?

What happens if goals are too challenging?

What factor can help you determine how challenging to make your goals?

What are moderately challenging goals?

What is another word for realistic?
What is an example of an unrealistic goal?

CHARACTERISTICS OF GOALS

To be both useful and motivating, the goals you set must have some important characteristics. Your goals should be self-chosen, moderately challenging, realistic, measurable, specific, finite, and positive. ← STEP 1: Identify information

1. **Goals should be self-chosen.** Goals that are set by your parents, teachers, or friends may not always work for you. You need to determine or choose your own goals; *you* need to decide what you want to accomplish. If you set your own goals, you will be more motivated to achieve them.

2. **Goals should be moderately challenging.** You probably were told to set high or even exceptionally high goals for yourself in college; you may have been told to "shoot for the stars" or "go for straight As." In fact, this may not be the best advice. If your goal is to achieve all As during your first semester in college, you may be disappointed. As soon as you "lose your A" in one class, you may feel that you failed to achieve your goal, and you may be tempted to give up.

One way to set moderately challenging goals is to consider what you have done in the past. Of course, everyone is different, but high school grades are fairly good predictors of college success. Why were you successful in some classes yet unsuccessful in others? You may have been more motivated, so you may have worked harder. Of course, if you didn't work very hard in high school, you can do better in college if you choose to apply yourself; study skills can make a big difference. Even so, you should set goals that are moderately challenging—goals that will require you to achieve more than you did before but will not place undue pressure on you. Goals can always be revised if you discover you can achieve more than you originally set out to accomplish.

3. **Goals should be realistic.** Think about whether your goals are attainable. It would be unrealistic to expect to get a B or better in Calculus if your math background is very weak and your high school grades in math were never higher than a C. To set realistic goals, you must carefully evaluate your chances of achieving each goal. Using the five-step approach to setting goals (discussed later in this chapter) can help you make this decision.

and narrow questions. Write a broad question for each heading or subheading and then as many specific questions as you can in the space available. If your text doesn't have wide margins, you can still use this strategy. Write the questions on a long strip of paper (about 3 inches wide), which you can line up with the top of the text page. Keep the question strip in the text on that page for later review (note the page number on each strip). You can also write each question on the front of an index card and the answer on the back (note the page number on the back, too).

You may find it helpful to use some of the innovations my students developed. You could write every other question in a different color (red then blue) and underline the answer with the same color. This helps separate your questions and their answers. You could also number each question and answer. Brittney wrote questions for her Educational Psychology course. If you look at the first sentence (see Figure 8.9), you'll notice that Brittney used part of the information that she highlighted to frame her question and then used the key information she wanted to remember as her answer. Because there was so much information in this section, Brittney felt that numbering her questions and answers would help keep the information more organized. If you have definitions or other material in the margin, you might want to put a post-it note over them and write your questions on top. That way you can lift the note and study the material underneath.

Predicting questions in the margin of your text provides you with at least three more interactions with the text material. You reread the highlighted material, think about its importance, turn it into a question, and then underline the answer. Of course, when you use the questions to quiz yourself—to check your learning— you're getting even more practice with the material. When I ask my students at the end of the semester to list the one strategy that they think has helped them the most, more than twenty-five percent list predicting questions in the margin.

Activity 8-11

Predict Quiz Questions

Read and highlight the text material in Figure 8.10, which is a continuation of the political science material that you read earlier in Figure 8.3. Predict and write questions in the margin of the text and then underline the answer to each. Compare your marking, questions, and underlined answers to others in your group. How closely did your marking match that of the others in the group? How many of your questions were the same or similar to those of the others in the group? Did you understand and remember the information better than the material that you marked in the first part of this selection in Figure 8.3? Take turns quizzing each other on the material. Did you know most of the answers to your questions?

HOW TO EVALUATE YOUR TEXT MARKING

Each time you evaluate your marking, you should consider whether you have marked the material in a meaningful way, whether you have condensed the text material, and whether the method you used was efficient and effective. There are a number of ways to evaluate how well you mark your textbook. You can test your marking before an exam and again after the exam. Each evaluation will give you more information about how well you are marking your textbook.

FIGURE 8.9
Brittney's Predicted Questions
and Answers

1. How many Americans under 18 live in poverty?

2. How is poverty level defined?

3. What developed country has highest poverty level?

4. How much higher?

5. What % of children live in poverty?

6. What was significant about poverty level in 2000?

7. How many US families lived in poverty in 2000?

8. What % of White children live in poverty?

9. What % are Hispanic American?

10. What % are African American?

11. What do we know about high-SES students?

12. When does poverty have greatest negative impact?

13. Which group is most likely to be poor?

14. Why?

15. What increases with every year children live in poverty?

16. What factors maintain the cycle of poverty?

BEING POOR

About ① one in four Americans under the age of 18 lives in poverty, defined in 2002 by the United States Department of Health and Human Services as ② an income of $18,100 for a family of four ($22,630 in Alaska and $20,820 in Hawaii). The ③ United States has the highest rate of poverty for children of all developed nations, as much as ④ five to eight times higher than other industrialized countries. And almost half of these children can be classified as living in deep poverty—in families with incomes ⑤ 50% below the poverty threshold. Recently, there seem to be improvements. In 2000, the number of families in poverty was the ⑥ lowest in 21 years—about ⑦ 6.2 million (U.S. Census Bureau, September 25, 2001).

The majority of these poor children, about ⑧ 65%, are White, because the total number of poor White families is greater than any other ethnic group. But even though the total number of poor African American and Hispanic American children is smaller than the number of poor White children, the percentages are higher. According to the 2000 United States Census, about ⑨ 21% of all Hispanic American families and ⑩ 22% of all African American families live in poverty. Compare this to an overall poverty rate of 11% for all families in the United States.

SES AND ACHIEVEMENT

There are many relationships between SES and school performance. For example, it is well documented that high-SES students of all ethnic groups show ⑪ higher average levels of achievement on test scores and stay in school longer than low-SES students (Conger, Conger, & Elder, 1997; McLoyd, 1998). Poverty ⑫ during a child's preschool years appears to have the greatest negative impact. Unfortunately, ⑬ families with young children are the most likely to be poor because ⑭ young parents have the lowest paying jobs or no jobs at all (Bronfenbrenner, McClelland, Wethington, Moen, & Ceci, 1996). And the longer the child is in poverty, the stronger the impact on achievement. For example, even when we take into account parents' education, the ⑮ chance that children will be retained in grades or placed in special education increases 2% to 3% for every year the children live in poverty (Sherman, 1994).

What are the effects of low socioeconomic status that might explain the lower school achievement of these students? Many factors maintain a cycle of poverty. ⑯ Poor health care for mother and child, limited resources, family stress, interruptions in schooling, exposure to violence, overcrowding, homelessness, discrimination, and other factors lead to school failures, low-paying jobs—and another generation born in poverty. Garcia (1991) and McLoyd (1998) describe other possible explanations. Let's take a closer look at each of them.

Text material from Anita Woolfolk, *Educational Psychology,* 9th ed. (Boston, MA: Allyn and Bacon, 2004), p. 158.

Be Sure Your Marking Makes Sense

The first way to test your marking is to see whether it makes sense. Look back at a marked page in one of your textbooks. Read only the words that you marked. Does the information make sense? Now choose a page that you marked more than two weeks ago. Do you still understand the information that you marked? Reread the entire page. Does the marking retain the meaning of the selection? If it doesn't, check to see if you marked too little (only key words) or too selectively. Repeat this activity with material that you marked a month ago. If your marking doesn't make sense or include all of the important information in the text, you won't be able to properly prepare for your exam.

FIGURE 8.10
Continuation of Political
Science Excerpt

The Electors' Commitment

If a plurality of voters in a state chooses one slate of electors, then those electors are pledged to cast their ballots on the first Monday after the second Wednesday in December in the state capital for the presidential and vice presidential candidates for the winning party.[10] The Constitution does not, however, require the electors to cast their ballots for the candidate of their party.

The ballots are counted and certified before a joint session of Congress early in January. The candidates who receive a majority of the electoral votes (270) are certified as president-elect and vice president–elect. According to the Constitution, if

[10]In Maine and Nebraska, electoral votes are based on congressional districts. Each district chooses one elector. The remaining two electors are chosen statewide.

FIGURE 9-3
How Presidents and
Vice Presidents Are Chosen

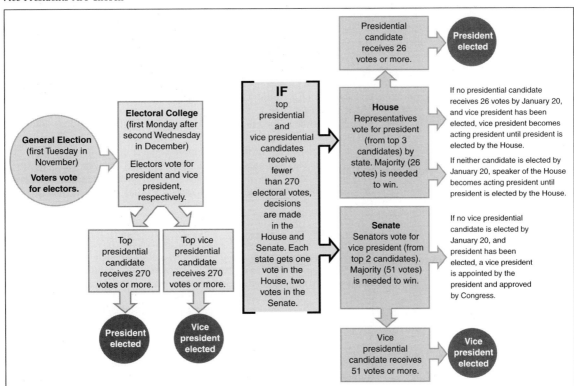

SOURCE: Adapted from Michael J. Glennon, *When No Majority Rules: The Electoral College and Presidential Succession* (Washington, D.C.: Congressional Quarterly Press, 1993), p. 20.

continued

FIGURE 8.10 (continued)
Continuation of Political
Science Excerpt

no candidate receives a majority of the electoral votes, the election of the president is decided in the House from among the candidates with the three highest number of votes (decided by a plurality of each state delegation), each state having one vote. The selection of the vice president is determined by the Senate in a choice between the two highest candidates, each senator having one vote. Congress was required to choose the president and vice president in 1801 (Thomas Jefferson and Aaron Burr), and the House chose the president in 1825 (John Quincy Adams). The entire process is outlined in Figure 9–3.

It is possible for a candidate to become president without obtaining a majority of the popular vote. There have been numerous minority presidents in our history, including Abraham Lincoln, Woodrow Wilson, Harry Truman, John F. Kennedy, Richard Nixon (in 1968), and Bill Clinton. Such an event can always occur when there are third-party candidates.

Perhaps more distressing is the possibility of a candidate's being elected when the opposing candidate receives a larger share of the popular vote. This occurred on three occasions—in the elections of John Quincy Adams in 1824, Rutherford B. Hayes in 1876, and Benjamin Harrison in 1888, all of whom won elections without obtaining a plurality of the popular vote.

Criticisms of the Electoral College

Besides the possibility of a candidate's becoming president even though his or her major opponent obtains more popular votes, there are other complaints about the electoral college. The idea of the Constitution's framers was to have electors use their own discretion to decide who would make the best president. But electors no longer perform the selecting function envisioned by the founders, because they are committed to the candidate who has a plurality of popular votes in their state in the general election.[11]

One can also argue that the current system, which gives all of the electoral votes to the candidate who has a statewide plurality, is unfair to other candidates and their supporters. The current system of voting also means that presidential campaigning will be concentrated in those states that have the largest number of electoral votes and in those states in which the outcome is likely to be close. All of the other states generally get second-class treatment during the presidential campaign.

It can also be argued that there is something of a less-populous-state bias in the electoral college, because including Senate seats in the electoral vote total partly offsets the edge of the more populous states in the House. A state such as Alaska (with two senators and one representative) gets an electoral vote for roughly each 209,644 people (based on the 2000 census), whereas Iowa gets one vote for each 418,846 people, and New York has a vote for every 613,064 inhabitants.

Proposed Reforms

Many proposals for reform of the electoral college system have been advanced particularly after the turmoil resulting from the 2000 elections. The most obvious is to get rid of it completely and simply allow candidates to be elected on a popular-vote basis; in other words, have a direct election, by the people, for president and vice president. Because abolishing the electoral college would require a constitutional amendment, however, the chances of electing the president by a direct vote are remote.

The major parties are not in favor of eliminating the electoral college, fearing that it would give minor parties a more influential role. Also, less populous states are not in favor of direct election of the president, because they feel they would be overwhelmed by the large urban vote.

Text material adapted from S. Schmidt, M. Shelley, and B. Bardes, *American Government and Politics Today,* 2004-2005 ed. (Belmont, CA: Wadsworth, 2004), pp. 296–298.

Get Feedback on Your Marking

Another way to test your marking is to compare your marked section of text to a classmate's marking. Read your classmate's marked page. How does it compare to yours? Does it make more sense than yours? If it does, compare the marked information. You may find that your classmate included more information or was better able to create meaningful phrases than you were. Talk about why each of you chose to include or leave out specific information or words.

You can also evaluate your text marking by talking to your professor or to someone in your campus learning or tutoring center. Take your textbook with you and ask whether you're picking out the important information in the selection. If you aren't hitting the right material, ask your professor or learning center staff member to mark a portion of a page of text for you. Then you mark a section, while that person observes. Stop and ask questions about anything you aren't sure about. If you're just getting started marking a textbook, this additional feedback can let you know whether you're using effective strategies.

Test Your Marking After an Exam

You also can test your marking after an exam using the **T Method.** That's often the time that students appreciate how much they condensed the material for review. Take your textbook with you when you go to take your exam. As soon as the exam is over, rush out into the hall, find a quiet corner, and sit down. Turn to any chapter that was heavily tested upon. Begin to reread that chapter. Read the unmarked and the marked areas of the page. Every time you come across something that was on the test, put a "T" in the margin of your book.

After you read through about a half of the chapter, stop and look at where the Ts appear. How many of them are in highlighted or marked areas? How many are in unmarked areas? If all the Ts are in the marked areas, you did a good job of marking. You were able to recognize as important the same pieces of information that the professor thought were important. By marking those points, you identified them for later review. If, on the other hand, a number of your Ts are in unmarked areas, you probably marked too little or too selectively as you read the chapter. Because those pieces of information were unmarked, you probably didn't review them before the test. Were you able to answer those questions correctly on the test?

Activity 8-12

Practice Marking Text Material

Read and mark the text selection in Figure 8.11, which is an excerpt from a psychology textbook. Compare your marking to that of the other members of your group. Did you include the key information? Did you use meaningful phrases? Did you condense the selection to its essence? What changes do you plan to make? Use index cards or strips of paper to predict questions about the key information.

FIGURE 8.11
Excerpt from a Psychology
Textbook

Motivational Theories and Concepts

PREVIEW QUESTIONS

● What is the distinction between drive and incentive theories of motivation?

● How do evolutionary theories explain various motives?

● What are the two major categories of human motives?

Motives are the needs, wants, interests, and desires that propel people in certain directions. In short, *motivation* **involves goal-directed behavior**. There are a number of theoretical approaches to motivation. Let's look at some of these theories and the concepts they employ.

Drive Theories

Many theories view motivational forces in terms of *drives*. The drive concept appears in a diverse array of theories that otherwise have little in common, such as psychoanalytic (Freud, 1915) and behaviorist formulations (Hull, 1943). This approach to understanding motivation was explored most fully by Clark Hull in the 1940s and 1950s.

Hull's concept of drive was derived from Walter Cannon's (1932) observation that organisms seek to maintain *homeostasis,* **a state of physiological equilibrium or stability**. The body maintains homeostasis in various ways. For example, human body temperature normally fluctuates around 98.6 degrees Fahrenheit (see Figure 10.1). If your body temperature rises or drops noticeably, automatic responses occur: If your temperature goes up, you'll perspire; if you temperature goes down, you'll shiver. These reactions are designed to move your temperature back toward 98.6 degrees. Thus, your body reacts to many disturbances in physiological stability by trying to restore equilibrium.

Drive theories apply the concept of homeostasis to behavior. **A** *drive* **is an internal state of tension that motivates an organism to engage in activities that should reduce this tension.** These unpleasant states of tension are viewed as disruptions of the preferred equilibrium. According to drive theories, when individuals experience a drive, they're motivated to pursue actions that will lead to *drive reduction*. For example, the hunger motive has usually been conceptualized as a drive system. If you go without food for a while, you begin to experience some discomfort. This internal tension (the drive) motivates you to obtain food. Eating reduces the drive and restores physiological equilibrium.

Drive theories have been very influential, and the drive concept continues to be widely used in modern psychology. *However, drive theories cannot explain all motivation.* Homeostasis appears irrelevant to some human motives, such as a "thirst for knowledge." Also, motivation may exist without drive arousal. This point is easy to illustrate. Think of all the times that you've eaten when you weren't the least bit hungry. You're driving or walking home from class, amply filled by a solid lunch, when an ice cream parlor beckons seductively. You stop in and have a couple of scoops of your favorite flavor. Not only are you motivated to eat in the absence of internal tension, you may cause yourself some internal tension—from overeating. Because drive theories assume that people always try to reduce internal tension, they can't explain this behavior very well. Incentive theories, which represent a different approach to motivation, can account for this behavior more readily.

Incentive Theories

Incentive theories propose that external stimuli regulate motivational states (Bolles, 1975; McClelland, 1975; Skinner, 1953). **An** *incentive* **is an external goal that has the capacity to motivate behavior.** Ice cream, a juicy steak, a monetary prize, approval from friends, an A on an exam, and a promotion at work are all incentives. Some of these incentives may reduce drives, but others may not.

Drive and incentive models of motivation are often contrasted as *push versus pull* theories. Drive theories emphasize how *internal* states of tension push people in certain directions. Incentive theories emphasize how *external* stimuli *pull* people in certain directions. According to drive theories, the source of motivation lies *within* the organism. According to incentive theories, the source of motivation lies *outside* the organism, in the environment. This means that incentive models don't operate according to the principle of homeostasis, which hinges on internal changes in the organism. Thus, in comparison to drive theories, incentive theories emphasize environmental factors and downplay the biological bases of human motivation.

As you're painfully aware, people can't always obtain the goals they desire, such as good grades or choice promotions. *Expectancy-value models* of motivation are incentive theories that take this reality

Figure 10.1

Temperature regulation as an example of homeostasis. The regulation of body temperature provides a simple example of how organisms often seek to maintain homeostasis, or a state of physiological equilibrium. When your temperature moves out of an acceptable range, automatic bodily reactions (such as sweating or shivering) occur that help restore equilibrium. Of course, these automatic reactions may not be sufficient by themselves, so you may have to take other actions (such as turning a furnace up or down) to bring your body temperature back into its comfort zone.

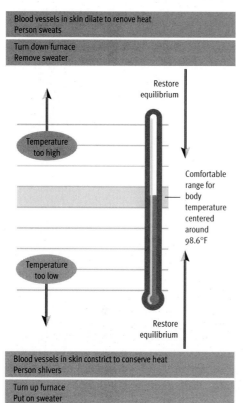

FIGURE 8.11 (continued)
Excerpt from a Psychology
Textbook

into account (Atkinson & Birch, 1978). According to expectancy-value models, one's motivation to pursue a particular course of action will depend on two factors: (1) *expectancy* about one's chances of attaining the incentive and (2) the *value* of the desired incentive. Thus, your motivation to pursue a promotion at work will depend on your estimate of the likelihood that you can snare the promotion (expectancy) and on how appealing the promotions is to you (value).

Evolutionary Theories

Psychologists who take an evolutionary perspective assert that human motives and those of other species are the products of evolution, just as anatomical characteristics are. They argue that natural selection favors behaviors that maximize reproductive success—that is, passing on genes to the next generation. Thus, they explain motives such as affiliation, achievement, dominance, aggression, and sex drive in terms of their adaptive value. If dominance is a crucial motive for a species, they say, it's because dominance provides a reproductive or survival advantage.

Evolutionary analyses of motivation are based on the premise that motives can best be understood in terms of the adaptive problems they have solved over the course of human history. For example, the need for dominance is thought to be greater in men than women because it could facilitate males' reproductive success in a variety of ways including (1) females may prefer mating with dominant males, (2) dominant males may poach females from subordinate males, (3) dominant males may intimidate male rivals in competition for sexual access, and (4) dominant males may acquire more material resources, which may increase mating opportunities (Buss, 1999). Consider, also, the *affiliation motive,* or need for belongingness. As we will discuss later, the adaptive benefits of affiliation for our ancestors probably included help with offspring, collaboration in hunting or defense, opportunities for sexual interaction, and so forth (Baumeister & Leary, 1995). David Buss (1995) points out that it is not by accident that achievement, power (dominance), and intimacy are among the most heavily studied social motives, as the satisfaction of each of these motives is likely to affect one's reproductive success.

The Range and Diversity of Human Motives

Motivational theorists of all persuasions agree on one point: Humans display an enormous diversity of motives. Most theories (evolutionary theories being a notable exception) distinguish between *biological motives* that originate in bodily needs, such as hunger, and *social motives* that originate in social experiences, such as the need for achievement.

People have a limited number of biological needs. According to K. B. Madsen (1968, 1973), most theories identify 10 to 15 such needs, some of which are listed on the left side of Figure 10.2 on the next page. As you can see, most biological motives reflect needs that are essential to survival, such as the needs for food, water, and maintenance of body temperature within an acceptable range.

People all share the same biological motives, but their social motives vary depending on their experiences. For example, we all need to eat, but not everyone acquires a need for orderliness. Although people have a limited number of biological motives, they can acquire an unlimited number of social motives through learning and socialization. Some examples of social motives—from an influential list compiled by Henry Murray (1938)—are shown on the right side of figure 10.2. He theorized that most people have needs for achievement, autonomy, affiliation, dominance, exhibition, and order, among other things. Of course, the strength of these motives varies from person to person, depending on personal history.

Although the distinction between biological and social needs is not absolute, this dichotomy allows us to impose some organization on the diverse motives seen in human behavior. Given the range and diversity of human motives, we can examine only a handful in depth. To a large degree, our choices reflect the motives psychologists have studied the most. Specifically, we'll draw two examples each from the two broad classes of human needs, biological and social. We'll focus on hunger and sexual motivation to show how researchers have dissected biological needs. Then we'll examine affiliation and achievement to illustrate how psychologists have analyzed social motives.

Figure 10.2

The diversity of human motives. People are motivated by a wide range of needs, which can be divided into two broad classes: biological motives and social motives. The list on the left (adapted from Madsen, 1973) shows some important biological motives in humans. The list on the right (adapted from Murray, 1938) provides examples of prominent social motives in humans. The distinction between biological and social motives is not absolute.

Examples of Biological Motives in Humans	Examples of Social Motives in Humans
Hunger motive	Achievement motive (need to excel)
Thirst motive	Affiliation motive (need for social bonds)
Sex motive	Autonomy motive (need for independence)
Temperature motive (need for appropriate body temperature)	Nurturance motive (need to nourish and protect others)
Excretory motive (need to eliminate bodily wastes)	Dominance motive (need to influence or control others)
Sleep and rest motive	Exhibition motive (need to make an impression on others)
Activity motive (need for optimal level of stimulation and arousal)	Order motive (need for orderliness, tidiness, organization)
Aggression motive	Play motive (need for fun, relaxation, amusement)

Text material from Wayne Weiten, *Psychology: Themes and Variations,* 6th ed. (Belmont, CA: Wadsworth, 2004), pp. 382–384.

Activity 8-13

Evaluate After an Exam

After your next exam, use the T Method to evaluate your marking. Write a paragraph explaining what you found. What do you plan to do differently the next time?

Activity 8-14

Where Are You Now?

Now that you have completed Chapter 8, take a few minutes to repeat the "Where Are You Now?" activity, located on the *College Study Skills* Web site. What changes did you make as a result of reading this chapter? How are you planning to apply what you've learned in this chapter?

SUMMARY

Marking your textbook increases your comprehension, your understanding, of the material because it promotes active reading. Because many students don't really know how to mark their textbooks, they tend to mark too little, too selectively, or mark almost everything. Strategic text marking involves thinking about what's important, deciding what to mark, and then using a simple method to identify that information. Reading to the end of the paragraph before you begin to highlight, underline, or take marginal notes will help you mark more efficiently and effectively. Avoid complex marking systems; you may find that you spend more time thinking about how to mark than about what you are reading and marking. Marking your text also allows you to condense the material for later review. If you predict questions in the margin, you'll improve your comprehension and be able to monitor your learning. Mark meaningful phrases and include main ideas as well as supporting details (much as you do when you take lecture notes). Learning how much to mark takes time and practice, so monitor your text marking after your first exam. If you missed a lot of questions because you never even marked the appropriate material, you may need to mark more information. Re-marking your text, taking notes, and predicting questions are just a few ways to stay actively involved as you review your text marking.

REVIEW QUESTIONS

Terms You Should Know: Make a flash card for each term.

Complex marking systems	Marginal notes	Signal words
Highlighting	Marking too little	Stated main ideas
Implied main ideas	Marking too selectively	T Method
Linking	Meaningful phrases	Underlining
Main Ideas	Overmarking	Undermarking

Completion: Fill in the blank to complete each of the following statements.

1. You should read to the end of the _____ before you begin marking your text.

2. Complex marking systems can interfere with your _____.

3. One way to review your text marking is to _____ questions in the margin of your text.

4. Marking only one sentence per paragraph is referred to as marking too _____.

5. When you are marking your text, you should read, _____, _____, and then mark.

Multiple Choice: Circle the letter of the best answer for each of the following questions. Be sure to underline key words and eliminate wrong answers.

6. _____ main ideas are not directly stated in the text.
   A. Applied
   B. Implied
   C. Comprehensive
   D. Critical

7. _____ _____ help(s) you summarize the key information in your text.
   A. Marginal notes
   B. Underlining words
   C. Meaningful phrases
   D. T Method

Short Answer–Essay: On a separate sheet, answer each of the following questions.

8. What are the four main reasons you should mark your text?

9. Why do some students have difficulty marking their textbooks? What should they do differently?

10. How should students evaluate their text marking?

"In my study skills class, we had to make a map of something that we were studying in another class. At the time, I was studying psychoactive drugs in psychology class, so I decided to make a map of the drugs. I am now studying psychoactive drugs in social problems, and I can still remember that whole map and how I set it up. I used the same map to review for the social problems test."

Amy Shaulis

ORGANIZING TEXT INFORMATION

In this chapter you will learn more about:

- Why you need to organize text information
- When to take text notes
- Three methods for taking text notes
- How to review your text notes

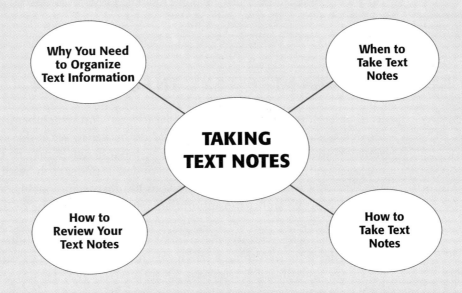

Activity 9-1

Where Are You Now?

Take a few minutes to answer *yes* or *no* to the following questions.

	YES	NO
1. Do you take notes on textbook material after you've highlighted the chapter or section?	_____	_____
2. Do you take text notes when you read the chapter for the first time?	_____	_____
3 Do you read the whole paragraph before you begin to take notes?	_____	_____
4. Do you evaluate your text notes after an exam?	_____	_____
5. Do you usually copy information from the text in the same wording that the author used in the book?	_____	_____
6. Do you recite your text notes when you review for an exam?	_____	_____
7. Do you create concept maps when you take notes on the textbook material?	_____	_____
8. Are your text notes a good summary of the text material?	_____	_____
9. Do you tend to write down only key words when you take notes?	_____	_____
10. Do you create headings and/or subheadings in your notes to better organize the information?	_____	_____

Total Points   _____

Give yourself 1 point for each *yes* answer to questions 1, 3, 4, 6, 7, and 8 and 1 point for each *no* answer to questions 2, 5, 9, and 10. Now total up your points. A low score indicates that you need some help in taking notes on text material. A high score indicates that you are already using many good note-taking strategies.

WHY YOU NEED TO ORGANIZE TEXT INFORMATION

In Chapter 4, you learned that it's easier to learn and remember information when it's well organized. Have you found that it's harder to recall the information from your text than your lecture notes? One of the differences may be that your lecture notes are well organized with a short list of details under each heading. Look back at a recent set of your lecture notes. Do your headings stand out? Did you group all of the related details under the appropriate headings (this is one of the major reasons for editing your notes). Do you take notes when you read your textbooks? You've probably discovered already that a lot of your text material is not as well organized as you'd like it to be. Although taking text notes is more time consuming than highlighting or underlining, it has many advantages, too. When you write out the text information, you have an opportunity to change it—to act on it. You can condense it, organize it, put it in your own words, and add other information to it. This helps increase your comprehension and prepares your text for later review. For a list of ways that taking text notes is better than highlighting see Figure 9.1. Research studies have found that taking notes on difficult material is helpful because you're forced to organize the information in a way that makes sense to you. That helps you understand the material you're reading, learn it, and recall it during quizzes and exams.

Some Texts Lack Subheadings

Take a look at some of your own textbooks. Are there any long selections of material with only a single heading? Are they a page long, two pages long? Even though it's only about a page long, the text excerpt in Figure 9.2 is a good example. Take a few minutes and read through it. You may have noticed that there are no subheadings in this section to separate and organize all of the information about asteroids. Without subheadings, you might find yourself confused by the information presented in the section. All of the details seem to blur together. Can you recall the specific characteristics of each type of asteroid? Can you even remember the different shapes of asteroids? Do you know which example goes with which shape? Although highlighting the information would help you condense it, it can't reorganize the details. **Headings** let you know what a section of text is about. They also serve as cues to help you recall the information (the details) later when you're preparing for quizzes and exams. However, if you have only one heading to cue twenty or thirty details, you won't be able to remember them all. **Subheadings** are the smaller headings that divide the information in a headed section into smaller chunks. What subheadings could this author have included that would have better organized the material? Take another look at the section and ask yourself what common information is provided about asteroids. You may have said color or shape. What other subheadings would you include? You also might have said Gaspra and Ida. Did you? You could organize this information by the names of the asteroids or by the characteristics of them. Either method would have been fine. One of the advantages of taking text notes is that you can organize the material your way—the way that makes the most sense to you.

FIGURE 9.1
Why Taking Text Notes Is Better Than Highlighting

- You can organize the material your way—a way that makes sense to you

- You can create headings or subheadings to group and organize details

- You can put the information in your own words to make it more meaningful

- You can show how information from one section is connected to information in another section of the chapter

- You can condense the material more

- You can connect the new information to your prior knowledge

- You can generate examples from your own experiences to make the information more relevant and memorable

- You are writing—an active strategy that aids memory

- You build cues that lead to better retrieval

FIGURE 9.2

Text Excerpt on Asteroids

Properties of Asteroids Asteroids are too small to be resolved by Earth-based telescopes, so we see no details of their shape or composition. Yet astronomers have learned a surprising amount about these little worlds, and spacecraft are giving us a few close-ups.

From the infrared radiation emitted by asteroids, astronomers can calculate their sizes. Ceres, the largest, is about 30 percent the diameter of our moon, and Pallas, next largest, is only 15 percent the diameter of the moon. Most are much smaller.

Because the brightness of the typical asteroid varies over periods of hours, astronomers concluded that most asteroids are not spherical. As their irregular shapes rotate, they reflect varying amounts of sunlight and their brightness varies. Presumably, most are irregularly shaped worlds with too little gravity to pull themselves into a spherical form.

Recent observations have confirmed that asteroids are irregular in shape. The Galileo spacecraft on its way to Jupiter passed through the asteroid belt twice as it looped through the inner solar system. By very careful planning, controllers directed Galileo to pass only 16,000 km from the asteroid Gaspra in late 1990. Galileo found the asteroid an oblong world 20 by 12 by 11 km covered by a layer of shattered rock soil about a meter deep and marked by numerous craters (see, Figure 16-11). Again in August 1993, Galileo passed only 3500 km from the asteroid Ida and returned photos of an irregularly shaped, cratered world 52 km long (Figure 19-6a). In fact, the photos reveal that Ida is orbited by a 1.5-km diameter moon, apparently the product of an ancient collision.

Earth-based radar confirms the irregular shape of asteroids. Asteroid Castalia (Figure 19-6b) was imaged repeatedly at 9-minute intervals as it passed near Earth, and the radar images clearly show a dumbbell shape tumbling through space. The asteroid Toutatis (Figure 19-6c) has also been imaged by radar, and it appears to be two objects 4 and 2.5 km in diameter held together by their weak gravity like two peanuts. Some experts now suspect that many asteroids are binary objects, two bodies that collided and are now loosely bonded together.

Not all asteroids lie in the asteroid belt. Spacewatch, a program searching for small asteroids passing near Earth, has found about 100 times more near-Earth asteroids than astronomers had expected. Limited to objects smaller than 100 meters in diameter, the study suggests that as many as 50 such asteroids pass within the moon's orbit each day. The danger of impacts by such objects is small but significant, and this has even led to a hearing before Congress (The Threat of Large Earth-Orbit-Crossing Asteroids, March 24, 1993). The actual danger seems small, and astronomers are more interested in the origin of these bodies. The best guess is that they are fragments from the main asteroid belt.

The color and spectra of asteroids help us understand their composition. From their bright, reddish colors astronomers classify some asteroids, including Gaspra, as S types (Figure 19-7). They may be silicates mixed with metals, or they may resemble chondrites. C-type asteroids are very dark—about as bright as a lump of coal. They appear to be carbonaceous. M-type asteroids, bright but not red, appear to be mostly iron-nickel alloys. S types are common in the inner belt, and C types are common in the outer belt. That distribution is a clue to the origin of asteroids.

From Michael A. Seeds, *Horizons: Exploring the Universe* (Belmont, CA: Wadsworth, 1995).

Activity 9-2

Create Subheadings to Organize Text Information

Now go back to the text material on asteroids in Figure 9.2 and jot down a list of subheadings that you would use to better organize the information. Compare your list of subheadings with the lists of the other members of your group. Did you include the same subheadings? Work together to generate a list of subheadings that you all agree on.

Some Texts Include Details Under Multiple Headings

Did you recently read a chapter that included details on the same topic spread across a number of headed sections? Would you find it confusing to read more about asteroids five pages later when you were reading a section on meteorites? Would you remember that those details related back to the information on asteroids, or would you confuse them with the details on meteorites on your exam? Many textbook authors refer back to earlier topics in later headed sections to make comparisons or show contrasts. Although this may help you better understand the similarities and differences between the topics, it can lead to confusion (the heading doesn't serve well as a cue for the details that refer to the other topic). Take a few minutes and read a portion of the text material in Figure 9.3, which is from a World History text. The author discussed details on the Old Kingdom and the Middle Kingdom, often mixing them in the same section (information on the New Kingdom is described five pages later, along with more information about the Old and Middle Kingdoms). When I asked my students to take notes on that section, some of them just copied the details down in the same order in which they were presented, mixing the details about the Old Kingdom and the Middle Kingdom within the same section of their notes. Others organized the material by creating the subheadings, "Old Kingdom" and "Middle Kingdom" and grouping the appropriate details under each.

Activity 9-3

Highlight to Better Organize the Details

Although I don't usually encourage students to use multiple colors when highlighting, here's a case where it will help you see how to organize the text material. Use one color to mark all of the details that relate to the Old Kingdom and another color for details related to the Middle Kingdom. Did you find that you had to use the two colors across headed sections? Did this help you sort out the information and identify the details related to each heading?

Activity 9-4

Take Notes to Organize the Details

Go back to the text material you marked in Activity 9-3 and take notes. Use the headings *Old Kingdom* and *Middle Kingdom* and list the details that you highlighted under the appropriate headings.

Some Material Is Better Organized with Graphic Displays

Some text material is easier to remember when it's organized by creating graphic displays. Many authors include charts, graphs, and concept maps of one form or another to help students see how information is organized. You've probably seen them in your science, history, and economics texts. However, they don't appear for all of the material you need to learn. Although the text material on Piaget's Stage Theory (see Figure 9.4) does include a graphic that describes some of the features of each of the four stages, it doesn't include all of the details about each stage. Read the sections

FIGURE 9.3

Excerpt from a History Textbook

The Old and Middle Kingdoms

The basic framework for the study of Egyptian history was provided by Manetho, an Egyptian priest and historian who lived in the early third century B.C.E. He divided Egyptian history into thirty-one dynasties of kings. Based on Manetho and other king lists, modern historians have divided Egyptian history into three major periods, known as the Old Kingdom, the Middle Kingdom, and the New Kingdom. These were periods of long-term stability characterized by strong monarchical authority, competent bureaucracy, freedom from invasion, much construction of temples and pyramids, and considerable intellectual and cultural activity. But between the periods of stability were times of political chaos known as the Intermediate periods, which were characterized by weak political structures and rivalry for leadership, invasions, a decline in building activity, and a restructuring of society.

According to the Egyptians' own tradition, their land consisted initially of numerous populated areas ruled by tribal chieftains. Around 3100 B.C.E., the first Egyptian royal dynasty, under a king called Menes, united both Upper and Lower Egypt into a single kingdom. Henceforth, the king would be called "King of Upper and King of Lower Egypt," and the royal crown would be a double diadem, signifying the unification of all Egypt. Just as the Nile served to unite Upper and Lower Egypt physically, kingship served to unite the two areas politically.

The Old Kingdom encompassed the third through sixth dynasties of Egyptian kings, lasting from around 2700 to 2200 B.C.E. It was an age of prosperity and splendor, made visible in the construction of the greatest and largest pyramids in Egypt's history. The capital of the Old Kingdom was located at Memphis, south of the delta.

Kingship was a divine institution in ancient Egypt and formed part of a universal cosmic scheme. "What is the king of Upper and Lower Egypt? He is a god by whose dealings one lives, the father and mother of all men, alone by himself, without an equal."[4] In obeying their king, subjects helped to maintain the cosmic order. A breakdown in royal power could only mean that citizens were offending divinity and weakening the universal structure. Among the various titles of Egyptian kings, that of pharaoh (originally meaning "great house" or "palace") eventually came to be the most common.

Although they possessed absolute power, Egyptian kings were not supposed to rule arbitrarily, but according to set principles. The chief principle was called Ma'at, a spiritual precept that conveyed the ideas of truth and justice but especially right order and harmony. To ancient Egyptians, this fundamental order and harmony had existed throughout the universe since the beginning of time. Pharaohs were the divine instruments who maintained it and were themselves subject to it.

Despite the theory of divine order, the Old Kingdom eventually collapsed, ushering in a period of chaos. Finally,

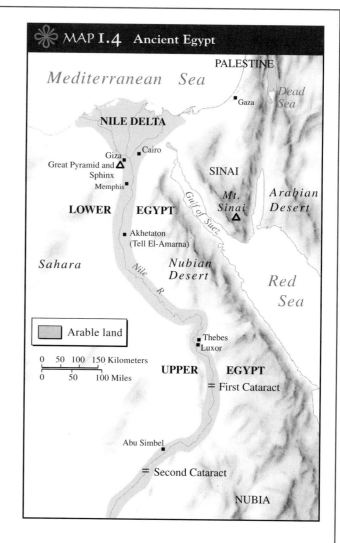

MAP 1.4 Ancient Egypt

a new royal dynasty managed to pacify all Egypt and inaugurated the Middle Kingdom, a new period of stability lasting from c. 2050 to 1652 B.C.E. Egyptians later portrayed the Middle Kingdom as a golden age, a clear indication of its stability. Several factors contributed to its vitality. The nome structure was reorganized. The boundaries of each nome were now settled precisely, and the obligations of the nomes to the state were clearly delineated. Nomarchs were confirmed as hereditary officeholders but with the understanding that their duties must be performed faithfully. These included the collection of taxes for the state and the recruitment of labor forces for royal projects, such as stone quarrying.

The Middle Kingdom was characterized by a new concern of the pharaohs for the people. In the Old Kingdom, the pharaoh had been viewed as an inaccessible god-king. Now he was portrayed as the shepherd of his people with the responsibility to build public works and provide for the public welfare. As one pharaoh expressed it: "He [a particular god] created me as one who should do that which he had done, and to carry out that which he commanded

FIGURE 9.3 (continued)
Excerpt from a History Textbook

should be done. He appointed me herdsman of this land, for he knew who would keep it in order for him."[5]

Society and Economy in Ancient Egypt

Egyptian society had a simple structure in the Old and Middle Kingdoms; basically, it was organized along hierarchical lines with the god-king at the top. The king was surrounded by an upper class of nobles and priests who participated in the elaborate rituals of life that surrounded the pharaoh. This ruling class ran the government and managed its own landed estates, which provided much of its wealth.

Below the upper classes were merchants and artisans. Within Egypt, merchants engaged in an active trade up and down the Nile as well as in town and village markets. Some merchants also engaged in international trade; they were sent by the king to Crete and Syria, where they obtained wood and other products. Expeditions traveled into Nubia for ivory and down the Red Sea to Punt for incense and spices. Egyptian artisans exhibited unusually high standards of artisanship and physical beauty while producing an incredible variety of goods: stone dishes; beautifully painted boxes made of clay; wooden furniture; gold, silver, and copper tools and containers; paper and rope made of papyrus; and linen clothes.

By far the largest number of people in Egypt simply worked the land. In theory, the king owned all the land but granted out portions of it to his subjects. Large sections were in the possession of nobles and the temple

CHRONOLOGY
THE EGYPTIANS

Early Dynastic Period (Dynasties 1–2)	c. 3100–2700 B.C.E.
Old Kingdom (Dynasties 3–6)	c. 2700–2200 B.C.E.
First Intermediate Period (Dynasties 7–10)	c. 2200–2050 B.C.E.
Middle Kingdom (Dynasties 11–12)	c. 2050–1652 B.C.E.
Second Intermediate Period (Dynasties 13–17)	c. 1652–1567 B.C.E.
New Kingdom (Dynasties 18–20)	c. 1567–1085 B.C.E.
Post-Empire (Dynasties 21–31)	c. 1085–30 B.C.E.

complexes. Moreover, although free farmers who owned their own land had once existed, by the end of the Old Kingdom, this group had disappeared. Most of the lower classes were serfs, or common people bound to the land, who cultivated the estates. They paid taxes in the form of crops to the king, nobles, and priests, lived in small villages or towns, and provided military service and forced labor for building projects.

Adapted from William J. Duiker, and Jackson J. Spielvogel, *World History,* 3rd ed. (Belmont, CA: West/Wadsworth, 2001), pp. 16–19.
Note: In the next edition of the text, the authors created subheadings for the Old, Middle, and New Kingdoms.

on the four periods and think about how you might organize the details for each. Would you just list them? Would you add them to the graphic display in the text? Later in this chapter, you'll learn to create maps and charts to organize and separate closely related details and will have an opportunity to create your own system for organizing this information. You'll find that when you do create your own organizational system for the text material, you'll be able to learn and remember it better.

Activity 9-5
List the Details for Closely Related Material

Read and highlight the important details for each of Piaget's four stages of cognitive development in Figure 9.4. Compare your marking with that of the other members of

Continued

Activity 9-5

List the Details for Closely Related Material (continued)

your group. Then list the details under each of the headings. Later in the chapter, you'll have an opportunity to organize the details using graphic displays so you can decide which method works best for you.

FIGURE 9.4

Text Excerpt on Stage Theory

The Growth of Thought: Cognitive Development

Cognitive development **refers to transitions in youngsters' patterns of thinking, including reasoning, remembering, and problem solving.** The investigation of cognitive development was dominated in most of the second half of the 20th century by the theory of Jean Piaget (Kessen, 1996). Much of our discussion of cognitive development is devoted to Piaget's theory and the research it generated, although we'll also delve into other approaches to cognitive development.

Overview of Piaget's Stage Theory

Jean Piaget (1929, 1952, 1983) was an interdisciplinary scholar whose own cognitive development was exceptionally rapid. In his early 20s, after he had earned a doctorate in natural science and published a novel, Piaget's interest turned to psychology. He met Theodore Simon, who had collaborated with Alfred Binet in devising the first useful intelligence tests (see Chapter 9). Working in Simon's Paris laboratory, Piaget administered intelligence tests to many children to develop better test norms. In doing this testing, Piaget became intrigued by the reasoning underlying the children's *wrong* answers. He decided that measuring children's intelligence was less interesting than studying how children *use* their intelligence. In 1921 he moved to Geneva, where he spent the rest of his life studying cognitive development. Many of his ideas were based on insights gleaned from careful observations of his own three children during their infancy.

Like Erikson's theory, Piaget's model is a *stage theory* of development. Piaget proposed that youngsters progress through four major stages of cognitive development, which are characterized by fundamentally different thought processes: (1) the *sensorimotor period* (birth to age 2), (2) the *preoperational period* (ages 2 to 7), (3) the *concrete operational period* (ages 7 to 11), and (4) the *formal operational period* (age 11 onward). Figure 11.11 provides an overview of each of these periods. Piaget regarded his age norms as approximations and acknowledged that transitional ages may vary, but he was convinced that all children progress through the stages of cognitive development in the same order.

Noting that children actively explore the world around them, Piaget asserted that interaction with the environment and maturation gradually alter the way children think. According to Piaget, children progress in their thinking through the complementary processes of assimilation and accommodation. *Assimilation* **involves interpreting new experiences in terms of existing mental structures without**

Figure 11.11

Piaget's stage theory. Piaget's theory of cognitive development identifies four stages marked by fundamentally different modes of thinking through which youngsters evolve. The approximate age norms and some key characteristics of thought at each stage are summarized here.

Stage 1	Stage 2	Stage 3	Stage 4
Sensorimotor period	**Preoperational period**	**Concrete operational period**	**Formal operational period**
Coordination of sensory input and motor responses; development of object permanence	Development of symbolic thought marked by irreversibility, centration, and egocentrism	Mental operations applied to concrete events; mastery of conservation, hierarchical classification	Mental operations applied to abstract ideas; logical, systematic thinking
Birth to 2 years	2 to 7 years	7 to 11 years	Age 11 through adulthood

FIGURE 9.4 (continued)
Text Excerpt on Stage Theory

changing them. In contrast, *accommodation* involves changing existing mental structures to explain new experiences. Accommodation and assimilation often occur interactively. For instance, a child who has learned to call four-legged pets "puppies" may apply this scheme the first time she encounters a cat (assimilation), but she will eventually discover that puppies and cats are different types of animals and make adjustments to her mental scheme (accommodation). With the companion processes of assimilation and accommodation in mind, let's turn now to the four stages in Piaget's theory.

Sensorimotor Period. One of Piaget's foremost contributions was to greatly enhance our understanding of mental development in the earliest months of life. The first stage in his theory is the *sensorimotor period*, which lasts from birth to about age 2. Piaget called this stage *sensorimotor* because infants are developing the ability to coordinate their sensory input with their motor actions.

The major development during the sensorimotor stage is the gradual appearance of symbolic thought. At the beginning of this stage, a child's behavior is dominated by innate reflexes. But by the end of the stage, the child can use mental symbols to represent objects (for example, a mental image of a favorite toy). The key to this transition is the acquisition of the concept of object permanence.

Object permanence develops when a child recognizes that objects continue to exist even when they are no longer visible. Although you surely take the permanence of objects for granted, infants aren't aware of this permanence at first. If you show a 4-month-old an eye-catching toy and then cover the toy with a pillow, the child will not attempt to search for the toy. Piaget inferred from this observation that the child does not understand that the toy continues to exist under the pillow. The notion of object permanence does not dawn on children overnight. The first signs of this insight usually appear between 4 and 8 months of age, when children will often pursue an object that is *partially* covered in their presence. Progress is gradual, and Piaget believed that children typically don't master the concept of object permanence until they're about 18 months old.

Preoperational Period. During the *preoperational period*, which extends roughly from age 2 to age 7, children gradually improve in their use of mental images. Although progress in symbolic thought continues, Piaget emphasized the *shortcomings* in preoperational thought.

Consider a simple problem that Piaget presented to youngsters. He would take two identical beakers and fill each with the same amount of water. After a child had agreed that the two beakers contained the same amount of water, he would pour the water from one of the beakers into a much taller and thinner beaker (see Figure 11.12). He would then ask the child whether the two differently shaped beakers still contained the same amount of water. Confronted with a problem like this, children in the preoperational period generally said no. They typically focused on the higher water line in the taller beaker and insisted that there was more water in the slender beaker. They had not yet mastered the principle of conservation. *Conservation* is Piaget's term for the awareness that physical quantities remain constant in spite of changes in their shape or appearance.

Why are preoperational children unable to solve conservation problems? According to Piaget, their inability to understand conservation is due to some basic flaws in preoperational thinking. These flaws include centration, irreversibility, and egocentrism.

Centration is the tendency to focus on just one feature of a problem, neglecting other important aspects. When working on the conservation problem with water, preoperational children tend to concentrate on the height of the water while ignoring the width. They have difficulty focusing on several aspects of a problem at once.

Irreversibility is the inability to envision reversing an action. Preoperational children can't mentally "undo" something. For instance, in grappling with the conservation of water, they don't think about what would happen if the water were poured back from the tall beaker into the original beaker.

Egocentrism in thinking is characterized by a limited ability to share another person's viewpoint. Indeed, Piaget felt that preoperational children fail to appreciate that there are points of view other than their own. For instance, if you ask a preoperation girl whether her sister has a sister, she'll probably say no if they are the only two girls in the family. She's unable to view sisterhood from her sister's perspective (this also shows irreversibility).

A notable feature of egocentrism is *animism*—the belief that all things are living, just like oneself. Thus, youngsters attribute lifelike, human qualities to inanimate objects, asking questions such as, "When does the ocean stop to rest?" or "Why does the wind get so mad?"

As you can see, Piaget emphasized the weaknesses apparent in preoperational thought. Indeed, that is

Figure 11.12

Piaget's conservation task. After watching the transformation shown, a preoperational child will usually answer that the taller beaker contains more water. In contrast, the child in the concrete operational period tends to respond correctly, recognizing that the amount of water in beaker C remains the same as the amount in beaker A.

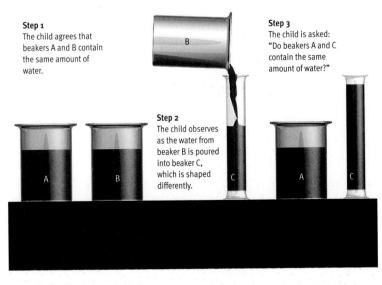

Step 1
The child agrees that beakers A and B contain the same amount of water.

Step 2
The child observes as the water from beaker B is poured into beaker C, which is shaped differently.

Step 3
The child is asked: "Do beakers A and C contain the same amount of water?"

FIGURE 9.4 (continued)
Text Excerpt on Stage Theory

why he called this stage *pre*operational. The ability to perform *operations*—internal transformations, manipulations, and reorganizations of mental structures—emerges in the next stage.

Concrete Operational Period. The development of mental operations marks the beginning of the *concrete operational period*, which usually lasts from about age 7 to age 11. Piaget called this stage *concrete* operations because children can perform operations only on images of tangible objects and actual events.

Among the operations that children master during this stage are reversibility and decentration. *Reversibility* permits a child to mentally undo an action. *Decentration* allows the child to focus on more than one feature of a problem simultaneously. The new found ability to coordinate several aspects of a problem helps the child appreciate that there are several ways to look at things. This ability in turn leads to a *decline in egocentrism* and *gradual mastery of conservation* as it applies to liquid, mass, number, volume, area, and length (see Figure 11.13 on the next page).

As children master concrete operations, they develop a variety of new problem-solving capacities. Let's examine another problem studied by Piaget. Give a preoperational child seven carnations and three daisies. Tell the child the names for the two types of flowers and ask the child to sort them into carnations and daisies. That should be no problem. Now ask the child whether there are more carnations or more daisies. Most children will correctly respond that there are more carnations. Now ask the child whether there are more carnations or more flowers. At this point, most preoperational children will stumble and respond incorrectly that there are more carnations than flowers. Generally, preoperational

children can't handle *hierarchical classification* problems that require them to focus simultaneously on two levels of classification. However, the child who has advanced to the concrete operational stage is not as limited by centration and can work successfully with hierarchical classification problems.

Formal Operational Period. The final stage in Piaget's theory is the *formal operational period*, which typically begins around 11 years of age. In this stage, children begin to apply their operations to *abstract* concepts in addition to concrete objects. Indeed, during this stage, youngsters come to *enjoy* the heady contemplation of abstract concepts. Many adolescents spend hours mulling over hypothetical possibilities related to abstractions such as justice, love, and free will.

According to Piaget, youngsters graduate to relatively adult modes of thinking in the formal operations stage. He did *not* mean to suggest that no further cognitive development occurs once children reach this stage. However, he believed that after children achieve formal operations, further developments in thinking are changes in *degree* rather than fundamental changes in the *nature* of thinking.

Adolescents in the formal operational period become more *systematic* in their problem-solving efforts. Children in earlier developmental stages tend to attack problems quickly, with a trial-and-error approach. In contrast, children who have achieved formal operations are more likely to think things through. They envision possible courses of action and try to use logic to reason out the likely consequences of each possible solution before they act. Thus, thought processes in the formal operational period can be characterized as abstract, systematic, logical, and reflective.

Text material from Wayne Weiten, *Psychology: Themes and Variations,* 6th ed. (Belmont, CA: Wadsworth, 2004), pp. 441–443.

WHEN TO TAKE TEXT NOTES

There are benefits to taking notes at different points in your reading and study of the textbook. You can take notes when you first read the chapter, after the lecture, or before the exam.

As You Read the Chapter

Some students take notes as they read the chapter instead of highlighting or underlining. They find that it helps them better understand what they're reading. If you decide to take notes the first time you read the chapter, you may find that you write down more information than you'll need. After all, all the information will be new to you, and everything may seem important. You'll also find that note taking takes more time than highlighting. If you highlight the text when you first read it and then take notes, you'll save time and have a better set of text notes. If you're using the S-RUN-R reading/study system, for example, you already may have discovered that taking notes after highlighting or underlining saves time and helps you condense the information even more.

After the Lecture

Taking text notes right after the lecture has several advantages. If you wait until after the lecture to take your text notes, you'll avoid duplicating the information in your lecture notes. That will save you time. Then you can condense the information in the text while editing your lecture notes. If your professor's lecture follows the text fairly closely, you can fill in information that you missed during the lecture and at the same time note important points that were never touched on in class. Write your text notes in another notebook or on looseleaf notebook paper so that you can lay your text notes and your lecture notes out side by side when you're studying.

When You Prepare for the Exam

Another good time to take your text notes is when you're preparing for your exam. Instead of just reading over the highlighted or underlined text material, take notes on it. As you know, just reading without some form of marking is a passive activity that results in little actual learning. By the time you're ready to prepare for the exam, you already may have learned a lot of the information that you originally highlighted or underlined. Not only will you save time by waiting to take notes, but you'll also benefit from the active review that requires you to determine what you still need to learn. Writing down this information will help you organize it so you can learn it, and allows you to condense what you need to study for the exam. Of course, you still need to practice the information in your notes to learn it.

Activity 9-6

Take Notes at Different Times

During the next week of classes, experiment with taking notes at different times. Try taking notes on one part of a text chapter as you first read the chapter. Then try taking notes on a different part of the chapter after the lecture. Finally, wait until you're preparing for an exam and take notes on another section of the chapter. Note the time it took you to complete each task. What did you find? Which set of notes do you think is most useful? Why?

HOW TO TAKE TEXT NOTES

There are many different ways to take notes on text material. In Chapter 8, you learned how to create marginal notes and predicted questions to **annotate** (add comments or summary notes) the text. Some other useful methods are taking written notes in outline, modified-block, or summary formats. You may also find that mapping and charting text material helps you organize it more effectively.

In this section, you'll learn how to use each of these note-taking techniques. Try each method as you do your own reading. Then decide which one works best for you.

Take Written Notes

Taking written notes is probably the most common method students use for taking notes from text material. You already may be making notes in the margin of your text as you read. These **marginal notes** help you focus your reading and can serve as recall cues for your highlighting, but they don't restructure the information. Do you prefer to take notes outside of the text (on an index card or sheet of paper) in outline, modified-block, or summary form?

Outlining

One popular method of taking notes on text material is outlining. If you want to use **formal outlining** to take your notes, you may want to use the author's organization to structure your notes. Refer to the table of contents at the beginning of the book to find the main headings to use in your outline. These may be the chapter subdivisions or the main headings. Use Roman numerals (I, II, III, IV, and so on) for them in your outline.

Read and mark the first section in the chapter. Then write down the heading and use a capital letter (A, B, C, D) to indicate that it's a main point in your outline. Go back and jot down any other important information that you want to include. Number these points using Arabic numerals (1, 2, 3, and so on). If you wish, you can further break down your outline and indicate subpoints with lowercase letters (a, b, c). Dividing the material into main points and subpoints helps you condense and organize it for study, as shown here:

```
  I. Main division of the chapter
     A. First heading
        1. Main point
           a.  Supporting detail
           b.  Supporting detail
        2. Main point
           a.  Supporting detail
           b.  Supporting detail
     B. Second heading
        1. Main point
        2. Main point
 II. Main division of the chapter
```

Although formal outlining is useful, informal outlining is more efficient for taking notes (Figure 9.5). If you've been using the outline method for taking lecture notes, you already are familiar with the basic format for informally outlining text material. When you take notes on your text, you can rely on the author's organization or you can create your own. You can use the chapter subdivisions as your main points. You don't have to use every heading as a main point; some of them may be combined or omitted. Write the heading next to the left margin, go to the next line, and then indent to indicate supporting information. You don't need to use any numbers or letters in your **informal outline.** Although outlines

FIGURE 9.5

Sample Notes in Informal
Outline Form

```
                              Benthic Communities
          Rocky Intertidal Communities
               Intertidal zone
                    land between highest and lowest marshes
                    hundreds of species
               Problems living there
                    wave shock — force of crashing waves
                    temperature change
                    ice grinding against shoreline
                         higher altitudes
                    intense sunlight
                         in tropics
               Reasons for diversity
                    large quantities of food available
                         strong currents keep nutrients stirred
                    large number of habitats available
                         high, salty splash pools
                    cool, dark crevices
                    provide hiding places
                         rest places
                         attachment sites
                         mating nooks
          Sand Beach and Cobble Communities
               Three types
                    Sand beaches
                         forbidding place for small organisms
```

generally lend themselves to organizing information, you need to create headings
and/or subheadings, even when the author hasn't included them. You also need to
dig through the material and gather the details under each appropriate heading.
Don't forget, your outline will be much more helpful if you think about what you
want to write down and condense the information into meaningful phrases instead
of copying entire sentences.

Activity 9-7

Take Notes in Outline Form

Work as a group to take notes. Use the text excerpt in Figure 9.2 to generate a set of
text notes using either formal or informal outlining. Be sure you create subheadings to
organize the details.

Block Notes

If you already are using the block method to take lecture notes, you may want to
use it to take your text notes, too.

The **block method,** however, may not be the best method for taking text notes.
If you're a visual learner, you may have difficulty picturing the information in your
notes because the information is crowded together, rather than spaced out in an

easy-to-recall format. You may also find that it's harder to write questions in the margin of your notes if you have several details on the same line.

Modified-Block Notes

The **modified-block method** may be even more effective. In this case you list all the important details directly under each other. Some students put a dash in front of each meaningful phrase, whereas others simply indent the list slightly. Look at the sample of modified-block notes in Figure 9.6. The information is well organized and includes sufficient detail to make it useful for later study. If there are too many details to list under just one heading, you can create additional headings or subheadings to organize the material in a way that makes it easier to study and learn.

Summarizing

Some students prefer to summarize text information when taking notes. A **summary** is a condensed version of the information, generally written in sentence or paragraph form. If you decide to summarize your text information, you need to break down the chapter into shorter segments. You could write short summaries of each headed section or combine the information from several sections under a new heading that you create yourself. In any case, before you start writing your summary, read the entire section, think about what the author is saying, and decide

FIGURE 9.6

Sample Notes in Modified-Block Form

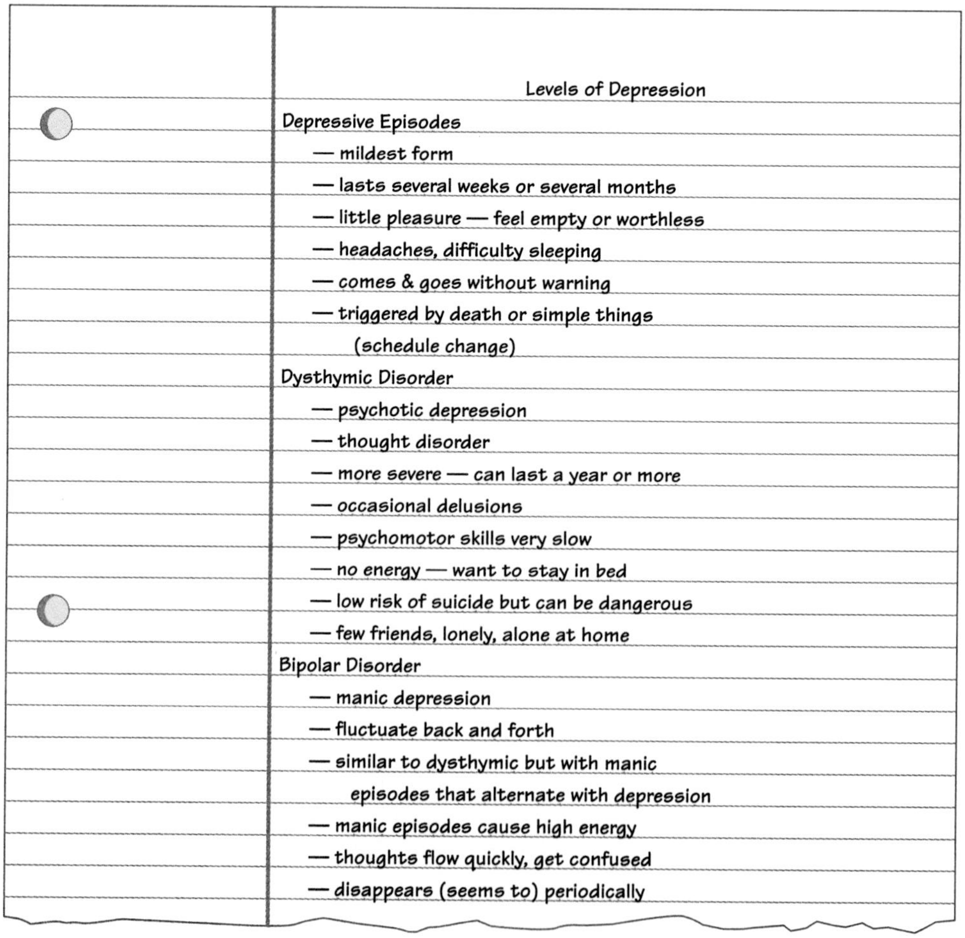

Levels of Depression

Depressive Episodes
— mildest form
— lasts several weeks or several months
— little pleasure — feel empty or worthless
— headaches, difficulty sleeping
— comes & goes without warning
— triggered by death or simple things
    (schedule change)

Dysthymic Disorder
— psychotic depression
— thought disorder
— more severe — can last a year or more
— occasional delusions
— psychomotor skills very slow
— no energy — want to stay in bed
— low risk of suicide but can be dangerous
— few friends, lonely, alone at home

Bipolar Disorder
— manic depression
— fluctuate back and forth
— similar to dysthymic but with manic
    episodes that alternate with depression
— manic episodes cause high energy
— thoughts flow quickly, get confused
— disappears (seems to) periodically

what you think is important. Then write out the main points or key information in your own words. Of course, if you underline or highlight as you read the section, you may find that it's easier to focus on the key information to include in your summary.

Read the summary in Figure 9.7. Although Laura's summary is well written, it refers only to the key points made in the text; it doesn't contain the actual information. Many students make this same mistake when they begin writing summaries. Remember to include the actual points that the author is making. Don't just say that the text gives the reasons that you should mark your text—you need to list the reasons. Remember that your purpose for writing a summary is to take notes on the text. You need all of the important information so you can study for your exam. "Vague" summaries are a common problem when students try to summarize an entire chapter in one or two paragraphs. However, some students make the same error even when dealing with shorter segments. (A better example of a summary is shown later in card A of Figure 9.8. It includes the main points and details contained in the text.)

Summarizing may not be the best method for taking notes on certain types of material. A biology textbook, for example, includes so many facts and technical terms that summarizing isn't a very effective note-taking method. On the other hand, literature, history, philosophy, and anthropology texts lend themselves more appropriately to summarization because they include more general ideas, theories, and issues. Summaries are also very useful when taking notes on library reference materials and other outside reading assignments.

End-of-chapter summaries found in many college textbooks only touch on the main concepts and ideas presented in the chapter. They don't include enough specific information to use them as a test review. However, as you learned in Chapter 7, reading the chapter summary is an important part of previewing your text.

Although you shouldn't try to write a summary for the entire chapter of your textbooks, you can effectively summarize headed sections.

FIGURE 9.7
Poor Example of a Summary

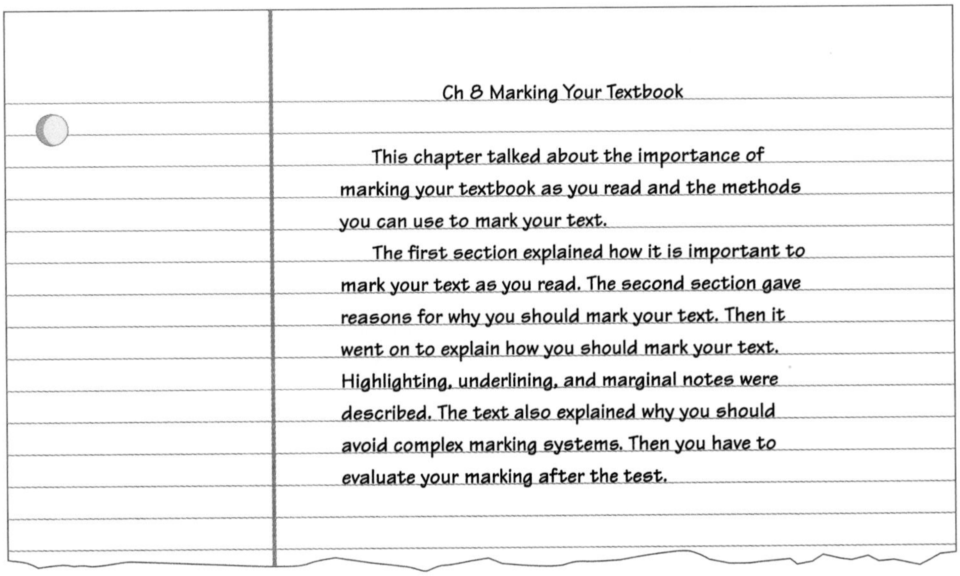

Ch 8 Marking Your Textbook

This chapter talked about the importance of marking your textbook as you read and the methods you can use to mark your text.
The first section explained how it is important to mark your text as you read. The second section gave reasons for why you should mark your text. Then it went on to explain how you should mark your text. Highlighting, underlining, and marginal notes were described. The text also explained why you should avoid complex marking systems. Then you have to evaluate your marking after the test.

Laura's Summary

Activity 9-8

Take Written Text Notes

Refer back to the text selection "The Old and Middle Kingdoms" in Figure 9.3. Ask each member of your group to take text notes using one of the following formats: outline, modified-block, or summary. Then compare the information in your notes. Which method organized the material better? Which method do you prefer?

Use Note Cards to Organize Your Text Material

Some students prefer to take notes on index cards rather than on notebook paper. As you'll see in later chapters, note cards or index cards can be used for many study techniques. They're especially effective for taking notes, though, because they make it easy to organize information and they're so easy to carry around. You can use note cards to organize all the important information on one particular heading or topic.

Write the heading at the top of the card and then jot down any important supporting information that you want to review. You may want to write a summary of the text material or take notes in outline or modified-block formats. Look at the sample note cards in Figure 9.8. Card A summarizes the text information that you read in Activity 8-8. Look back at the actual excerpt and then read the summary on the card. Does the summary include the main ideas presented in the text material? Card B contains modified-block notes on the same information. Which method do you think would work best for you?

FIGURE 9.8
Sample Note Cards

> Further Evolution
>
> Major geologic events had an effect on land and sea life. During the Paleozoic Period the land masses Gondwana and Laurasia joined to form Pangea, a single world continent. All of the remaining surface of the Earth was covered by water — the Tethys Sea.
> As the continents collided, the overall diversity of species declined, and many habitats were lost. This resulted in a 96% reduction of marine species 240 million years ago. Climatic changes and changes in ocean currents affected all land & sea organisms.

Card A

> Further Evolution
>
> Paleozoic Period
>   – Major geologic events
>   – Led to effects on evolution of life
>   – Gondwana & Laurasia → Pangea
>   – Rest of surface covered by Tethys Sea
>
> Collision of landmasses
>   – habitats lost
>   – diversity of life declined
>   – reduced # species of marine animals by 96% (240 m yrs ago)
>   – led to changes in climate & currents, which affected all lifeforms

Card B

If you do take notes on index cards, you may also find it helpful to write questions on the back of each note card. By doing this, you're reinforcing the important information and, at the same time, creating a set of self-test question cards for later review.

Activity 9-9

Take Notes on Note Cards

Read the text material on rock types in Figure 9.9 and take notes on your own index cards. Use one card for each rock type. Then compare your notes to those of the other members in your group. As a group, develop questions to write on the back of each card. Then take turns quizzing each other on the material.

FIGURE 9.9
Excerpt from an Environmental
Science Text

10-3 MINERALS, ROCKS, AND THE ROCK CYCLE

What Are Minerals and Rocks? The earth's crust, still forming in various places, is composed of minerals and rocks. It is the source of almost all the nonrenewable resources we use: fossil fuels, metallic minerals, and nonmetallic minerals. It is also the source of soil and of the elements that make up our bodies and those of other living organisms.

A **mineral** is an element or inorganic compound that occurs naturally and is solid. Some minerals consist of a single element, such as gold, silver, diamond (carbon), and sulfur. However, most of the more than 2,000 identified minerals occur as inorganic compounds formed by various combinations of elements. Examples are salt, mica, and quartz.

Rock is any material that makes up a large, natural, continuous part of the earth's crust. Some kinds of rock, such as limestone (calcium carbonate, or $CaCO_3$) and quartzite (silicon dioxide, or SiO_2), contain only one mineral, but most rocks consist of two or more minerals.

What Are the Three Major Rock Types? Based on the way it forms, rock is placed in three broad classes:

■ **Igneous rock** formed below or on the earth's surface when molten rock material (magma) **(1)** wells up from the earth's upper mantle or deep crust, **(2)** cools, and **(3)** hardens into rock. Examples are **(1)** granite (formed underground) and **(2)** lava rock (formed above ground when molten lava cools and hardens). Although often covered by sedimentary rocks or soil, igneous rocks form the bulk of the earth's crust. They also are the main souce of many nonfuel mineral resources.

■ **Sedimentary rock** formed from sediment when preexisting rocks are **(1)** weathered and eroded into small pieces, **(2)** transported from their sources, and **(3)** deposited in a body of surface water. Examples are **(1)** sandstone and shale formed from pressure created by deposited layers of sediment, **(2)** dolomite and limestone formed from the compacted shells, skeletons, and other remains of dead organisms, and **(3)** lignite and bituminous coal derived from plant remains.

■ **Metamorphic rock** produced when a preexisting rock is subjected to **(1)** high temperatures (which may cause it to melt partially), **(2)** high pressures, **(3)** chemically active fluids, or **(4)** a combination of these agents. Examples are anthracite (a form of coal), slate, and marble.

What Is the Rock Cycle? Rocks are constantly exposed to various physical and chemical conditions that can change them over time. The interaction of processes that change rocks from one type to another is called the **rock cycle** (Figure 10-8).

The slowest of the earth's cyclic processes, the rock cycle recycles material over millions of years. It concentrates the planet's nonrenewable mineral resources on which we depend.

Text material adapted from G. T. Miller, *Living in the Environment: Principles, Connections, and Solutions,* 13th ed. (Pacific Grove, CA: Brooks/Cole, 2004), pp. 209–210.

Create Concept Maps

Maps are visual displays of text information. They are a way of organizing the key information in the text into easy-to-read and easy-to-remember pictures or diagrams. Although there are many different types of concept maps, only *line maps, hierarchical maps, and semantic webs,* will be described in this chapter. You may find that mapping is a great way to take notes. When you take exams, this strategy may help you recall the information that you learned because of the way you organized it. You may also find that you can visualize it in your mind or remember how you set it up. Mapping is an even more active method than some of the ones we've discussed because you have to move outside the author's organizational framework and create your own.

Line or Wheel Maps

One of the easiest types of maps to create is the line or wheel map. A **line map** is a visual display of information drawn by adding lines or spokes that radiate out from a central hub. You already may be familiar with time lines from history class. To create a line map for other types of text material, write the topic in the center of the paper and then add subordinate points on lines that radiate up, down, or out from it. Add supporting details by inserting lines that extend out from the previous lines. Many students like using line maps because they provide more space to write meaningful phrases.

Although they seem easy to create, it's also easy to make mistakes when designing your line map. First, don't turn the paper as you draw the lines. You want the information to be written horizontally across the paper so that you can easily study and learn it. If you turn the paper, you may find that half of your information is upside down when you're ready to study. There's also a tendency to simply list all of the details on individual lines that extend directly from the heading. For texts that contain only a few details this is fine. However, some text material is so detailed that you could have fifteen or twenty lines all connected to one heading.

Instead, you need to create subheadings as you map the text information. The subheadings organize the information, separate the details into easier-to-remember chunks, and serve as additional cues to help you learn and retrieve the information. Although the author didn't include the subheadings food source, social practices, and technology, Christy created her own subheadings to better organize the text material in Figure 9.10. You may have also noticed that Christy made some notes on the introductory material from the text at the top of her map. As you create your own line maps to take notes on text material, feel free to move outside of the author's organizational structure and create one that will make your map a well-organized study tool.

Hierarchical Maps

One of the most common forms of maps is the hierarchical map. **Hierarchical maps** provide a top-down display of information. You often see this form of map in science texts in the form of flowcharts or process charts. To create a hierarchical map, write the topic at the top of the page and put a box around it. Then draw lines to indicate the subdivisions (the next level of headings) and write and box each of them. You can then further divide each of these points into one or more subheadings and then add supporting points. Look at Figure 9.11, the hierarchical map that Wendy developed from the text material from a Special Education textbook. Look for the excerpt entitled "Chemically Dependent Youth" on the *College Study Skills* Web site. You can see the natural progression from the main topic of the selection down to the supporting details.

FIGURE 9-10
Christy's Line Map

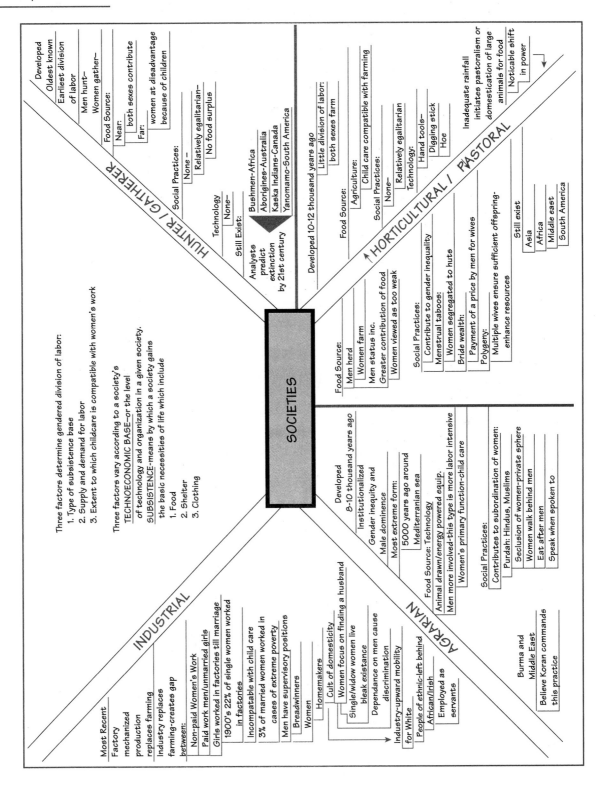

SOCIETIES

Three factors determine gendered division of labor:
1. Type of subsistence base
2. Supply and demand for labor
3. Extent to which childcare is compatible with women's work

Three factors vary according to a society's
TECHNOECONOMIC BASE—or the level
of technology and organization in a given society.
SUBSISTENCE—means by which a society gains
the basic necessities of life which include
1. Food
2. Shelter
3. Clothing

HUNTER / GATHERER

Developed
Oldest known
Earliest division
of labor
Men hunt—
Women gather—
Food Source:
Near:
Far:
both sexes contribute
women at disadvantage
because of children
Social Practices:
None –
Relatively egalitarian–
No food surplus
Technology
None–
Still Exist:
Bushmen–Africa
Aborigines–Australia
Kaska Indians–Canada
Yanomamo–South America
Analysts predict extinction by 21st century

HORTICULTURAL / PASTORAL

Developed 10-12 thousand years ago
Little division of labor:
both sexes farm
Food Source:
Agriculture:
Child care compatible with farming
Social Practices:
None–
Relatively egalitarian
Technology:
Hand tools—
Digging stick
Hoe
Inadequate rainfall
initiates pastoralism or
domestication of large
animals for food
Noticable shift
in power
Food Source:
Men herd
Women farm
Men status inc.
Greater contribution of food
Women viewed as too weak
Social Practices:
Contribute to gender inequality
Menstrual taboos:
Women segregated to huts
Bride wealth:
Payment of a price by men for wives
Polygeny:
Multiple wives ensure sufficient offspring-
enhance resources
Still exist
Asia
Africa
Middle east
South America

INDUSTRIAL

Most Recent
Factory
mechanized
production
replaces farming
Industry replaces
farming–creates gap
between:
Non-paid Women's Work
Paid work men/unmarried girls
Girls worked in factories till marriage
1900's 22% of single women worked
in factories
Incompatable with child care
3% of married women worked in
cases of extreme poverty
Men have supervisory positions
Breadwinners
Women
Homemakers
Cult of domesticity
Women focus on finding a husband
Single/widow women live
bleak existance
Dependance on men cause
discrimination
Industry–upward mobility
for White
People of ethnic–left behind
African/Irish
Employed as
servants

AGRARIAN

Developed
8-10 thousand years ago
Institutionalized
Gender inequity and
Male dominence
Most extreme form:
5000 years ago around
Mediterranean sea
Food Source: Technology
Animal drawn/energy powered equip.
Men more involved–this type is more labor intensive
Women's primary function–child care
Social Practices:
Contributes to subordination of women:
Purdah: Hindus, Muslims
Seclusion of women–private sphere
Women walk behind men
Eat after men
Speak when spoken to
Burma and
Middle East
Believe Koran commands
this practice

FIGURE 9.11

Wendy's Hierarchical Map

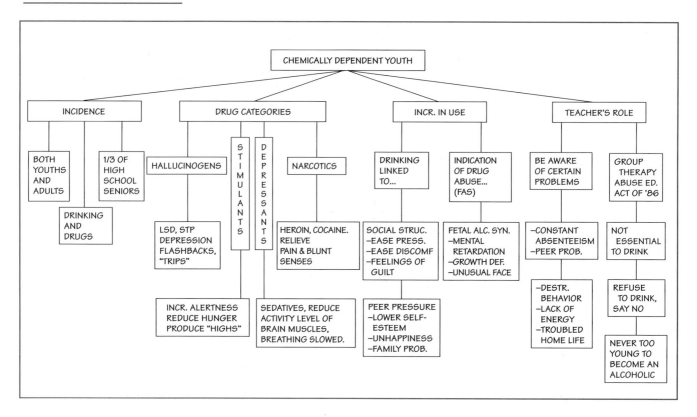

Mapping is a very individual method of note taking. Feel free to make your map fit the material; don't try to make the material fit the map. In their map (Figure 9.12), Rayna, Barbara, and Amy put the greatest emphasis on the four types of drugs rather than focusing equally on all sections of the material. What else do you notice that is different about their map? If you said that they didn't use boxes, you're correct. What other differences do you notice?

Semantic Webs

One of the newest styles of mapping is the Semantic Web. Instead of using a top-down display, as in the hierarchical map, **Semantic Webs** radiate from a central focal point. There are four main components in a Semantic Web: the Core Question or Concept, the Web Strands, the Strand Supports, and the Strand Ties. The **Core Question** or **Concept** is the main focus of the text chapter or section. It may be the title of an article or a major division of the chapter or heading of a section that you decide to map. To start your web, write this word, phrase, or question in the center of a piece of paper and draw a circle or oval around it. The second component, the **Web Strands,** show the headings or subheadings that subdivide the Core Concept. They are joined to the Core Concept by lines that radiate from it. Circle each Web Strand as well. The **Strand Supports** do just what their title implies; they support the Web Strands. They include the details that support the Web Strands. Finally, the **Strand Ties** are words or phrases that are written on the lines that connect some of the information. They define the relationships between some of the Web Strands or Strand Supports.[1]

---

[1]Adapted from G. Freeman and E. G. Reynolds, "Enriching Basal Reader Lessons with Semantic Webbing," *The Reading Teacher* 33 (1980): 677–684.

FIGURE 9.12

Rayna, Barbara, and Amy's
Hierarchical Map

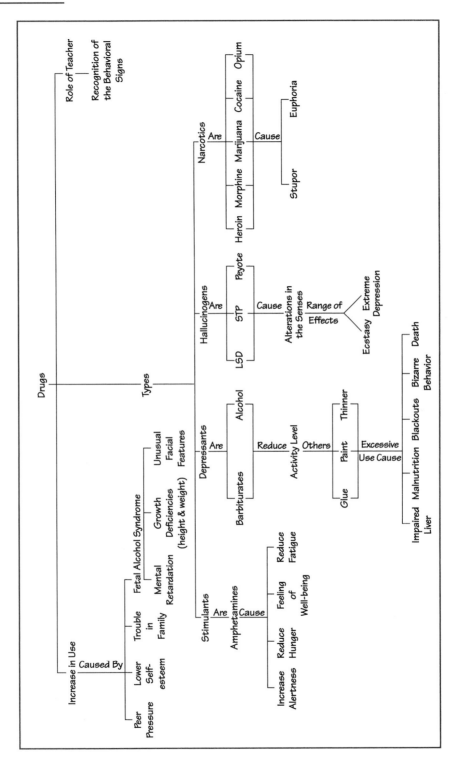

Look at Figure 9.13, the Semantic Web that Kelly produced for the "Chemically Dependent Youth" selection. Can you locate each of the components mentioned above? First, what is the Core Concept? If you look at the center of Kelly's web, you'll see that she used the phrase "Drug Categories." It also is easy to find the four Web Strands because Kelly used double lines to connect them to the center focal point. You may have noticed that Kelly used several levels of Strand Supports. She moved from "Narcotics" (a Web Strand) to "Examples" (a Strand Support) to "marijuana" (a detail supporting the Strand Support). Even though this last level of support wasn't in the "rules" for how to construct a Semantic Web, Kelly felt that the text information demanded further division. Don't leave out information you think is important just because it doesn't fit the formula for a particular type of map. Instead, adapt the mapping technique to fit your text material. You can have second-level, third-level, and fourth-level strand supports if the text demands it. Because college text material is so detailed, you should have more layers of Strand Supports. Remember, you're going to use these maps to study for your exams. You may have noticed that Kelly didn't add Strand Ties to her map. She could have written "used to" on the line between "Narcotics" and "relieve pain," or "leads to" on the line that connects "Narcotics" to "blunt senses."

After you complete your web, review the information that you noted. If you aren't sure how some of your information related to the information connected to it, you may need to add Strand Ties to your map.

Color coding your maps can also help you recall the information. Color coding will work on any type of map, but it's especially effective for Semantic Webs because you create "clusters" of information for each of the sections of the text ma-

FIGURE 9.13
Kelly's Semantic Map

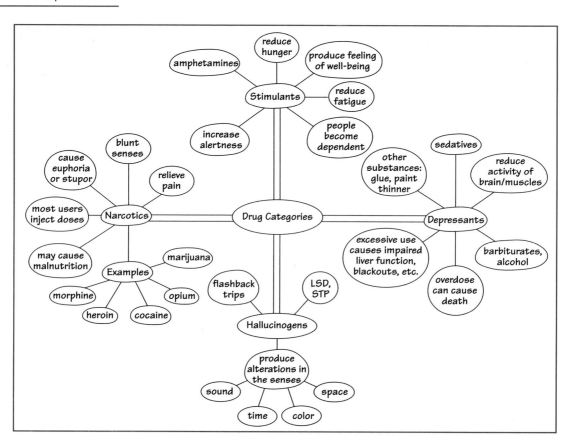

terial. You can either draw the ovals in color or use a highlighter or colored pencil to fill in each portion of the map. For example, you could color code all of the information related to narcotics orange, stimulants red, depressants blue, and hallucinogens green. Using a different color for each of the clusters in your map helps separate the details and provides you with an additional cue to trigger your memory of the material. It's important to use light colors if you're going to shade the information that you write—you still want to be able to read it clearly. For some material, you may find that the colors you choose are related to the material itself, providing even more associations with the material.

Activity 9-10

Experiment with Mapping Techniques

Using the text material on Piaget's Stage Theories in Figure 9-4, work as a group to take text notes. First, highlight the text material and discuss what you think are the important points you want to include in the map. Once you know what you want to include in your map, ask each group member to create a line map, a semantic web, or a hierarchical map. Compare your map to the others to evaluate the organizational structure and the content you included. Which method do you think will work best for you?

Create Charts

A **chart** is a graphic display of information that shows the similarities and differences of closely related information. You can't chart an entire chapter because so many unrelated topics are presented; however, you can chart some sections of chapters. For example, you just read about the Piaget's Stage Theory and earlier you read about different types of asteroids, rocks, and drug categories. In each text selection, you read about similar types or forms of the same thing. Charting information forces you to organize the information more than any of the other forms of note taking, because you have to develop categories for comparison and contrast. By separating the distinct features of each type of rock, for example, you'll be able to better learn their differences for an exam.

One of the most common types of charts is the **matrix,** a chart with rows and columns. A portion of Melissa's chart is shown in Figure 9.14. To set up the chart, you need to first include the things that you are reading about. If you decided to chart the four drug categories, you would write the names of each along the left margin of your paper. These would be like the headings in written notes. The next step is not as easy. To complete the framework of your chart, you need to create categories for comparison across the top. They are the subheadings you would have to create to better organize your written notes. To do this, you need to read and think about the material in the text selection to determine what kind of information is presented about each one that is similar (yet different) from the others. The final step in creating a chart is to fill in the details. Go back to the text material and write them in the correct box in your chart. You'll notice that each one (in most cases) will be different.

Go back to the text material on asteroids that you read at the beginning of the chapter. As you read that material, you had to organize it so that you could sort out the various details about each type of asteroid. In each case, there was information

FIGURE 9.14

A Portion of Melissa's Chart

Overview of Piaget's Stage Theory

Period	Age	Definition	Development	Key Concept or Flaw
Sensorimotor	birth to age 2	Ability to coordinate sensory inputs with motor actions	Symbolic thought Behavior dominated by innate reflexes	Key concept: Object permanence Recognizing that object continues to exist even when no longer visible
Preoperational	age 2 to age 7	Improve use of mental images Preoperational because of all the weaknesses	Development of symbolic thinking Not yet grasped concept of conservation: quantities remain constant regardless of shape or appearance	Key flaws: Centration: Focus on one part of problem Irreversibility: Inability to undo an action Egocentrism: Inability to share other's viewpoints Animism: Believe all things are living

about the color, the shape, and the size of the different types of asteroids. What other types of information would you also include? The advantage of charting is that you really must create subheadings to create a chart—you have to organize and categorize the information. In written notes, you aren't forced to—you could simply list all of the details under the heading. Because the information is better organized in a chart, you can learn it more easily.

When you create a chart, you need to make the chart fit the material. In one matrix you could have four categories across the top, and in another you might have seven. It all depends on how many aspects of the topic are presented. If you must, turn the paper sideways, write smaller, or create your chart on the computer (use the table menu). You can color code your charts just as you do your concept maps. Be sure to color all of the details about each type of rock or drug category the same color. You want to be able to remember which details go with each type.

Activity 9-11

Create a Chart

Refer back to the text excerpt on Piaget's Stage Theory (Figure 9.4) and create a chart to separate and organize the important information. You can use some or all of Melissa's categories (see Figure 9.14), or you can create your own. Compare your chart with the maps you created in Activity 9-10. Which method do you think will help you learn and remember the information? Which method worked best for you?

MORE TIPS FOR ORGANIZING TEXT INFORMATION

CREATE WORD CARDS. As you read (or even before you read) the chapter, make out a set of word cards for all of the new technical terminology. Write the word on the front of the card and the definition on the back (one per card). This will help improve your understanding of the terms and the text material. You can begin working on learning the definitions immediately.

TAKE NOTES ON DIFFICULT MATERIAL ON NOTE CARDS. Writing your notes on index cards serves two purposes. First, you organize the information from one headed section (or one specific topic) on each card. This may make the information easier for you to learn and remember. Second, you can carry your cards with you for quick reviews during work breaks, while commuting, or even before class begins.

ADD QUESTIONS TO YOUR NOTE CARDS. If you take notes only on the front of each card, you can write recall questions on the back. You can study the material on the front of the card and then check your learning by answering the questions on the back. Feel free to shuffle the cards to make sure you aren't learning the information in order.

TAKE NOTES ON LITERARY ASSIGNMENTS. Use a separate index card for each play, short story, or novel you read. Develop a list of categories of information that you want to record for each work. You may want to include the title, author, setting, theme, main characters, symbolism, and a brief summary or diagram of the plot line. Jot down any other important information that stands out and include your own reaction to what you read.

CREATE A TEMPLATE ON YOUR COMPUTER. If you plan to use the same format for your note cards for a particular text, create a template on your computer and simply type in the notes for each section and print out your cards.

TAKE NOTES ON OUTSIDE READING ASSIGNMENTS. Use note cards to take notes on any outside reading material. Include the title of the article and the author at the top of the card and then jot down the important material using any of the note-taking methods.

EXPAND CONCEPT MAPS. Many textbooks, like this one, have concept maps at the beginning of every chapter. They serve as an overview of what the chapter is about. In most cases these maps include only the topics and main points that you will be reading about. Copy the map onto your own paper so that you can add details to it as you read.

COMPARE YOUR TEXT NOTES WITH THOSE OF ANOTHER CLASSMATE. Until you feel more confident about the content and organization of your text notes, get together with a classmate or study group to compare notes.

GET HELP FROM YOUR PROFESSOR OR LEARNING ASSISTANCE CENTER. If you haven't taken text notes before, ask your professor or someone in your college learning center to evaluate your text notes. The feedback you get can help you take better notes in the future.

HOW TO REVIEW YOUR TEXT NOTES

There are three main ways to review text notes, but simply "reading over them" is not one of them. Try reciting your notes, replicating your notes, and creating recall questions.

Recite Your Notes

One way to transfer the information in your notes into your long-term memory is to recite it. First, practice the information by reviewing the main and supporting points. Try to recall and recite the headings that you used to set up the information in your notes. Then recite the details under each heading. Look back at your notes to see whether you are correct. Then cover your notes and practice again. If you made note cards, carry them with you. Review them whenever you have a few minutes to spare. Then look away and try to recite (or mumble) the information. Try taping your notes to a mirror, or tack them to a bulletin board. Review them in the morning and then recite them as you walk to class.

Replicate Your Notes

Another way to review text notes is to replicate them. Take a blank sheet of paper and try to reconstruct your notes. If you mapped the information in the text, you probably will find that it's fairly easy to recall the visual image that you created; try to remember the map and also how you set it up. If you made a detailed map, practice drawing it one section at a time. You also can practice writing out your modified-block notes, outlines, or charts. When you review charts or matrixes, don't try to learn all the information at once. Work on one column at a time. Practice matrixes by reciting them first, column by column or row by row. Then use a blank sheet of paper and write in the headings and the categories. Then try to fill in one row across or one column down. Keep working on the matrix until you can write it from memory.

Add Recall Questions

If you took written notes, you can also write recall questions in the margin as a way of reviewing your notes. Be sure you create both general and specific questions in the recall column so that you can test yourself on all of the important information. You can develop the recall column when you first take notes or when you review for your exam. Just developing the questions requires you to go back and review the notes you took. Then you get another review of the material each time you test yourself. If you've already written your recall questions, review by covering your notes and writing or reciting the answers to the questions. Gavin, Beth, Chris, and Sara developed a set of notes and recall questions on text material from an anthropology textbook. A portion of those notes is shown in Figure 9.15. Did you notice that both general and specific questions are included?

Activity 9-12

Review Your Text Notes

Select a set of text notes that you took recently. Then divide the notes into three sections. Review the first section by reciting the information using the headings to prompt your memory. Review the second section by replicating your notes—rewriting them from memory. Finally, review the last section of notes by creating recall questions in the margin and reciting the answers from memory. Which review strategy was the most effective in learning the information? Write a paragraph or two describing what you found.

FIGURE 9.15
Text Notes with Recall Questions

	Types of Political Organizations
◑	**Band Societies**
What are the characteristics of band societies?	Characteristics
	• Least complex
What is the occupation of bands?	• small, nomadic groups of food collectors
How large are the groups?	• can range from 20 to several hundred
	• members share all belongings
How much role specialization is there?	• very little role specializations
What is egalitarian?	• egalitarian—few differences in status and wealth
How much political integration occurs?	Political Integration
	• have least —bands are independent
What is the political integration based on?	• based on kinship and marriage
What ties members of bands together?	• bound together by language and culture
◑ What type of leadership occurs in bands?	Leadership roles
	• informal—no designated authority
Who serves as leader? Why?	• older men are leaders—respected for their wisdom and experience
Who makes decisions?	• decisions made by adult men
What are the powers of a head man?	• head man advises—has no power
What is an example of a band society?	Example
	! Kung of the Kalahari
What are the characteristics of tribal societies?	**Tribal Societies**
	Characteristics
What is their occupation?	• food producers
What are pop. like?	• populations—large, dense, sedentary

Activity 9-13

Where Are You Now?

Now that you have completed Chapter 9, take a few minutes to repeat the "Where Are You Now?" activity, located on the *College Study Skills* Web site. What changes did you make as a result of reading this chapter? How are you planning to apply what you've learned in this chapter?

SUMMARY

Because you can learn and remember information better when it's well organized, you need to take notes on your text chapters. A great deal of text material is not very well organized (making it difficult to learn and remember), so you need to organize it by creating your own organizational system. You may need to add headings and/or subheadings, move information around to group it under the appropriate heading, or separate and label closely related material. You can accomplish all of these tasks and, at the same time, condense the material and improve your comprehension if you take notes on your text.

Although many students take notes as they read the chapter for the first time, that's not the most efficient time to take notes on your text. Since everything seems important during a first reading, students tend to write down much more information than they would after hearing the lecture, or while reviewing to prepare for an exam. Taking written notes using the outline or modified-block methods, writing a summary, predicting questions, or making marginal notes are effective ways to take text notes. Concept maps and charts are especially effective for some students and some types of material. Creating hierarchical maps, Semantic Webs, line maps, and charts allows you to organize material in ways that can more easily be recalled for later use. Just taking written notes or creating maps and charts doesn't automatically mean that you have learned the information, though. Review your notes on a regular basis by reciting them, writing them from memory, or creating recall questions to test your learning.

REVIEW QUESTIONS

Terms You Should Know: Make a flash card for each term.

Annotate	Informal outlining	Strand Supports
Block method	Line map	Strand Ties
Chart	Maps	Subheading
Core Concept	Marginal Notes	Summary
Formal outlining	Matrix	Web Strands
Heading	Modified-block method	Wheel map
Hierarchical map	Semantic Web	

Completion: Fill in the blank to complete each of the following statements.

1. You may not want to take text notes as you read the chapter for the first time because everything seems _____.

2. You can edit your _____ notes as you take your text notes.

3. Some students like to take text notes on _____ _____ because they can carry them around to review when they have a few extra minutes.

4. _____ _____ show the supporting details in a Semantic Web.

5. _____ cannot be used to take notes on entire chapters.

Multiple Choice: Circle the letter of the best answer for each of the following questions. Be sure to underline key words and eliminate wrong answers.

6. When you are writing a summary, be sure you use
   A. meaningful phrases.
   B. main ideas.
   C. paragraph form.
   D. recall questions in the margin.

7. Which of the following is a top-down method of taking text notes?
   A. Summaries
   B. Hierarchical maps
   C. Semantic Webs
   D. Charts

Short Answer–Essay: On a separate sheet, answer each of the following questions.

8. Why do students need to organize their text material?

9. Why is charting an effective method for some text material?

10. How should students review their text notes?

"Recently I had a Psychology test. I made study sheets and question cards. Then I put myself on a five-day preparation schedule. I wrote and recited a lot. Going into the test, I felt very confident about my ability to do well on the test. I received a C-average on my first couple of tests, but on this one I got a B. This proves to me if I can get myself to prepare properly now that I know how to, I can get the grades that I want."

Nelson Hernandez
Student

PREPARING FOR EXAMS

In this chapter you will learn more about:

- **What you need to know before you begin to study**
- **How to use the Five-Day Study Plan**
- **How to use a variety of active learning strategies**
- **How to evaluate your exam preparation**

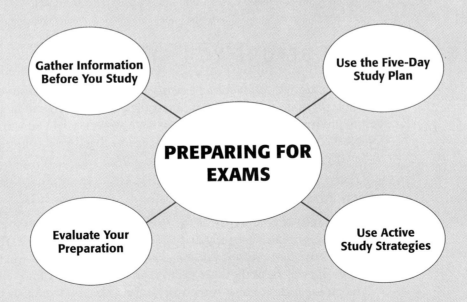

Activity 10-1

Where Are You Now?

Take a few minutes to answer *yes* or *no* to the following questions.

		YES	NO
1.	When preparing for exams, is your primary study method to read over the material?		✓
2.	Do you tend to miss class the day before the exam?		✓
3.	After an exam are you unsure of how well you did?	✓	
4.	Do you make up self-tests as a way of studying for exams?	✓	
5.	Do you study both by yourself and with a group before a very difficult exam?		✓
6.	Do you tend to study only the day or night before the exam?		✓
7.	Do you review your lecture notes and text material together according to the topic?	✓	
8.	Do you often know the answers to multiple-choice questions even before you look at the alternatives?	✓	
9.	Do you review by reciting out loud or by making up study sheets?	✓	
10.	Do you space your study time over several days?	✓	
	Total Points		

Give yourself 1 point for each *yes* answer to questions 4, 5, 7, 8, 9, and 10 and 1 point for each *no* answer to questions 1, 2, 3, and 6. Now total up your points. A low score indicates that you need to learn how to study for college exams. A high score indicates that you are already using many good test preparation strategies.

GATHER INFORMATION BEFORE YOU STUDY

Before you begin to study for an exam, gather information about both the test and yourself. Learning about the type of test that will be given will help you know how best to prepare for it. In addition, knowing how you learn best can help you choose the most effective ways to prepare for an exam. Together, this information can lead to better grades.

Learn About the Exam

The first thing to do in preparing for an exam is find out what the exam will be like. If your professor hasn't already discussed the exam, ask about it. You need to know what types of questions you will be expected to answer. Ask whether the exam is objective or essay or both. If the exam is an objective one, find out if all questions will be multiple choice or if some will be true/false, matching, or completion. The more you know, the better you can prepare.

You also need to know how many questions will be on the exam. If you have 100 questions on four chapters of Life Science, you can expect about 25 questions

FIGURE 10.1
Levels of Questions

on each chapter. On the other hand, if you have only 20 questions on the same four chapters, you'll have only 5 questions per chapter. The more questions you have from each chapter, the greater the probability that they'll cover not only main ideas but also less important points from the chapters and your notes. If there are only a few questions from each chapter, they are more likely to cover the main ideas or concepts. However, you can't depend on this. Some professors who ask only three or four questions per chapter still test on "picky little things." And, don't forget: Even one essay question can cover a great deal of material.

Levels of Questions

Many college students don't realize that professors test their understanding of the material at many different levels. Although most of the questions on your high school tests depended only on your ability to memorize, six different levels of questions are often found on college exams (see Figure 10.1). Read the description of each in the paragraphs that follow. Then look closely at the sample questions after each paragraph. They are based on the text selection "The Growth of Thought: Cognitive Development," which you read in the last chapter (Figure 9.4).

1. **Knowledge-level questions** require only rote memory; they're the easiest type of question to answer. They include remembering terms, facts, dates, lists, and so on. To answer this type of question, you need only to recognize the information as it was written in the text or spoken in the lecture. Without even reviewing the material, you can probably recognize the answer to the following sample question.[1]

   According to Jean Piaget, the four levels of cognitive development are the sensorimotor period, the preoperational period, concrete operations, and

   a. advanced operations.
   b. the abstract period.
   c. formal operations.
   d. the adult period.[2]

---

[1]Based on Bloom's Taxonomy in B. S. Bloom, ed., *Taxonomy of Educational Objectives: The Classification of Educational Goals. Handbook 1. Cognitive Domain* (New York: McKay, 1956).
[2]Sample test items prepared by Dr. Malcolm Van Blerkom. Used with permission.

2. **Comprehension-level questions** require you to understand the material well enough to be able to identify concepts and issues even when they're phrased differently from the way you read them or heard them presented. To answer a comprehension-level question, you need to check its meaning carefully against what you learned. How does the following question rephrase the issue of age and cognitive development?

At which of Piaget's periods of cognitive development would we expect most kindergarten students to be operating?

   a. concrete operations
   b. formal operations
   c. preoperational
   d. sensorimotor

3. **Application-level questions** require you to apply the information that you learned to a new situation. Application questions are common in math and science courses, but as you can see below, they may appear on any exam. What information do you have to know in order to answer the following application-level question?

Four-year-old Bobby insists that his mother give him a big glass of orange juice as she does for his older brother. But Bobby will drink only about three to four ounces of orange juice. Fortunately, Bobby's mother remembers Piaget's theory from her college child development course. How does she satisfy Bobby's wishes without wasting most of the orange juice?

   a. Promise to refill Bobby's glass if he finishes his juice.
   b. Give him his juice in a tall, thin glass.
   c. Allow him to pour as much juice as he wants.
   d. Hide the orange juice from him during breakfast.

4. **Analysis-level questions** require you to break down a complex concept into its components or parts. Many essay questions involve analysis. Look at the sample essay question below. Think about how you might go about answering it. What information do you need to answer this question?

Five-year-old Sally and her seven-year-old sister, Jill, each have a ball of clay exactly the same size to play with. Jill flattens her clay into a pancake, and Sally insists that Jill now has more clay than she does. Explain, using the concepts of centration and irreversibility, how Sally came to that conclusion.

5. **Synthesis-level questions** require you to bring information together into a single unit or whole. Many essay questions involve synthesis. What information from the selection do you need to know in order to answer this question? How would you combine the information to answer the question?

You are designing a curriculum for first-, second-, and third-grade science classes. Assuming that one of your goals is to increase the students' abilities to solve conservation problems, describe some science demonstrations that could help achieve that goal.

6. **Evaluation-level questions** require you to make judgments about the value or worth of an idea. In most cases, both analysis and synthesis are required to answer an evaluation-level question. They are the most difficult type of question to answer and require the highest-level thinking skills. What information would you need to know to answer the following question?

Some educators have argued that algebra, which involves abstract concepts, could actually be taught as early as third grade. Do you think that such a proposal is reasonable? Why, or why not?

Learn About Yourself

As you decide which strategies to use when you prepare for an exam, you should also consider how you learn best. Refer to the section on learning styles in Chapter 1. Using your preferred learning style as you prepare for exams may help you stay more focused on the material and may make your study sessions more productive. Don't forget, though, that using a combination of learning styles is often most effective when you're dealing with a new type of course, a professor who doesn't teach to your style, or a type of test that you've had difficulty with in the past.

Think about how you currently prepare for exams. Do you generally prepare for all exams the same way, or do you prepare for different exams in different ways? You may, for example, spend more time, put in more effort, or use better strategies for exams that are in your major or for those that you feel are more important or critical to your college success. Think about the different ways that you and your classmates or friends prepare for exams.

Activity 10-2

What Study Strategies Do You Use Now?

Describe the strategies or methods of preparation that you generally use when preparing for exams. Are you satisfied with the results? Why? Or why not? What changes would you like to see?

Activity 10-3

List Test-Preparation Strategies of Successful Students

Make a list of strategies that successful students use when preparing for exams. Then compare your responses with other members of your group. Select the twenty best exam preparation strategies and create a list. Then look back at the strategies you listed in Activity 10-2. Put a check mark next to each one you use now. Put a dot next to each one you'd like to use.

USE THE FIVE-DAY STUDY PLAN

Once you find out what the exam will be like, you should organize your study time. In this section, you will learn how to use the Five-Day Study Plan. This plan has several main ingredients that will help you learn and remember the course information. The **Five-Day Study Plan** provides you with a mechanism to space your learning over a period of days, divide the material so that you can work on it in small chunks, use active learning strategies to study the material, and self-testing strategies to monitor your learning.

Many students who have used this plan have reported dramatic improvements in their grades from one test to the next. The Five-Day Study Plan is not a magic solution to all of your problems; rather, it is a well-structured plan that puts into practice what we know about how people learn and remember.

Increase Your Study Time

One reason many new college students get poor grades on exams is that they don't put in enough time studying the material. How much time do you think you should spend studying for a four-chapter exam? How much time did you study for your last exam? Many students study about one to three hours the night before the exam. Compared with the time they put in on high school exams, this seems like a lot. Remember, though, that college exams may cover ten to twenty times as much information as high school tests. Most college students need to spend eight to ten hours studying to get an A or B on a college exam. Of course, this is only a general guideline. Some students constantly review material (daily and weekly) so that they don't need to put in quite as much time just before the exam. Other students may need to study even more. If you're taking a very challenging class (like Anatomy and Physiology or Organic Chemistry), you may need to double or even triple the suggested study time. As you'll see later in the chapter, it's not just the amount of time that makes the difference in your mastery of the material, but it's also what you do with that time.

Space Your Study

If you're trying to figure out when you can find time to study eight to twenty hours for one exam, don't panic. You don't need or really want to put in all of your study time on one day. It's much more effective to study over several days than to cram one day before an exam. Research studies have demonstrated that we learn better by spacing out our study over time. Instead of trying to study for ten hours the night before an exam, try studying for two hours each day for five days before the exam (Figure 10.2). If you need to put in more time, add more time to each day's study session or add more days to your study plan.

To set up your study plan, count backward from your exam date to decide when you should begin to study. To get in five days of study before a Friday exam, you would need to start studying on Sunday. When would you begin to study for a Monday exam? If you said Wednesday, you're right. If you said Tuesday, you could still be right. This is a flexible plan. If you work or even if you party on Saturdays, you can still use this plan. Just count back one more day to make up for the day that you decide to omit. However, never omit the day right before the exam; it's imperative to do a final review the day before the exam. Remember, we forget rapidly.

Divide the Material

The next step is to divide the material that will be on the exam. Make a list of the chapters, lecture topics, and outside readings that will be covered on the test. Then group or chunk them so that you study the lectures and readings covering the same topic at the same time. If your professor gave three lectures that related to the material in Chapter 1, you should study those lecture notes at the same time that you study Chapter 1 of the text. If your exam will cover four chapters, you can divide

FIGURE 10.2
Framework for the Five-Day
Study Plan

Tuesday			
	Prepare	CH 1	2 hrs
Wednesday			
	Prepare	CH 2	2 hrs
	Review	CH 1	30 min
Thursday			
	Prepare	CH 3	1-1/2 hrs
	Review	CH 2	30 min
	Review	CH 1	15 min
Friday			
	Prepare	CH 4	1 hr
	Review	CH 3	30 min
	Review	CH 2	15 min
	Review	CH 1	10 min
Sunday			
	Review	CH 4	30 min
	Review	CH 3	20 min
	Review	CH 2	10 min
	Review	CH 1	10 min
	Self-test		1 hr

the material into four chunks, studying one chapter per day and then conducting a final review on the last day. How would you divide the material if your test covered only two chapters? You could study the first half of Chapter 1 on day 1, the second half of Chapter 1 on day 2, and so on. If you only had three chapters on the exam, you could use a four-day plan instead, or you could divide the oldest (or most difficult) chapter in half. How would you set up a plan for six chapters or eight chapters? Working on smaller units of material each day allows you to work on it more actively and concentrate all of your effort on it.

When you set up your five-day plan, be sure to start with the oldest chapter first. When you look carefully at the framework of the Five-Day Study Plan, you'll notice that the oldest chapters are given the most preparation time and the most review time. You need to spend more time on the old material because it's not as fresh in your mind. Even though you may have read it, marked it, and even taken notes on it, much of that material may seem new to you when you begin to review. If you covered Chapter 1 four weeks ago, you won't remember very much of it.

In Figure 10.2, Chapters 3 and 4 are more familiar and therefore may require less preparation time and review. However, if Chapter 3 or 4 happens to be an especially difficult chapter, you may need to modify the plan and add some additional time for preparation and review. In the sample plan, how much time is spent studying (preparing and reviewing) each chapter? Remember, this plan is only a model. It can work as it's written for many of your exams, but it may need to be adjusted for other exams. If you had an exam covering only three chapters, you could eliminate one day and prepare effectively in four days instead. If your test covered five chapters, you could add a day. However, if your exam covers only two chapters, break them in half and use a five-day plan. Studying for only three days wouldn't provide you with enough opportunities to review and self-test.

Activity 10-4

Set Up a Framework for Your Study Plan

Set up a framework for a Five-Day Study Plan for an exam that you have coming up in the next few weeks. Decide when you're going to study; then divide up the material into four chunks. Use the framework in Figure 10.2 as a model. In a later activity, you'll have a chance to add active study strategies to your study plan.

Plan Active Study Tasks

Look again at the framework for the Five-Day Study Plan in Figure 10.2. It includes both time to prepare a chapter and time to review that chapter several times before the exam. (Remember that "CH 1" means the text chapter, the lecture notes, and any other related material.) The Five-Day Study Plan is a task-oriented plan. In many ways, it's like creating a "To Do" list for your study plan.

If you've been rereading your text and lecture notes for hours before an exam and still not getting the grades you want, you need to change your strategy. Unlike reading over the material, writing and reciting strategies are excellent ways of putting information into long-term memory. In Figure 10.3 you can see some suggested preparation and review tasks for Wednesday and Thursday, the second and third days of this Five-Day Study Plan. Unfortunately, most students can't learn all the important information in their notes and in the chapter by going over it a few times. To prepare well for an exam, you need to use a variety of active study strategies.

FIGURE 10.3

Actual Tasks for Five-Day Study Plan

Wednesday Prepare CH 2	1. Re-mark highlighting 2. Make study sheets 3. Make word cards 4. Make question cards
Review CH 1	1. Recite rehighlighted material *unknowns (recite main points) 2. Mark and recite study sheets 3. Recite word cards 4. Recite question cards
Thursday Prepare CH 3	1. Re-mark highlighting 2. Make study sheets 3. Make word cards 4. Make question cards
Review CH 2	1. Recite rehighlighted material *unknowns (recite main points) 2. Mark and recite study sheets 3. Recite word cards 4. Recite question cards

Review CH 1	1. Make a list of information still not
	   known from text or study
	   sheets—recite
	2. Recite cards still not known
	3. Make self-test questions

Use Active Preparation Strategies

Preparation strategies help you identify what you need to learn, condense it, organize it, and write it. You can use the mnemonic ICOW to help you remember the role of preparation strategies. Preparation strategies are primarily writing strategies. If you're a kinesthetic or visual learner, you'll find that preparation strategies are especially effective. Using at least three different preparation strategies allows you to work on the material in different ways. You can make word or question cards to learn key terms, facts, and details. You may also take notes on your text marking or even condense your lecture notes further as you reread them. Although these are all good preparation strategies, they tend to focus on the material in an isolated way. You should also include at least one integrated study strategy in your plan. Making study sheets or planning possible essay questions allows you to study and learn the material in a more integrated manner. As you gather and organize the information on one topic or one question, you form many additional associations with the material. This helps you create additional cues to long-term memory, which makes it easier to retrieve the information during the exam. Preparation strategies are effective learning strategies because they force you to identify, condense, organize, and write the material.

Although the preparation strategies tend to emphasize the visual and kinesthetic learning styles, auditory learners still need to identify and condense the key information for later review. To use your preferred learning style, you may find it useful to read out loud as you re-mark your text or to recite key points as you create word cards or prepare concept maps and study sheets, for example.

Use Active Review Strategies

During the review stage, you need to practice the material that you prepared each day in your study plan. **Review strategies** are mainly recitation strategies that help you rehearse, understand, self-test and evaluate your learning. We can use the mnemonic R-USE (recite to use them) to remember the role of review strategies. They force you to recite the information out loud, so they're especially effective for auditory learners. You could get the same level of practice by writing the material again, but that is a bit more time-consuming. By reciting the information in your predicted questions, word cards, and study sheets, for example, from the previous chapters each day, you can continue working on the material (often forming additional cues), gain a better understanding of it, keep it fresh in long-term memory, and monitor your learning. Each day, as you review the material, you can continue to condense what you still don't know.

The review strategies tend to emphasize the auditory learning style because they rely so heavily on recitation (reciting out loud from memory). However, visual and kinesthetic learners can review by writing down the material, picturing the material, and looking at the material before and after reciting it out loud. As you'll see, many of the review strategies incorporate hands-on activities such as recreating maps and charts, taking self-tests, working problems, and so on.

Since you'll be reviewing some of the material three or four times, it's also a good idea to vary your review strategies. Although you should use the same three or four strategies to prepare each chapter and to review each chapter the first time, you need to select different strategies to review the chapter the second, third, and fourth time. By working on the material different ways, you can create more new connections to it, use the learning style that may be the most effective, and make studying fun and interesting.

The activities that Crystal used to prepare and review one of the chapters for her sociology exam are shown in Figure 10.4. Notice how she continues to work

FIGURE 10.4
Crystal's Daily Review Strategies
for Chapter 4

Day 1 Prepare Ch. 4

	Thursday (Feb 28th) Prepare Ch. 4	(1) Reread and re-mark highlighting
		(2) Write answers to study guide
		(3) Predict essay questions
		(4) Make "fact" cards w/statistics + people of importance

Day 2 First Review of Ch. 4

	Friday (March 1st) Review Ch. 4	(1) Recite the rehighlighted w/attention to charts + diagrams
		(2) Recite fact cards
		(3) Write main points for essays
		(4) Recite answers to study guide

Day 3 Second Review of Ch. 4

	Saturday (March 2nd) Review Ch. 4	(1) Recite main points for essays
		(2) Recite troubling fact cards
		(3) Reread highlighting for details missed. Take notes on key pts.

Day 4 Third Review of Ch. 4

	Sunday (March 3rd) Review Ch. 4	(1) Write answers to essay questions
		(2) Recite fact cards + study guide questions

Day 5 Final Review of Ch. 4

	Monday (March 4th) Review Ch. 4	(1) Recite outlines for essays
		(2) Self-test

---

on the "troubling" or still unlearned information on each day of her five-day plan.

As you review, you're actively involved in practicing the material and self-testing. By reviewing the old material each day, you have more opportunities to learn it and keep it fresh in your long-term memory. Many students find that they really don't learn the course material until they've worked on it several times. Each time you review, you can also test your mastery of the material. If you can't recite the main points in the study sheets on day 2 that you prepared on day 1, you don't know the information. However, it's better to find that out on day 2 of your plan (instead of during the exam) because you will have three more days to work on the material.

The tasks listed in Figure 10.3 are just a few examples of the types of tasks that you could use to study for an exam. The menu of active preparation and review strategies includes many other excellent strategies you can use in your study plan (Figure 10.5). You also may develop some excellent strategies of your own. Varying the activities you use when you study can keep you from feeling bored. You also may discover that many of these active strategies are fun and make learning interesting and exciting.

It's easy to modify the format of your study plan. You can include specific times to study, check off tasks, or include specific topics or concepts that you want to learn during a specific study session.

Activity 10-5

Evaluate Sample Study Plans

Look at the four study plans available on the *College Study Skills* Web site. What are the strengths and weaknesses in each plan? Write down your ideas and then discuss your analysis with other members of your group.

Monitor Your Learning

One of the reasons that the Five-Day Study Plan is so effective is the built-in self-testing. As you review the old material each day, you should be testing your mastery of it. If you can't say it out loud or write it from memory, you don't really know it. Each time you recite your flash cards or practice the main points in your essay answer, you're checking to see what you do know and what you don't know. Although you may be disappointed that you don't get all the question cards correct the first time you review them, you will get some right. That tells you that you are learning the material and lets you know the strategies you're using are working. Have you ever tried to check your learning after just reading over the material? You may find that you don't really know very much of it.

Activity 10-6

Add Active Study Tasks to Your Study Plan

Select some active study tasks to add to your study plan from the menu in Figure 10.5. This list is not exhaustive, so use some preparation and review strategies from the list but feel free to create other strategies of your own. Exchange plans with another member of your group. What are the strengths and weaknesses of each plan? Discuss your responses with other members of your group.

USE ACTIVE STUDY STRATEGIES

In this section, you'll learn about a variety of active study strategies. Some of these strategies lend themselves to the preparation stage and others lend themselves to the review stage. You won't use all of these strategies to study for one exam; there

FIGURE 10.5
Menu of Active Study Tasks

PREPARATION STRATEGIES	REVIEW STRATEGIES
develop study sheets	recite study sheets
develop concept maps	replicate concept maps
make word cards	recite word cards
make question cards	recite question cards
make formula cards	practice writing formulas
make problem cards	work problems
make self-tests	take self-tests
do study guides	practice study guide info out loud
re-mark text material	take notes on re-marked text
do problems	make a list of 20 (30 or 40)
outline	recite list of 20 (30 or 40)
take notes	do "missed" problems
predict questions in the margin	recite main points from outline
chart related material	recite notes from recall cues
list steps in the process	recite out loud
predict essay questions	re-create chart from memory
plan essay answers	recite steps from memory
write essay answers	answer essay questions
answer end-of-chapter questions	practice reciting main points
prepare material for study group	write essay answers from memory
	recite answers
	explain material to group members

are just too many of them. What you should do, however, is try each of them as you prepare for different exams during the semester. You probably will find that some strategies work better for you than others. You also may find that certain strategies work well for one type of exam or course material but others are better for another.

Your learning style, your professor's teaching style, and the type of exam you are going to have all influence how you need to study. Figure 10.6 includes many of the active study strategies that are discussed in the remainder of this chapter. Notice how each of the "Study Tools" can be used in both the preparation and the review stages. As you read about how to use these strategies, think about which ones you would use to prepare for exams in each of your courses this semester.

Condense Your Text and Notes

A good way to start preparing for a test is to read through your text and lecture notes and condense the material that you'll need to review again. Think about what you do know and what you don't know. It certainly is possible that after several weeks of class, some of the information in the early chapters will be "old hat." You may not have to spend any more time on it at all. Don't spend time rereading the text material that you didn't mark, though. Some students have trouble skipping this unmarked material, but you must learn to trust the marking that you did. You

FIGURE 10.6
Effective Study Tools and
Strategies for the Five-Day
Study Plan

STUDY TOOL	PREPARATION STRATEGY	REVIEW STRATEGY*
Highlighting	Re-mark text and * unknowns	Recite main points out loud
Text notes	Dig through text and write main points and supporting details; develop recall column	Recite information, identifying connections among ideas from headings and/or recall columns
Predicted questions in the margin	Predict questions and underline the answers	Recite the answers out loud
Concept maps	Design and draw	Sketch from memory or recite key points
Charts	Create charts	Re-create charts from memory on scrap paper
Geographic maps	Prepare copy of map without answers for self-test	Recite and/or write out answers; check original
Study sheets	Dig through text and lecture notes to select, condense, and organize material under main topics	Practice reciting out loud or in writing
End-of-chapter questions	Write out answers	Practice reciting answers
Word cards, question cards, formula cards, problem cards	Select information and write out cards	Recite out loud or in writing; shuffle cards and retest; test in reverse; retest missed items
Study groups	Prepare materials as agreed to by group	Explain your material to group and take notes on others' explanations; discuss
Self-tests	Select information and construct test	Take test in writing and/or recite out loud—retest
Predict essay questions	Predict specific essay questions; plan and prepare answers	Practice reciting main points and writing out answers
List of 20, 30, or 40+	Determine content and write out list	Recite out loud and write out troubling items

*Goal for review strategies is to recite and write out material from memory.
Adapted from chart developed by Patricia Luberto. Used with permission.

can re-highlight, take notes, create questions, prepare study sheets, or write word cards on the material.

Identify the important information in your lecture notes as you reread them, too. You can condense them just as you did your text material. However, this is just the first step in learning the material. Remember, you need to write and recite to get the information into long-term memory—to learn it at the **recall level of learning.** At this level, you'll be able to recall the information without any additional cues.

If you took notes as you read or after you marked, you should review your text notes and mark them as your first step. However, if your professor tends to ask picky questions on small details, you may benefit from one quick rereading of your highlighting. This can be especially helpful if your exam is a multiple-choice test. To answer multiple-choice questions correctly, you often can rely on **recognition-level learning.** That means you don't need to recall the actual answer; you need only to *recognize* it from among the answers listed on the exam. If you've recently read that material, the answer may stand out or seem familiar to you. However, many instructors rephrase the information on multiple-choice tests, so you may not be able to recognize the correct answer. Of course, if your exam is completion, short answer, or essay in design, that quick rereading won't be very helpful because you'll have to supply the answers from memory.

Prepare Word Cards

Think back to the last objective test that you took. How many of the questions on the test required you to know the meaning of a word that was part of the specialized vocabulary for that unit of material? You may have been surprised to find a technical term somewhere in the question or in at least one of the possible answers. Many students don't spend much time on technical terminology because they know that they won't have to actually write out the definitions for an exam. What they don't realize, though, is that they're expected to know the meanings of those terms, and this understanding is necessary for answering many of the questions on the exam.

How do you learn all those terms? One way is to make **word cards.** By going through the chapter and writing out word cards, you're actively involved with the material. Just the process of writing them will help you learn them. Put the word on the front of a three-by-five card and then write a brief definition on the back. Put only one word on a card. You want to use them like flash cards, so they shouldn't be cluttered with information. If you're trying to save money, cut your cards in half.

Use Word Cards for Any Subject

You can make word cards for just about any subject. If you're in a psychology class, you may have forty or fifty technical terms for just one chapter. In addition, you may want to make cards for famous psychologists and what they did, theories, or even research studies that were emphasized by your professor. In History, put people, dates, events, treaties, or anything else you need to learn on the cards. Make formula cards for math and science classes. Put the formula on one side and the name of the formula or when it's used on the other side. Of course, word cards are a great way to learn foreign-language vocabulary terms. Some students even put diagrams or sketches of things that they'll have to identify on the front of the card and the explanations on the back. Look at the examples of word cards from History, Biology, and Psychology in Figure 10.7. Word cards are easy to make, and they're quite effective in getting information into long-term memory.

Make Word Cards Early

If, like some students, you make as many as fifty word cards for just one chapter, you may find that this activity takes up most of your preparation time. If this is the case, you may want to make your cards before you begin to study. Some students make word cards even before they read a chapter for the first time. Making word cards provides you with an excellent preview before reading and allows you plenty of time to learn all of the definitions. You can also make your cards as you read the

FIGURE 10.7

Examples of Word Cards

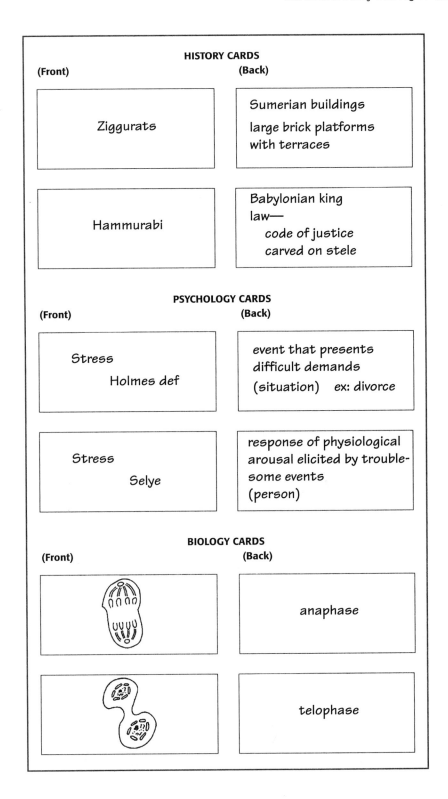

chapter. After you have read the chapter and gone to the lecture, you'll have a better understanding of the material and may find that making the cards provides you with a good review.

Practice Your Word Cards

After you make your word cards, you need to learn them. Although you'll learn some of them just from writing them out, you won't learn all of them that way.

Study them by practicing ten or fifteen at a time. Carry them around with you and recite or mumble them whenever you have a few minutes to spare. After you know that group, start on the next pack of fifteen.

Hold the stack of cards in your hand and look at the first term. Try to recite the definition out loud. Turn the card over to check your answer. If you were right, set that card aside. If you couldn't think of the answer or were not completely correct, read the definition out loud. Then put it on the bottom of the pile. Continue practicing the cards until you have none left in your hand. After you know all the terms, shuffle the cards to check your learning. Sometimes you remember the definition of one word because you got a clue to it from the previous term. Although it is good to learn information in chunks, sometimes you need to separate closely related information to make sure that you can distinguish among similar terms. If you also include the word card information in your maps, charts, study sheets, or outlines, you'll find that you can tie the information to a major concept. This will help reduce the effects of learning the information in isolation.

You also may want to practice your cards in reverse. Students usually look at the name of a term and then try to recite the definition. You also can review by looking at the definition and saying the word or name or date. It's especially important to review math or science formulas both ways, backward and forward. You need to be able to identify a formula if it's given as part of a test question and also write that formula if it's not given.

Incidentally, it's very important to recite the answer rather than just "think of it." Our brains can play tricks on us. In a class experiment, I asked students to study ten word cards and practice their definitions. After about fifteen minutes, I asked if anyone knew all ten terms. Several students volunteered to be tested. I asked the students to say the definitions out loud. Interestingly, several of the students who thought they knew the definitions couldn't say them. If you can say it out loud, then you can be sure that you know it.

Activity 10-7

Learn Technical Vocabulary

Prepare a set of word cards for all the technical terms from one chapter in any of your texts. Practice reviewing the cards using the reciting and writing methods described previously. Then try to write or recite the definitions. How many did you get right? How many times did you need to practice the terms? Which strategy worked best for you?

Make Question Cards

Making **question cards** is another active strategy for preparing for exams. Instead of just concentrating on terms, names, dates, and events, you can dig through your text and lecture notes and write questions on all types of information. By making question cards, you actually are focusing on specific details you may need to know for the exam. You also may approach the material in a slightly different manner and focus more on understanding rather than on simple memorization.

If you already wrote questions in the margin of your text or lecture notes, you can write different questions on cards (or put the ones you keep getting wrong on cards). The practice you get from writing out the questions and answers may help you learn the information.

You can make question cards on any type of information. Write the question on the front of the card and then write the answer on the back. Make at least twenty-five per chapter. If you already have prepared a stack of word cards for the chapter, concentrate on different information for your question cards. Focus on lists or on how things relate or how they differ. Look at the sample question cards for Business, History, and Biology in Figure 10.8. These questions emphasize steps in a process, lists of things, and causes and effects.

Practice Your Question Cards

Use your question cards as you would flash cards. Practice answering the questions aloud until you know them all. You can use your question cards if you work in groups or with a study partner. If both you and your partner make question cards on the chapters, you'll be able to test each other on the material. You may be surprised because each of you will write different questions on the same material. Although you may have questions on the same information, each of you may approach it from a different angle. This can be helpful in preparing for the exam because you can test your learning in several ways. Your question cards are in fact another form of a self-test. Each time you recite the answer, you're prompting your memory for the information—you're practicing retrieval.

Make Math or Science Problem Cards

Using question cards is especially helpful for students who are taking math and science classes. If you have to solve problems on your exams, you may find that

FIGURE 10.8
Sample Question Cards

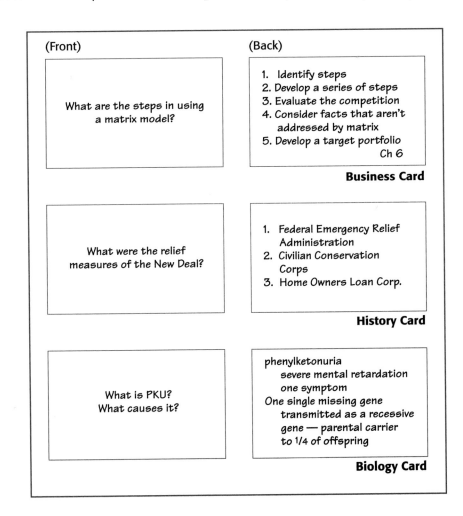

(Front)   (Back)

What are the steps in using a matrix model?

1. Identify steps
2. Develop a series of steps
3. Evaluate the competition
4. Consider facts that aren't addressed by matrix
5. Develop a target portfolio
   Ch 6

Business Card

What were the relief measures of the New Deal?

1. Federal Emergency Relief Administration
2. Civilian Conservation Corps
3. Home Owners Loan Corp.

History Card

What is PKU?
What causes it?

phenylketonuria
    severe mental retardation
    one symptom
One single missing gene
    transmitted as a recessive
    gene — parental carrier
    to 1/4 of offspring

Biology Card

making problem cards is essential to getting a good grade. Have you ever started a math, chemistry, or physics problem on a test and realized you weren't sure which kind of problem it was? Even though you knew how to do all of the problems when you reviewed, their random order on the exam may have left you confused.

One of the problems with reviewing for math or problem-related tests is that we tend to review within the context of the book. If you were going to have an exam on two chapters of Algebra, for example, you probably would review the information in the first part of Chapter 1 and then do some of the sample problems. Then you might review the next section and do some of those problems. The trouble, though, is that you always "know" what type of problem you're doing because you pick up clues or cues from the section of the text in which you're working. What you need to do is learn to recognize the special features of each problem so that you'll be able to identify the problems when they appear out of context on a test.

One way you can do this is by creating your own test bank, a series of sample problems on cards. After you've studied for the exam, put three of each kind of problem on the front of an index card (one problem per card). Don't put any other information on the front of the card; you don't want to give yourself any clues that won't be on the test. Then, on the back of the card, put four things (Figure 10.9). First, at the top of the card write the type of problem that it is. After that, write the first step that you need to take to solve the problem. Then put the answer or solution on the card. Finally, in the bottom corner put the page number where you got the problem or where you can go for help.

After you've prepared all of your cards, shuffle them to mix them up. Go through the cards orally a few times. Look at each problem and try to state the type of problem it is and the first step you have to take to solve it. If you're wrong, look at the problem and try to determine a way to remember which type of problem it is. Don't try to memorize the solution and page number; they're there only for reference. If you've prepared well, you should be able to solve the problem once you identify its type. Next, test yourself by solving the problems on paper. Take the stack and work each problem as though it were a test question. Turn the card over

FIGURE 10.9
Sample Math Problem Cards

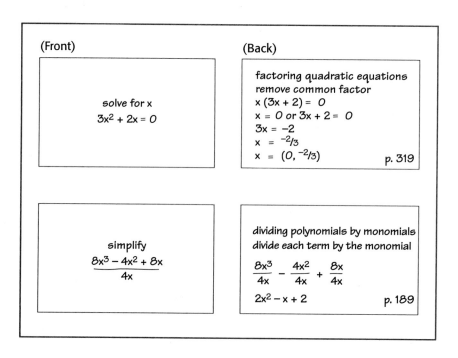

and check your work. Continue until you can do all of the problems. Problem cards provide an excellent self-test.

Create Study Sheets

Developing study sheets is one of the best ways to prepare for an exam. A **study sheet** is a one-page compilation (a synthesis) of all the important information on a particular topic. The sample study sheet on Mesopotamia in Figure 10.10 is the first of four study sheets prepared for the first chapter of a Western Civilization exam.

It's easy to make study sheets. Put a specific topic at the top of a sheet of paper and go through your text and lecture notes looking for all of the important information about that topic. Then combine the information in an organized manner. Creating a study sheet requires you to identify, condense, organize, and integrate the important information from both the text and your lecture notes into a single study sheet. By the way, this is an excellent way to prepare for an open-book exam. When you create study sheets, include both the material you already know and the material you need to learn. The already learned information will help you learn and remember the new information because it will serve as hooks and cues to help you store and retrieve the new information. Study sheets allow you to work on information using high-level rehearsal strategies combined with organizational and elaboration strategies.

FIGURE 10.10
Sample Study Sheet

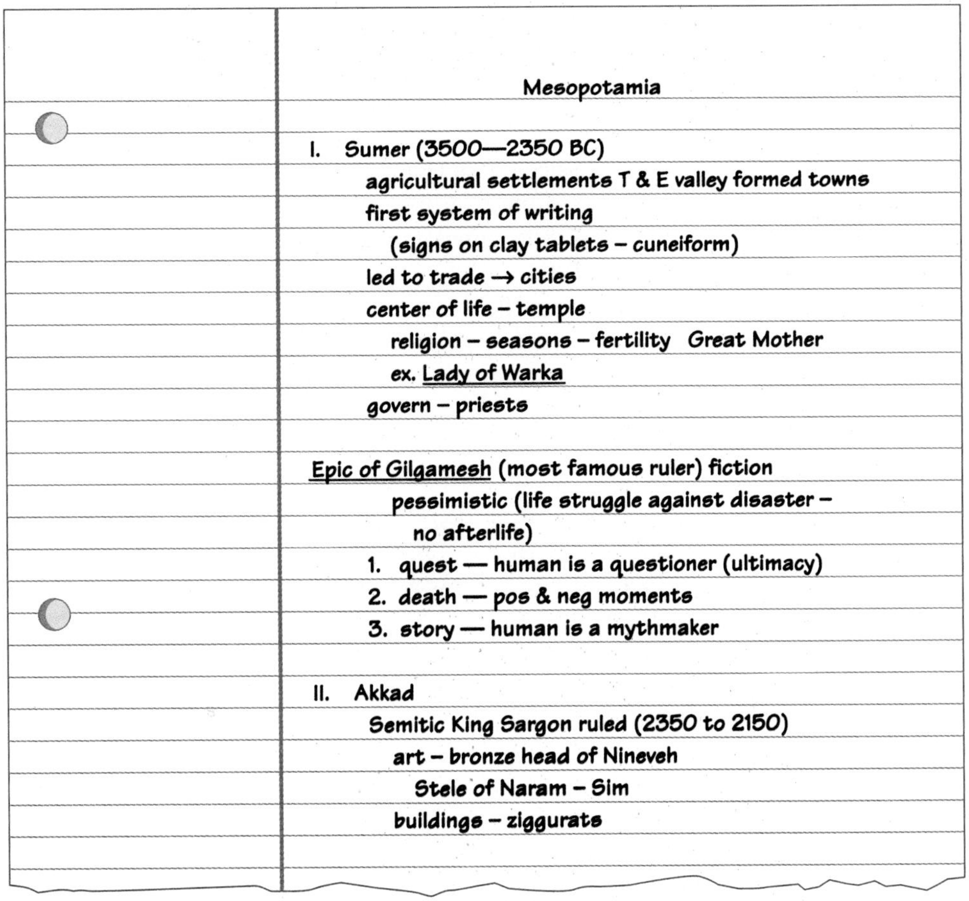

Mesopotamia

I. Sumer (3500—2350 BC)
agricultural settlements T & E valley formed towns
first system of writing
(signs on clay tablets – cuneiform)
led to trade → cities
center of life – temple
religion – seasons – fertility   Great Mother
ex. Lady of Warka
govern – priests

Epic of Gilgamesh (most famous ruler) fiction
pessimistic (life struggle against disaster –
no afterlife)
1. quest — human is a questioner (ultimacy)
2. death — pos & neg moments
3. story — human is a mythmaker

II. Akkad
Semitic King Sargon ruled (2350 to 2150)
art – bronze head of Nineveh
Stele of Naram – Sim
buildings – ziggurats

As you'll see later, you can use written formats, maps, or charts. If you're using an outline or modified-block format, it's important to include headings and subheadings in your study sheet. The headings help you break up the information into manageable units and serve as cues to help you learn and remember the main points and details in your study sheet. How many study sheets you prepare depends a lot on how you organize or divide the information you need to learn. If you're preparing for a History exam, for example, you can make a study sheet on each main topic that was covered in lecture or each main subdivision of the chapter. You might have three study sheets for one chapter, or you could have six or seven.

Many students get confused when they make study sheets. They simply jot down bits and pieces of information that seem important as they review the text and lecture material. These study sheets, as they call them, often contain long lists of unrelated details. Because the information is not organized under headings, it rarely contains sufficient detail about any one topic. These isolated facts, definitions, and theories are hard to learn and remember because they aren't connected or related to anything else. It's important to work on information in both an isolated way (using word or question cards) and in an integrated way (using study sheets and by preparing essay questions and answers, which will be discussed in Chapter 12). Learning information in an integrated or connected way helps you prepare well for both objective and essay exams.

The second advantage of preparing study sheets is that you have concise "summaries" of the information, which can be used for review. Study sheets provide a quick way to review as you progress through your Five-Day Study Plan, and they're useful when you prepare for comprehensive finals. After you prepare your study sheets, use them to review the important information. Practice reciting the information. If you have a lot of information on a study sheet, focus on the main headings first. Learn them and then use them as cues to help you recall the details.

You may also find it helpful to write questions in the margin of your study sheets to cue your recall of specific facts, statistics, and details. Look back at the study sheet on Mesopotamia (Figure 10.9). What questions would you write in the margin? Hollie developed another strategy for her study sheets for Science for Elementary Teachers. She added definitions for her technical terms in the margin instead (see Figure 10.11).

Hollie highlighted the words in her study sheet and wrote the definitions in the margin directly across from them. This saves space on the study sheet and provides another way of self-testing the technical terms.

Use Different Formats

You can use different formats in designing your study sheets. You may use a written format, a chart (or matrix) format, or even a map format. Look at a portion of the study sheets that Angela and Juanita prepared to study for their exams (Figures 10.12 and 10.13). Angela worked directly from her text and lecture notes to prepare a chart on the material. Juanita combined information from her text and her lecture notes when she prepared a Semantic Web for an accounting class in Figure 10.12. She used the text to help organize her map and then used information from her notes to fill in the details. You also should include diagrams, formulas, and even sample problems, as Pete did in his study sheet for a physics exam in Figure 10.14. Which method do you like better? If you already have been using one or more of these techniques for taking notes, you'll find that it doesn't take long to prepare your study sheets.

FIGURE 10.11
Hollie's Study Sheet with
Definitions in the Margin

Muticellular organisms that capture and consume molecules of other organisms	**Animals**
	General Information
	over 1.3 million species
	greatest diversity
	include more than 30 phyla
	breathe in oxygen + exhale carbon dioxide
organisms without backbones	**Invertebrates**
	coral and sponges
	can be broken into separate minute
	organisms that function independently
	worms, mollusks, + microscopic organisms
invertebrates with a hard exoskeleton, specialized segments, and jointed appendages	**Arthropods**
	most successful phylum
crabs, shrimp, lobsters	spiders, insects, crustacea
	segmented bodies + jointed limbs
	70% of all animals
hard external covering used to support and protect	have an exoskeleton for support
	shed exoskeletons when growing
central segment with legs	body—head, thorax, and heart
have spinal cord encased in a backbone	**Vertebrates**
	rabbits, frogs, fish, birds
	Bony fish
	skeletons made from bones
	gills supply oxygen in stagnant water
vertebrates with a body plan and reproductive mode between fishes and reptiles	**Amphibians**
	life cycle on land and in water
	tadpoles evolve into frogs
	3 chambered heart + circulatory system

FIGURE 10.12
Angela's Study Sheet

TYPES OF TERRESTRIAL BIOMES	DEFINITION	CLIMATE	TYPES OF PLANTS	TYPES OF ANIMALS
TUNDRA	A biome found in polar regions and characterized by permafrost and a brief summer.	– average monthly temp –10°C – winter is a way of life – summers are short and cool	– sphagnum mosses – lichens – herbs, grasses, flowers	– arctic hares – lemmings – arctic foxes – snowy owls – arctic wolves – polar bears
TAIGA	A biome characterized by harsh winters, warmer summers, and a diverse array of plants.	– similar to tundra but summers are warmer – temperatures fluctuate wildly	– evergreens: spruce, fir, pine, and larch – deciduous trees: beech, aspen, willow and ash	– rodents, rabbits, moose, elk, deer – weasel, mink, lynx, wolves, bears – birds: eagles, falcons, buzzards, ducks
TEMPERATE FOREST	A biome found in the middle latitudes with rich soil and ample rainfall.	– mild winters – year-round rainfall	– shrubs, herbs – douglas fir – oak, hickory	– deer, boar, foxes, wildcats, martens, lynx, elk, moose, caribou – birds

FIGURE 10.13
Juanita's Study Map

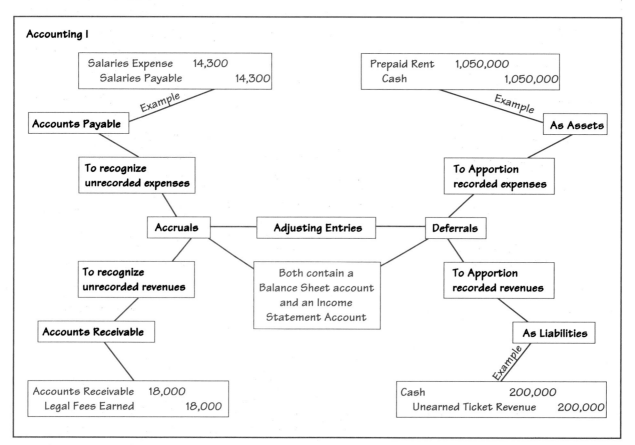

Note: Blue represents information taken from lecture notes.

FIGURE 10.14
Pete's Study Sheet

<u>RESISTANCE</u>

Resistance comes from many things in a circuit. The most common source of resistance comes from a resistor. The symbol for a resistor is:

A variable resistor or Rheostat is given by:

The equation $I = V/R$ can be used to solve for R (Resistance)

To find total resistance in a circuit several rules apply
— For resistors in series, the currents are all the same
— Resistors in series add directly to get total resistance
— Resistors in parallel, the voltages are the same
— Resistors in parallel add reciprocally

Resistors in Series   Resistors in Parallel

Total Resistance   Total Resistance
for Series   for Parallel
$R = R_1 + R_2$ $1/R = 1/R_1 + 1/R_2$

Activity 10-8

Work Together to Prepare a Study Sheet

Work together to prepare a study sheet on the Five-Day Study Plan. Be sure that you combine the information from your text and your lecture notes. Share your study sheet with other members of the class. Did you include the same topics? What changes would you make the next time?

Make Self-Tests

Making **self-tests** is another active way to prepare for an exam. To make a self-test, you have to decide what information you need to know for the exam and then formulate questions about it. Most students tend to write either short answer or completion questions.

Use the Same Type of Questions

Although you may have already written questions in the margin or on question cards, you can benefit even more from your self-tests if they're composed of the same types of questions that will be on the exam. For example, if you're going to have a Psychology exam that's fifty multiple-choice questions, you may be able to improve your score by writing multiple-choice test items rather than completion items. One advantage of actually making up multiple-choice items is that you have to generate three or four wrong answers in addition to the right answer. This can help you improve your score on the exam because you're learning to distinguish between the correct answer and several possible but incorrect answers. In a sense you're predicting the incorrect answers or **distractors** that your professor may also use. If you choose the same ones that are on the actual test, you'll be able to eliminate them immediately.

If you write questions only at the knowledge level, you may be unable to answer higher-level questions. That may explain why you may have felt well prepared for an exam but couldn't answer some of the questions. If you have to answer comprehension- or application-level questions on an exam, you should try to write questions at that level for your self-test. Writing higher-level questions does require more time and effort than writing knowledge-level questions, but it will better prepare you for the types of questions that you'll actually have to answer.

In the same way, writing your own true/false items can help you tune in to key words that can be used or changed to make a statement false. Making up matching tests helps you make fine distinctions among terms, concepts, people, and so on. If you'll have to answer essay questions, you need to prepare by predicting and practicing possible essay test questions. A detailed discussion of how to prepare for essay tests will follow in Chapter 12.

Use Your Self-Test to Monitor Your Learning

You can use your self-test to monitor your learning. One benefit of making self-tests is that you can use them over and over again to test your knowledge of the information. Write the answers on another sheet of paper or on the back of your self-test. Once you mark the answers on the test, you have changed the test into a review sheet. As you prepare the chapter, make a self-test and then take the test as a way of reviewing what you have learned. Many students create their self-tests as a review strategy on day 2 or day 3 of the plan. Then they can take the test several times before the real exam. Self-testing gives you a feeling of accomplishment—makes you feel like all the hard work is paying off. That motivates you to keep going. You also will find that as you test your learning, you won't know some of the material. Identifying what you still don't know allows you to focus your efforts the next day on that material. Self-testing also allows you to practice retrieving information from your long-term memory. Since that's exactly what you'll have to do on the exam, the retrieval practice better prepares you for the test. According to Halpern and Hakel, "The single most important variable in promoting long-term retention and transfer is practice at retrieval."[3] Finally, taking a self-test on the last day of your study plan can help reduce any anxiety that you may be feeling about the exam. After all, if you take your test and do well, you'll know that you know the material.

---

[3]Diane Halpern and Milton Hakel, "Applying the Science of Learning," *Change* (July/August 2003): 36–41.

MORE ACTIVE STUDY STRATEGIES

PREPARE REVIEW CARDS. In some classes, students are permitted to take one index card to the exam with anything on it they wish. Even if you aren't permitted to do so, creating a review card may be an excellent final review strategy. To do it you need to identify those key pieces of information that are the most critical or that you still don't know. Writing and organizing the information on the card are active ways to review for your exam.

TURN DIAGRAMS INTO A SELF-TEST. Photocopy or trace any important diagrams that may be on the exam and label them with numbers instead of names. Then use them to test your learning by reciting or writing the actual names of the bones, structures, or muscles, for example. You can use your labeled version as your answer key.

FORM STUDY GROUPS. Adult learners are accustomed to working in groups or teams in the workplace and at home. Find students in your classes who are interested in working together to prepare for exams. But rather than just getting together just before the exam, work as a team throughout the semester. Take turns asking and answering questions, share notes, study sheets, and self-tests.

MAKE A LIST OF 20, 30, OR 40 OR MORE. Another final review strategy is to list the 20 to 40 or more most important things that you think will be on the test. It's important to list the actual information and not just the topic. Then review your list just before the exam as a final review and a way to focus your concentration. After the exam, check to see how many items on your list were on the exam. This strategy also helps you monitor your ability to predict what will be on the exam.

USE STUDY GUIDES TO TEST YOUR LEARNING. Many textbooks come with a study guide that includes word lists, questions, and practice tests. Don't actually fill in your study guide as you read the chapter. Instead, write the words on cards so you can shuffle them to learn them without cues. Then answer the questions and take the tests on notebook paper. That way you can use the study guide again to test your learning before the exam.

USE OLD EXAMS AS A RESOURCE. Use copies of old exams, which are often available in the library or your college learning center, to get more information about what the test will be like. You can get an idea about the kinds of questions the instructor uses, the topics that were emphasized, and the level of detail of questions. If the tests closely parallel your current material, take them for extra practice.

PREPARE TAPED SELF-TESTS. Read your test questions into a tape recorder, pause after each question while letting the tape run, and then read the answer. As you commute to school or work, you can take your tests. Try to answer the question out loud during the paused portion of the tape, listen to the answer, and check your learning.

GET YOUR FAMILY AND FRIENDS INVOLVED. Your family and friends can be a great resource to you as you prepare for tests. Ask a friend or family member to help you with your word or question cards. Teach the material to your friends, parents, or older children. Ask someone to quiz you by asking you the word or question cards or questions from the study sheets or self-tests that you prepared.

Activity 10-9

Create a Taped Self-Test

 Develop a self-test on a cassette tape to play as you commute to and from school or work. Be sure to let the tape run for a few seconds after you record your question. Then record the correct answer. As you listen to the tape, recite the answer to each

Continued

Activity 10-9

Create a Taped Self-Test (continued)

question out loud and then check it against the correct answer that you recorded. How did making the tape help you learn the information? How often were you able to play the tape and take your own self-test? How effective was this strategy in preparing you for the exam? Would you use this strategy again? Why, or why not?

Use Recitation Strategies

If you've been practicing your word or question cards, you've probably discovered that reciting is one of the best ways to get information into long-term memory. If you like using recitation strategies, there are a number of them that you can try. First, practice the important information by reciting it by using the headings in your notes, text, or study sheets as cues. Cover the information with your hand or look away, and then try to recite it, or use the questions in your recall column to test your memory. Seeing, saying, and hearing the information help you put it into long-term memory.

Teaching the information to someone else is another effective recitation strategy. If you're lucky enough to have a friend or relative who is willing to be your "guinea pig," you can take on the role of instructor and explain everything you know about the subject. One advantage of a human partner is that he or she can easily signal understanding or confusion. If your partner doesn't understand the information, you can try to explain it in another way. This may force you to re-phrase the information in your own words, which helps you learn it, too.

You can teach the material to anything—a dog, a plant, or even a stuffed animal. Explaining the material out loud helps you clarify the information for yourself. Sit with your book and notes open and pretend that you're trying to explain the information to someone who doesn't understand it. Pretend that someone asked you a question about a particular topic and answer it.

If you're being tutored or are part of a study group, remember one thing: The person who does the talking is the one who does the learning. Just listening to someone else explain something is a passive activity. When I was taking statistics in college, I walked to and from the parking lot with another classmate. I asked questions about something we had just covered, and he explained it to me. He then asked if I understood, and I always said, "yes," but often I was still not sure I did understand. Finally, one day I stopped my friend in the middle of explaining something and said, "Wait a minute. Let *me* explain it to you. If I make a mistake, stop me." After that I did the explaining. I found that I truly understood the information because I had to put it into my own words.

Activity 10-10

Review by Recitation

Select two headed sections from one of your texts or from one of the excerpts in this text. Review one section by reading over it a few times. Then review the second section by reciting the information or "teaching" it to someone or something else. Which method was more effective in helping you learn the information? Why?

EVALUATE YOUR PREPARATION

Now that you've experimented with many of the test-preparation strategies, you need to evaluate their effectiveness. How comfortable you feel when you use certain strategies may indicate whether they fit your preferred learning style. How effective they are in helping you learn and master the material may indicate how well they fit your instructor's teaching style, and the course material itself. Finally, your performance on the exam may indicate how well your study strategies match your instructor's testing style.

Evaluate as You Prepare

You can evaluate your study strategies even as you prepare for the exam. Monitor your learning each day of your Five-Day Study Plan. By reviewing the previously prepared and reviewed material the next day, you have an opportunity to test your learning. By reciting, writing, or taking self-tests, you can find out what you do know and what you don't know—what you need to continue to review. In addition, you can find out how successful your strategies actually are. If you study your lecture notes by simply reading over them for two hours, you may find that the next day you can't recall the key information when you try to recite the answers to the questions in the margin. If, on the other hand, you study your lecture notes by further condensing them and reciting key points, you may find that the next day you can easily recite the key information by using your recall questions. It's easy to see which strategy works when you monitor your learning each day.

Evaluate After You Complete Your Plan

You can also evaluate your preparation strategies after you complete your study plan. Conducting a final review, taking a self-test, and even assessing how well prepared you feel are methods of evaluating your study plan. If you find yourself moving through the exam at a steady pace, knowing most of the answers, and thinking to yourself, "I knew this would be on the test," you did a good job of preparing. If, on the other hand, you find yourself moving slowly through the exam, skipping a lot of questions, and asking, "Where did these questions come from?" you probably didn't prepare properly for the exam. When things aren't going well during exams, many students tell themselves that they should have studied more (to them that means longer). Sometimes, though, it's not the time spent, but rather the way that time was spent and the strategies used that are the keys to success.

Evaluate After the Exam

After each exam, you should evaluate your entire study plan. Consider how much time you spent studying, the material you stressed or omitted, and the strategies that you used. Once your exam is graded and returned, you can make even better decisions about what worked and what didn't. Be sure to look at both the questions that you got right and those that you got wrong. Evaluating your study plan and your study strategies can help you do better on your next exam. By continuing to use the strategies that do work and replacing the ones that are less successful, you can improve your performance on future exams. You can't prepare for every exam the same way, though. Different courses, different professors, and even different types of material require you to tailor your study plan and study strategies to each specific exam.

Activity 10-11

Evaluate Your Exam-Preparation Strategies

Evaluate the preparation strategies that you used to prepare for one of your exams. Consider the following questions as you analyze your study plan.

1. What study strategies did you use to prepare for the exam?

2. How effective were each of the strategies that you used?

3. After you finished taking your exam, how did you feel about your preparation?

4. When your exam was returned, did you feel that you used effective strategies?

5. What changes do you plan to make when you prepare for your next exam?

Activity 10-12

Where Are You Now?

Now that you have completed Chapter 10, take a few minutes to repeat the "Where Are You Now?" activity, located on the *College Study Skills* Web site. What changes did you make as a result of reading this chapter? How are you planning to apply what you've learned in this chapter?

SUMMARY

Preparing for exams requires you to be a strategic learner. If you prepare the same way that you did for high school tests, use the same strategies for all of your courses, or prepare the same way as your friends or classmates do, you may not get the grades you want or deserve. Before you prepare for an exam, you need to learn as much about the exam as you can. That way, you can design your study plan correctly. You need to plan what to study, when to study, and how to study. You may decide to study with a group for a math exam but study alone for your history exam. That's fine; you need to consider your learning style as well as the type of exam you'll have to determine how you can learn best. In any case, you should set up a Five-Day Study Plan to organize your study efforts and space out your learning. Divide the material into smaller units so that you can concentrate your efforts and incorporate daily reviews. Use active study strategies as you prepare and review each of the chapters or units of material. Re-marking the text, taking notes, predicting questions in the margin, preparing word and question cards, making study sheets, developing self-tests, and reciting are just a few of the active strategies that will help you learn the material for your exam. You shouldn't study for every exam the same way. Choose the strategies and techniques that you think will work the best for you. Try different strategies for different subjects. Forget about just "reading over" the material, though; that won't help you remember it for the exam. By using a variety of active learning strategies, you can achieve your goal. You must be actively involved with the material to get it into long-term memory—to really learn it. Finally, evaluate your study plan as you prepare, during the exam, and before your next exam, and make some changes if your performance doesn't match your goals.

REVIEW QUESTIONS

Terms You Should Know: Make a flash card for each term.

Analysis-level questions	Question cards
Application-level questions	Recall-level learning
Comprehension-level questions	Recognition-level learning
Distractors	Review strategies
Evaluation-level questions	Self-tests
Five-Day Study Plan	Study sheet
Knowledge-level questions	Synthesis-level questions
Preparation strategies	Word cards

Completion: Fill in the blank to complete each of the following statements.

1. You should study the _____ chapter on day 1 of the Five-Day Study Plan.

2. You should study for _____ to _____ hours for a college exam.

3. Studying your text and lecture material together is known as _____ study.

4. If you only have two chapters to study for an exam, you should prepare _____ on day 1.

5. The review strategies give you more opportunities for _____ your learning.

Multiple Choice: Circle the letter of the best answer for each of the following questions. Be sure to underline key words and eliminate wrong answers.

6. _____-level questions require you to understand the information so you can select the answer even when it is phrased differently on the exam.
   - **A.** Knowledge
   - **B.** Comprehension
   - **C.** Application
   - **D.** Analysis

7. Which of the following is the least effective time to evaluate your exam preparation?
   - **A.** As you prepare for the exam
   - **B.** After you finish studying
   - **C.** During the exam
   - **D.** After the exam

Short Answer–Essay: On a separate sheet, answer each of the following questions.

8. How are preparation strategies and review strategies different?

9. Why do some students have difficulty preparing for exams? What should they do differently?

10. Why is the Five-Day Study Plan so effective?

"Today I took my psychology exam. Before I took the exam, I decided I would try the strategy of answering the easiest questions first. As I answered the questions I knew and skipped the ones that I didn't know, my confidence grew. I felt like I actually knew the material. I realized later that my test anxiety had subsided. I'm glad that I tried this strategy; now I know it will be useful for future exams."

Alison Marney
Student

TAKING OBJECTIVE TESTS

In this chapter you will learn more about:
- **How to reduce test anxiety**
- **General test-taking strategies**
- **Specific test-taking strategies**
- **Learning from exams**

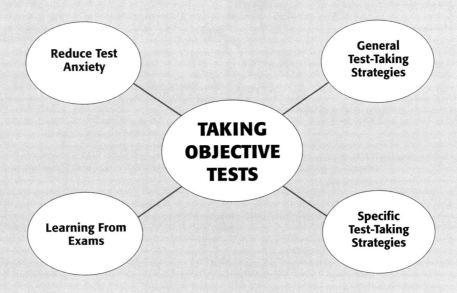

Activity 11-1

Where Are You Now?

Take a few minutes to answer *yes* or *no* to the following questions.

	YES	NO
1. Do you always read the directions before you begin to answer the questions on an objective exam?	_____	_____
2. Do you eliminate wrong answers on multiple-choice exams?	_____	_____
3. Does test anxiety interfere with your performance on exams?	_____	_____
4. Do you ever leave blanks on exams?	_____	_____
5. Do you use strategies to help you figure out the correct answer when you are unsure of it?	_____	_____
6. Do you ever find that you're unable to finish an exam before time runs out?	_____	_____
7. Do you go back over the entire exam before you turn it in?	_____	_____
8. After your exam is returned, do you go over it to evaluate your preparation and clarify your errors?	_____	_____
9. When you get your exam back, are you often surprised by the grade that you received?	_____	_____
10. Do you usually make careless errors on your exams?	_____	_____
Total Points	_____	

Give yourself 1 point for each *yes* answer to questions 1, 2, 5, 7, and 8 and 1 point for each *no* answer to questions 3, 4, 6, 9, and 10. Now total up your points. A low score indicates that you need to develop some new skills for taking objective tests. A high score indicates that you are already using many good strategies.

REDUCE TEST ANXIETY

To perform well on objective tests, you have to be well prepared. However, several other factors also may contribute to your success or failure. One of these factors often is referred to as your "test-taking ability." Some students are more skilled at taking tests than others. They have learned strategies and techniques that improve their performance on exams. Another factor that can affect test performance is your level of comfort when you take an exam. Some students view exams as everyday events, whereas other students consider them to be monumental obstacles that must be overcome. These different attitudes toward exams may be, in part, a result of students' varying levels of test anxiety.

All students experience a certain level of test anxiety at one time or another, but some students experience high levels of anxiety, fear, and frustration before, during, and after taking exams. Understanding the real causes of test anxiety and developing coping techniques can help you reduce the amount of test anxiety you experience.

What Is Test Anxiety?

Some students come into an exam feeling well prepared, well rested, and highly motivated. Other students, however, feel uncertain about their level of preparation and anxious about their performance on the test. We could say that they are experiencing test anxiety. **Test anxiety** involves both physical responses, such as headache, nausea, rapid heart beat and shallow breathing, and emotional responses, such as worry and negative thoughts. What are some common symptoms of test anxiety? The following list was suggested by college students:

nausea	fainting	throwing up
light-headedness	going blank	shaking
sweaty palms	worrying about failing	headaches
butterflies	trouble concentrating	feeling tense
heart pounding	diarrhea	crying

Of course, not everyone exhibits all of these symptoms of test anxiety, but some students do experience one or more of them. Can you think of any others that could be added to the list?

Although many students experience test anxiety, we don't know for sure whether test anxiety really causes some students to perform less well on exams. The connection between test anxiety and poor test performance still is being investigated by many researchers. However, test anxiety does appear to be related to poor test performance in students who exhibit very high levels of anxiety. For most of us, though, test anxiety alone does not cause test failure. Instead, lack of preparation (which can in fact increase text anxiety) is the real cause of test failure.

What Causes Test Anxiety?

What causes some students to experience test anxiety while others appear calm and collected on exams? Although there's no real answer to this question, several possible explanations may help us understand the problem. For some students, past experiences during exams lead to anxious feelings about subsequent exams. Failure accompanied by embarrassment and frustration in one testing situation can lead to anxiety in the next. Failure, by the way, doesn't mean the same thing for every student. When most people talk about failing an exam, they mean getting a grade that is below passing. For some students, however, getting a C or even a B is like failing; they fail to get the grade they wanted or needed. Excellent students often exhibit high levels of test anxiety because of the pressure they (or others) put on themselves to be the best.

The amount or level of anxiety that students experience also may depend on the value that they place on the exam. If doing well in the course is very important to you personally or professionally, you may view the exam as a critical or "must win" situation. On the other hand, if the class is seen as having little value or being unimportant to your future, you may experience little anxiety. This may explain why you may experience test anxiety in one class but not in others. Often, the greater the risk, the greater the stress.

Sometimes the type of test being given can lead to test anxiety. Some students become anxious during exams that require them to demonstrate their knowledge in ways in which they do not feel comfortable. For example, some students panic when they find that they have to take essay tests. Others become anxious over oral exams. And, some, like me, hate true/false tests. Different types of tests cause feelings of anxiety for different people. The added pressure of having to complete an exam within a limited time period also creates feelings of anxiety for many students.

Some professors make students anxious because of things that they do during the exam. Telling the class that the test is the hardest they've ever made up or that no one in the other class got above a D can lead to feelings of anxiety. Some instructors think that they are helping the students pace themselves by announcing the time every five minutes, but that behavior makes the already anxious students feel even more pressured. Even going to a special "testing room" to take the exam can produce anxiety in some students.

Is Test Anxiety Normal?

With all of these factors contributing to test anxiety, it's hard to believe that any student doesn't feel some level of anxiety. Actually, just about everyone does. It's perfectly normal to be anxious about an exam. If you weren't a little anxious about your performance, you probably wouldn't study at all. A small amount of test anxiety is good. We can describe this state of anxiety as **facilitating test anxiety**—anxiety that facilitates or helps motivate us to prepare before and work hard during the exam. On the other hand, a high level of test anxiety can interfere with your performance on an exam. We call this type of anxiety **debilitating test anxiety.** Like a debilitating illness, it prevents us from functioning in a normal way. High levels of test anxiety may interfere with your ability to concentrate on the exam, take the exam, or even to prepare for it. If you're out in the hall throwing up, you're losing time you could have spent completing the exam.

Some students find that they really can't prepare for exams because they're so anxious about them. When they begin to study, they start to think about the exam, and they experience some of the physical and emotional symptoms that we've discussed. They have difficulty concentrating on the material during the study session in much the same way that they do during the exam. This leads to poor preparation, which then leads to another poor test grade, and so the cycle continues (Figure 11.1).

Coping with Test Anxiety

There are a number of ways that you can learn to cope with test anxiety. First of all, remember that some test anxiety is good, so your goal should be to reduce higher levels of anxiety to a level that becomes facilitating. Look again at the **test-anxiety cycle** in Figure 11.1. There really is only one point at which a test-anxious student could interrupt the cycle and therefore change the outcome. Where is it? If you said, "can't study effectively," you were correct. This is the only point at which you can effectively change the outcome of your next exam. There are a number of strategies that can help you reduce your test anxiety.

1. **Prepare Well**
   The best way to lower your level of anxiety is to be well prepared for the exam and to know that you are well prepared. By developing a structured study plan (such as the Five-Day Study Plan), you can be well prepared for the next exam. By using active study strategies like writing and reciting, you can master the

FIGURE 11.1
Test-Anxiety Cycle

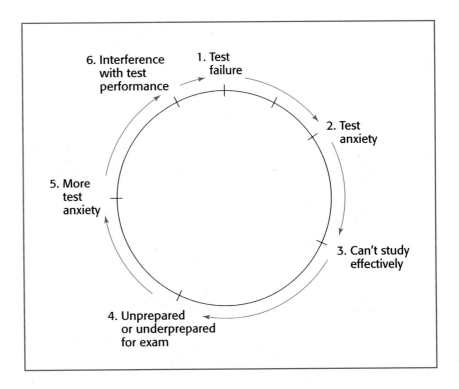

material for your exam. With good preparation and good concentration, you should do well. Once you know that you can do well on that exam, you won't be so anxious the next time—you'll be able to break the test-anxiety cycle.

2. **Monitor Your Learning**
If you quiz yourself each day, you'll also find out what you do know and what you don't know. Then you can review that material until you do know it, and by test time you'll be well prepared and confident about your preparation.

3. **Use Relaxation Strategies**
During an exam, use relaxation exercises to help reduce your anxiety level. Use breathing or muscle-relaxing techniques to calm yourself. Just taking a few deep breaths can help you calm down. If that doesn't work, try taking a breath and then blowing it out very slowly as if you had built a house of cards and didn't want to knock it over. Do this a few times until you find that you're able to control your breathing.

Practicing tensing and relaxing your muscles is another excellent strategy for reducing anxiety. Try this experiment. Make a fist. Squeeze it as tightly as you can and feel how tense your hand and arm feel. Then very slowly let your hand unfold. Feel how relaxed and loose your hand is now. Shake it out and let your arm dangle at your side. Practice tensing and relaxing the muscles in your hands, shoulders, stomach, feet, and so on. Hold the muscles in a tense position for five to ten seconds and then, as you relax them, say the word *relax* very slowly in your mind (reeee laaaa xxxxx). By using this silent command as you practice the relaxation exercises, you may find that during exams you can loosen your tensed muscles just by telling yourself to relax. Practice this exercise on a regular basis (two or three times a week) until you can do it fairly automatically. If you begin to feel tense during an exam, stop and go through your relaxation exercises until you feel more relaxed. Cassette tapes that include an entire routine of relaxation exercises are available at book and music stores.

4. **Avoid Negative Thoughts**

   One of the most common problems that students experience during exams is negative thoughts. They think about failing the test, start worrying about whether they studied the right material, or tell themselves that they don't belong in school. All of these negative thoughts interfere with their ability to concentrate on the test itself. If your attention is occupied by negative thoughts, you can't effectively think about the questions and retrieve the answers you need to complete the exam. Negative thoughts compete with and distract you from concentrating on the exam, so you need to avoid them.

5. **Recite a Positive Mental Script**

   After you study for the test, prepare a positive mental script. Practice saying it over and over again and think about why it's true. Everyone's script will be different, but yours might go something like this: "I'm going to do well on this exam because I really know this stuff. I studied for eight hours for this exam, and I got As on all my homework papers and on my self-test. I know how to take tests, and I'm well prepared." As soon you begin to think any negative thoughts during the exam, yell "STOP" or "STOP IT" in your mind and then immediately start to repeat your positive script.

6. **Use Visualization**

   You can also reduce anxiety by dealing with it ahead of time. Several days before the exam, put yourself in the exam situation. You can actually go to the classroom or testing room and pretend that you're there to take the exam, or you can just pretend you're there and visualize the room. Try to imagine the professor walking in with the exam, giving directions, and passing out the tests. Picture yourself starting the exam. As you go through this role playing, monitor your level of anxiety. If you begin to feel anxious, use one of the stress-reduction activities to calm yourself. Putting yourself in the testing situation before the test can help you reduce a lot of your anxiety ahead of time.

7. **Don't Arrive Too Early**

   Sometimes you can change your own behavior to help reduce test anxiety. A lot of students who feel nervous about exams think that getting to the classroom early will give them time to calm down and feel relaxed. Although this may work for some students, arriving too early can actually increase the anxiety level for others. The longer you have to wait for something that you're apprehensive about, the higher your anxiety level may rise. Enter the classroom about five minutes before the exam is to start. You'll have time to settle in and do a quick review, but not enough time to allow yourself or others to make you nervous.

8. **Identify Your Triggers**

   Identifying what triggers your feelings of anxiety can help you cope with them. Some students who always get nervous when they read the first question on an exam find that starting at the end helps them relax. If essay questions are your troublesome area, do the objective part of the test first. If your instructor makes you nervous by announcing the time every five minutes, tell him or her about your problem; the two of you should be able to work out a better arrangement that will reduce your anxiety.

9. **Answer the Questions You Know First**

   Test anxiety doesn't last forever; for most students the symptoms subside after about fifteen or twenty minutes. If you use strategies to help reduce your anxiety and at the same time answer the ones you know, your anxiety need not affect your grade.

10. **Don't Let Test Anxiety Become an Excuse**
Some students blame test anxiety instead of themselves when things aren't going well. They blame their test failure on their anxiety rather than on their lack of preparation, poor class attendance, or poor preparation in high school. After all, that's easier than having to work hard and face the results of their efforts. Be sure you don't fall into that trap.

Activity 11-2

Check Your Test Anxiety Level

Go to the *College Study Skills* Web site and follow the link to the Test Anxiety Scale. Answer each of the questions on line or by printing a copy of the questionnaire. Then follow the scoring instructions to determine your test anxiety level. What did you find?

GENERAL TEST-TAKING STRATEGIES

Now that you've developed many good strategies for test preparation, you need to learn how to approach and take objective tests. Learning how to approach tests in a calm, logical way can help you increase your score.

Follow Directions

Reading the directions before beginning an exam can make the difference between getting a good grade and failing the exam. The directions give you information on how many questions to answer, what form the answers must take, and special directions for some parts of the test. The directions for all parts of an exam are not necessarily the same. Some sections of a multiple-choice exam, for example, may ask you to choose the best answer. Other sections may ask you to select all the correct answers or the only incorrect answer. Marking only the best answer when all correct choices are required may cost you 2 or 3 points per question. Occasionally, students lose points on true/false exams because they don't read the directions. If you mark the statement false without correcting the false statement (as required in the directions), you may not get credit for the answer. Errors like these can result in failure.

Activity 11-3

Follow Directions

Read all the following statements before completing any of the items.

1. Write your birth date. _____

2. Cross out all of the vowels in the word *serendipity.*

Continued

Activity 11-3

Follow Directions (continued)

3. Add the following numbers: 37, 12, 64, 58, 83. _____

4. Write down the first word on each of the last five pages of this text.

   _____

5. Write your ID number or your Social Security number. _____

6. Add the last three numbers in your answer to question 5 to the total from question 3. _____

7. If the total from question 6 is over 500, subtract 300 from it. If it is under 500, add 300 to it. Write your new number here. _____

8. Circle all *Es*, cross out the *Is*, and underline the *Os* in the word *Mesopotamia*.

9. Write a good abbreviation for the word *marshmallow*. _____

10. Write your name instead of your birth date for question 1 and skip all the other items.

Budget Your Time

If you budget your time during a test, you should be able to complete the entire test before time runs out. If you lose track of time or spend too much time on one part of the exam, you may end up leaving some questions undone. Being unable to finish even five 2-point questions on a fifty-item test can mean the difference of one letter grade. Pacing yourself during the test also helps you maximize your score by letting you devote the most time to those parts of the exam that have the highest point values.

Consider Point Values

Previewing the exam gives you an idea of what you need to accomplish during the test period. Count the total number of questions that you have to answer. Then look at each section of the exam and check the point value for each question. Some students ignore the differences in point values among questions and treat all questions as if they were of equal weight. Occasionally, this has disastrous effects. One student failed a test in a religion course because she treated identification items as if they were essays. Her test was composed of ten 5-point identification items and two 25-point essay questions. She looked at the exam and saw twelve questions and decided to space out her time equally. She spent fifty minutes on questions that accounted for only 50 percent of the test points (the ten identifications) and only ten minutes on questions that accounted for the other 50 percent of the points (the two essays). Even though she wrote excellent answers for all of the identification items, she failed the exam because she couldn't fully develop the answers for her essay questions.

Divide Your Time Accordingly

Divide your time appropriately based on the point values of the test questions. Some professors tend to ask forty or fifty multiple-choice (or true/false) questions on an exam and two short essay questions. As soon as some students see the essay questions, they think that they need to spend half of their time on them. How would you divide your time if you were given the following exam?

40 multiple-choice worth 2 points each = 80 points

2 essays worth 10 points each = 20 points

You have 1 hour and 40 minutes for the exam.

In this case you have 100 points on the test and 100 minutes to take the test, so you should spend 80 minutes on the multiple-choice questions (or 2 minutes each) and 20 minutes on the essays (or 10 minutes on each). If you need a little more time for the essays, you could steal a little time from the objective section. You might spend 70 minutes on the multiple-choice items and 30 minutes on the essay questions. You also could steal a little time to allow for a final review of entire exam. In this case you would spend 60 minutes on the multiple-choice items ($1\frac{1}{2}$ minutes each), 30 minutes on the essay section (15 minutes each), and 10 minutes for a final review. If you use the following rule, you'll be able to determine how much time to spend on each question or section of the test:

> **Rule:** Percentage of the total points = Percentage of total time

If you had only 70 minutes for the above exam, you would multiply .80 (80 points out of 100 points is 80 percent) × 70 (total time) = 56 minutes for the multiple-choice questions.

Pace Yourself During the Exam

Even if your exam is all multiple-choice questions, you still need to budget your time. You want to complete the entire test and still have time to go back over it. Divide the time you have by the total number of questions and then shave off some for your review. You may have forty questions to answer in a fifty-minute period. If you allow ten minutes for review, you can spend one minute on each question. Many students lose track of time because they spend too much time on one question; they find that they have fifteen questions left to answer when the professor announces that they have five minutes left. You can prevent this from happening by **pacing** yourself during the exam—by dividing up the test and setting time goals for each third, fourth, or fifth of the exam. For example, if you had forty questions to answer in forty minutes, you might divide the test at the end of each ten-question chunk. If your exam started at 2:00, you might jot 2:10 in the margin next to question 10, 2:20 in the margin next to 20, and 2:30 in the margin next to question 30. Each time you moved to the next chunk of questions, you would see the time in the margin, check your watch, and monitor your progress. If you were working slowly, you would realize it early enough to speed up. If you realized that you were racing through the questions, you could slow down and spend more time on each question.

What to Do If Time Runs Out

What would you do if you aren't finished with the exam when time runs out? If you have one or two questions left to do, ask the professor for a few more minutes. Even though some professors are sticklers about time, they may allow you to finish the exam while they gather up their materials. If you know that you often have difficulty completing exams in the required time, discuss this with your professor ahead of time. Some professors allow students to arrive early and begin the exam before the rest of the class. If you have a learning disability or if English is your second language, you often can make special arrangements through your campus disability office, learning center, or academic dean. Most professors are willing to make accommodations to help you succeed on exams, but you need to tell them what your needs are.

Activity 11-4

Budget Your Time

Work as a group to determine how much time you should spend on each section in the following practice tests. (For this exercise, don't allow time to review the entire test.)

PRACTICE TEST A:	CASE 1	CASE 2
10 multiple-choice items worth 20 points	_____	_____
20 identification items worth 40 points	_____	_____
2 essay questions worth 40 points	_____	_____

(Case 1: You have 100 minutes for the test.)

(Case 2: You have 50 minutes for the test.)

PRACTICE TEST B:	CASE 1	CASE 2
30 multiple-choice items worth 2 points each	_____	_____
10 completion items worth 2 points each	_____	_____
1 essay worth 10 points	_____	_____

(Case 1: You have 80 minutes for the test.)

(Case 2: You have 50 minutes for the test.)

Work Logically Through The Exam

You can improve your score on objective exams by working logically and methodically through the exam. To maximize your score, you should answer the questions you know (the easy questions) first and use strategies to figure out the ones you don't know immediately. In any case, don't leave blanks—answer all questions to maximize your score.

Answer the Easiest Questions First

Another strategy for improving your grade on an exam is to answer the easiest questions first. By immediately answering all of the questions that you know, you can maximize your score on the test. If you do run out of time, you'll be sure to receive points for the questions that you did know. In addition, you can reduce your test anxiety by answering the easiest questions first. By the time you go back to work on the more difficult questions, you'll feel more relaxed. This is because you build up your confidence as you complete the easy questions; you know that you know at least some or even many of the answers. One student reported that she used this strategy on an algebra exam. By the time she went back to the "difficult" questions, they didn't seem nearly as hard. Because she was more relaxed, she was able to think through the problems more logically and solve them correctly.

Some students panic if they read the first question on the test and realize they don't know the answer. Instead of allowing yourself to start thinking negative thoughts, just tell yourself "This is a hard question—I'll come back to it later." This type of positive thinking allows you to stay calm and focus on the rest of the test.

Work Strategically to Answer All Questions

As you move through the exam, skip the questions you aren't sure of and go on to the easier questions. If you know that you don't know an answer, don't spend a lot of time on the question. Mark the questions you skip by putting a dash or question mark in the margin or by circling the number. After you complete the rest of the test, go back to them. (If you're using an answer sheet, be sure you skip the same spaces there, too.) When you return to the questions you skipped, try to figure out the answers strategically. Think through each question. Underline key words in the question to focus your thinking. Eliminate any answer that you know is wrong and then try to figure out the correct answer. Do a **memory search** to try to retrieve the information about the topic. Ask yourself questions about the material. Try to determine whether the answer came from the lecture or from the text. Try to remember where you saw it on the page, where it was written in your notes or study sheets, or what the professor was talking about just before or after that topic was presented. By searching your memory, you may be able to find a clue or cue that helps you recall the information.

Look for Clues in Other Questions

Many students find clues to difficult questions as they move through the test. You may even find the answer to an early question in one of the possible answers to a question three pages away. Even if you don't find the answer itself, you may find a clue or cue to help you answer the question. You may read a word in another question or in another possible answer that triggers your memory and helps you retrieve the information that you need. Even if you pick up a clue to only one or two questions as you move through the test, that can often make a difference in your grade.

Guess Strategically

Even if you're well prepared for a test and use good test-taking strategies, you still may find that you can't answer some questions. When none of your test-taking strategies work, then you should guess. Let's say there are four questions that you can't figure out on a fifty-item multiple-choice test. Because each of those questions is worth 2 points, your unanswered questions add up to 8 points or almost one letter grade. Not answering them will result in at least an 8-point loss in your grade. Guessing doesn't guarantee that you'll get all of the questions right, but it certainly improves your odds of getting some of them right.

What is a guess anyway? Some students describe a guess as just putting down any letter they can think of to fill the slot. They choose randomly from among the alternatives. However, **strategic guessing** involves more active processes. There are a number of strategies that you can use to pick up a few more points on a test even when you don't know the correct answer.

Look for Patterns

Pretend that you answered all of the easy questions on an exam and then went back and used problem-solving strategies to figure out the answers for a few more.

Rather than just guessing randomly, look for patterns in the answers. Many professors never use the same letter more than two or three times in a row before shifting to a different response. So if you know that B is the correct response for the three previous questions and you eliminated C and D, A would be a more strategic guess than B. Go back and look at some of your old exams to see what types of patterns your professors use. You may find that your professor tends to use more false statements on true/false tests or more D answers on multiple-choice items. If you have five or six blanks at the end of the test, you could mark them all false or all D (assuming you didn't already eliminate D as a wrong answer). Although you won't get all of the questions right, you should be able to get at least a few of the answers right—adding several points to your total test score.

Activity 11-5

Guess at True/False Questions

Pretend that you answered all the easy questions on an exam and then went back and figured out a few more by using problem-solving strategies. There are still seven items on the following answer sheet that you can't answer. In the empty spaces below, write T for true or F for false for each of the unanswered questions. Although you don't have the actual questions, try to guess the actual answers from a real exam.

1. _T_	6. _F_	11. _T_	16. _____	21. _F_
2. _____	7. _F_	12. _T_	17. _F_	22. _F_
3. _F_	8. _____	13. _F_	18. _F_	23. _T_
4. _F_	9. _T_	14. _____	19. _F_	24. _____
5. _____	10. _F_	15. _T_	20. _____	25. _T_

List any strategies that you used to figure out the correct answers. Jot them in the margin.

Now check your answers to Activity 11-5 in the key at the end of the chapter. Your score before you guessed was 72 out of 100, a low C. Add up the number of guesses that you got right and multiply that number by 4 (the point value for each question). Add your total points to 72 to get your new score. Were you able to increase your score by one letter grade (80–89 is a B) or by two letter grades (90–100 is an A)? Did you use any strategies to guess the correct answers in Activity 11-5? Although guessing is not a recommended strategy for early in a test, it certainly can help you pick up a few points when you absolutely don't know the answer.

Activity 11-6

Guess at Multiple-Choice Questions

Pretend that you answered all the easy questions on a multiple-choice exam and then went back and figured out a few more by using problem-solving strategies. There are still fourteen items on the following answer sheet that are blank. In the empty spaces

Continued

below, write A, B, C, or D for each of the unanswered questions. Although you don't have the actual questions, try to guess the actual answers from a real exam.

1. _A_	11. _B_	21. _D_	31. ____	41. ____
2. ____	12. _A_	22. _D_	32. _B_	42. _C_
3. _C_	13. _C_	23. _A_	33. ____	43. ____
4. _C_	14. ____	24. ____	34. _B_	44. _D_
5. _B_	15. _B_	25. _A_	35. _D_	45. _A_
6. _D_	16. ____	26. _C_	36. ____	46. _B_
7. _C_	17. _C_	27. _A_	37. ____	47. _A_
8. ____	18. _C_	28. _B_	38. _D_	48. ____
9. _B_	19. _D_	29. _D_	39. _A_	49. _D_
10. _D_	20. _A_	30. ____	40. ____	50. _C_

List any strategies that you used to figure out the correct answers. Jot them in the margin.

Now check your score in Activity 11-6 from the key at the end of the chapter. Add up the number of correct answers and multiply by 2 (each question is worth 2 points). Then add your total points to 72 to get your new score. Did you improve your score? How much? You may be disappointed that your score is lower this time than it was for the true/false test. The odds of guessing correctly on this multiple-choice test were only 1 in 4; on the true/false test you had a 50-50 (or 1 in 2) chance of being correct. You can increase your odds of guessing right on multiple-choice exams by eliminating answers that you know are wrong. Can't you often eliminate two of the alternatives? Then you have the same chance of guessing correctly as you did on a true/false test.

Check for Balanced Answer Keys

Some professors always have **balanced answer keys;** they use exactly the same number of As, Bs, Cs, and Ds. If you find that there are three or four questions that you can't answer, count how many of each letter you've already used. You may find that you have fewer As than any other letter. By marking your remaining answers "A," you probably will pick up several additional points. Although this sounds like a great strategy, it works only if you're well enough prepared to get most of the answers right, thus revealing the pattern. By looking at old exams or watching for patterns on each exam that you have in the course, you'll be able to determine whether you can use this strategy. As you probably noticed, it didn't work for the sample test in Activity 11-6 because I didn't use a balanced answer key.

Guessing Doesn't Replace Proper Preparation

Remember, guessing strategies are designed to help you pick up a few additional points when you absolutely can't figure out the correct answer any other way. They're *not* designed to replace proper preparation or substitute for more active problem-solving strategies that can lead you to the correct answer by providing you with clues or aiding your recall of the answer. Use them *only* after all other attempts to figure out the correct answer have failed. In fact, the students who are the best prepared to take an exam can benefit the most since they have only a small number of unanswered questions.

SPECIFIC TEST-TAKING STRATEGIES

Although you should be able to correctly answer the majority of the test questions right if you're well prepared, you won't know the answer to all of them the instant you read them. There are four levels of strategies that you should use when approaching an exam question (Figure 11.2). First, if you prepare well enough, you should be able to recall the correct answer to many of the questions without even looking for it—you should be able to think of it and then go find it. If you don't know the correct answer to all of the questions, you should be able to use problem-solving strategies to figure some of them out. If you still can't identify the correct answer to some of the test questions, your third option is to use test-wise clues. Finally, if all else fails, use strategic guessing to get a few of those that you can't figure out correct.

Strategies for Multiple-Choice Tests

The most common type of objective test is the multiple-choice test. Many new college students have difficulty on multiple-choice exams because they expect all questions to be at the knowledge level. They prepare by memorizing the material and often don't take the time to really learn and understand it. If you're able to recall the correct answers from memory without cues, multiple-choice exams will be easy for you. Most multiple-choice exams contain a **stem,** which is composed of a question or an incomplete sentence, and several **alternatives** or possible answers.

Many strategies are effective for taking multiple-choice exams; however, these strategies come in two different forms. The first group includes **problem-solving strategies** that can help you figure out the correct answer from the various distractors or decoys. The other group involves **test-wise strategies** that should be used only after you've tried all the other strategies first. Some students think of test-wise strategies as rules; they aren't. They should be used *only* when you can't figure out the answer using problem-solving strategies. After you read the directions and budget your time, use the following strategies for multiple-choice items.

FIGURE 11.2
Levels of Strategies

Problem-Solving Strategies

Problem-solving strategies can help you logically and methodically identify the correct answer even if you don't know it when you first read the question.

1. **Read the question and all answers before you select the "correct" answer.** Some students lose points on multiple-choice exams because they don't read all possible answers before selecting the one that they think is correct. Many times the first or second alternative may appear to be the correct answer, but one of the other answers may in fact be an even better choice. In most multiple-choice tests, you generally are asked to select the *best* answer. In that case, several of the choices may be correct or good answers, but only one answer is the "best" answer.

2. **Underline key words.** By underlining key words in the question, you can better focus your attention on what's being asked. In addition, you may find that underlining key words helps you identify a cue that triggers your long-term memory. Finally, taking the time to underline key words in both the question and the possible answers forces you to slow down and read the question and answers more carefully. If you rush through the test, you may misread questions or answers. You may make careless errors that cost you points you should have had.

3. **Work to eliminate incorrect alternatives rather than looking for the "right" answer.** After reading the question and all alternatives, begin looking for those that you know are wrong. When you're sure that one possible answer is a **distractor** (incorrect answer designed to appear correct), cross it off. Continue eliminating choices until only one answer remains. If you can eliminate all alternatives except one, you know you've found the correct answer.

4. **Connect the stem of the question to each alternative answer; then treat each statement as a true/false item.** In a way, all multiple-choice exams are really composed of a series of true/false items. If you're good at taking true/false tests, use the same strategies that work for you on the true/false items for the multiple-choice items. Identify key words, underline words or phrases that make the statement false, and watch for absolute, qualifying, and negative words (discussed in the next section). By examining each alternative as a separate statement, you may be able to improve your test score.

5. **Read the question, cover the alternatives, and think of the answer.** Some students find multiple-choice tests difficult because they allow the distractors to confuse them. Some professors are so good at writing distractors that, even if you know the correct answer, you begin to have doubts about it after reading the alternatives. To avoid this problem, cover the answers with your hand, read the question, and think of the answer. Then read each alternative and ask yourself, "Does this mean the same thing as the answer that I know is correct?" This strategy is especially effective when the question is written at the comprehension level. In this situation, the information is rephrased or put in different words. By comparing your answer to each of those listed, you should be able to identify the correct choice.

6. **Use caution when "all of the above" and "none of the above" are included as choices.** If you can eliminate even *one* alternative, you can eliminate "all of the above" as the correct answer. Similarly, if you're sure that at least one choice is correct, you can eliminate "none of the above." If you have three alternatives and you know that two of them are correct but aren't sure of the third, "all of the above" must be correct (assuming you can choose only one answer). If "all of the

above" and "none of the above" are used only occasionally on the test, they are probably the correct choices. Watch for patterns like this on each exam.

Test-Wise Strategies

Use test-wise strategies to help you determine the correct choice when you can't figure it out. Many courses that are designed to prepare students to take the SATs or other standardized tests seem to specialize in these "test-smart" strategies. Some of them are very helpful; others are not so useful. The key to using these strategies is to use them sparingly. Never follow a test-wise strategy that would require you to select one alternative when you are fairly sure that another alternative is the correct answer. Use these strategies only when you can't determine the correct answer by using the more conventional strategies.

Some of the more effective and useful test-wise strategies follow. Use them to answer the multiple-choice questions that follow each tip. You aren't expected to *know* the correct answers, but rather to figure them out by following the test-wise strategy. The correct answers are at the end of the chapter.

1. **An answer that contains more specific, detailed information probably is correct. Vague or general alternatives are often used as distractors.**

   According to studies on alcohol consumption,

   a. young people drink more than they used to.

   b. Americans drink more than ever.

   c. as many as 23 percent of all young people between the ages of twelve and eighteen have a serious drinking problem.

   d. drinking has filtered down to preteen groups.

2. **An answer that contains the most words, especially if it also contains the most specific information, probably is correct.**

   Depressants may be defined as

   a. downers.

   b. sedatives, substances that reduce the activity of the brain and muscles.

   c. drugs that increase alertness.

   d. none of the above.

3. **An answer that's in the middle probably is correct, especially if it has the most words.**

   Increased drug use among youth has been attributed to

   a. biochemical differences.

   b. alcoholic parents.

   c. peer pressure, lowered self-esteem, and, often, trouble in the family.

   d. feelings of guilt.

4. **An answer that's about in the middle numerically probably is correct.** Instructors often surround the correct choice by a range of lower and higher alternatives.

   About _____ percent of high school students tried at least one illegal drug.

   a. ten

   b. fifteen

c. thirty

d. fifty

5. **An answer that contains an unfamiliar term probably is wrong.** Instructors often make up words or take terms from other material to generate additional distractors.

Which of the following is not one of the four drug categories?

a. Stimulants

b. Depressants

c. Hallucinogens

d. Nallohines

6. **An answer that contains a "typo," especially if there are very few typos in the test, probably is wrong.** Instructors often catch typos in correct answers when they make out the answer key; often they don't even look at the incorrect choices during this process.

Which of the following is not a characteristic of concrete operations?

a. Mental operations appliet to concrete objects and events

b. Little or no capacity for symbolic representation

c. Development of conversation

d. Mastery of the concept of raversibity

7. **An answer that is grammatically correct probably is right if the other choices are not grammatically correct.** Occasionally, instructors end the stem of the question with the word *a* or *an* instead of *a(n)*. Words that start with vowels follow *an* (an apple); words that start with consonants follow *a* (a book). Sometimes you also may notice that the stem of the question includes a singular subject and one or more of the alternatives contains a plural verb.

PACs were created by organized labor in response to a

a. prohibition against using union treasury money to finance elections.

b. action by the government that made donations illegal.

c. one-year moratorium on collecting dues from its members.

d. interest group that tried to bar labor unions from involvement in federal elections.

8. **An answer that contains a form of the word or a word similar to one in the stem of the question is probably correct.**

Which of the following describes Hamilton's plan to improve the government's financial situation through funding and assumption?

a. The federal government would pay off the states' debts at full value.

b. The federal government would take over or assume the states' debts.

c. The federal government would pay off the states' debts with cash.

d. The federal government would tax the rich states to pay the debts of the states that were in debt.

9. **If a question contains two opposite alternatives, one of them is probably correct.**

As political parties declined in their ability to finance campaigns, PACs

a. moved in rapidly to fill the gap.

b. moved in slowly to fill the gap.

    c. declined as well.

    d. focused on national elections.

10. If a question contains two alternatives that are almost identical (perhaps only one word is different), then one of them is probably correct. Which of the following is the correct definition for irreversibility?

    a. Irreversibility is a problem that leads to the decline in egocentrism.

    b. Irreversibility is the inability to envision reversing an action.

    c. Irreversibility is the ability to envision reversing an action.

    d. Irreversibility is the inability to grasp the principle of reversibility.

Activity 11-7

Take a Multiple-Choice Test

Without looking back at Chapter 4, circle the best answer for each of the following questions. The answers are given in the key at the end of the chapter. What strategies did you use to answer each question?

1. Which memory theory is concerned with how old memories affect newer memories?

    a. Decay theory

    b. Interference theory

    c. Reconstructive theory

    d. Schema theory

2. According to the Information Processing Model, we are able to pay attention to about _____ thing(s) at any one time.

    a. one

    b. two

    c. three

    d. several

3. Bonnie, a waitress, takes the order from a table of eight customers. She must remember the order until she gets to the kitchen where she can write it down. This whole process takes about five minutes. How might she accomplish this feat?

    a. Iconic memory will do the trick.

    b. Immediate memory will do the job for her.

    c. She can rely on her sensory registers.

    d. She will need to move that material into long-term memory.

4. According to the Information Processing Model, the process of finding material in long-term memory is known as

    a. encoding.

    b. mnemonics.

    c. retrieval.

    d. storage.

Strategies for True/False Tests

Many students like true/false tests because they provide excellent odds for guessing correctly. However, some students have difficulty dealing with this type of test because the statements can be tricky. To make a statement incorrect, professors may change key words, omit key words, add absolute or qualifying words, add negative words, add extraneous information, and so on. Because there are so many ways to make a statement "false," students must consider all of them as they examine each statement.

Use the following basic guidelines when taking true/false tests:

1. **Always read the directions before beginning a true/false test.** Some instructors are very particular about how they expect students to mark true/false items. If you don't complete the exam according to the directions, you may not get credit for your answers.

2. **For a statement to be true, it must be all true.** If any part of the statement is false, the entire statement is false. Even if a statement is composed of two or three parts or entire sentences, if one part or even one word is incorrect, the entire statement is false.

   EXAMPLE:

   True or False   To do well on college exams, you must become actively involved with the material, which can be accomplished by reading over the material several times.

   The correct answer is *false*. Even though the first part of the statement is correct, the second part is not.

3. **True/false items are not all tricky.** Some students start to look for "tricks" or read too much into the question when a true/false item seems "too easy." If you're properly prepared for a test, some true/false items should appear to be easy.

   EXAMPLE:

   True or False   Knowledge-level questions require only rote memory.

4. **Identify the key words or phrases.** Many professors make a statement false by substituting another word or phrase for the correct one. Which words are the key words in examples 2 and 3? In example 2, the words *actively involved* and *reading over* are the most important words. In example 3, the key words are *Knowledge-level* and *rote memory*. By identifying and verifying the accuracy of key words, you can more easily decide whether a statement is true or false. What are the key words in the following statement?

   EXAMPLE:

   True or False   Application-level questions involve a rephrasing of the information that you learned.

5. **Statements that contain absolute words are usually false.** Words like *always, all, none, never, only, every,* and *no* are examples of **absolute words.** Each of these words implies that there are no exceptions. Although the inclusion of these words in a true/false item does not guarantee that it's false, it usually indicates a false statement. In fact, other than changing one or more key words in the statement, this is one of the most common ways to turn a true statement into a false one.

   EXAMPLES:

   True or False   All adults are auditory learners.

True or False   Students should always study by reciting out loud.

True or False   You should never study more than two chapters on the same day.

6. **Statements that contain qualifying words are usually true statements.** Words like *usually, often, may, can, sometimes, frequently, rarely, most, some, many, few,* and *generally* are examples of **qualifying words.** These words qualify or "temper" the statement to allow for exceptions and are generally associated with true statements. However, if you *know* that a statement is false, mark it *false,* even though it contains a qualifying word.

EXAMPLES:

True or False   Some adults are auditory learners.

True or False   Reciting out loud is often a good study strategy.

True or False   You should rarely study more than two chapters on the same day.

7. **Statements that contain negative words often are tricky and require careful attention.** Double negatives, which generally include the word *not* plus another word that contains a negative prefix, such as *incoherent, illogical, irresponsible, unhelpful,* and so on, often confuse students. If a statement contains a double negative, cross off the word *not* and the negative prefix (*in, il, ir,* or *un*) and then reread the statement in order to determine whether it's true or false.

EXAMPLE:

True or False   It is not illegal to smoke in the dormitory rooms on this college campus.

By eliminating the negative words, the statement becomes: It is legal to smoke in the dormitory rooms on this college campus.

8. **Always underline the word or words that make a statement false.** If you can't identify and mark the actual key words, absolute words, qualifiers, and so on that cause the statement to be incorrect, assume that it is correct and mark it true. There is one exception, however. If you know that a statement is false by omission (because a key word or phrase has been left out), mark the statement *false* even though you can't actually underline the words that make it false.

EXAMPLES:

True or False   You can improve your test scores by using the Seven-Day Study Plan that was recommended in the text.

True or False   If you learn information to the recognition level of learning, you can think of the answer without additional cues.

True or False   Word cards should be made up for technical terms and names of people.

Although the last item is true, some students might wonder whether it implies that word cards should be used *only* for these two types of information. According to the text, you can use word cards for many other types of material, including dates, events, theories, and formulas. Some students might think that the third example therefore is false by omission. In instances like this one, you should ask the professor whether he or she means that these are the *only* uses of word cards.

9. **Correct all false items on the exam if you have time to do so.** By correcting the statement, you show the professor, and remind yourself, what you were thinking during the exam. (By the time you get the exam back, you may not remember why you thought the item was false.) Use this strategy only when you have plenty of time to complete the test or if you can make the correction quickly.

   You might correct each of the statements in number 8 by crossing out the incorrect words and substituting or adding:

   Five-Day Study Plan

   recall level

   to learn terms, names, dates, events, theories, formulas, and so on.

10. **Professors usually include more true items than false items on an exam.** Many professors use tests to reinforce the main ideas that were presented in the course. If you absolutely can't figure out whether a statement is true or false, mark it true. Watch for patterns on each test.

Activity 11-8

Take a True/False Test

Work with a partner to indicate whether each item in the following section is true or false. If it is false, underline the word or words that make it false and then correct the statement. Circle any absolute words. Compare your responses to those in another group.

_____ 1. Reading and active reading involve exactly the same processes.

_____ 2. You should always make maps when studying for exams.

_____ 3. You may find it helpful to read the summary before reading the chapter.

_____ 4. Sitting in the front of the room will assure you of getting a good grade.

_____ 5. When skimming a chapter, you should have complete comprehension.

_____ 6. Once you learn something, you never have to review it again.

_____ 7. Some students use recall columns when they take lecture notes.

_____ 8. Recopying notes verbatim is an active study strategy.

_____ 9. All students should take self-tests to reduce test anxiety.

_____ 10. All students who fail exams have high levels of test anxiety.

Strategies for Matching Tests

With proper preparation and test-taking strategies, you should be able to get top scores on matching tests. Matching tests require you to recognize the correct answer from a list of alternatives. The answers to all questions are given; you don't have to "pull" the answer from memory. Before beginning a matching test, be sure that you read the directions. Usually, you're instructed to use each letter only once, but some matching tests allow for or require the repeated use of some letters. Although you probably aren't familiar with the terms and definitions in the matching test in Activity 11-9, try it now. By taking the test and then reading about how to figure out many of the answers, you can learn a number of test-taking strategies.

Activity 11-9

Practice Answering Matching Questions

Match the terms and definitions from a psychology chapter on the biological basis of behavior.[1] Write the letter of the correct definition on the line in front of each term. Each letter is used only once. How many were you able to get correct? What strategies did you use?

TERMS   DEFINITIONS

_____ 1. ablation

_____ 2. action potential

_____ 3. aphasia

_____ 4. cerebral cortex

_____ 5. endorphins

_____ 6. genotype

_____ 7. myelin sheath

_____ 8. neurons

_____ 9. soma

_____ 10. thalamus

A. a disorder characterized by language and speech disorders attributed to brain damage

B. individual cells of the nervous system

C. a person's genetic makeup

D. surgical removal of a piece of the brain

E. the convoluted outer layer of the cerebrum

F. a structure in the forebrain through which all sensory information must pass

G. insulating material that encases some axons

H. the family of internally produced chemicals that resemble opiates in structure and effects

I. the body of a cell, which contains the nucleus

J. a brief change in a neuron's electrical charge that travels along the axon

Work from One Side

Matching tests often include a list of names or terms in one column and then a list of identifications, accomplishments, or definitions in the other column. When you take a matching test like the one in Activity 11-9, always work from one side only. Crossing off items in both columns leads to confusion and often results in careless errors or wasted time. From which side did you work in that test? You may have been taught that you should always work from the left column or the right column. Neither is correct. Actually, you should always work from the column that has the most words. In the sample test, there are thirteen words in the term column and over eighty words in the definition column. If you worked from the term column, you would have to scan more than eighty words in the definition column to find a correct match. If, instead, you worked from the definition column, you would have

---

[1]Test items prepared by Dr. Malcolm Van Blerkom based on information from W. Weiten, *Psychology: Themes and Variations* (Pacific Grove, CA: Brooks/Cole, 1989). Used with permission.

to scan only thirteen words on each pass—saving you time for other parts of the exam.

Answer the Questions You're Sure of First

When taking a matching test, it's crucial that you answer the questions or make the matches that you're absolutely sure of first. By eliminating all choices that you're sure of, you can narrow the alternatives for the remaining choices. When I took the test in Activity 11-9, I hadn't studied or prepared for it. Even though I didn't prepare, I still was able to make all matches correctly. In the next three sections, I'll tell you how I figured out each match.

Eliminate and Cross Off Alternatives

As you go through the list of definitions, cross off the letter (not the word) of the ones that you use. Just put one diagonal line through the letter so that you can recheck your matches later. If you can eliminate five of the ten alternatives on your first pass through the list, you've improved your chances of getting the others right. The first time I read through the definitions in Activity 11-9, I was able to make only three matches. I knew that aphasia was "A," a disorder that caused speech problems. I knew that endorphins had to match with "H" because I learned that the good feeling I get from exercise is caused by the release of a chemical, endorphins. I also figured out that myelin sheath had to be "G" because a sheath is a covering, so it *encases* or covers something, and the word *encases* is used in answer "G."

After you match all of the items you're sure of, start with the first unmatched definition that you have and try to match it with each remaining term. If you're sure of a match, make it; if not, skip over that definition and go on to the next one. Continue down the list until you can make one more match. Then go back through the list again. Having eliminated one more alternative, you may find that only one other term could possibly be correct for one of the definitions. Through the process of elimination, you should be able to make all the matches.

On my second pass through Activity 11-9, I matched "C" with *genotype* because *genetic makeup* had *gene* in it, as did *genotype*. I also matched "E" with *cerebral cortex* because I knew it was a part of the brain and it had a similar word part in it, too (*cerebrum*). I also matched "D" with *ablation* because I had never heard of the word *ablation* and no other term appeared to fit the definition. I had some idea about the meaning of most of the other terms. I matched "J" with *action potential* because the definition involved a change in the charge, and change to me seemed to fit with *action*. Also, it didn't seem to fit well with any of the other choices.

Jot Down Alternatives That You're Sure Don't Match

Sometimes you actually can figure out a correct choice by making notes about which terms are definitely wrong for each definition. For example, after my second pass through the test in Activity 11-9, I had three items left to match (8, 9, and 10) and three definitions ("B," "F," and "I"). I knew that *thalamus* was a part of the brain and not a cell, so it couldn't be matched with "B" or "I." Therefore, "F" had to match with number 10. I also knew that "B" and "I" had to match with *neurons* and *soma*. It was difficult to determine which was correct because I had not prepared for this test; however, I vaguely remembered that neurons were like connections in the brain, so I matched "B" with *neurons*. Also "B" contained a plural noun, cells, and *neurons* was also plural. The only remaining alternative was to match "I" with *soma*.

Although I didn't expect to get them all right, I did. Did you use any of these strategies to figure out the correct matches? If you prepare properly for an exam, you should be able to match most of the items without difficulty. Then, by using some of the previous strategies, you should be able to figure out the other matches. Don't be afraid to draw on information from other courses and your own experiences to help you figure out correct answers, just as I did.

Recheck Your Work

After you've matched all items on the list, go back and check to be sure that you've not accidentally used the same letter or number twice. Going through the letters or numbers and crossing off each one again can help you avoid careless errors. If you do find that you have one term left and one definition left, and you know that they don't match, you need to go back and recheck your work, especially because it is unlikely that this is your only error. Go back through the list looking for any term that could fit the remaining definition. If necessary, rewrite the letters or numbers next to the original list and cross them off again.

Strategies for Math Tests

Many students experience anxiety on math exams—those with math anxiety and those without it. Math tests are a little like essay tests—you can't just guess A or C; you have to know how to get to the answer. There are a number of strategies you can use to earn a high grade. The first thing you should do when you get your test paper is write down the formulas that have caused you the most trouble. We call this doing a *memory dump*. Once you jot down some notes on the exam paper, you'll feel a little better. If you can't bring a 3- by 5-inch card to the exam, bring it in your head and write it out when you get your test paper. After you read the directions, take a look at the whole exam to see how many problems you need to answer and set up a strategy to budget your time.

Take a look at the first problem. If you can immediately identify it, go ahead and do the problem. If you're not sure about it, skip it. Trying to solve the problem when you really don't even know where to begin will only frustrate you and heighten your anxiety level (and waste too much time). Go through the exam and do the easy problems first. By completing all of the problems you can solve easily, you'll guarantee yourself points for those answers. Have you ever spent so much time trying to figure out one or two hard problems that you couldn't finish the exam? Maybe the last three problems would have been ones that you could have easily solved. Then go back, if you have time, and try the "hard" ones again. You may find that you can solve them once you have calmed down.

As you approach each of the problems, try to identify which type of problem it is. Then think about the model problems you created on your problem cards. How did you solve the problem like this one? Picture it in your head or even jot it down on your scrap paper or in the margin. Math teachers tell students to draw a diagram of what is given and what is needed to solve a problem. That works for some types of problems, but writing down your model is a type of diagram, too. Follow the steps line by line to solve your new problem.

If you complete the exam and have some time left, go back over your work. Many students make careless errors on math exams because they're nervous or rushing. Don't just look over your solution. You'll probably see what you expect to see, not what's there. Instead, put your hand or a piece of paper over your solution and rework the problem. Check your answer. If it's the same, move on to the next problem. If it's different; however, check your original problem and your new one line by line. I've found many careless errors using exactly this method. Remember, do all of the problems on the exam before you take the time to go back to recheck your work. You want to finish the exam to maximize your grade.

Activity 11-10

Describe Your Test-Taking Experiences

 Describe your test-taking experiences in high school. How did you do on tests? What strategies did you use when taking objective tests? How successful were the strategies? What changes do you plan to make in order to be as successful or more successful on college exams?

END-OF-EXAM STRATEGIES

DON'T LEAVE THE EXAM EARLY. Some students rush through the exam because they are afraid of running out of time. Others begin to panic as soon as the first student turns in his or her paper. You need to use all of the exam time to get the best grade you can. You may be able to pick up a few more points by using problem-solving strategies, test-wise clues, and guessing strategies.

GO BACK OVER DIFFICULT QUESTIONS. Use any additional time to rethink difficult questions on the exam. Underline key words in the question and in the alternatives. Eliminate wrong answers. Look for clues in other questions. Rephrase the question or the alternatives.

REDO MATH PROBLEMS TO CHECK YOUR WORK. Some students lose points on exams because of careless errors. If you have time, cover the problem with your hand and rework it. Then compare your answers. If they differ, check your work line by line until you locate your mistake.

DO A MEMORY SEARCH. When you can't figure out the answer to a question, try doing a memory search. Ask yourself whether the information was presented during the lecture or if it came from the text. Try to figure out from which topic the question came. Sometimes you can trigger a cue to long-term memory by identifying where or when you studied it.

USE CAUTION WHEN CHANGING ANSWERS. During a final review of the test, many students change answers because they start to have second thoughts about their original choices. This strategy often leads to changing correct answers to incorrect ones. Instead, use this rule: Don't change an answer unless you find that you misread the question or actually find the correct answer or a clue to it somewhere else on the exam.

REVIEW THE ENTIRE EXAM. When you complete the exam, take a few minutes to go back over it and check your answers. Some students make careless errors when they begin the exam because they're anxious; others do the same toward the end of the exam when they think they're running out of time. By reviewing your test, you may be able to correct some careless mistakes that would have cost you valuable points.

CODE YOUR TEST. If you have time, put a line through the letters of answers that you eliminate. Circle the letter of the answer that you select and leave blank the letters of any answers that you aren't sure about. After the exam is over, you can see how effectively you were able to eliminate wrong answers. You should also put a dot next to the answer when you guess. You can monitor your guessing ability after the exam, too by **coding your answers.**

CHECK YOUR ANSWER SHEET AGAINST YOUR EXAM. Before you turn in your test paper, take a minute or two to check to be sure that you marked the correct answers on your answer sheet. It's easy to make mistakes when you're nervous or in a hurry. You want to get the points for all your correct answers.

ESTIMATE YOUR GRADE. Before leaving the exam, take a few minutes to estimate your grade. Learning to accurately predict your test score can help you eliminate feelings of panic that often occur after taking the exam. Some students become so nervous about the outcome of an exam that it interferes with their ability to concentrate on their other work.

LEARNING FROM EXAMS

Many students think that once an exam is over, the only thing that matters is the grade. However, exams are learning opportunities. Professors often use them to help reinforce the critical concepts that they are trying to present. Reviewing an exam after it's returned can help you learn more about the course content and clarify any errors that you made. You also can learn a great deal about your professor's testing methods and about your own test-taking skills.

Evaluate Your Preparation

Your graded exam can be used to help you evaluate your preparation. By finding out where each question came from (the lecture or the textbook), you can determine whether you're focusing on the same topics and concepts as your professor. You also can check how well you mark and take notes by scanning the text or your text notes and looking for questions that were on the test. If you find that few of the test questions are contained in material that you highlighted or noted, you can adjust for the next test. Determining how many of the questions came from the text and how many came from the lecture can help you decide how much time to spend on each type of material the next time you prepare. If, for example, your professor took 80 percent of the test questions from the lecture material, then you should have spent 80 percent of your study time on lecture notes and only 20 percent on text material.

You also can evaluate how well you were able to anticipate or predict test questions. Check your predicted questions to see how many of the items were actually on the exam. How many of the test questions did you predict? Think back to how you felt as you took the exam. Did you feel surprised by many of the items, or did you often find yourself thinking, "I knew this would be on the test"?

Finally, evaluate your test-taking skills. Did you read the directions, budget your time well, and answer the easy questions first? Did you work through the difficult items in a logical, systematic way, eliminating wrong answers? Were you able to identify key words in the questions that helped you figure out the correct answers? Did you review the exam and rework the difficult items? Knowing how effectively you were able to use the various test-taking strategies can help you improve your performance on the next exam.

Learn from Your Mistakes

Understanding why you were wrong about a particular answer can be critical to your success on the next exam. In some cases, you may need to clarify or correct some of the information that you learned. By discussing your mistakes with your professor, you may find that you hadn't really understood the material after all. By examining your errors, you also can determine whether they resulted from poor preparation or from carelessness or poor test-taking strategies. Locating the questions that you missed in the text or in your notes can help you determine whether you spent enough time on that material.

Get Help Before the Next Exam

If your grade on the exam isn't up to par, go for help immediately. Your first stop should be your professor. Set up an appointment to discuss your exam. Go over the exam question by question until you have a clear understanding of what you need to do to improve your grade for the next exam. Tell your professor exactly what you did to prepare and ask for suggestions about what you may need to do differently.

Your next stop should be your college learning center. Many learning centers offer individual assistance or workshops on test preparation, test anxiety, and test-taking strategies. You may need to request tutorial assistance. Check to see if your learning center, department, or organizations offer tutoring services. Waiting to see if you do better on your next test can be very risky. If you don't do any better, you'll have two low grades to pull up.

Activity 11-11

Learn from Your Exam

Review one of the exams that recently was returned to you. Write a paragraph or two discussing what you were able to learn from the exam. Include information about how the test was designed, your preparation, and your test-taking skills.

Activity 11-12

Where Are You Now?

Now that you have completed Chapter 11, take a few minutes to repeat the "Where Are You Now?" activity, located on the *College Study Skills* Web site. What changes did you make as a result of reading this chapter? How are you planning to apply what you've learned in this chapter?

SUMMARY

Your preparation for exams is only one factor that influences your final grade. Some students appear to be good test takers and others don't. Why? One explanation involves how effectively they can handle the stress of taking exams. Test anxiety can affect your ability to prepare for and take exams. Some students get queasy, feel faint, worry, or even "go blank" during exams. Because of test anxiety, they can't completely focus on the exam questions and their grades suffer. Coping techniques such as doing relaxation exercises, visualizing, using positive self-scripts, and identifying anxiety triggers can help reduce your test anxiety. However, the most effective way to reduce test anxiety is being well prepared.

Following directions carefully is crucial during any testing situation. Too often, though, students skip this important step in order to save time or because of high levels of test anxiety. Budgeting your time during exams is also important so that you can complete all of the questions and still have time for a final review of the test. You can maximize your test score and pick up clues to more difficult questions by answering the easiest questions first. Using both problem-solving and test-wise strategies will help you gain points on matching, true/false, completion, and multiple-choice exams. Doing memory searches, eliminating wrong answers, and underlining key words are just a few ways to "figure out" the correct answer when you're not sure of it. However, when you still can't come up with the right choice, you should guess. You can often improve your exam score by using strategic guessing. If you've taken the time to prepare properly for your exam, take the time to "take" it, too. Use the full amount of time that's been allotted for the exam. Students who persevere—continue to work on difficult questions, think through confusing items, look for clues in other questions, and use other problem-solving strategies—do better on exams. By estimating your grade and evaluating your preparation and performance, you can learn how to improve your grade on the next exam.

Answer Key

Activity 11-5 Guess at True/False Questions
2. T   5. T   8. F   14. T   16. F   20. T   24. T

Activity 11-6 Guess at Multiple-Choice Questions
2. B   8. C   14. B   16. D   24. B   30. D   31. C
33. A   36. C   37. C   40. A   41. C   43. A   48. D

Activity 11-7 Take a Multiple-Choice Test
1. B   2. A   3. D   4. C

Activity 11-8 Take a True/False Test
1. F   2. F   3. T   4. F   5. F   6. F   7. T   8. F
9. F   10. F

Test-Wise Strategies
1. C 2. B   3. C   4. C   5. D   6. B   7. A   8. B
9. A   10. B

REVIEW QUESTIONS

Terms You Should Know: Make a flash card for each term.

Absolute words	Facilitating test anxiety	Stem
Alternatives	Memory search	Strategic guessing
Balanced answer keys	Pacing	Test anxiety
Coding your answers	Problem-solving strategies	Test-anxiety cycle
Debilitating test anxiety	Qualifying words	Test-wise strategies
Distractors		

Completion: Fill in the blank to complete each of the following statements.

1. The real cause of test anxiety is _____ _____.

2. The best way to reduce test anxiety is to _____ _____.

3. The most important factor in determining how much time to spend on a question is the _____ _____.

4. On a matching test, you should always work from the side with the _____ words.

5. Unless you _____ the question or find the correct answer (or a clue to it) somewhere else on the test, you shouldn't change your answer.

Multiple Choice: Circle the letter of the best answer for each of the following questions. Be sure to underline key words and eliminate wrong answers.

6. _____ test anxiety is helpful because it makes you study for a test.
   - **A.** Motivating
   - **B.** Affective
   - **C.** Facilitating
   - **D.** Debilitating

7. _____ words generally make a statement false.
   - **A.** Negative
   - **B.** Absolute
   - **C.** Qualifying
   - **D.** Italicized

Short Answer–Essay: On a separate sheet, answer each of the following questions.

8. Why should students answer the easiest questions first?

9. How should students cope with test anxiety in order to improve their performance on exams?

10. What strategies should students use to maximize their scores on objective tests?

"A few days ago I got back my exam on political process. I got 9 out of 10 on the essay. This professor never gives 9 out of 10 on essays. I was shocked. We are given the essay question ahead of time, but up to now I just used to write from the top of my head. Now, I plan out my essay before the exam. I read through the material and list important ideas in a logical order."

Valerie Jones
Student

PREPARING FOR ESSAY TESTS

In this chapter you will learn more about:

- **How to predict essay questions**
- **How to plan essay answers**
- **How to practice essay answers**

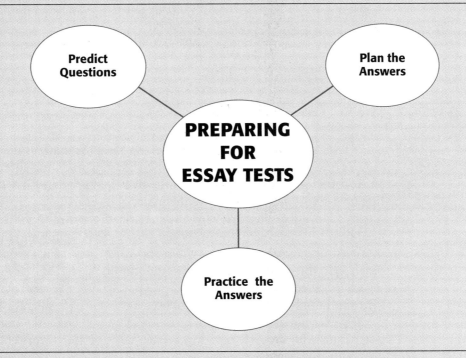

Predict Questions

Plan the Answers

PREPARING FOR ESSAY TESTS

Practice the Answers

Activity 12-1

Where Are You Now?

Take a few minutes to answer *yes* or *no* to the following questions.

	YES	NO
1. Do you study differently for essay tests and objective tests?	_____	_____
2. Do you generally plan out your answers in your head rather than on paper?	_____	_____
3. Do you always write out essays before the test if the professor gives you the questions?	_____	_____
4. Do you predict possible essay questions before an exam?	_____	_____
5. Are you usually able to predict accurately which essay questions the professor will include?	_____	_____
6. Do you use memory techniques to help you remember the main points that you want to make in your answer?	_____	_____
7. Do you tend to rely on old exams and hope that the same questions will be used again?	_____	_____
8. Do you prepare sample essay answers and ask your professor to evaluate them before the exam?	_____	_____
9. Are you generally well prepared for essay exams?	_____	_____
10. Do you know how to study for an essay exam?	_____	_____
Total Points	_____	

Give yourself 1 point for each *yes* answer to all of the questions except 2 and 7 and 1 point for each *no* answer to questions 2 and 7. Now total up your points. A low score indicates that you need to develop some new skills for preparing for essay tests. A high score indicates that you already are using many good strategies.

PREDICT QUESTIONS

Essay tests are more difficult than objective tests for many students because they require recall learning. You need to *know* what you're writing about. To prepare for an essay test, you should use many of the strategies presented in Chapter 10 for setting up a study plan and learning the material. Preparing for an essay test, though, involves more than just knowing the material. To write a good essay answer, you need to be able to organize your thoughts and ideas rapidly and then present them in a well-developed and well-written form. All these skills require training and practice. In this chapter you'll learn some additional strategies for preparing for essay exams. Predicting, planning, and practicing your answers before the exam can help you improve your performance on essay exams. (See Figure 12.1.)

If you're not given the actual questions that will be on the exam, then the best way to study for an essay test is to predict test questions yourself. By anticipating questions that could be on the exam, you increase your chances of studying the

FIGURE 12.1
Three Steps to Preparing
for an Essay Exam

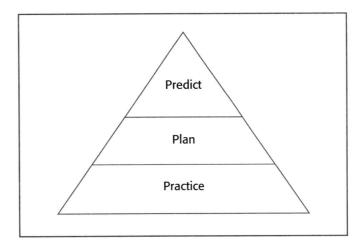

same information on which you'll be tested. Of course, it's also to your advantage to prepare the answers in essay form so that you study the information in the same format that you'll be required to use on the test.

Predict Extra Questions

Deciding how many questions to predict isn't easy. Many factors need to be considered. A test that covers two chapters may require more or fewer questions than one that covers six chapters; the difference involves the depth or breadth of the questions. A good rule of thumb is to predict at least four to five times the number of questions that will be on the exam. If you'll have to answer two essay questions on the exam, then you should predict eight to ten questions. Another approach is to predict three or four questions from each chapter. This is especially effective if you have only one essay question to answer. The more questions you predict, the greater your chances of accurately predicting the questions on the exam. Also, even if you don't predict the exact questions, you may find that you've predicted a question similar to the one on the test. In the process of preparing to answer your question, you may learn the information that you need to answer the question that the professor asks. The more questions that you predict and prepare, the better you'll do on the test.

Predict the Right Kinds of Questions

You should predict **broad questions** if the exam will cover large amounts of material. If the essay test will include ten questions on only two chapters of text, however, the questions may be more specific and require more detail about a specific topic. If you're well prepared to answer broad questions, you should be able to answer the specific questions, too. Study guides (purchased guides or study guides provided by the professor), major topics in your lecture notes, and end-of-chapter questions in the text are valuable sources of essay questions. Asking the professor for sample questions and reviewing old exams can help you determine the types of questions that you should be predicting.

    Narrow questions that focus on why or how something happened often are too limited in scope. Most essay questions ask you to discuss causes and effects, compare and contrast, explain the steps in a process, and so on. You'll be able to predict and answer essay questions more effectively if you understand the terms

FIGURE 12.2

Frequently Used Terms in Essay Questions

Term	Definition
compare	Tell how two or more subjects are alike; provide similarities. Some professors also expect you to discuss differences—ask.
contrast	Tell how two or more subjects are different.
define	Give the meaning or definition.
describe	Provide details or characteristics about a subject.
discuss or explain	Give a detailed answer that may include definitions, main and supporting points, reasons, and examples.
evaluate	Discuss both positive and negative aspects of the topic and then make a judgment.
illustrate	Explain by giving examples.
justify	Prove by giving evidence that backs up or supports a point.
list or enumerate	Number and list the information rather than writing in paragraph form.
summarize	Provide a brief review of the main points.
trace	Describe the events or steps in order of occurrence.

that commonly are used in essay questions. A chart of frequently used terms is presented in Figure 12.2. Although you don't need to memorize the terms and their definitions, you should become familiar with them.

Activity 12-2

Predict Three Essay Questions

Refer to Chapter 5, "Taking Lecture Notes," and predict at least three questions that might be on an exam. (*Hints:* Were three types of note-taking systems described? Did the chapter present a series of reasons for taking notes? Did it present lists of things to do or not to do?) Compare your questions to those of others in your group. Did you have the same questions?

1. _____

   _____

   _____

2. _____

   _____

   _____

3. _____

   _____

   _____

Predict Challenging Questions

Predicting good essay questions requires some practice; they must be not only thoughtful but also penetrating and challenging. Look at the questions that you predicted in Activity 12-2. Are they questions that require only brief, one-word or one-sentence answers? Many students predict only knowledge-level questions—questions that require only the repetition of the information as it was stated in the text or the lecture. Although some professors do include some of these short-answer essays, most ask questions that require analysis, synthesis, and application. Look at these three questions:

1. What are two types of note-taking systems used for lecture classes?

2. Describe two types of note-taking systems that are used for lecture classes.

3. Compare and contrast the outline method and the block method of taking notes in lecture classes.

The first question isn't really an essay question at all. It requires only a short answer and little other information about the topic. The second and third questions, on the other hand, require more in-depth mastery of the material. Several paragraphs or several pages may be needed to answer them properly.

Students often get into the habit of predicting one essay question for each main topic or main heading in the text or lecture. One problem with this practice is that it may be too limiting for some essay tests. Learning the material in isolation, heading by heading, may not prepare you to answer a more general question that requires you to integrate the information. To prepare for tests where you may have only one or two long essays to answer, you need to learn to connect two or more of the main topics.

As an in-class exercise, I asked students to read a short text excerpt on Federalism and then to predict five essay questions on the material. You can get a good idea of what the material was about by looking at an outline of the headings that were included in the excerpt in Figure 12.3. Can you predict any essay questions on this text

FIGURE 12.3
Outline of Excerpt on Federalism

I. Why Federalism?
   A. Advantages of Federalism
   B. Disadvantages of Federalism

II. Constitutional History of Federalism
   A. Implied Federal Powers
   B. National Supremacy
   C. Secession and Civil War
   D. Civil Rights
   E. Interstate Commerce
   F. Loss of Reserved Powers
   G. Federalism's Constitutional Status Today

III. Essentials: The Framework of American Federalism
   A. Delegated Powers
   B. Reserved Powers
   C. Powers Denied to the Nation and States
   D. State Role in National Government

FIGURE 12.4

Predicted Essay Questions on Federalism

1. Explain the impact of the Thirteenth, Fourteenth, and Fifteenth Amendments with respect to limiting state power for individual freedom.

2. What are the advantages and disadvantages of Federalism?

3. How does Federalism increase political participation?

4. Name the three amendments passed by the Reconstruction Congress and describe what each amendment did to delegate Congress's power of security.

5. Explain the differences between delegated and reserved powers.

6. Explain both Hamilton's and Jefferson's views on Federalism and the Constitution; tell which one you agree with and why.

7. What was the greatest crisis of the American Federal system? Why did it happen? What were the results?

8. Name the court case in 1819 that involved the state of Maryland and the National Bank and tell what it established.

9. What is Federalism? How does it affect the American people?

10. Discuss the 1954 Supreme court case *Brown* v. *Board of Education*. What effect did this case have on civil rights in the United States?

material? Then look at the questions that one group of students predicted after reading the actual text material (Figure 12.4). Are any of your questions on the list? Which of these questions are broad, general questions, and which are specific?

Although almost all of my students included questions on the advantages and disadvantages of Federalism, they also predicted an impressive number of other essay questions from this material. Many of the questions were limited to headed sections, but others were broad questions that involved several headed sections. Which of the questions do you think are good predicted essay questions for this material? If you'd like, you can read the text excerpt on the *College Study Skills* Web site.

Activity 12-3

Read and Predict Essay Questions

 Read and mark the text excerpt "Political Systems in Global Perspective," in Figure 12.5, and then work with your group to predict three essay questions. Include at least one broad question.

1. _____

_____

_____

2. _____

_____

_____

3. _____

_____

_____

FIGURE 12.5
Excerpt from a Sociology Text

POLITICAL SYSTEMS IN GLOBAL PERSPECTIVE

Political systems as we know them today have evolved slowly. In the earliest societies, politics was not an entity separate from other aspects of life. As we will see, however, all groups have some means of legitimizing power.

Hunting and gathering societies do not have political institutions as such because they have very little division of labor or social inequality. Leadership and authority are centered in the family and clan. Individuals acquire leadership roles due to personal attributes such as great physical strength, exceptional skills, and charisma (Nolan and Lenski, 1999).

Political institutions first emerged in agrarian societies as they acquired surpluses and developed greater social inequality. Elites took control of politics and used custom or traditional authority to justify their position. When cities developed circa 3500–3000 B.C.E., the *city-state*—a city whose power extended to adjacent areas—became the center of political power. Both the Roman and Persian empires were composed of a number of city-states, each of which had its own monarchy. Thus, in these societies, political authority was decentralized. After each of these empires fell, the individual city-states lived on.

Nation-states as we know them began to develop in Europe between the twelfth and fifteenth centuries (see Tilly, 1975). A *nation-state* is a unit of political organization that has recognizable national boundaries and whose citizens possess specific legal rights and obligations. Nation-states emerge as countries develop specific geographic territories and acquire greater ability to defend their borders. Improvements in communication and transportation make it possible for people in a larger geographic area to share a common language and culture. As charismatic and traditional authority are superseded by rational—legal authority, legal standards come to prevail in all areas of life, and the nation-state claims a monopoly over the legitimate use of force (P. Kennedy, 1993).

Approximately 190 nation-states currently exist throughout the world; today, everyone is born, lives, and dies under the auspices of a nation-state (see Skocpol and Amenta, 1986). Four main types of political systems are found in nation-states: monarchy, authoritarianism, totalitarianism, and democracy.

Monarchy

Monarchy **is a political system in which power resides in one person or family and is passed from generation to generation through lines of inheritance.** Monarchies are most common in agrarian societies and are associated with traditional authority patterns. However, the relative power of monarchs has varied across nations, depending on religious, political, and economic conditions.

Absolute monarchs claim a hereditary right to rule (based on membership in a noble family) or a divine right to rule (a God-given right to rule that legitimizes the exercise of power). In limited monarchies, rulers depend on powerful members of the nobility to retain their thrones. Unlike absolute monarchs, *limited monarchs* are not considered to be above the law. In *constitutional monarchies,* the royalty serve as symbolic rulers or heads of state while actual authority is held by elected officials in national parliaments. In present-day monarchies such as the United Kingdom, Sweden, Spain, and the Netherlands, members of royal families primarily perform ceremonial functions. In the United Kingdom, for example, the media often focus large amounts of time and attention on the royal family, especially the personal lives of its members. Recently, the European Union (of which the United Kingdom, Spain, Sweden, and the Netherlands are all members) has also received media attention as a form of governmental cooperation across national boundaries but not one that weakens the powers of the present-day monarchies (see Box 14.2, "Sociology in Global Perspective").

Authoritarianism

Authoritarianism **is a political system controlled by rulers who deny popular participation in government.** A few authoritarian regimes have been absolute monarchies who rulers claimed a hereditary right to their position. Today, Saudi Arabia and Kuwait are examples of authoritarian absolute monarchies. In *dictatorships,* power is gained and held by a single individual. Pure dictatorships are rare; all rulers need the support of the military and the backing of business elites to maintain their position. *Military juntas* result when military officers seize power from the government, as has happened in recent decades in Argentina, Chile, and Haiti. Today, authoritarian regimes exist in Fidel Castro's Cuba and in the People's Republic of China. Authoritarian regimes seek to control the media and to suppress coverage of any topics or information that does not reflect upon the regime in a favorable light.

Totalitarianism

Totalitarianism **is a political system in which the state seeks to regulate all aspects of people's public and private lives.** Totalitarianism relies on modern technology to monitor and control people; mass propaganda and electronic surveillance are widely used to influence people's thinking and control their actions. One example of a totalitarian regime was the National Socialist (Nazi) Party in Germany during World War II; military leaders there sought to control all aspects of national life, not just government operations. Other examples include the former Soviet Union and contemporary Iraq before the fall of Saddam Hussein's regime.

To keep people from rebelling, totalitarian governments enforce conformity: People are denied the right to assemble for political purposes, access to information is strictly controlled, and secret police enforce compliance, creating an environment of constant fear and suspicion.

Many nations do not recognize totalitarian regimes as being the legitimate government for a particular country. Afghanistan in the year 2001 was an example. As the war on terrorism began in the aftermath of the September 11 terrorist attacks on the United States, many people developed a heightened awareness of the Taliban regime, which ruled most of Afghanistan and was engaged in fierce fighting to capture the rest of the country. The Taliban regime maintained absolute control over the the Afghan people in most of that country. For example, it required that all Muslims take part in prayer five times each day and that men attend prayer at mosques, where women were forbidden (Marquis, 2001). Taliban leaders claimed that their actions were based on Muslim law and espoused a belief in never-ending *jihad*—a struggle against one's perceived enemies. Although the totalitarian nature of the Taliban regime was difficult for many people, it was particularly oppressive for women, who were viewed by this group as being "biologically, religiously and prophetically" inferior to men (McGeary, 2001: 41). Consequently, this regime made the veil obligatory and banned women from public life. U.S. government officials believed that the Taliban regimen was protecting Osama bin Laden, the man thought to

FIGURE 12.5 (continued)
Excerpt from a Sociology Text

have been the mastermind behind numerous terrorist attacks on U.S. citizens and facilities, both on the mainland and abroad. As a totalitarian regime, the Taliban leadership was recognized by only three other governments, despite controlling most of Afghanistan.

Once the military action commenced in Afghanistan, most of what U.S. residents knew about the Taliban and about the war on terrorism was based on media accounts and "expert opinions" that were voiced on television. According to the political analyst Michael Parenti (1998), the media play a significant role in framing the information we receive about the political systems of other countries. *Framing* refers to how news is packaged, including the amount of exposure given to a story, its placement, the positive or negative tone of the story, the headlines and photographs, and the accompanying visual and auditory effects if the story is being broadcast. The war in Afghanistan, like other wars in the past, was typically framed as a fight to save freedom and democracy.

Democracy

Democracy **is a political system in which the people hold the ruling power either directly or through elected representatives.** The literal meaning of *democracy* is "rule by the people" (from the Greek words *demos,* meaning "the people," and *kratein,* meaning "to rule"). In an ideal-type democracy, people would actively and directly rule themselves. *Direct participatory democracy* requires that citizens be able to meet together regularly to debate and decide the issues of the day. However, if all 292 million people in the United States came together in one place for a meeting, they would occupy an area of more than seventy square miles, and a single round of five-minute speeches would require more than five thousand years (based on Schattschneider, 1969).

In countries such as the United States, Canada, Australia, and the United Kingdom, people have a voice in the government through *representative democracy,* whereby citizens elect representatives to serve as bridges between themselves and the government. The U.S. Constitution requires that each state have two senators and a minimum of one member in the House of Representatives. The current size of the House (435 seats) has not changed since the apportionment following the 1910 census. Therefore, based on Census 2000, those 435 seats were reapportioned based on the increase or decrease in a state's population between 1990 and 2000 (see "Census Profiles: Political Representation and Shifts in the U.S. Population").

In a representative democracy, elected representatives are supposed to convey the concerns and interests of those they represent, and the government is expected to be responsive to the wishes of the people. Elected officials are held accountable to the people through elections. However, representative democracy is not always equally accessible to all people in a nation. Throughout U.S. history, members of subordinate racial–ethnic groups have been denied full participation in the democratic process. Gender and social class have also limited some people's democratic participation. For example, women have not always had the same rights as men. Full voting rights were not gained by women until the ratification of the Nineteenth Amendment in 1920. However, women were divided by class in their perceptions about the necessity of suffrage.

Even representative democracies are not all alike. As compared to the winner-takes-all elections in the United States, which are usually decided by who wins the most votes, the majority of European elections are based on a system of proportional representation, meaning that each party is represented in the national legislature according to the proportion of votes that party received. For example, a party that won 40 percent of the vote would receive 40 seats in a 100-seat legislative body, and a party receiving 20 percent of the votes would receive 20 seats.

Text material from Diana Kendall, *Sociology in Our Times,* 5th ed. (Belmont, CA: Wadsworth, 2005), pp. 460–465.

PLAN THE ANSWERS

Predicting essay questions is not the end of your preparation for an essay exam; it's just the beginning. The second step in preparing for an essay exam is to plan your answer. Dig through your text and lecture notes and gather information that you would use in your answer. Then take a few minutes and organize it. Finally, outline your answer. Think back to the active study strategies that you learned in Chapter 10. Planning your answer is an active preparation strategy that incorporates all of the ICOW strategies (identify, condense, organize, and write).

Gather Information

The first step in planning your answer is to **gather information.** You need to find the main and supporting points required to answer the question. You probably know some information to include in your answer, but you need to refer to your text and lecture notes for more. This process of gathering information is valuable because it forces you to dig through the text and your lecture notes looking for relevant information. This active study technique may help you learn some of the other text information at the same time. Putting the information from the

FIGURE 12.6
Basic Format for Planned
Essay Questions

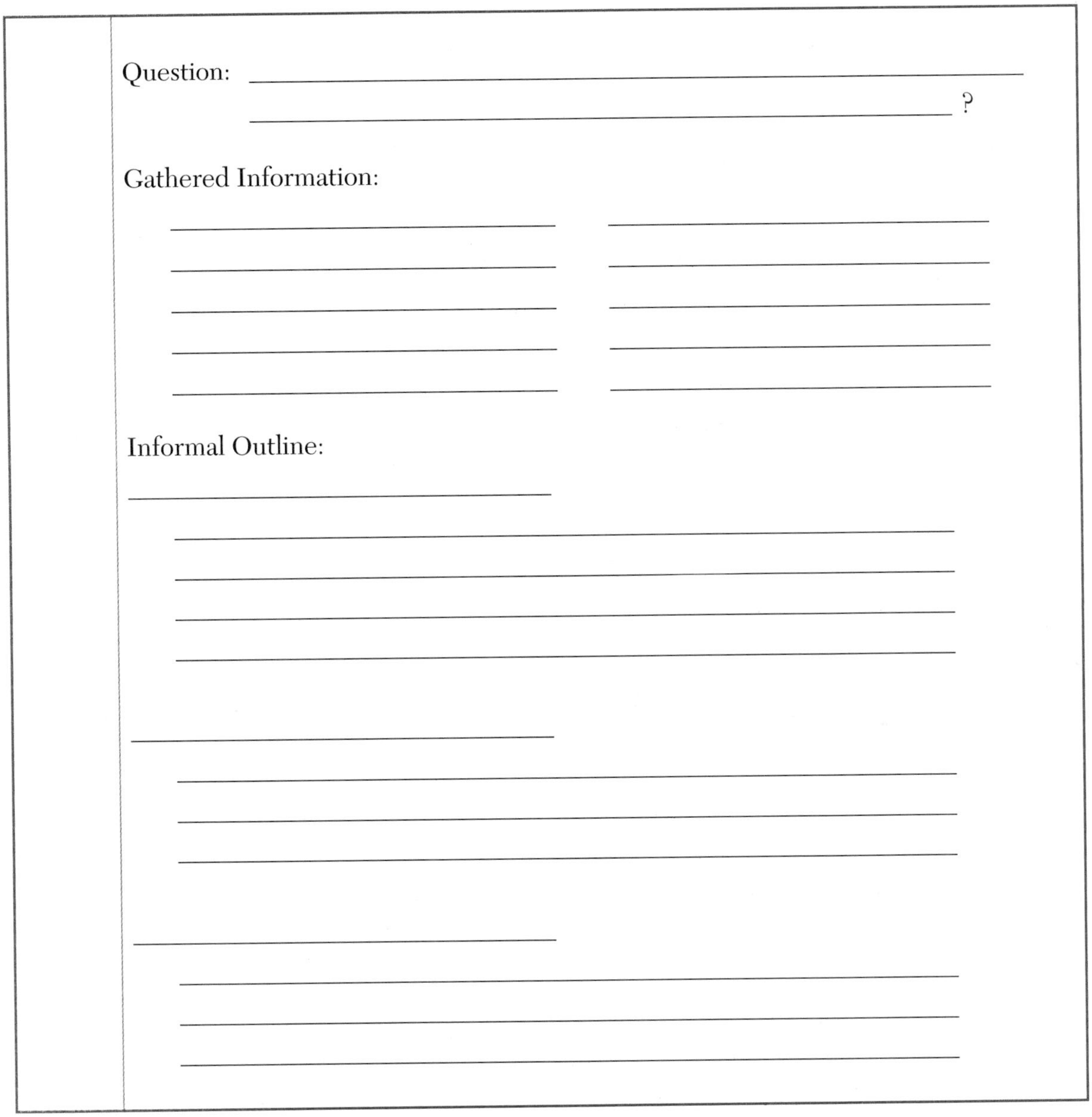

Question: _____

_____ ?

Gathered Information:

_____   _____
_____   _____
_____   _____
_____   _____
_____   _____

Informal Outline:

_____

_____

_____

_____

_____

_____

_____

_____

_____

_____

_____

_____

_____

_____

text and the lecture together also is a good technique for preparing for an essay test.

An easy way to gather information is to treat each question separately. Write each question across the top of a large piece of paper. Then open your text and your notes to that section of the material. Start to look for information that you would use if you had to answer that question. Pretend that it's an open-book exam and you have the opportunity to look for the material that you're going to use. As you locate important points and details that would be useful in answering the question, write them down on your sheet of paper. Don't copy the information; rather, write it in meaningful phrases. If you use a two-column format, you'll be forced to condense the material. Afterward, outline your answer. Figure 12.6 contains the basic format for your essay plan.

Addie and DaShawn listed the information from both their textbooks and lecture notes. Figure 12.7 shows the information Addie and DaShawn gathered for the

FIGURE 12.7

Addie's and DaShawn's Examples
of Gathered Information

What are the stages in the evolution and growth of American cities?	
From beginning to about 1800s (T)	Urban population swelled (T)
Manifest Destiny (L)	Industrialization continued after Civil War (T)
Cities grew and developed (T)	1860s to World War I (T)
The Great Depression (L)	Urban decay (L)
Suburbs grew and flourished (T)	SMSAs became MSAs (T)
NYC became national metropolis (L)	Construction of canals and
1800 to 1860s (T)	railroads (L)
Cities served as outposts of	World War I to World War II (L)
Western Europe (T)	Development of coastal cities (T)
Returning veterans (L)	Northeastern cities developed as
Cities developed before commercial	industrial centers (T)
agriculture (L)	Post World War II (T)
Programs instituted by Pres. F.D.R. to	9,000 banks closed losing
help the unemployed (T)	$2.5 billion (L)

Addie's Gathered Information

How did we obtain Alaska?	
Seward (L)	exercise commercial domination (T)
72 mill (L)	less than 2 cents an acre (T)
greatest steal (L)	feared Brit would buy it (T)
gold, fishery, timber (L)	convince British colonies to (T)
Folly or Icebox (L)	request annexation as well (T)
Bribe money (L)	
Union in 1960 (L)	
Russia (L)	

DaShawn's Gathered Information

essay questions that they predicted would be on their Geography and History exams. As you can see, these lists of information are still far from the organized essay answers that you need to write. There are many ways to arrange the information that you pull from your text and notes. Some students prefer to organize the information as they gather it. Many students find, though, that it's too difficult to jump directly to the outlined answer. In the next section, you'll learn how to organize and outline your essay answer.

Some students get confused about how to plan an essay answer. Instead of writing down the actual information that they need to answer the question, they

FIGURE 12.8
Poor Examples of Planned
Essay Questions

Question: What tasks do specialized processors perform?
Plan: 1. Explain what a specialized processor is.
2. Give examples of different kinds of specialized processors.
3. Give exact operations of different kinds of specialized processors.
4. Compare other processors with a specialized processor.

Vashon's Plan

Question: Explain why you should answer the easy questions on a test first.
Plan: Use the information given in class to explain why you should answer the easy questions first.

Bev's Plan

Question: What are the main causes of low savings in the United States?
Plan: people live for present
Social Security
capital markets

Martin's Plan

---

make a list of what they must do to answer the question. Look at the examples in Figure 12.8.

Neither Vashon's nor Bev's plan actually answers the questions to which it refers. The information that must be discussed in order to earn points on the exam is never actually stated. The first example, however, does demonstrate that Vashon thought about the answer and knew what type of information was needed. Listing the details under each of the four statements would have filled in the necessary information. How would you have answered the second question? Couldn't you list some points that you would make? Martin did include three main points in his gathered information, but he didn't include any of the specific details that he would need to write his essay answer. Be sure that you gather main ideas and details so that you know exactly what you want to put into your answer.

Activity 12-4

Gather Information

As a group choose one of the questions that you wrote in Activity 12-3 and gather the information that you would need to answer the question if it were on an essay test. Compare your gathered information to that of others in your group.

Organize Information

After gathering information for a number of questions, you may find that you have a huge amount of information to remember. By organizing the information for each question, you'll find it is easier to learn and remember the points you want to make for each question.

You can organize your gathered information by *labeling* each point. Look at each piece of information that you wrote down and decide where it should go in your essay. Find the point that you want to make first and label it 1. Any points that support it should be marked 1A, 1B, and so on. You may find that after you organize the information, you'll find that you don't have any supporting points for some of your main points or too few for others. You can go back to your text or lecture notes and dig for more support. Two excellent ways to organize your essay notes are shown in Figure 12.9. Do Karen and Addie have sufficient support for each of their main points?

Outline Your Answer

Although both Addie and Karen did organize their information (Figure 12.8), it still is not in a form that's easy to practice and remember. An informal outline is much more useful for remembering the points that you want to make in your es-

FIGURE 12.9

Two Examples of Organized Information

Explain the research done by the experimenters at Santa Barbara University. What conclusion was found?

L **significant differences in time 2C1
L **learned drive theory 3A
L **videotaped joggers 1
L **timed in two sections 1A
L **joggers—unaware experiment 1B
L **fear of evaluation increases drive 3C

L **three groups 2
L **saw no one 2A
L **saw woman reading 2B
L **saw woman watching 2C
L **Cotrell 3B
L **conclusion 3

Karen's Plan

What are the stages in the evolution and growth of American cities?

1 From beginning to about 1800s (T)
2A Manifest Destiny (L)
3B Cities grew and developed (T)
4A The Great Depression (L)
5B Suburbs grew and flourished (T)
2C NYC became national metropolis (L)
2 1800 to 1860s (T)
1B Cities served as outposts of
   Western Europe (T)
5A Returning veterans (L)
1A Cities developed before commercial
   agriculture (L)
4D Programs instituted by Pres. F.D.R. to
   help the unemployed (T)

(L) 5D Urban population swelled (T)
3A Industrialization continued after Civil War (T)
3 1860s to World War I (T)
4C Urban decay (L)
5C SMSAs became MSAs (T)
2B Construction of canals and
   railroads (L)
4 World War I to World War II (L)
1C Development of coastal cities (T)
2D Northeastern cities developed as
   industrial centers (T)
5 Post World War II (T)
4B 9,000 banks closed losing
   $2.5 billion (L)

Addie's Plan

say answer. The easiest way to outline your answer is simply to list the **main points** (most important points) next to the margin and then list the **supporting details** indented slightly underneath. Try to limit your main points to seven or fewer so you can remember them. Three or four main points with good support for each should be sufficient for most answers. Of course, if you need to know the five causes of something, then you'll have five main points.

Look at the outlines that Todd and Addie developed from the information that they gathered (Figures 12.10 and 12.11). Todd used **formal outlining** to organize his information. Addie used an **informal outline** style in which she listed main points and then indented the secondary or supporting points.

Some students become confused or careless when preparing outlines for their essay answers. Although Casey and Emily (Figure 12.12A and 12.12B) did gather a wide variety of specific information to answer their predicted questions, they didn't include any of the actual main points or supporting details in their outlines. These outlines demonstrate that the students thought about how to organize the information for their answers but they didn't develop effective outlines to use to learn the information.

Activity 12-5

Organize and Outline Information

Work as a group to organize and then outline the information that you gathered in Activity 12-4 for the question on "Political Systems in Global Perspective." What were your main points? Did you have supporting details or examples for each?

FIGURE 12.10
Example of Formal Outlining

I. What is a mechanistic system?
  A. Characteristics
    1. centralized—top management
    2. have a lot of rules and policies
    3. jobs are highly specialized
    4. communication is vertical coming down from mgmt.
    5. goals are based on top management
    6. uses system 1
    7. bureaucratic
  B. Mechanistic work is very cold and informal

II. What is an organic system?
  A. Characteristics
    1. decentralized—have a lot of options
    2. have few rules and policies
    3. jobs are enriched—more central in their job
    4. communication is horizontal as well as vertical
    5. group goal setting
    6. uses system 4
    7. nonbureaucratic
  B. Organic work area is very warm and informal

Todd's Outline

FIGURE 12.11
Addie's Informal Outline

From beginning to about 1800s
    Cities developed before commercial agriculture
    Cities served as outposts of Western Europe
    Development of coastal cities

1800 to 1860s
    Manifest Destiny
    Construction of canals and railroads
    NYC became national metropolis
    Northeastern cities as industrial centers

1860s to World War I
    Industrialization continued after Civil War
    Cities grew and developed

World War I to World War II
    The Great Depression
    9,000 banks closed losing $2.5 billion
    Urban decay
    Programs instituted by Pres. F.D.R. to help urban unemployed

Post World War II
    Returning veterans
    Suburbs grew and flourished
    SMSAs became MSAs
    Urban population swelled

FIGURE 12.12A
Poor Example of Essay Outline

What is a political party? Explain the difference between Republicans and Democrats and give examples by using specific presidents.

Define a political party
    Define party
    Example of party
Explain difference between Rep & Dem
    Define Rep.
    Define Dem.
Name three Rep. & Dem. Presidents
    Name them
    Describe their political backgrounds

Casey's Outline

FIGURE 12.12B
Poor Example of Essay Outline

Describe the IK tribe of Northern Uganda from Colin Turbull's, "The Mountain People"

I. Before the move
   A. Where they lived
      1. Why live there
      2. Why did they leave
   B. Family life
      1. Children
      2. Elders
      3. Food

II. After the move
   A. Where they moved
      1. Who put them there
      2. Why they couldn't thrive there
   B. Family life changed
      1. Children
      2. Elders
      3. Food
   C. Survival

Emily's Outline

Activity 12-6

Evaluate Student Outlines

Evaluate each of the student outlines in Figure 12.13. Jot down your reaction to each outline and then rate each as excellent, good, fair, or poor. Compare your evaluations with those of others in your group.

EXAMPLE 1: _____

_____

RATING: _____

EXAMPLE 2: _____

_____

RATING: _____

EXAMPLE 3: _____

_____

RATING: _____

EXAMPLE 4: _____

_____

RATING: _____

FIGURE 12.13
Sample Student Outlines

Question: Why is the Five-Day Study Plan so effective in helping students prepare for exams?

Example 1
I. Active study strategies
   A. Set up a plan
      1. Plan actual tasks
      2. Divide up material
II. Modify the format
   A. Be creative
   B. Easier to get motivated
   C. Space study to aid retention
   D. Include specific topics
III. Lots of review
   A. Spaced out
   B. Study oldest material first
   C. Don't start too early

Example 2
Set up a plan
   Allow enough time
   Eight to ten hours
Divide up material
   Group material w/similar topics
   One chapter per day
Prepare new chapter each day
   Study old material first
Plan active tasks
   Make study sheets
   Make note cards
   Condense material

Example 3
Divides up material
Spaces learning
No cramming
Confidence booster
Reduces anxiety
Good time management

Example 4
I. Well-structured plan
   A. Emphasizes spaced study
      1. Breaks down material
      2. Promotes time management
      3. Prevents cramming the night
         before
II. Helps reduce anxiety
   A. Helps boost confidence
   B. Practices recall & retrieval
III. Emphasizes active learning
   A. Allows for self-testing
   B. Promotes a lot of repetition
   C. Writing and reciting

PRACTICE THE ANSWERS

Gathering, organizing, and outlining the information that you would use to answer a question doesn't guarantee that you'll be able to replicate the answer on the test. The next step is to practice your answer. By learning the key points you selected, you increase your chances of maximizing your score on the exam. It's not necessary to memorize your outline word for word. Practicing the main points and details in your outline should help you learn the answers to your predicted questions.

Practice Your Outline

Identify the main points in your outline and then learn them. The best way to learn the main points is to practice them over and over. Cover everything except the question with your hand or another sheet of paper. Ask yourself, "What are the main points that I want to make about this question?" Even better, try to write your outline without looking back. Practicing (reciting and writing) the information over a period of days will help you remember it during the exam. Once you know the main points, practice the details in your outline. Each of the main points can then serve as a cue to help you recall the details.

Use Mnemonics to Aid Recall

If you have difficulty recalling certain points or remembering them in order, try using a **mnemonic device** (a memory cue) to improve your recall. Identify a key word in each of the main points that you made in your outline. Underline the key words and then think of a way to remember them. Acrostics or catchphrases are useful for essay tests because they allow you to recall the information in order. Although these mnemonics don't replace learning the information, they do act as hooks or cues to help you recall what you learned. Lisa created the catchphrase, "Nancy sells every car for parts," to help her remember the six main points for her sociology answer (Figure 12.14). What mnemonics could you use to help you remember the main points in Todd's outline in Figure 12.10?

FIGURE 12.14
Lisa's Gathered Information and Outline with Mnemonic Cues

Explain the view Thomas Hobbes took on the problem of order and the social contract.

1 social order is political natural law	3 equality among people
2 state of nature	4 people form a social contract
2A people are selfish and violent	4A agreement b/w societies
2C people become power hungry	4B people give up natural liberty
2B central concept is power	4C laws tell us how to act
3A state of nature is condition of war	5 if break laws we are denied freedom
3B common fear of power	6 power of state is order

TS Thomas Hobbes viewed order in society as a hunger for power among people.

1. Social order is political natural law
2. State of nature
   - A. people are selfish & violent
   - B. central concept is power
   - C. people become power hungry
3. Equality among people
   - A. State of nature is condition of war
   - B. Common fear of power
4. People form a social contract
   - A. agreement b/w societies
   - B. people give up natural liberty
   - C. laws tell us how to act
5. If we break laws, we are deprived of freedom
6. Power of state is order

1. Natural
2. State
3. Equality
4. Contract
5. Freedom
6. Power

(Nancy sells every car for parts.)

Activity 12-7

Practice the Information

Make up a mnemonic to help you remember the main points that you selected for the question on "Political Systems in Global Perspective" in Activity 12-4 or for some other question that you planned. Practice learning the main points out loud. Then review out loud, or write the supporting points that you would like to add. Then use your mnemonic to replicate the main points in your outline. Which strategy was the most useful? How many times did you practice before you could replicate your outline?

Write Out Some Answers

Some students know how to answer a question; they know the information. However, when they actually are in the testing situation, they just can't seem to put that information on paper. If this has happened to you before, the problem may be about writing rather than about studying. To convincingly show the professor what you know, you need to practice writing out some of the answers in paragraph form.

Why You Should Write Out Some Answers

Writing out your answer before the exam will help you overcome some problems that cause students difficulty during exams. One of the most common problems is getting started. By practicing ahead of time, you can avoid this problem. When the test begins, although you may not remember your first sentence word for word, you'll know how to approach the question. Some students have difficulty deciding how to phrase what they want to say and how to tie their points together. Doing this before the exam will help you do a better job during the exam. Again, don't try to memorize your answer word for word. If you forget one word or phrase, you may find yourself unable to complete your answer. You want to practice writing out the answer just to get the feel for how the whole thing fits together.

Practice Using Your Outline

Practice writing your answer by referring to your outline. Your goal here is not to test your memory of the information but to practice stringing together your ideas. Turn each line from your outline (each meaningful phrase) into a sentence. Add additional sentences to provide more details, if you can. After you've successfully constructed an answer with the outline, try to write the answer again without it. On the evening before the exam, practice writing the answer one last time. By allowing yourself some time between your initial practice session and your final one, you test your ability both to recall the information and to present it in a well-written and well-organized manner. If you're able to construct a well-written answer without your outline the night before the exam, you'll feel reassured when you begin the actual exam.

Write Out the Most Difficult Questions

If you've predicted a large number of questions, you may not have time to write out all the answers ahead of time. If this happens, write out only the ones that you think you would have the greatest difficulty explaining. If a number of your questions seem fairly straightforward, you can probably eliminate this stage. Just be sure you review aloud the key points that you would make and think about how

FIGURE 12.15
Lisa's Practice Essay

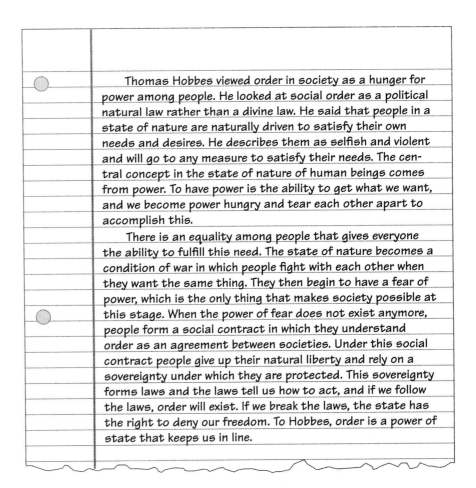

> Thomas Hobbes viewed order in society as a hunger for power among people. He looked at social order as a political natural law rather than a divine law. He said that people in a state of nature are naturally driven to satisfy their own needs and desires. He describes them as selfish and violent and will go to any measure to satisfy their needs. The central concept in the state of nature of human beings comes from power. To have power is the ability to get what we want, and we become power hungry and tear each other apart to accomplish this.
>
> There is an equality among people that gives everyone the ability to fulfill this need. The state of nature becomes a condition of war in which people fight with each other when they want the same thing. They then begin to have a fear of power, which is the only thing that makes society possible at this stage. When the power of fear does not exist anymore, people form a social contract in which they understand order as an agreement between societies. Under this social contract people give up their natural liberty and rely on a sovereignty under which they are protected. This sovereignty forms laws and the laws tell us how to act, and if we follow the laws, order will exist. If we break the laws, the state has the right to deny our freedom. To Hobbes, order is a power of state that keeps us in line.

you might start the answers. Choose more complex questions for written practice. If you can present the information in the difficult questions in a well-written form, you probably can do equally well or better on the easier questions.

Figure 12.15 shows the practice essay that Lisa constructed from her outline in Figure 12.14. Notice how she moved from one main point to the next in constructing her answer.

Prepare Answers for All Sample Questions

Some instructors pass out sample essay questions prior to an exam. You can use them to get an idea of the kinds of questions that will appear on the exam; however, they can be used to even greater advantage. Each sample question can be planned and practiced using the strategies described previously.

Even if the sample questions aren't the ones on the actual test, chances are they're closely related. In the process of preparing to answer the sample question, you probably will learn the information to answer the actual test question. A good general rule is always to treat sample questions as if they were the actual exam questions. Don't assume, however, that you should focus your study only on those questions. Go ahead and predict some additional questions just in case.

Get Feedback on Your Planned Answers

After you've prepared several questions and written out the answers, go see your professor. Ask him or her to take a look at your predicted questions (or the sample

Activity 12-8

Write Out Your Essay Answer

 Using the outline that you developed in Activity 12-5, work as a group to write out a practice answer for the essay question that you predicted.

TEN TIPS FOR PREPARING FOR ESSAY TESTS

PROPER PREPARATION IS THE KEY. Many students are anxious about essay tests, partially because they don't know how to prepare for them. Trying to write an essay answer requires recall learning. You can't just read over the material. Instead you need to predict questions, plan the answers, and learn the information.

REVIEW OLD EXAMS. Review old exams to get some ideas about the types of questions your professor tends to ask. Don't rely just on those questions, though, because few professors use the same questions over again. Use them, instead, as models to develop your own questions.

PREDICT YOUR OWN TEST QUESTIONS. Go through your text and lecture material and write eight to ten essay questions that you think could be on the exam. The more questions you write, the greater the possibility several of your questions will be on the exam.

PLAN THE ANSWERS TO YOUR QUESTIONS. Dig through the text and lecture material to find the information that you need to answer the questions that you predicted. Write the information on a sheet of paper and think about how you might use it to answer the question. Share your plans with members of your group.

DEVELOP AN INFORMAL OUTLINE. Organize your gathered information in an informal outline so that you can easily see the main points that you want to make when writing out your essay answer. List the main points of your answer and then several of the details in your outline. Keep your outline simple so that it's easy to recall.

RECITE THE MAIN POINTS OF YOUR ANSWER. Practice reciting the main points that you want to make for each of the answers that you developed. While you're driving to school or work, check your memory of the information. Just creating an outline doesn't mean you know the information.

USE MNEMONICS TO AID YOUR RETENTION. Developing catchwords and catchphrases can help you recall the main points in your sample essay answers (in your outline). Remember, mnemonics don't replace learning the information; they just help you get it back out of memory after you have learned it.

SET UP A STUDY GROUP. Some students find that working in a group is quite effective when preparing for essay exams. Compare your questions with those of the members of your study group or predict questions as a group. Other members of the group may find connections in the material that you hadn't considered.

WRITE AND COMPARE ESSAY ANSWERS. Ask each member of your study group to write out the answers to the several questions that were predicted in your study group. Then exchange answers during a group meeting and compare your answer to each of the answers written by the other members of your group.

GET SOME FEEDBACK ON YOUR ANSWERS. If you really aren't sure about the quality of your essay answers, ask your professor to take a look at one or two of them. Your professor can give you valuable feedback on how well you are preparing for the exam and how well you are able to communicate what you know.

test questions) and the answers that you wrote. Ask for feedback on how you approached the question and how you presented your answer. Don't expect your professor to "grade" the paper for you; instead, look for tips or suggestions for how you might improve your essay for the exam. Getting feedback on your answers before the exam may result in much higher test grades and a better relationship with your instructors.

Activity 12-9

Work as a Group to Predict Essay Questions

Work as a group to develop a list of predicted essay questions for the material in Chapter 11 of this text. Use the chart of frequently used terms in essay questions (Figure 12.1) to help you develop a variety of broad general questions. Then choose one question and gather information for the answer individually. Work together to develop a group essay plan, including an outline. Then write the answer from the outline that you developed.

Activity 12-10

Use Feedback to Revise Essay Answers

At least one week prior to your exam, prepare answers for the broad essay questions that you chose from major headings or lecture topics, old exams, study guides, or sample questions provided by your course instructor. Discuss your answers with either your professor or a staff member in your college learning center. Using the feedback that you received, revise your answers. What feedback did you get? What did you learn about the quality of your original answers? What changes did you make when you revised your answers? Include a copy of your original answer and your revised answer with your response.

Activity 12-11

Where Are You Now?

Now that you have completed Chapter 12, take a few minutes to repeat the "Where Are You Now?" activity, located on the *College Study Skills* Web site. What changes did you make as a result of reading this chapter? How are you planning to apply what you've learned in this chapter?

SUMMARY

Essay exams are often more difficult than objective exams because they require recall-level learning. You have to know the material well enough to write one paragraph, several paragraphs, or even several pages to answer the question. To be properly prepared for essay exams, you need to predict broad, challenging questions—questions that cover the main topics presented in the course. Developing questions that integrate or incorporate several headed sections of text or several topics presented during one or more lectures can help prepare you to answer the kinds of questions that often appear on essay exams.

After you predict a series of questions, you need to plan the answers. The first step is to gather information by digging through the text and your lecture notes. List any points that you would use to answer the question. Organize the information by labeling each point according to where you would use it in your answer. Then take a few minutes to write an outline of your answer. Seeing the information in this organized format will help you better learn and recall the points you want to make. Practice writing or reciting your outline to learn the main points you want to make and to test your ability to recall the details, too. Creating mnemonics can help you recall all of the points in your outline. Finally, write answers to one or two of the most difficult questions just to get the feel for how the information in your outline fits together. Writing out several practice answers can help you learn how to move from one point to the next and reduce your anxiety about taking essay exams. By predicting possible essay questions and planning and practicing their answers, you'll be well prepared for your next essay exam.

REVIEW QUESTIONS

Terms You Should Know: Make a flash card for each term.

Broad questions	Evaluate	Main points
Compare	Formal outline	Mnemonics
Contrast	Gather information	Narrow questions
Define	Illustrate	Summarize
Describe	Informal outline	Supporting details
Enumerate	Justify	Trace

Completion: Fill in the blank to complete each of the following statements.

1. One way to prepare for an essay exam is to predict _____ or _____ questions for every one that will be on the exam.

2. If you only have one essay question on an exam, you should predict _____ or _____ questions from every chapter.

3. Using a two-column format forces you to write the gathered information in _____ _____.

4. _____ are especially useful for recalling the main points in your outline.

5. After you create an outline for your answer, you must _____ the information.

Multiple Choice: Circle the letter of the best answer for each of the following questions. Be sure to underline key words and eliminate wrong answers.

6. If the word _____ is used in the question, you must explain by giving examples.
   A. describe
   B. illustrate
   C. justify
   D. trace

7. Which of the following is not a good source for predicted essay questions?
   A. Main headings in the textbook
   B. Main topics from your lecture notes
   C. Recall questions in your text and notes
   D. Old exams

Short Answer–Essay: On a separate sheet, answer each of the following questions.

8. How should you prepare for an exam that contains both objective and essay questions?

9. Why do some students have difficulty preparing for essay exams? What should they do differently?

10. What are the benefits of gathering information for predicted essay questions?

TAKING ESSAY TESTS

In this chapter you will learn more about:

- **How to take an essay test**
- **Factors that influence your grades**
- **Strategies for gaining more points**
- **Learning from exams**

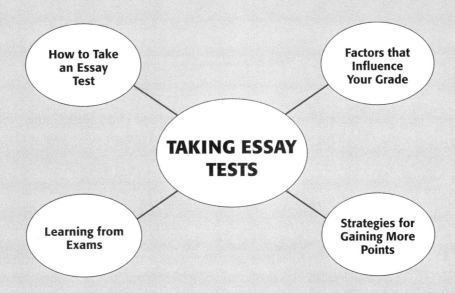

Activity 13-1

Where Are You Now?

Take a few minutes to answer *yes* or *no* to the following questions.

	YES	NO
1. Do you always read the directions before you begin to answer the questions on an essay exam?	_____	_____
2. Do you generally plan your answer in your head rather than on paper before you begin to write?	_____	_____
3. Do you usually score lower on essay exams than on objective exams?	_____	_____
4. Do you ever leave blanks on essay exams?	_____	_____
5. Do you organize your answer before you begin to write?	_____	_____
6. Do you generally find that you are unable to finish the exam before time runs out?	_____	_____
7. Do you go back over the entire exam before you turn it in?	_____	_____
8. After your exam is returned, do you go over it to evaluate your preparation and clarify your errors?	_____	_____
9. When you get your exam back, are you often surprised by the grade that you received?	_____	_____
10. Do you know how professors grade essay exams?	_____	_____
Total Points		_____

Give yourself 1 point for each *yes* answer to questions 1, 5, 7, 8, and 10 and 1 point for each *no* answer to questions 2, 3, 4, 6, and 9. Now total up your points. A low score indicates that you need to develop some new skills for taking essay tests. A high score indicates that you already are using many good strategies.

HOW TO TAKE AN ESSAY TEST

There are a number of strategies for taking essay exams that can help you retrieve, relate, and organize the information that you learned. After you read the directions, you should plan before you write and organize your answer to be more successful on essay exams.

Read the Directions Carefully

The first step in taking an essay exam is to read and follow the directions. Some students have actually failed essay exams, not because they didn't know the information, but because they didn't read and follow directions. Unfortunately, they just plunged into the exam without making sure they knew how to proceed.

Find Out How Many Questions You Have to Answer

When you read the directions, be sure that you look to see how many questions you're expected to answer. On many essay exams, you're given a choice of questions to answer. Consider the following set of directions: *1. Answer two of the following questions.* (Six questions are given in total.) *2. Answer two questions from set A and two questions from set B.* (Three questions are included in set A, and three questions are included in set B.) In each of these cases you are being limited to a certain number of questions and, in the latter case, to a certain number of questions from two different sets.

If you tried to answer all six questions in the time that you were given to answer two, you couldn't spend enough time on any one answer. As a result, you may earn a lower grade than your preparation warranted.

Don't Answer Additional Questions

Sometimes students who have extra time at the end of an exam go back and try to answer additional questions (more than the directions indicated). This is often a mistake. If the directions indicated that you were to answer two of the six questions, your professor isn't going to read all of your answers and pick the best two on which to base your grade. In most cases, the professor will grade the first two answers and merely cross off or ignore the rest. This can really hurt your grade if your best answers were the fourth and fifth ones.

Follow Formatting Instructions

The test directions also may include information about how the essay is to be formatted. For example, you may be expected to answer each question on one side of a blue book page. The directions also may tell you to write on every other line, to include an example, or to include a brief outline. In some cases, students are given length limitations for their answers. Not following formatting instructions can cost you points on essay exams.

How Much Should You Write?

Although essay answers are often only one paragraph long, they can range from a few sentences to ten pages long. The best guide for how much to write is how much space the professor provides on the examination paper. If there are three questions on one side of a page, a one-paragraph answer probably is expected. However, if you're not limited to just one side of the page, don't limit yourself to only the space that the professor has provided. Instead of trying to squeeze in or leave out additional information, continue your answer on the other side of the page. If there's only one question per page on your exam, then the professor probably expects you to fill the page in order to provide a satisfactory answer.

Many students are uncertain about how much to write when they're given only a sheet of questions and a blue book. If your professor has not stated a specific page limit for each question, you should consider the point value of the questions in order to determine how much to write. Obviously, a question worth 30 points will require a longer answer than one worth only 10 points. Occasionally, an essay test has only one question. This question is essentially worth 100 points. If you still feel unsure of how much to write, ask your professor what he or she expects.

Plan Before You Write

If you take a few minutes to plan your answers before you write them, you'll find that you write better essay answers in a shorter period of time. When you first look at the essay test, read *all* of the essay questions before you decide which ones you want to answer. Circle the number of a question if you think you may want to an-

FIGURE 13.1
Plan Before Writing

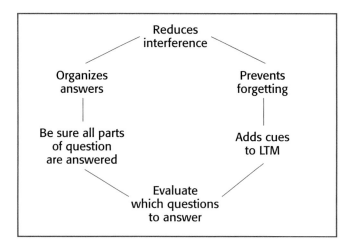

swer it. Then jot down your ideas in the margin. There are many advantages of planning before you write (Figure 13.1).

Jot Down Ideas in the Margin

As you read each question, make notes in the margin, **marginal notes,** as the ideas for an answer pop into your mind. If you predicted one or more of the questions, jot down your mnemonic device, the key words, or the main points from the outline that you planned. You'll be able to make a better decision about which question or questions you should answer after you look at your notes. Look at the student example in Figure 13.2. Kesha listed the ideas that she thought of when she read the question. As you can see, she wrote down only key words and phrases.

Making notes as you read the questions can be very helpful. Sometimes it's hard to remember what you wanted to say about a particular question when you're ready to answer it. Reading the other questions and thinking about whether you should answer them can cause interference. Have you ever gone back to begin answering a question only to realize that you couldn't remember what you were going to say? If you think back to the analogy of your long-term memory as a filing cabinet, you may be able to understand better why this happens. When you read the first question, something in the question triggers an association that opens a particular file drawer for you and makes the information on that subject accessible to you. As you read other questions, however, that drawer is closed and others are

FIGURE 13.2
Kesha's Marginal Notes

Question: What general and specific strategies should a student follow when taking a matching test?

Notes in margin:

- work from one side to other
- usually longest first
- don't work from side to side
- cross off answer if you use it
- do the ones you know 1st
- don't guess right away
- read directions
- read through all choices

opened. Sometimes, it's difficult to get the first drawer open again. The notes you jot in the margin also serve as additional cues to long-term memory. Each of the words you write down acts as an additional cue that can help you retrieve even more details for your answer. In addition to aiding your memory, making notes in the margin helps relieve test anxiety. Once you know that you can answer the question, you can relax and feel more comfortable about the exam.

Be Sure Your Notes Reflect All Parts of the Question

After you've chosen to answer a question and have jotted your ideas in the margin, you should reread the question to make sure that your notes reflect all parts of the question. If you find that you've planned for only a part of the question, make additional notes in the margin. Some essays require you to answer two or three questions within one question. In that case, number each part of the question (1, 2, 3, and so on) and then write the numbers in pencil in the space under the question to make sure you don't forget to answer any parts. After you complete each part, erase that number.

Consider the following essay question from a chemistry test: *What differences, if any, exist between morphine and heroin in terms of chemical makeup, pharmacological effects, legal availability, and abuse?* Because there really are four parts to this question, you could put a "1" above *chemical makeup,* a "2" above *pharmacological effects,* and so on. If you find that you tend to forget to answer some parts of your essay questions, these strategies may help you improve your score on the next exam.

Organize Your Ideas Before Writing

After jotting down your ideas in the margin, you can organize your essay in just a few seconds. Simply number your ideas in the margin as Kesha did in Figure 13.3. Look at the ideas that you jotted down and ask yourself, "What's the first thing that I want to talk about?" After that, you can decide what to put second, third, and so on. You also may decide that some of your ideas actually support some of the others. You can indicate that some of your ideas are supporting points by marking them with an "A" or a "B" after the number.

Some students don't feel that they can take the time to plan their answers in the margin because they feel pressured for time during exams. However, you should be able to plan and organize an answer in just one or two minutes. For a longer essay, you can organize your ideas even more by writing a brief outline in the margin.

FIGURE 13.3
Kesha's Numbered
Marginal Notes

Question: What general and specific strategies should a student follow when taking a matching test?

Notes in margin:

③ – work from one side to other ⑥ – do the ones you know 1st
④ – usually longest first   ⑦ – don't guess right away
⑤ – don't work from side to side ① – read directions
   – cross off answer if you use it ② – read through all choices

Activity 13-2

Organize Your Answers

Jot down your ideas in the margin as you read each of the following questions. Then work with a group to organize them by numbering the points.

1. Why should students answer the easiest questions first when taking objective exams?

2. What general and specific strategies should a student use when taking a true/false exam?

3. Compare and contrast short-term and long-term memory.

Write Your Answer

Getting started is often the hardest part of writing an essay answer. So, start with the easiest question first. Write your essay answer as you would write an essay for one of your English classes. State your first main idea and then back it up with supporting details and examples. Then go on to your next main point.

Use a Basic One-Paragraph Design

The general format for a one-paragraph essay is shown in the left-hand column of Figure 13.4. Begin your essay with a **topic sentence** (TS) that states the central idea of your paragraph. After the topic sentence, state your first main point (M1). After stating your first main point, back it up with one or more supporting sentences. Each of these sentences may include details, facts, or examples that further explain your main point. Next, state your second main point, followed by a sentence or two of support. Your third main point should be made next, followed by relevant support. Additional main points and secondary supporting information also can be included here. Finally, end your paragraph with a concluding sentence. A well-developed paragraph should be from eight to eleven sentences long. Of course, a paragraph can be shorter or longer, but by writing at least eight sentences, you can ensure that you are including both main points and details.

Modify the Design for Longer Essays

Not all essays can be answered in only one paragraph. You may be expected to write several paragraphs or several pages in order to answer a question properly. In that case, instead of having a topic sentence followed by several main points, each paragraph in your essay would focus on one of these main points. A one-paragraph answer can easily be expanded to a four- or five-paragraph answer simply by developing each point more fully. The topic sentence would be expanded to an introductory paragraph containing a thesis statement, each main-point sentence would be expanded to form a supporting paragraph, and the concluding sentence would become a concluding paragraph (see the right-hand column of Figure 13.4). A long essay, five or more pages, would be developed in much the same way. Remember, the shorter an essay answer is, the more general it tends to be. You can develop your ideas into a longer answer by adding more and more specific details and examples.

FIGURE 13.4

Sample Essay Design

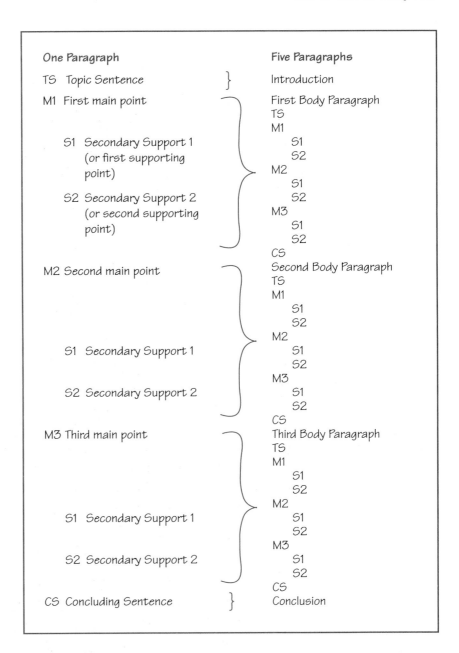

One Paragraph

TS Topic Sentence

M1 First main point

    S1 Secondary Support 1
        (or first supporting
        point)

    S2 Secondary Support 2
        (or second supporting
        point)

M2 Second main point

    S1 Secondary Support 1

    S2 Secondary Support 2

M3 Third main point

    S1 Secondary Support 1

    S2 Secondary Support 2

CS Concluding Sentence

Five Paragraphs

Introduction

First Body Paragraph
  TS
  M1
    S1
    S2
  M2
    S1
    S2
  M3
    S1
    S2
  CS

Second Body Paragraph
  TS
  M1
    S1
    S2
  M2
    S1
    S2
  M3
    S1
    S2
  CS

Third Body Paragraph
  TS
  M1
    S1
    S2
  M2
    S1
    S2
  M3
    S1
    S2
  CS

Conclusion

Turn the Question into a Statement

One strategy that may help you get started is to actually take the question, turn it into a statement, and add your answer to it. The resulting statement will become either your topic sentence (for a one-paragraph answer) or your **thesis statement** (for a short or long essay answer). Consider the following question: *How did Greek architecture and sculpture reflect the Greeks' concern for order, reason, and the ideal? What rules did they follow?* This question can be rephrased to form the following topic sentence: *The Greeks valued architecture and sculpture and tried to make them reflect their concern for order, reason, and the ideal.*

By generating a topic sentence or thesis statement that includes main points, you show your professor that you know the answer to the question. Turning the question into a topic sentence also helps you organize your own presentation of the material. In other words, you know where you're going with your answer.

Activity 13-3

Write Some Topic Sentences

Work with your group to change each of the questions in Activity 13-2 into a statement that could serve as the topic sentence for each answer.

1. _____

_____

2. _____

_____

3. _____

_____

Write Your First Main Point

The next step in writing your answer is to make your first **main point.** Refer to one of the plans that you made in Activity 13-2. Take the idea that you labeled number 1 (or put first in your informal outline) and convert it into a sentence. Make it a general statement that can then be supported by details and examples. Look back at the sample plan in Figure 13.3. Kesha decided that "read directions" was the first main point she wanted to make. She converted her notes to the following sentence: "The first and most important thing a student should do is always read the directions."

Activity 13-4

Turn Main Ideas into Sentences

Practice turning your ideas into sentences by converting your first numbered response to each question in Activity 13-2 into a sentence. Then compare each of your main point sentences to those of others in your group. How similar were your responses?

1. _____

_____

2. _____

_____

3. _____

_____

Support Your Main Points

After you write your first main point, you need to add one or more sentences that contain **supporting points,** the specific information to back up your main point. Next, add an example if you can. You may use an example that was presented in the text or lecture, or you could include an example of your own. By using examples, you demonstrate to your professor that you understand the abstract material. Don't stop after you make one good point. Continue with other main points and follow each of them with details and examples just as you did for the first one. Your job on an essay exam is to prove each of your points by including the information you learned in lecture or from your textbook.

Although Kesha didn't list any supporting points in her original plan, she did back up her first main point with several supporting sentences; her next two sentences explain *why* it's so important to read the directions: "Some students see that they have matching on a test and automatically start matching without reading the directions. Directions may help a student out because not all answers are always used, and also because some answers may be used twice." How could you back up the main point sentences that you wrote in Activity 13-4?

Activity 13-5

Write Supporting Sentences

Talk with others in your group about how you could support each main point. Then write two or three supporting sentences for one of the main points that you developed in Activity 13-4.

1. _____

   _____

2. _____

   _____

3. _____

   _____

Add Transitional Words

Add transitional words to indicate each of your main points and to help your reader move from one idea to the next. Words like *first, second, third, next,* and *finally* are **transition words** often used to introduce the main points in your essay. They let your reader know that you're making a main point. *Moreover, in addition, also,* and *furthermore* tell your reader that you are adding support to the points that you already made. Occasionally, you may want to change direction or say something that contradicts the previous statement. In this case, you should begin your statement with a word or phrase like *however, but, on the other hand, nevertheless,* or *on the contrary.* Words like *consequently, therefore,* and *thus* indicate that you've reached a conclusion based on previous information.

You also can show connections by restating some of the key words in your question or topic sentence as you make additional points in your essay. If you're writing a long essay, it often is effective to restate parts of the question in each of your main points. You might say, for example: *The first main reason to answer the easiest question first is to maximize your points.* After explaining how that can be accomplished, you might restate the question for your second point as follows: *The second main reason for answering the easiest question first is to relieve test anxiety.* Each time you make a main point you can restate the question. Repeating key words and phrases helps organize your essay and reinforces the points that you want to make.

FIGURE 13.5
Sample Essay

1 **rules of**	Question: How did Greek ①architecture and ②sculpture reflect the Greeks' concern for ªorder, ᵇreason, and the ᶜideal? What rules did they follow? (30 points)
proportion	Answer:
3 **Parthenon**	
2 **human-ideal**	The Greeks valued architecture and sculpture and tried to make them reflect their concern for order, reason, and the
4 **perfect image**	ideal. First, the Greeks followed very careful rules of proportion
5 **virtual image**	in creating their sculptures of gods and heroes. Every human figure was seven and one-half heads tall. The distances from the head to the chest, the chest to the groin, and the ankle to the foot all followed exact proportional measurements that had previously been determined. Also, the Greeks followed care-ful "rules" in the way they portrayed man and the gods in their sculpture. All works were idealized. They showed only the best human features. Second, the Greeks used the rules of propor-tion and measurement in creating their works of architecture. The Parthenon provides an excellent example of this order. The columns were spaced in proportion to the others in order to create a "perfect" image for the viewer. The number of columns across the side was equal to twice the number across the front plus one. This provided a sense of balance to the Greeks. Also, all of the columns leaned inward in order to maintain the illusion that they were exactly parallel and vertical. They were also thicker in the middle so that from the bottom of the hill, they appeared to be perfectly straight. Other similar "correc-tions" were made to the floor and the decorations in the frieze in order to maintain that "virtual image" that was so impor-tant to the Greeks. Both sculpture and architecture reflected the Greeks' concern for order, reason, and the ideal.

Add a Conclusion

Finally, you should end your paragraph or essay with a **conclusion,** a concluding sentence or paragraph that reminds your professor of the main points that you made. Professors form opinions of essays as they read, but they don't assign an ac-tual grade until after they've read the entire answer. If you've made some of your best points early in your answer, it helps remind your professor of them just before he or she assigns a grade. Also, the concluding sentence or paragraph helps bring the answer to a logical ending, making the entire essay appear well thought out. Look at the sample essay in Figure 13.5. Which sentence is the topic sentence? Which sentences present the main points? Which sentences provide the secondary support? Which sentence presents the conclusion? Are transitions used? Which ones?

Proofread and Revise Your Answer

Your job isn't done when you write the last sentence of your essay answer. If you take just a few additional minutes to reread your answer, you may catch careless errors in sentence construction, grammar, or mechanics. In addition, as you read your answer from start to finish, you may think of an additional point to make or a better way to phrase something.

Activity 13-6

Analyze Sample Essay Answers

Look at Kesha's and Amy's essays in Figures 13.6 and 13.7. Label each sentence, using a red or blue pen according to the sample essay design in Figure 13.3 (TS, M1, S1, S2, M2, . . . , CS). Note any problems with development that you find. Underline any transitional devices. (The essays appear exactly as written and do contain several grammatical and mechanical errors.) Then compare your responses to those of others in your group.

Activity 13-7

Write Your Essay Answer

Work as a group to write an answer to one of the essay questions in Activity 13-2, following the steps that were presented. Be sure to include a topic sentence, transitions to introduce each of your main points, and a concluding sentence.

FACTORS THAT INFLUENCE YOUR GRADE

Many factors can influence your grade. Although the content of your answer carries the most weight, other factors—such as the organization of your answer, the format that you use, your writing ability, and how neatly you write your answer—can affect your grade. Some professors are as interested in how well you present the information as they are in the information itself. Knowing what your professor will be looking for in your answer can help you write better essay exams.

Content

The **content**—the information that you include in your answer—is of course the most important factor in determining your grade. When you're planning and writing your answer, include as much **relevant information,** main points and supporting details related to the question, as you can. Many students make the mistake of including only some of the information that they know. They incorrectly assume that their professor will think that some information is just obvious and

FIGURE 13.6

Kesha's Essay Answer

---

1. What ① general and ② specific strategies should a student follow when taking a matching test?

When taking a matching test, there are various general and specific strategies that one can use to help himself. The first and most important thing a student should do is always read the directions. Some students see that they have matching on a test and automatically start matching without reading the directions. Directions may help a student out because not all answers are always used and also because some answers may be used twice. The second general strategy that students should do is skim down through column A and column B to get a general idea of what exactly they are matching. After the student has this broad idea, they can decide what way they are going to match. Most students match from left to right, or some match the longest answer column to the shortest column. Either one of these techniques is very good; however, a student should not jump from column to column, and go back and forth. The student should work his/her way down through the first answering the ones they are definitely sure of. After they use an answer, they should cross out the letter, circle it, or somehow mark it so they know that they have already used that choice. The student should proceed down through the column, skipping the ones they don't know. After they have gone through the column once, they should go back and now see if they can match the ones they previously skipped. A student should continue doing this process until every item has a match. You should not guess until you have only a few left and you absolutely can not figure out the answer. By guessing too soon, you could really mess up the entire section. After you have completed the section, you should go back through and make sure you did not use any letter twice. By following these specific and some what general strategies, a student should be able to do well on all of the matching sections on an exam.

---

should not be included in the answer. Assuming that your professor will know what you mean even with little explanation also may result in a lower test score. It's important to explain key terms and back up the statements that you make. One way to avoid being too general is to pretend that your professor doesn't know the answer to the question. If you tell yourself that you're writing the essay for someone who doesn't know anything about the topic, you'll be sure to include all the pertinent information. Remember, your job on an essay test is to show the professor how much you know about the question.

As tempting as it may be, avoid including irrelevant information. Some students try to impress the professor by including everything that they know about a topic even if it isn't relevant to the question. Some professors will simply overlook

FIGURE 13.7

Amy's Essay Answer

> 2. What general and specific strategies should a student
> follow when taking a multiple-choice test?
>
> There are general and specific strategies a student should
> follow when taking a multiple choice test. Always start off by read-
> ing the directions carefully. Make the statement into a true and
> false question by using the statement with each available answer
> and the one that sounds most logical will usually be correct. Put
> your hand over the answers and read the question, see if you can
> answer it before you read the answers. Always read all of the
> answers and eliminate by crossing off the ones that are not cor-
> rect. Do the easiest ones first then come back to the more difficult
> ones. Even if you have to guess on the harder ones, guessing can
> improve your grade. Make sure you answer all of the questions, Do
> not leave any blanks. You may even get the guessed answers right.
> Watch out for words such as not, a and an, qualifiers, absolute
> words, and maybe typos. Underline these to help you understand
> the question better. When you are all done taking the multiple
> choice test make sure you review your test completely to make sure
> everything is done correctly. These are basically the strategies
> students should follow when taking a multiple choice test.

the irrelevant information or make a note that it's unnecessary or off the topic. Other professors, however, may penalize students because, to them, it seems the students really don't know the answer to the question that was asked.

Organization

The **organization** (order) of your essay answer also is an important factor in the grade you receive. Try Activity 13-8 now. A discussion of the results will follow.

Activity 13-8

Grade Two Sample Essays

Read the two sample essay answers in Figure 13.8. After reading sample 1, assign it a grade of A, B, C, D, or F. Then read sample 2 and assign a grade for it also. Go back and jot your reasons for the grades in the margin. Compare your responses to those of the other members of your group.

FIGURE 13.8
Sample Essay Answers

Question: Compare and contrast short- and long-term memory.

Sample 1:

Short-term memory and long-term memory are much alike. They both allow you to remember information that you have read or heard. In short-term memory, we can only hold things for 15 to 30 seconds. Long-term memory is memory that has an unlimited capacity. You can get information into long-term memory by spacing study, using associations, using mnemonics, etc. Short-term memory is not permanent, and unless information is rehearsed, repeated, and meaningful it is lost. ROY G. BIV is an example of a mnemonic device for the color spectrum. Mnemonics like ROY G. BIV are devices that aid retrieval. We have limited capacity in our short-term memory. Its capacity is the magical number 7. A good example is a telephone number. Once we get information into our long-term memory it is permanent. To get it into long-term memory we must learn the information. We can expand our short-term memory by chunking. This is when we categorize information into one thing instead of leaving it separate. They are also both kinds of memory.

Grade _____

Sample 2:

Short- and long-term memory have some similarities and a number of differences. Short- and long-term memory are two types of memory. To get information into either short-term memory or long-term memory, you must encode it; you must make it meaningful. Short-term memory and long-term memory are also similar in that each is plagued by interference and forgetting. But short-term memory and long-term memory are different, too. Although it is easy to get information into short-term memory, you must rehearse and organize it in order to get it into long-term storage. The capacity of short-term memory is very limited. It can hold only seven plus or minus two bits of information at one time. If you try to hold onto more than five to nine things at a time, displacement of some of the earlier information will occur. However, we can increase the capacity of short-term memory by chunking the information. For example, it was easier to remember the list of letters after we put them into meaningful groups. Long-term memory, on the other hand, has an unlimited capacity. Long-term memory can hold billions of bits of information at one time. While information remains in long-term memory permanently, it can only be retained in short-term memory for about 15 to 30 seconds. Without rehearsal, the information is quickly forgotten. For example, if you look up a phone number and then get a busy signal after you dial it, you may have to look the number up again when you decide to try again. Although short- and long-term memory are similar in some ways, they are very different in both their capacity and durability.

Grade _____

How well an answer is organized does affect how it will be graded. After I ask the students in my class or a workshop to evaluate the sample essay answers, I tally the grades. The first sample almost always is assigned mostly Cs, Ds, and Fs, whereas the second sample receives As and Bs as the most common grades. When asked why the second answer was better, the most common response was that it had more information.

When you first read the two essays, sample 2 probably seemed to contain much more information. However, if you looked very closely, the two answers contain about the same information. The second essay appears to contain more information because it's so well organized. Some students think the first essay should receive a lower grade even though it did contain most of the relevant information because it was poorly organized. Do you think that some of your professors approach grading this way?

When professors grade essay exams, they expect to read a well-organized answer. If they are looking for particular points to be made, they expect those points to be noted easily as the answer is read. Few professors will take the time to read an essay over and over again to *find* the information that they are looking for. Some professors penalize students intentionally for poorly organized answers. They feel justified in giving a poorly organized answer a lower grade because they think the student who wrote it did not know the information as well as the student who wrote the more clearly organized answer. In other cases, though, students are *unintentionally* penalized because the essay answer is so jumbled that it becomes difficult to follow the argument, and the professor misses some of the information.

Format

The **format** of your answer may also affect your grade. The directions on an essay test are sometimes rather vague. Professors assume that students know how to write essays, and they don't go into detail about what form of answer they expect. In some classes, writing the correct information in list format would earn you an A. In other cases, though, you might be penalized for not answering the question in the appropriate form. Generally, professors expect you to write essay answers in paragraph form. You may be expected to write every other line, limit your answer to one side of a page, or use ink rather than pencil. Penalties for not formatting your answer correctly vary greatly from one professor to another.

Mechanics

Mechanics—sentence structure, grammar, punctuation, and spelling—are other factors that influence your grade. They probably are given more weight in English courses, but professors from every discipline—engineering, biology, business, and so on—are influenced by these factors. Poor sentence construction and grammar can make it difficult to understand the information that you're trying to relate. Even problems in punctuation and spelling affect how well your written answer matches what you want to say. Look at the essay answer in Figure 13.9. This essay includes so many sentence structure and mechanics errors that it's difficult to locate the points that the student is making.

Your professors also may be influenced by these kinds of errors in less obvious ways. How well you're able to write your answer—how free of errors in mechanics it is—says something about you as a student. Essay answers that include numerous errors in sentence construction, grammar, spelling, and punctuation can give your professor the impression that you're not a very well-educated student. Unfortunately, this impression can "spill over" to the evaluation of the content of your answer as well. This shouldn't happen, but it does. Some professors may find themselves thinking, "If this person can't even write a complete sentence, how can he or

FIGURE 13.9
Poorly Written Essay Answer

> Question: Why should students use spaced study when preparing for an exam?
>
> Answer:
>
>   You should use spaced study to prepare for an exam, one because it is not good to study everything the night before the test. If you have a study plan you tend to stick with it. If you prepare a chapter one nite prepare another the next plus review the chapter from the nite before you have the time to prepare and use study sheets and word/question cards. The first chapters that you do will be the ones that were covered first in class, so the last chapter or 2 do not need as much time because they are still fresh in memory. Spaced study lets you keep recalling and refiling info. into long term memory, so you recite and relearn to the point where you are over learning the information. When you 1) use this approach you are slowly but steadily moving info from short term to long term memory and moving toward the test day. If you use this method of study properly you should have nothing but a short review the night before the test and you can get a good nites sleep to ensure you will be awake to recall info for the test . . . .

she understand philosophy (or psychology, sociology, history, and so on)?" Did you find yourself thinking something like that when you read the sample essay answer in Figure 13.9?

Neatness

Neatness also may influence your grade. Most professors expect students to write clearly and neatly, observe margins, and present the material in a "professional" manner. Very few of them are willing to spend hours attempting to decipher unreadable handwriting. If your professor can't read your essay, you'll lose points simply because he or she won't be able to understand the points you're trying to make. You also may lose points just because you make a "bad impression" by writing in an awkward and messy manner. Nicely written papers have been getting better grades than messy ones for years. Teachers seem to believe that good students care about their work and take the time to write in a careful and skillful manner, whereas poor students don't.

STRATEGIES FOR GAINING MORE POINTS

In this section you'll learn some strategies that may help you gain additional points on an essay exam. Even if you're well prepared, you may find that during the test you have difficulty getting what you know down on paper. Occasionally, students draw a complete blank on an essay question, think of an important point after they've completed their answer, run out of time, or even run out of space. The following tips may be helpful if you find yourself in one of these situations.

Use the Exam as a Resource

Many college exams are a combination of objective and essay questions. Students sometimes overlook the objective questions, which are a valuable source of information. By referring to the multiple-choice, true/false, and matching questions, you may find a great deal of specific information that you can use in your essay. Don't be afraid to look back at them for names, dates, terms, or even key ideas. Professors often include in the objective part of the exam information that relates to the essay questions. In fact, some of these details may even be found in the incorrect choices for the multiple-choice items. Even if the actual information isn't available, reading some of the questions and possible alternatives may help you recall some of the information that you need. Words or phrases in the questions may act as cues for your long-term memory.

Always Write Something

There are times when even well-prepared students are surprised by an essay question and draw a complete blank. Before you give up and resign yourself to accepting a failing grade, try to think through the question. Look for key words in the question that might give you some clues to the answer. Think about the main topics of the lectures and the chapters that were covered. Try to recall the maps you made, the study sheets you prepared, and the questions you predicted. Sometimes you actually can recall the answer after you do a memory search. However, if you still have no idea what the answer to a question is, you should write something. Many professors give students a few points for just trying. In addition, you may find that you know more than you thought. Even though you may not think you know the information the professor is looking for, you may be right on target. Sometimes in the process of writing "anything" to fill the space, you trigger something in your memory that suddenly makes the actual answer pop into your head. This has happened to a number of students who used this technique and it can happen to you.

Leave Extra Space

When you're answering a question on the test paper itself, it's important to leave reasonable margins on all sides of the answer. First of all, this makes your answer look better. Also, it allows you to add information after you've completed your answer. If you must add further information at the end of your essay, place an asterisk (*) or number next to it and also in the paragraph at the spot where the information belongs. You may earn more points if the additional material is read within the context of the answer rather than at the end. You also benefit from leaving wide margins because your professor has space to provide you with feedback about your answer. If no space is available, professors tend to include comments only at the end or not at all.

If you're using a blue book for your answers, leave at least three lines between each answer. Again, you'll have room to write in another point if you think of something after completing the question.

Sometimes you may find that you need even more space than is provided on the exam. You may write larger than other students or have more information to present. Before writing on the back of the page or on additional blue book pages, check with your instructor to see whether there are any space limitations. If your instructor hasn't limited you to one side of a page or to the space provided on the exam sheet, continue your answer on the back. Be sure to indicate that you're continuing your answer. Use an arrow, write the word "over," or write "continued on back." If you write parts of several answers on the back, number them so that they'll be easily recognized.

What If You Run Out of Time?

No matter how carefully you budget your time, you occasionally may run out of time during an essay exam. The first thing you should do is ask your professor whether you can have additional time to complete the test. Some professors will allow you to continue working until the next class begins. Others may even allow you to come to the office to complete your test. If, however, your professor says that you must finish in the time allotted, you can still pick up most of the points on an essay answer. Let's say you've started writing your last essay answer out in paragraph form. Suddenly the professor announces that you have only five minutes left to complete the test. Instead of only writing down a few more sentences, list the remaining points that you wanted to make. Add a little note to the professor that says something like, "I'm sorry that I didn't have time to finish my essay. These are the additional points that I wanted to make." Some professors will give you full credit for your answer, assuming it's a good one, even though you didn't write all of it out. This is a better strategy than just writing until time runs out and answering only half of the question.

Activity 13-9

Evaluate Sample Essay Answers

Take a few minutes and answer the following essay question: *Compare and contrast a catchword and a catchphrase.* Then read each of the essay answers available on the *College Study Skills* Web site, and evaluate them using the criteria that were discussed in this chapter. Evaluate each answer and assign a grade from 1 to 10 points (no grade is used more than once). Jot down a few notes to justify your decision. Which are the three best essays, in order? _____ _____ _____. Which are the three worst essays, in order? _____ _____ _____. Be prepared to defend your choices with your group.

TEN TIPS FOR TAKING ESSAY TESTS

YOU CAN SUCCEED ON ESSAY EXAMS. Some students are intimidated by essay exams—perhaps because they haven't had to write an essay recently. It's true that you have to know the answer, but if you've predicted questions and prepared answers, you should be well prepared. By practicing writing your own essay answers, you've already taken your own self-test.

ASK ABOUT CONFUSING DIRECTIONS. One of the most common mistakes that students make when taking essay tests is not following directions. Make sure you find out how many questions you need to answer, format requirements, and any limitations on length. If you're confused about any of the directions, ask your instructor for clarification.

BUDGET YOUR TIME. It's critical to budget your time on essay exams. Wear a watch and pace yourself throughout the exam so that you don't spend too much time on one or two questions. You also need to consider the point value of each question.

ANSWER THE EASIEST QUESTIONS FIRST. As you preview the exam, look for questions that you predicted. Since you've already planned how to answer those questions, you should find them easy to do. Completing one or two easy questions will help build up your confidence and help you maximize your score if time runs out.

BE STRATEGIC WHEN ANSWERING DIFFICULT QUESTIONS. Put the question in your own words and do a memory search. Think about how some of the information that you learned when you prepared your predicted questions could be used to answer the exam questions. Just start writing—sometimes you can cue your memory of the material as you write.

PLAN IN THE MARGIN. Make notes in the margin before writing your answer. Then go back and reread the question to be sure that your notes reflect all parts of the question. You'll also find this reduces your anxiety because you already know you know the answer.

QUICKLY ORGANIZE YOUR ANSWER. Add numbers to the notes that you made in the margin to organize them before you write. Don't take the time to write another outline; a quick plan will do fine. Check off each point as you use it in your essay. You won't get points for the information unless you actually use it in the essay.

INCLUDE ALL RELEVANT INFORMATION. Some students leave out important information because they think it's obvious. Pretend that you're writing the answer for a friend or family member who knows very little about the topic. Go into enough detail to explain each point you make.

PROOFREAD YOUR ANSWER. Be sure you take a few minutes to reread your answer before you turn in your exam. Some students are so nervous at the beginning of an exam that they make careless errors and leave out words, make spelling or grammar errors, or even forget some of the information that they learned.

LEARN FROM YOUR MISTAKES. After the exam is over, monitor your preparation. Go back and find out where the questions came from. Evaluate how well your predicted questions compared with the questions that were on the exam. Rewrite one or two of your answers and ask your professor to look them over and give you more feedback on their quality.

Activity 13-10

Evaluate Your Essay Answer

Compare your answer to the ones listed in Activity 13-9. What criteria did you use as the basis for ranking your answer? What were the strengths of your answer? The weaknesses? What changes would you make after completing this activity?

LEARNING FROM EXAMS

You can learn a great deal from your essay answers after the test is returned to you. You may think that once the test is over, you should simply move on and concentrate on the next unit of work. You probably think that if you just try harder the next time, you'll be able to do a better job. Unfortunately, some students just don't know how to write an "A" answer for some of their classes. They may do very well on the exams in one class, but for some reason that they can't explain, they just aren't able to get the grades they want in another class. Looking carefully and analytically at your returned tests can provide you with information on how to improve your answers on future exams.

What Can You Learn?

One of the most important things you'll learn from your returned exam is how closely your answer matched what the professor wanted. If you got a good grade on the exam, you probably are doing a good job of presenting the information that the professor wanted. If, on the other hand, your grade was lower than you expected, you need to find out where you went wrong. It's important to understand why you got the grade you did. You may want to evaluate your answer on the basis of the factors that influence grades (described earlier in this chapter) and then discuss it with your professor. Of course, the key to improving your score on future exams is to find out what you need to do differently.

How to Evaluate Your Answer

There are several good ways to evaluate the quality of your essay answer. One method is to compare your answer with those of your peers. Sometimes just reading another student's essay can teach you a lot about what the professor expects. Find a student in your class who got an A on the exam. Explain to this student that you were disappointed in your grade and you just want to get a better idea of what you should do differently. Ask the student to explain how he or she answered the question and ask whether you may read his or her essay. Then read your answer again. What differences did you find? How did the content of your answer compare to your classmate's answer?

Once you get a better idea of what the professor expected, set up an appointment to discuss your test with your professor. Don't go into the meeting with the expectation of getting extra points. Instead, focus on finding out how you should have answered the question in order to gain the maximum number of points. In this way, you and the professor are on the same side; you're working toward the same goal. Often, when you "fight" for additional points, you and the professor may find yourselves acting as opponents or adversaries. If that type of atmosphere is generated, you may gain a point or two on the exam, but you'll probably lose the opportunity to learn how to write a better answer.

Another place you should go for help is your college learning center. The learning center staff can help you evaluate and improve your essay answers. Also, the learning center may offer tutorial services in the course content area and writing assistance that will help you learn to correct sentence construction, grammar, and mechanics errors.

Rewrite Your Answers for Comparison

An excellent strategy for learning to write better essay answers is to rewrite your answers to the test questions after you get the exam back. Use your text and your notes to put together the best answer that you can. Take time to organize the information and check your sentence structure, mechanics, and spelling. Then go back to your professor and ask him or her to read your new answer. Ask what your grade would have been if you had written *that answer* for the exam. You need to find out whether you understand what your professor expects for an "A" answer. If you still don't succeed in meeting your professor's expectations, you now have another opportunity to discuss why your answer was not a good one. You may want to rewrite the answer one more time and then meet with your professor to discuss it.

Students who use this strategy find that it provides several rewards. First, they learn what their professors expect for an "A" answer and how to prepare for and write one. They also demonstrate to their professors that they are motivated enough to do extra work in order to excel in the course. This leaves the professor with a very positive impression about them as students. Some are even rewarded with bonus points for demonstrating that they can write an excellent answer. In addition, most of these students report that they score much higher grades on the remainder of their essay exams.

Activity 13-11

Rewrite an Essay Answer

Analyze and critique the grade that you got on one of your essay answers from a recent exam. Consider some of the following questions as you examine your answer: What factors influenced your grade? What mistakes did you make? What did you learn from your peers and your professor?

Then rewrite your essay answer. Use your text and notes to locate the correct information for your answer. Improve or correct organization, sentence structure, grammar, spelling, and punctuation errors. Attach a photocopy of the original answer to your new answer and add a note describing the kinds of changes that you made.

Activity 13-12

Develop a Plan to Improve Performance on Essay Exams

Develop a two-column chart to list all your strengths and weaknesses when taking essay exams. Select three of the strengths on your list and describe how each can help you be successful when taking essay exams. Then select three of the weaknesses that you listed and develop a plan to improve or overcome them. List the steps in your plan.

Activity 13-13

Where Are You Now?

Now that you have completed Chapter 13, take a few minutes to repeat the "Where Are You Now?" activity, located on the *College Study Skills* Web site. What changes did you make as a result of reading this chapter? How are you planning to apply what you've learned in this chapter?

SUMMARY

If you're well prepared, essay tests can be even easier than objective tests. Some students lose points on essay tests, not because they don't know the material, but because they don't know how to take essay tests. First, read the directions to determine how many questions to answer, their point values, and any special limitations or formatting requirements. Most professors give students a choice of questions to answer, so consider them all before you decide which ones to answer. As you read each question, though, jot down any ideas that pop into your head. Use a basic essay design to construct your answer. Turn the question into a thesis statement or topic sentence (for one-paragraph answers) and then write your first main point. Be sure to back it up with reasons, details, facts, and examples. Continue in the same manner until you've included all the relevant information that you know. Take a few minutes to sum up your main points and then proofread your answer. Although many students believe that the content of their answer is the only factor the professor uses to determine their grade, it's only one of many factors that actually influence that decision.

Even the best-prepared students need to use some strategies to gain extra points on exams. You can use the objective part of your exam (if you have one) as a resource. If you don't know the answer to an essay question, you should still write something. Leaving a blank on an essay test can cost you one or more letter grades because essay questions generally carry high point values on exams. You may surprise yourself as you begin to formulate your answer and suddenly remember the answer—it can happen.

When your exam is returned to you, you can learn how well your preparation and your style of writing essay answers match your professor's expectations. Discuss your answer with your professor or compare your answer with those of several classmates. If you didn't get the grade you expected or feel you deserved, you need to find out what you did wrong so that you can improve your score on future exams.

REVIEW QUESTIONS

Terms You Should Know: Make a flash card for each term.

Conclusion	Mechanics	Thesis statement
Content	Neatness	Topic sentence
Format	Organization	Transition words
Main point	Relevant information	
Marginal notes	Supporting points	

Completion: Fill in the blank to complete each of the following statements.

1. You should answer the _____ questions first on an essay exam.

2. Doing an informal outline in the margin can help you _____ your essay answer before you begin to write.

3. Jotting ideas in the margin can actually help you _____ which questions to answer.

4. It's important to include all _____ information on an essay exam.

5. A good essay answer includes both _____ and _____ points.

Multiple Choice: Circle the letter of the best answer for each of the following questions. Be sure to underline key words and eliminate wrong answers.

6. A good _____ tells the professor you know the answer to the question.
   A. outline
   B. paragraph
   C. thesis statement
   D. transition

7. Which of the following is the second most important factor in determining your grade?
   A. Sentence structure
   B. Organization
   C. Spelling
   D. Neatness

Short Answer–Essay: On a separate sheet, answer each of the following questions.

8. Why should students plan in the margin before answering essay questions?

9. Why do some students have difficulty taking essay exams? What should they do differently?

10. Why should students rewrite their answers after the exam is returned?

> "Preparing for finals would have been so much harder had I not planned and spaced out my studying. I also set up a specific time to start studying and I stuck to it. I'm not even worried about finals because of this. When my friends are running around cramming for finals, I just have to check my calendar to see exactly what I have scheduled to do. It's so easy."
>
> *Brian Shomo*
> *Student*

Chapter

14

PREPARING FOR FINAL EXAMS

In this chapter you will learn more about:

- **Different types of final exams**
- **How to prepare for final exams**
- **How to set up a final exam plan**
- **How to prepare for comprehensive finals**

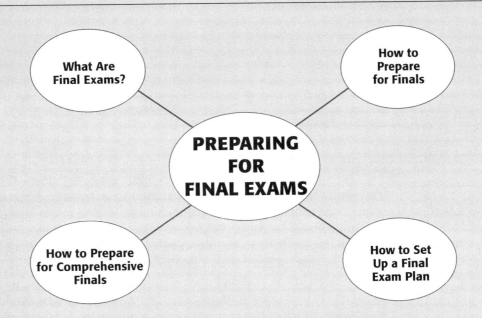

Activity 14-1

Where Are You Now?

Take a few minutes to answer *yes* or *no* to the following questions.

	YES	NO
1. Do you work ahead before finals to free up study time?	_____	_____
2. Do you tend to give up at the end of the semester and spend little or no time preparing for finals?	_____	_____
3. Do you usually score lower on final exams than on the other exams given during the semester?	_____	_____
4. Do you set up a plan to prepare for your finals?	_____	_____
5. Do you put most of your effort into the course in which you have the lowest grade?	_____	_____
6. Do you generally spend a lot of time partying at the end of the semester when you know you should be studying?	_____	_____
7. Do you review all your old exams before your final?	_____	_____
8. Do you use a four- or five-day study plan to prepare for each of your finals?	_____	_____
9. Do you put so much effort into one exam that you don't have the time or energy to prepare for one or more of the others?	_____	_____
10. Do you realistically consider your chances of success before preparing for final exams?	_____	_____
Total Points	_____	

Give yourself 1 point for each *yes* answer to questions 1, 4, 7, 8, and 10 and 1 point for each *no* answer to questions 2, 3, 5, 6, and 9. Now total up your points. A low score indicates that you need to develop some new skills for preparing for final exams. A high score indicates that you already are using many good strategies.

WHAT ARE FINAL EXAMS?

Final exams are end-of-semester tests that help professors evaluate your progress. They are used by some professors to monitor your mastery of the concepts and ideas presented in the course. Other professors use them to make decisions about grades, to determine whether students should move on to the next class, or even to monitor their own teaching. Although final exams may be one of many routine exams given during the semester, they often are longer, both in number of questions and in time allotted for the test, and more difficult. Comprehensive final exams may survey all of the material covered in the course. Final exams range in value from about 20 percent of your grade all the way up to 100 percent. In some courses they count as much as two regular exams; in others, they are the *only* exam and determine your entire grade.

Many courses include only a midterm and a final, with each one determining half of the course grade. However, sometimes the final carries more weight in determining your grade because it's the second exam. If you score higher on the final, you'll probably receive a higher grade in the course, and vice versa. Although finals are more challenging than most of the regular exams that you have during the semester, you can still use many of the same strategies that you used for your other exams to prepare for them. However, if you have four or five final exams in a one-week period, you need to begin your preparation even earlier—perhaps several weeks before your first exam.

Activity 14-2

Describe Your Preparation Strategies

Write a paragraph that describes how you prepared in previous semesters or how you think you will prepare for final exams this semester. Then list five things that you generally do differently (or that you think you will do differently) to prepare for final exams as compared with other exams.

HOW TO PREPARE FOR FINAL EXAMS

Many students change their patterns of sleeping, eating, studying, socializing, working, and so on before final exams. For example, they may limit their time with friends, cut out television, and spend more time in the library in order to fit more study time into each day. They believe that their performance on finals is critical to their ultimate success in one or more of their courses. By starting your preparation early and managing your time efficiently, making academics your first priority, putting your effort into the right courses, and using other good preparation strategies (see Figure 14.1), you can improve your grades on your final exams as well as your overall GPA.

Look at the list in Figure 14.2, which shows many students' suggestions about what to do differently before finals. Some ideas are good ones; others may not be very helpful in preparing for final exams. How many of your ideas were on the list? Are there any ideas that you would like to adopt?

FIGURE 14.1
General Preparation Strategies

- Manage your time efficiently
- Make academics your top priority
- Set priorities for exams
- Attend all classes
- Reduce anxiety
- Use active study strategies
- Stay motivated
- Work hard during each exam
- Monitor your progress

FIGURE 14.2
Student Suggestions for Preparing for Final Exams

study harder	make self-tests	get homework out of way	don't talk on phone
work less hours at job	no visitors or phone calls	start studying on weekends	study almost twice as much
go out less	meditate when I get stressed	not sleep	spend less time in game room
study longer hours	not go to work	be very stressed, feel anxious	watch TV only as a reward
get up earlier	worry about grades a lot more	live at the library	be uptight
eat better	less socializing	don't go out as much	bite my nails
go to sleep earlier	won't watch TV as much	feel upset, not hungry	cram
don't go home	study during day more often	eat less	go to bed at a decent hour
study in library more	study with a partner	sleep less	stay up later studying
stay away from friends	swim at night	unplug Nintendo	review material more often
stop lifting	go home to study	go to library more often	think "It's only a test"
do not party so much	study extremely hard	drink no beer	cut down on work hours
do not smoke as much	make a plan and follow it	go to the library every night	do study plans for every final
exercise more to relieve stress	not procrastinate	study from dinner until bed	put all new strategies into use
don't go out	get lots of sleep	manage my time more wisely	space out my study time
make very accurate "To Do" lists	eat healthier	limit socializing	get more irritated
go out less	less recreational activities	study at all available times	feel more nervous
unplug TV	be more stressed	be less irritable	feel more pressure
make study sheets	schedule my time differently	skip meals	go to bed before midnight

Activity 14-3

Select Effective Strategies

Work as a group to list ten strategies that students should use when preparing for final exams. As you look through the list of suggested strategies in Figure 14.2, cross off those strategies that are poor ways of dealing with final exams. How many of the strategies do you already use?

Manage Your Time Efficiently

You can make the end of the semester much less stressful by using time-management techniques to reduce the overload that many students experience. Two or three weeks before your first final, sit down and make out an **End-of-Semester Assignment Calendar.** Write down all assignments, papers, projects, and exams that you still need to complete. Then make a list of all of your outstanding assignments and realistically estimate the amount of time that you think you'll need to complete them.

Pick several assignments to complete early. Even if they aren't due for two weeks, finish them as soon as possible to reduce the amount of work that you'll have to complete right before exams begin. You need to be able to begin concentrating on your finals at least five days before the first one is scheduled. That means you need to complete most of your regular work about a week before it's due. Doing some of your reading early, completing a term paper, or working ahead in several classes can help create the extra time that you'll need.

Go back and take another look at the Fixed-Commitment Calendar you created at the beginning of the semester (see Chapter 3). Do you need to make some changes to your calendar for the last three weeks of the semester? The best way to find more time for study is to create more available study time. Can you reduce your work hours? Your social time? Your extracurricular activities?

Activity 14-4

Manage Your Time

Complete the End-of-Semester Assignment Calendar in Figure 14.3, listing all assignments, exams, and projects that you need to complete before the end of the semester. Do you have enough time to complete all your work? Do you have any additional time left for relaxation and personal goals? Do you need to make any changes in your time plan to prepare for your final exams? If so, what changes do you plan to make?

Make Academics Your Top Priority

Many students get tired at the end of the semester. College is hard work, and it takes its toll on many students. One of the biggest mistakes that some students make, though, is to decide to rest up before finals week. They slack off and even get behind in their work just when they need to be pushing harder to get ahead. Although they may feel better for a day or two after this hiatus from work, most of them realize too late that it was a mistake. Suddenly they have only a few days to complete all of the assignments that have piled up and to prepare for their finals. They feel overwhelmed and stressed out. Even though they push hard at the end, they just don't have enough hours in the day to do all of their work, so something suffers. Often they give up on one or more assignments or on one of their courses, and their grades drop.

Rather than easing off at the end of the semester, you need to push hard. If you work as hard as you can for one week about two weeks before your first final, you'll be able to complete many of the assignments on your list and still have a few days to rest up before you begin to study for your final exams. During this week, plan daily tasks. Some students still like to use "To Do" lists; others get really serious and use hourly calendars to schedule their assignments. In either event, schedule regular study hours and set daily study goals.

The two weeks before finals tend to be a rather slow period for end-of-semester projects, so it's a good time to get ahead in your work. Look at your assignment calendar and locate a "light" week near the end of the semester. It may be three weeks before finals for you. Whichever week is the lightest week for you, that's when you should get a head start on your outstanding assignments. Don't forget to break down tasks, switch subjects, and plan rewards to maintain your motivation.

Activity 14-5

Make Academics the Top Priority

Make a list of all your study tasks, home responsibilities, and work assignments for the ten days before your first final exam. What tasks can you postpone until your finals are over? Mark them and assign a date following the end of your exams for each task.

Continued

FIGURE 14.3

End-of-Semester Assignment
Calendar

Sunday	Monday	Tuesday	Wednesday	Thursday	Friday	Saturday

Month _____

Activity 14-5

Make Academics the Top Priority (continued)

What tasks can you complete early? Mark them and decide when you will complete each of them. What tasks can you omit entirely? Develop a plan that you can use to manage your time more effectively for the two-week period surrounding final exams.

Set Priorities for Exams

You can increase your chances for academic success by **setting priorities.** Reevaluate your goals for each of your classes. Look closely at where you stand in each course. You may be able to figure out exactly what your grade is by averaging all your scores on exams, homework, and papers. If you can't determine your grade on your own, set up an appointment with your professor to go over your grade. You need to know what your grade is before you can determine how much time and effort you need to put into each of your final exams.

Calculate Your Course Grade

In many classes, your grade is based on a variety of factors such as attendance and participation (A/P), homework assignments (H), quizzes (Q), exams (E), and papers or projects (P), for example. In some classes, each of the factors is worth a specific percentage of the course grade. How can you determine your class grade when it's that complex? Perhaps the following formula will help. Find the average (percentage grade) you have for each factor and multiply it by the percentage of the total grade for each factor and add them together to determine your current average.

$$A/P \times (\% \text{ of grade}) + H \times (\% \text{ of grade}) + Q \times (\% \text{ of grade}) + E \times (\% \text{ of grade}) + P \times (\% \text{ of grade}) = \textbf{Grade}$$

Look at the following example. Let's assume that you currently have 100% of the attendance/participation points, which are worth 10% of your grade; 100% of the homework points, which are also worth 10% of your grade; 80% on the quizzes, which are worth 20% of your grade, and so on.

A/P	H	Q	E	P	G
$100 \times (10\%)$ +	$100\,(10\%)$ +	$80\,(20\%)$ +	$85\,(50\%)$ +	$90\,(10\%)$ =	87.5*

To calculate the grade you need on your final, you need to determine how the final will impact on your grade. Use the following formula:

$$(\%CG \times CG) + (\%FE \times SFE) = FG$$

(Percentage of Current Grade times Current Grade) plus (Percent the Final Exam Is Worth times Score on Final Exam) equals Final Grade.

If your final counts the same as the other tests and all four of them together count as 50% of your grade, the final exam is worth 12.5% of your total grade. On

---

*87.5 would be a high B if grades between 80 to 89 are assigned a B grade.

the other hand, your final may be worth 25% or more of the course grade in some classes. Look at another example:

Participation		Homework		Quizzes		Midterm		Final
$100 \times (10\%)$	+	$90 \times (10\%)$	+	$85\ (20\%)$	+	$85\ (25\%)$	+	SFE (35%)
10	+	9	+	17	+	21.25	+	? =

Your current grade is 57.25/65 (the percentage of grade you earned before final) divided by 65 (the percentage of points available before the final), which when calculated equals 88%. The grade you need on the final can be determined by plugging in the percentage of the total grade times your current grade plus the percentage of the final and the grade you think you need to earn on the final. For example:

$$(0.65 \times 88) + (0.35 \times \underline{\qquad}) = FG$$

To calculate what you need on the final, plug various scores into the blank until you find the grade you'll need on the final exam to earn the course grade you're hoping to achieve. In the previous example, you would need a 94% on the final exam to earn an A in the course if 90 to 100 is an A in the course: $(0.65 \times 88) + (0.35 \times 94) = 90$. To find that score, I tried a 90, 91, 92, and 93 looking for the lowest possible score on the final exam that would earn the A.

Activity 14-6

Calculate Your Current Course Grade

Using the formulas (and examples) listed above, calculate your grade in each of your courses. Show your work.

Do a Practice Exercise

Some course grades are calculated based only on exam grades. Pretend that you have the following test grades in your classes so far this semester. The final exam in each class has the same weight as the other exams. For which final exam or exams should you work the hardest, put in the most time? Make a decision before you go on with your reading.

Exams deserving the most preparation time: _____, _____.

Class A	82	84	83
Class B	81	76	79
Class C	74	84	85
Class D	14	40	56

Most students think they should put the greatest amount of time and effort into the final for class D. For the second most important final exam, some students select class A and others choose between B and C. The majority of students, however, select A and D as the finals that they would put ahead of the others. Why? They realize that they are failing class D. To pass the class, they need to get a good grade on the final.

Unfortunately, some college students actually let all of their other exams go (spend very little, if any, time on them) in order to "ace" the final in their worst class and "save" their grade. In most cases, however, students who have failed all previous exams in a course are unlikely to score high enough on the final exam to improve their grade. In this exercise, what grade would you have to get in order to pass class D? Because each exam carries the same weight, it's easy to figure this out. Add up the points that you already have (14 + 40 + 56). After the first three exams, you have accumulated 110 points in class D. To score a passing grade (with 60 as passing), you would need a total of 240 points (4 times 60). So what would you need to get on the final to achieve your goal of 240 points? If you said 130 points, you were right. As you can see, not only is it impossible to score 130 points, it also is highly unlikely that any student with scores of 14, 40, and 56 would even score 100 on the final exam.

Consider All Your Options

By evaluating your grade in each of your classes before you begin to study, you can determine whether or not you can pass the class. It might be better to try to drop (withdraw from) a class you are failing and concentrate on your other courses. Check with your professor before you drop a class, though. Some professors do take improvement into consideration and may actually "drop" the first exam when calculating your grade. If only the second, third, and final exams were counted, there could be hope of passing class D. Before dropping a class, ask your professor whether there is any chance that you can pass the class. If the answer is no, then drop the course or just forget about it. Don't study for the exam; don't even go to take it unless you're planning to retake the course. If that's your plan, just getting an idea of what the final exam is like will help you prepare even better the next time around. Instead, put your time and energy into your other classes. It's a mistake to believe that you should *never* give up on a course.

Setting Priorities Can Improve Your GPA

By setting your priorities appropriately, you actually may improve your GPA. You should put the greatest effort into the courses in which you have a borderline grade, in courses where the final actually can make a difference. Many students think that they should put their greatest effort into class A because it is the class with the highest grade (an 83 average). Although class A is the course in which you have the highest grade, the grade is a pretty solid B. What grade would you have to get on the final in order to get an A (90 average) in this class? Look at the following calculation:

360	what you need for an A (if all four exams are given equal weight)
−249	the total points you now have in Class A
111	total points that you need

As you can see, here again it's impossible to gain enough points on the final to significantly affect the grade; an A cannot be achieved, even with a perfect score. The two classes where you should put your effort are the middle two classes (B and C). In each of these courses, you have a borderline grade (78.6 in class B and 81 in class C). Because your grade is close to the cutoff for a B, the results of your final exam will determine your grade. If you want to get a B in class B, you need to score only an 84 (320 minus 236) on the final. With previous grades of 81, 76, and 79, an 84 seems to be a realistic goal requiring only a little extra effort. To keep the low B that you already have in class C, you need to get only a 77 (320 minus 243). Putting in the extra effort in class C certainly could pay off.

You can determine the grade you need in each of your courses by adding up all scores that you have so far and subtracting that total from the total points that you need. If you want an A in a course that has only three exams, you need 270 points, assuming a 90 is an A ($3 \times 90 = 270$). In a course with five exams, you need 460 points, assuming a 92 is an A ($5 \times 92 = 460$). The total points that you need can be calculated by multiplying the total number of exams by the lowest numerical value for the grade that you want to earn. If your grade is composed of homework, quizzes, papers, and other assignments, in addition to exam grades, use the earlier formula or ask your professor how to calculate your grade and how to determine what you need on the final.

Activity 14-7

Practice Setting Priorities

Complete the following table. What score do you need to earn on the final to earn the next highest letter grade for each course? Compare your responses to those of others in your group. In each of these examples, the final is worth 25% of the course grade. Use the formula (%CG $\times$ CG) + (%FE $\times$ SFE) = FG.

		%CG	CG	%FE	SFE	FG	Priority
Class A	76, 82, 82	_____	_____	_____	_____	_____	_____
Class B	66, 72, 74	_____	_____	_____	_____	_____	_____
Class C	80, 85, 90	_____	_____	_____	_____	_____	_____
Class D	80, 66, 78	_____	_____	_____	_____	_____	_____

Which two courses should be your highest priorities during finals? Why?

_____

_____

_____

Activity 14-8

Set Priorities for Your Own Courses

List the scores that you have received in each of your classes and total your points earned. Then decide which grade you think you could earn in the course and determine what score you would need to get on the final to earn the next highest letter grade. Again, use the formula (%CG $\times$ CG) + (%FE $\times$ SFE) = FG.

	Class	%CG	CG	%FE	SFE	FG	Priority
1.	_____	_____	_____	_____	_____	_____	_____
2.	_____	_____	_____	_____	_____	_____	_____

Continued

3. _____ _____ _____ _____ _____ _____ _____
4. _____ _____ _____ _____ _____ _____ _____
5. _____ _____ _____ _____ _____ _____ _____

Which courses should be your highest priorities during finals? Why?

_____

_____

_____

Attend All Classes

You can improve your performance on final exams by attending class. Missing class is never a good idea, but missing class just before finals is extremely unwise. Some students miss class because they feel they need that time to catch up or study for other courses. This may be a wise choice once in a while, but it's not a good choice before final exams. Many professors squeeze extra information into their lectures during the last week or two of classes in order to present all of the material that will be on the final. Others review or discuss what will be on the final, as well as what won't be on the final. Knowing what to study and also knowing what you don't have to spend time on can help you use your study time more effectively. In addition, you may benefit from questions that other students ask during class and the answers that the professor gives.

Reduce Anxiety

Don't let the thought of final exams make you panic. Many students experience test anxiety during final exams. Why do you think this happens? For one thing, final exams, especially comprehensive finals, are a new experience for many students. Some students see final exams as their last chance to pull up their grade. In addition, finals are more important than most exams because they can determine your grade in the course. Because they carry more value, they involve more risk. Because they involve more risk, they cause more feelings of anxiety. Finally, students experience more anxiety during finals because they are tired and "run down" at the end of the semester.

Some anxiety is a normal part of finals week. Although you can't expect to eliminate all feelings of anxiety, you can do things to keep test anxiety from interfering with your performance on exams. If final exams are a new experience for you, talk to your professor, advisor, or someone in your college learning center about what to expect. Ask some of your friends to describe their experiences with final exams and how they compared with regular exams. The more you know about the exams, the more prepared you'll be for them. If one of your finals will determine your grade in the course, be sure to make that exam your top priority. The strategies for test preparation that you learned will help you be well prepared for the exam, and being well prepared is the best way to reduce your feelings of anxiety. Finally, get lots of rest, eat well, and plan some time to relax during finals week so that you don't feel stressed out. If you used some stress-reduction exercises to help lower your anxiety on previous exams, use them again as soon as you feel anxious. Although anxiety may be an obstacle during final exams, you have many resources to help you overcome it.

Use Active Study Strategies

Use active strategies when you review your text and lecture materials. Write and recite in order to move information into long-term memory. Test your understanding of the material by using flash cards, self-tests, and recitation. If you already took good notes on your textbook and prepared study sheets combining the information from your text and lecture notes, you won't need to go back and review the text again. If you prepared questions in the margin or word and question cards for each of your chapters, take them out again to review for your final. Rather than rereading the notes that you took and the study sheets or maps that you prepared, create new ones. This time use your notes and study sheets as your starting points. In the process of making new study sheets, you'll effectively review the material. If you made self-tests for each chapter, use them again to find out what you already know and what you still need to learn.

Stay Motivated

As you prepare for each of your finals, use strategies to stay motivated. If you get tired or discouraged, give yourself a pep talk. Plan rewards that will help you stay on task. Surround yourself with other motivated people. Join a study group or check in with friends who also have made a commitment to work hard during finals week. One of the worst things you can do is hang around with other students who don't have very many exams or who don't plan to study. They will constantly distract you and may, without meaning to, tempt you to neglect your studies and "party" with them. Even though it's hard to say no to your friends, you have to. Remember that your academic goals must come first. If you have a heavy exam schedule, save the partying for when you're finished. Many students don't realize that partying every night after they study can be very harmful. Don't drink during finals preparation; hangovers can throw off your study schedule, interfere with your concentration and retrieval during exams, and affect whether you get to the exam on time.

Activity 14-9

Plan Ways to Stay Motivated

List some of the obstacles that you'll have to overcome during finals week, along with the strategies or resources that you plan to use to overcome them, and the rewards that you anticipate.

Work Hard During Each Exam

Work hard during each of your exams. Stay in the testing room for the entire time period. Review your answers and use problem-solving strategies to try to figure out the correct answer for any question that you're not sure about. Concentrate on only one exam at a time. Don't think about the exam that you had yesterday or the one that's coming up tomorrow. If you feel anxious, use one of the relaxation strategies that you learned. Focus all your energy and all your effort on the exam. After the exam, take a break before beginning your next study session. Don't allow

TEN TIPS FOR PREPARING FOR FINAL EXAMS

FINAL EXAMS CAN CHANGE YOUR GRADE. For many students, final exams can improve or lower your grade in a course. Many professors take improvement into consideration when determining your course grade, so it is important to do your best. In some classes, your final exam is worth 50 percent of your grade or more.

USE STRESS-MANAGEMENT STRATEGIES. Many students panic at the end of the semester. You may have so much to do in such a short time that you aren't sure you can get it all done. You may be worried about comprehensive finals or your grades. If you let it, stress can interfere with your ability to prepare for and take your final exams.

USE GOOD TIME-MANAGEMENT STRATEGIES. At the end of the semester, it is even more important to make the best use of your time. You need to set up a schedule to complete all your outstanding assignments. Write down what you plan to do each hour of the day.

MAKE A "TO DO" LIST. About ten days before your first final, make a list of all your outstanding assignments. Then push hard for one week to complete as many of the tasks ahead of time as you can. This will free up time at the end of the semester, to devote to preparing for your final exams.

SET PRIORITIES FOR STUDY. You don't need to study for every final exam the same way. If the final is unlikely to change your grade in the course, spend less time preparing for that exam. Put more effort, instead, into those exams where the final will determine the grade. You still need to study for all your exams, but use your time to your best advantage.

USE THE FIVE-DAY STUDY PLAN. Most students have two to five exams spaced within a three- or four-day time period. Some students have two exams on the same day. Although it's tempting to study for one exam at a time by cramming, you already know that's not the most effective way to learn. Split your day to use the Five-Day Study Plan for each of your exams.

PUT ACADEMICS FIRST THIS WEEK. Put family activities, cleaning, and social events on hold until after your last exam. You'll have several weeks between semesters to catch up on things once your exams are over. By focusing your attention on your final exams, you can increase your chances for academic success.

ASK FOR TIME OFF IF YOU NEED IT. You may need to take a vacation day from work or even from household tasks in order to prepare for one or two of your most important final exams. Think about how hard you worked the entire semester to get to this point. With a little extra time to prepare, you can make all that hard work pay off.

STAY HEALTHY TO DO YOUR BEST. Some students skip meals and pull one all-nighter after another to cram for finals. This strategy often results in poor test preparation and performance. You need to eat properly, get enough sleep, and get some exercise during final exam week so that you can do your best on each exam.

PLAN REWARDS. Make a list of things you want to do when finals are over. Ask your family and friends what they'd like to do, too. Setting goals for special activities or even some rest and relaxation can help keep you motivated through your exams.

your performance on one exam to interfere with your ability or commitment to prepare for another one. If you leave an exam angry or upset about your performance, accept the fact that you may not achieve your goal in that class, but don't give up on all of your other classes. You may be able to do even better than you expected on one of your other exams.

Monitor Your Progress

After the exam is over, evaluate your performance. Write down a few notes about how you thought you did on the exam. Note any areas where you think you had difficulty and then review your notes or study sheets to check your answers. At the beginning of the next semester, visit your professor and ask to look at your exam. If you had problems with some areas, ask your professor to go over them with you. Even though the course is over and your grade is already assigned, you still may benefit from this review. You can decide whether the plan that you set up or the strategies that you used were effective. If they were, use those strategies again in a similar class. If they weren't effective, revise them for future exams.

HOW TO SET UP A FINAL EXAM PLAN

Although cramming for finals is a common phenomenon, it's not the best way to prepare for finals. If you cram for finals, you may find that after one or two days it becomes very hard to keep up that kind of pace. You may get tired of the long days and nights of study and give up on later exams. Cramming makes inefficient use of your time, causes feelings of frustration, and results in lots of memory interference. It's a form of massed practice, and massed practice isn't an efficient method of learning information. You have less opportunity to organize, practice, and test your retrieval of the information.

Cramming is especially ineffective when you have more than one exam on the same day. Few students have a finals schedule that includes only one exam per day; usually, students have at least two exams on the same day. In most cases, then, cramming is not a useful strategy for preparing for exams. What alternatives are there? By spacing your study over several days, you can study for each of your exams using the Five-Day Study Plan and, at the same time, maintain your motivation throughout exam week.

Make a Final Exam Study Plan

One of the first things you need to do is set up a plan for your exams. Check your syllabi or final exam schedule several weeks in advance and write each exam time on a calendar. Occasionally, students find that they have more than one exam scheduled for the same time. If this happens, check with your professors about alternative exam times. More often, students find that they have more than one exam on the same day. It's relatively common to have two exams on one day, but some students find that they have three exams (or more) on one day. Having too many exams on the same day can negatively affect your performance during finals. By the time you begin the third exam, you may be exhausted, frazzled, or emotionally drained. To put it another way, you won't be at your best. Some schools have policies that help eliminate these conflicts; the faculty and administration recognize that students can't properly demonstrate what they've learned if the testing situation works against them. Check with your professor, academic dean, or someone in the registrar's office if you have exam conflicts.

Make out a **reminder sheet** (on 8½-by-11-inch paper) for each exam that you have to take. Write the name of the course, day and date, time, place, and any materials that you need to take with you. Post these on your door or bulletin board. Some students get so stressed out during finals week that they forget when or where their exams are scheduled. Having all the information for each of your exams clearly organized and posted may help reduce some of your anxiety. If your final exams are scheduled for times and places that are different from your regular class hours, these reminder sheets will be especially helpful.

Set Up a Final Exam Planning Calendar

By setting up a **Final Exam Planning Calendar,** you can properly prepare for each of your exams without feeling rushed or anxious. Use the **Five-Day Study Plan** to space out your study. By dividing up your day, you can prepare for several exams at the same time.

Don't Start to Prepare Too Early

When you start to study can affect your performance on final exams. Some students decide to get a jump on finals by preparing several weeks in advance. This strategy has both positive and negative effects. On the positive side, you can review a lot more material a lot more times if you start early. On the negative side, though, you can forget a lot of the material before the exam if you begin to prepare *too* early. If you do begin your preparation more than a week before the exam, you need to review the material that you prepared first when you're closer to the exam. One way to make good use of early preparation time is by preparing study sheets, maps, self-tests, word cards, and so on. Begin your actual review of these materials four to five days before the exam.

Space Your Study to Aid Retention

Spacing your study as you prepare for finals is crucial to getting information into your long-term memory in a logical and organized manner. Because of the large amount of information that you may need to master for a comprehensive final, you need to learn information in small chunks and review it often. If you try to cram fifteen chapters of biology into one long (eight- to ten-hour) study session, you may find that you only partially know the material. By studying one chunk of the material each day and then reviewing it again over the next few days, you can monitor your learning and reinforce the information that you still don't know.

Split Your Day When Preparing for Several Exams

Rather than studying for one exam at a time, you need to learn how to prepare for several exams at the same time. This isn't an impossible task as some students think, but rather one that requires a little planning and a lot of perseverance. Count back five or six days from each of your final exams to determine your starting date. You may find that you're on day 3 of your study plan for Biology when you start day 1 of your study plan for English Literature.

By splitting your day, you can effectively prepare for several exams at the same time. If you have your other work done, you should be able to devote all of your time to preparing for exams. This doesn't mean that you'll study nonstop from the time you wake up until the time you go to sleep. Rather, **splitting your day** means that you should be able to schedule three or four two-hour blocks of time each day to prepare for your exams. Let's pretend that you have the finals schedule shown in Figure 14.4. If you use a Five-Day Study Plan, you can prepare for all of your exams at one time. Your hardest and busiest days on this schedule are Sunday, Monday, and Wednesday. By carefully planning your time, you can prepare for each exam and still have sufficient time for sleep, meals, and some relaxation.

Students often ask me to help them figure out when to study for finals. If I were helping you plan a study schedule, I would recommend that you divide your day according to the courses on which you're working. Assigning one course to the morning, two to the afternoon, and one to the evening allows you to study for each test in a regular time slot. By studying the same material at the same time of day, you can separate course material for one exam from that of your other courses and

FIGURE 14.4
Final Exam Study Plan

Algebra	Monday	December 14	9:00 to 11:00
English	Wednesday	December 16	9:00 to 11:00
Biology	Thursday	December 17	12:30 to 2:30
Study Skills	Friday	December 18	12:30 to 2:30

Final Exam Study Plan

Wed Dec. 9	Thurs Dec. 10	Fri Dec. 11	Sat Dec. 12	Sun Dec. 13	Mon Dec. 14	Tues Dec. 15	Wed Dec. 16	Thurs Dec. 17	Fri Dec. 18
Day 1 Algebra	Day 2 Algebra	Day 3 Algebra	Day 4 Algebra	Day 5 Algebra	Extra Review Algebra				
		Day 1 English	Day 2 English	Day 3 English	Day 4 English	Day 5 English	Extra Review English		
			Day 1 Biology	Day 2 Biology	Day 3 Biology	Day 4 Biology	Day 5 Biology	Extra Review Biology	
				Day 1 SS	Day 2 SS	Day 3 SS	Day 4 SS	Day 5 SS	Extra Review SS
					Take Alg Final	No Exam	Take Engl Final	Take Bio Final	Take SS Final

thereby prevent some of the interference that often occurs during finals week. It's also a good idea to work on your hardest subject early in the day, when you're the most alert. By the time you spend four to six hours on your other two classes, you won't be able to concentrate as well on the material from the third class.

Create a Final Exam Planning Calendar

Look at the Final Exam Planning Calendar in Figure 14.5. If this were your exam schedule, I would suggest that you set up your study time this way. Because you have finals early in the final exam period, begin to prepare for your final exams during the last week of regular classes. You may still be busy completing reading assignments or even papers or projects that are due at the end of the semester. If you need to prepare for more than one exam during this week, try to complete your regular assignments early. By Sunday of exam week, schedule time to prepare for four final exams. Even in this schedule you have some flexibility.

You could eliminate one of the afternoon study blocks and move it to the 10:00 to 12:00 block, or you could use the optional study time for extra review for your highest priority class or classes. Because Biology is a very difficult class, I would schedule that study time first. Notice, incidentally, how each study block is followed by at least a one-hour break. You need time to rest and allow the informa-

FIGURE 14.5

Final Exam Planning Calendar

Time	⑨ Wednesday	⑩ Thursday	⑪ Friday	⑫ Saturday	⑬ Sunday	⑭ Monday	⑮ Tuesday	⑯ Wednesday	⑰ Thursday	⑱ Friday	⑲ Saturday
7:00											
8:00						Extra Review Alg		Extra Review English			
9:00	English		English		Day 5	Algebra		English	Extra	Extra	
10:00			Biology		Alg	Final		Final	Review Bio	Review Bio	
11:00	Biology								Lunch	Lunch	
12:00	Lunch	Lunch	Lunch	Lunch	Lunch	Lunch	Lunch	Lunch			
1:00	College Algebra	Study Skills →	College Algebra	Day 1	Day 2	Day 3	Day 4	Day 5	Bio Final	Study Skills	
2:00				Bio	Bio	Bio	Bio	Bio		Final	
3:00				break	break	break	break	break			
4:00			Day 1	Day 2	Day 3	Day 4	Day 5				
5:00	Dinner	Dinner	English	English	English	English	English				
6:00			Dinner	Dinner	Dinner	Dinner	Dinner	Dinner	Dinner	Dinner	
7:00	Day 1	Day 2	Day 3	Day 4	Day 1	Day 2	Day 3	Day 4	Day 5		
8:00	Alg	Alg	Alg	Alg	Study Skills	Study Skills	Study Skills	Study Skills	Study Skills		
9:00			break	break	break	break	break	break	break		
10:00			Optional	Optional	Optional	Optional	Optional	Optional	Optional		
11:00			Study time	Study time	Study time	Study time	Study time	Study time	Study time		

Note: Do not use the words *Optional Study Time* on your plan. Instead, indicate how that time will be used.

tion to **consolidate** (get organized in long-term memory) or "sink in" before you start to study again.

Color Code Your Calendar On the calendar in Figure 14.5, all of the study blocks are outlined in blue. However, when you create your own planning color, select a different color for each of your exams. You many want to outline the exam and all of the study blocks related to Biology with a red marker. Then use blue for College Algebra, green for English, and perhaps orange for Study Skills. This color coding helps you make up your plan and lets you see clearly what you're studying and when. The time block from 10:00 P.M. to 12:00 P.M. is designated optional study time on this calendar. You can use it a number of ways. If Biology is your top priority class, you could spend an extra two hours each day preparing for your exam. You could spend the early afternoon preparing and reviewing material and the late night block for more review and self-testing. If you have two high priority classes, use the first hour for extra review for one of them, take a ten- or fifteen-minute break and spend the last forty-five minutes on the other class. You could also use the optional study time block for a fifth exam. Do you prefer to stay up late studying rather than get up early? Photocopy the calendar and add more time blocks at the bottom so you can schedule some of your study blocks from 1:00 to 3:00 A.M., if that fits your time schedule. Other students may need to add time early in the morning. When I was in college, I was accustomed to 8:00 A.M. classes, so I often got up at 6:00 A.M. during finals to get in an extra review before my 8:00 exams.

Plan an Extra Review Although the Biology exam isn't scheduled until 12:30 P.M. on Thursday, day 5 for Biology on this study plan is scheduled for Wednesday. Because the exam is scheduled for an afternoon time slot, you may think that you should do your final review that morning. If you do have afternoon or evening exams, doing an extra review (two-hour review or one-hour review if your schedule is really tight) just before the exam is a good way to keep the information fresh in memory. However, it's not the best time to take your self-test. If you don't know a lot of the material that morning, there isn't enough time left to learn it. Instead, do your self-test on day 5, the day before the exam. Then you'll have time to work on any information you miss and do an extra review the day of the exam.

Set Up a Plan for Multiple Finals Did you notice as you looked at the planning calendar in Figure 14.5 that the student had only one exam per day during the final exam period? When I check each semester with my students, many of them aren't so fortuante. A lot of my students have two exams on one of the days and a few (especially if they are taking day classes and night classes) have three on the same day. If you have more than one exam on the same day, you can still use the Final Exam Planning Calendar to schedule your study time. Hollie set up five study blocks to prepare for her exams last semester (see Figure 14.6). Even though she had both her Educational Psychology and her Math for Elementary Teachers exams on Wednesday, it really didn't change her strategy of scheduling her study time. Because the finals at our university are scheduled in two-hour blocks with only a half hour in between the two afternoon time slots, Hollie didn't have time for an extra review before her Math exam. If Math had been a higher priority than Ed. Psych., she could have used the time before the Ed. Psych. exam to review more for her Math exam. In this case though, Hollie's top priority class was her Ed. Psych. class.

FIGURE 14-6

Hollie's Final Exam Planning Calendar

	Wednesday	Thursday	Friday	Saturday	Sunday	Monday	Tuesday	Wednesday	Thursday	Friday	Saturday
7:00											
8:00									Extra Rev Study Skills	Extra Review	
9:00	Math	Ed	Math	Day 2	Day 3	Day 4	Day 5	Extra Rev	Study Skills	Science	
10:00	Study Skills	Psych	Study Skills	Ed Psych	Ed Psych	Ed Psych	Ed Psych	Ed Psych	Final	Science	
11:00	Lunch	Lunch	Lunch	Lunch	Lunch	Lunch	Lunch	Lunch	Lunch	Lunch	
12:00	Comp		Comp	Day 1	Day 2	Day 3	Day 4	↑	Day 5	Science Final	
1:00				Sci	Sci	Sci	Sci	Ed Psych Final ↓	Sci		
2:00	Science		Science								
3:00			Day 1	Day 2	Day 3	Day 4	Day 5	Math			
4:00			Math	Math	Math	Math	Math	Final			
5:00	Dinner	Dinner	Dinner	Dinner	Dinner	Dinner	Dinner	Dinner	Dinner	Dinner	
6:00			Day 1	Day 1	Day 2	Day 3	Day 4	Day 5			
7:00			Ed Psych	SS	SS	SS	SS	SS			
8:00											
9:00			Extra Rev	Extra Rev	Extra Rev	Extra Rev	Extra Rev				
10:00			Ed Psych	Ed Psych	Ed Psych	Ed Psych	Ed Psych				
11:00											

Note: Hollie did not have a final in English Composition.

Activity 14-10

Compare Student Study Schedules

Print out Tanya's and Joel's Final Exam Planning Calendars, available on the *College Study Skills* Web site, and bring them to class. Although both students attempted to develop a good study plan for their final exams, they made some common mistakes. In your group, discuss the strengths and weaknesses of each plan. What changes would you make if they asked you to set up a study schedule for them?

Activity 14-11

Practice Setting Up a Final Exam Planning Calendar

Pretend that you have the following final exams this semester. Use the calendar in Figure 14.7 to make up a schedule that shows when you would prepare for each exam. Don't forget to split your day, space your study, plan breaks between study blocks, and use consistent time frames when possible.

COURSE	CLASS TIME		DATE OF FINAL		TIME OF FINAL
Math	MWF	9 to 10	Mon	Dec 14	3:00 to 5:00
English	MWF	11 to 12	Thur	Dec 17	12:30 to 2:30
Study Skills	TH	2 to 3:20	Fri	Dec 18	12:20 to 2:30
Biology	MTWF	3 to 4	Tues	Dec 15	9:00 to 11:00
Sociology	W	6 to 8:40	Wed	Dec 16	6:00 to 8:00

Activity 14-12

Set Up Your Study Schedule

Fill in information about your final exam schedule and then use the calendar in Figure 14.8 to set up your own final exam study schedule. Change the times to suit your study schedule and don't forget to set priorities.

	COURSE	DATE OF FINAL	TIME OF FINAL
1.	_____	_____	_____
2.	_____	_____	_____
3.	_____	_____	_____
4.	_____	_____	_____
5.	_____	_____	_____

FIGURE 14.7

Blank Final Exam Planning Calendar

	Wednesday	Thursday	Friday	Saturday	Sunday	Monday	Tuesday	Wednesday	Thursday	Friday	Saturday
7:00											
8:00											
9:00											
10:00											
11:00											
12:00											
1:00											
2:00											
3:00											
4:00											
5:00											
6:00											
7:00											
8:00											
9:00											
10:00											
11:00											

FIGURE 14.8
Blank Final Exam Planning
Calendar

	Wednesday	Thursday	Friday	Saturday	Sunday	Monday	Tuesday	Wednesday	Thursday	Friday	Saturday
7:00											
8:00											
9:00											
10:00											
11:00											
12:00											
1:00											
2:00											
3:00											
4:00											
5:00											
6:00											
7:00											
8:00											
9:00											
10:00											
11:00											

HOW TO PREPARE FOR COMPREHENSIVE FINALS

Check to see whether your final is **comprehensive** (includes previously tested material) or covers only new material. Some professors include both old and new material on final exams. Knowing how much of the exam is based on old material is critical to effective preparation. If you have a comprehensive final, find out *how much* of the exam is comprehensive. Many instructors give final exams that are partially comprehensive. If, for example, you had an exam that covered twelve chapters (and accompanying lecture notes and so on), you would prepare differently depending on whether the exam was 100 percent comprehensive, 75 percent comprehensive, 50 percent comprehensive, or 25 percent comprehensive.

Preparing for 25 Percent Comprehensive Finals

Let's say that you're going to have an exam that is only **25 percent comprehensive.** That means that 75 percent of the test questions cover **new** (not yet tested) **material,** while 25 percent of the test questions cover **old** (already tested) **material.** If the exam is composed of 100 multiple-choice items that cover twelve chapters, how many of the questions will be on old material? Of course, 25 of them will be. That means that 75 questions will be on the new material, which, for this example, will be Chapters 10, 11, and 12.

If you were going to set up a Five-Day Study Plan for this final, which chapters would you study on each of the first four days, assuming that you save the last day for a final review and self-test? Many students make the mistake of dividing the material into four equal chunks (as they did for regular exams). In the case of a comprehensive final, however, this would be very poor planning. Because 75 percent of the questions will come from the new material, 75 percent of your time should be spent on those chapters.

It may seem strange to spend only 25 percent of your study time on the first nine chapters of the text (and accompanying lecture notes, and so on); however, that is the appropriate time to devote to the old material. Look at the three study plans in Figure 14.9. In the first plan, the student divided up the study time equally. In the second study plan, the student divided the study time equally but reversed the order of the review. She thought that by beginning with the new material, she would get to spend five days reviewing it. Even so, the total time spent on the old material is still disproportionate to the number of related questions on the test. In the third study plan, the proportion of time spent on each section of the material is more appropriately divided to reflect the weight (number of test questions and point value) of each section. The correct way to divide the time would be to spend day 1 preparing Chapters 1–9, day 2 on Chapter 10, day 3 on Chapter 11, and

FIGURE 14.9
Sample Study Plans

Plan 1		Plan 2		Plan 3	
Day 1	Ch 1–3	Day 1	Ch 10–12	Day 1	Ch 1–9
Day 2	CH 4–6	Day 2	CH 7–9	Day 2	CH 10
Day 3	CH 7–9	Day 3	CH 4–6	Day 3	CH 11
Day 4	CH 10–12	Day 4	CH 1–3	Day 4	CH 12

day 4 on Chapter 12. Because each of the four chunks of material (1–9, 10, 11, and 12) is weighted the same on the exam, they should be given equal preparation time.

The number of questions taken from each chapter often signals how detailed or specific each question will be. Typically, the fewer the questions from each chapter, the more general they tend to be. If you have only twenty-five questions covering nine chapters of text, you have less than three questions per chapter on the exam. On the other hand, if you have seventy-five test questions based on the last three chapters, you have approximately twenty-five questions for each chapter. Although the student who spends three days preparing and reviewing the first nine chapters may know that material very well, he or she will not know the last three chapters well enough (with only one day of preparation) to get a high score on the exam. A quick review of the old material followed by intense study of the new material is necessary for exams that are only slightly comprehensive.

How can you review nine (or more) chapters of material in only a two- or three-hour study session? Obviously, you don't have time to reread all your highlighting or even all your lecture notes (and rereading is not a good way to review anyway). If you prepared properly for each of the exams that covered those chapters, you should have study sheets, word and question cards, and self-tests from which to study. The best way to prepare for those chapters, then, is to review the material that you already prepared when studying for the earlier exams. In addition, if you have copies of your old tests or are permitted to review them in your professor's office, do so. Many instructors use questions from the original exams again on the final.

Preparing for Other Comprehensive Finals

Now that you know how to divide your time correctly between old and new material for 25 percent comprehensive finals, let's look at other combinations. Let's say that you're going to have a **50 percent comprehensive** final. One-half of the test questions will be based on Chapters 1–14 and the other half will come from the last four chapters in the text (15–18). How would you divide your study time, assuming you have the same four days to prepare and one day for a final review of the material? To figure out the proper ratio of time to chapters, think about how many chapters will be covered in each quarter of the exam. Because half of the test questions will come from the first fourteen chapters, you can effectively divide those chapters in two. You would prepare Chapters 1–7 on day 1 and Chapters 8–14 on day 2. You would then prepare Chapters 15 and 16 on day 3 and Chapters 17 and 18 on day 4. Deciding which chunk of chapters to review first depends on your past performance. If you got high grades on the exams on Chapters 1 to 14, you may want to work on the new chapters first, to get more repetition on that material. If you didn't do well on the old tests, you should start with those chapters because they're less fresh in your mind and will require even more review. Remember to review each chunk of material on each day of your study plan.

An exam that's **75 percent comprehensive** requires more time on old material than on new material. Let's use the following example. If you had 100 questions that covered nineteen chapters of text, how much time would you spend on the old material if only Chapters 16–19 were still untested? In this case, you would spend the first three days of your study plan reviewing the first fifteen chapters (because 75 percent of the questions will come from those chapters) and only the last day on the new material (because only 25 percent of the questions will be drawn from those chapters). Even though you have not yet been tested on the last three chapters, you shouldn't spend a disproportionate amount of your time on them because so few questions will be taken from each one. However, if you did really well on the exams for the "old" chapters, you should review Chapters 16 to 19 first. That way you'll have more time to learn the "new," not-yet-tested material during each daily review. By spacing your study and allocating the appropriate amount of time to each of the chapters, you can maximize your test score on any type of comprehensive final exam.

Activity 14-13

Practice Planning for Comprehensive Finals

Work as a group to make up study plans that demonstrate your understanding of how to divide the material based on how much of the exam is comprehensive. In each of the following cases, assume that you have 100 questions on the exam and each question is worth 1 point. Use the Five-Day Study Plan with day 5 as a final review. For more practice, consider your success on previous exams.

1. You have a 50 percent comprehensive exam covering seven old chapters and three new chapters (Chapters 8–10).

2. You have a 75 percent comprehensive exam covering twelve chapters of old material and three new chapters (Chapters 13–15).

3. You have a 25 percent comprehensive exam covering ten chapters of old material and four chapters of new material (Chapters 10–13).

4. You have a 100 percent comprehensive exam covering fourteen chapters (Chapters 1–14).

5. You have a noncomprehensive exam covering four chapters (Chapters 12–15).

Activity 14-14

Where Are You Now?

Now that you have completed Chapter 14, take a few minutes to repeat the "Where Are You Now?" activity, located on the *College Study Skills* Web site. What changes did you make as a result of reading this chapter? How are you planning to apply what you've learned in this chapter?

SUMMARY

The key to preparing for final exams is good time management. Most students are still attending classes, preparing daily assignments, and completing term papers and projects as final exam period approaches. Because final exams are often critical in determining your final course grade, you need enough time to prepare for each one as carefully as or more carefully than you did for your regular exams. To do this, you may need to make some changes in your daily routine. About two weeks before your first final, you need to make academics your first priority. You should push hard about two weeks before the end of the semester and get ahead in your work. Your goal is to complete most of your outstanding assignments five days before your first exam. At the same time, you need to evaluate your status in each course. By calculating your current grade, you can determine whether the final exam will make a difference in your overall course grade. Setting your priorities before you begin to study can help you decide how much time to put into studying for each of your final exams.

Use the Five-Day Study Plan to prepare for each exam. Set up a Final Exam Planning Calendar. With most of your regular assignments already completed, you should have plenty of time to schedule three to four (two-hour) study blocks each day. Spacing your study and splitting your day will help you stay on task, reduce anxiety, and prevent interference as you prepare for several exams at the same time. Cramming for one exam after another just doesn't work. Developing strategies to stay motivated is also especially important during final exam week. As you take each of your finals, put forth your best effort. Concentrate on each exam, monitor your progress to evaluate the strategies you used, and then make any necessary adjustments for the next exam.

Comprehensive final exams are more difficult than other tests because they cover so much material. However, if you divide your study time properly and use the material that you prepared from each of your old exams, you can do as well or even better on the finals. If you learn from your successes and your mistakes, the experience you gain will help you cope with the intensity and the stress of final exams—each semester, you'll do it even better!

REVIEW QUESTIONS

Terms You Should Know: Make a flash card for each term.

Comprehensive final exam	Five-Day Study Plan
Consolidation	New material
End-of-Semester Assignment Calendar	Old material
Exam reminder sheet	Setting priorities
50 percent comprehensive	75 percent comprehensive
Final Exam Planning Calendar	Splitting your day
Final exams	25 percent comprehensive

Completion: Fill in the blank to complete each of the following statements.

1. You can prepare for several final exams at the same time by _____ your day.

2. You should generally review the _____ material early in your study plan so that you can get more repetition on it.

3. When setting up your Final Exam Planning Calendar, plan _____ hour(s) for each exam each day.

4. Courses with _____ grades should be your highest priority.

5. A twenty-five percent comprehensive final includes _____ questions out of one hundred on the old material.

Multiple Choice: Circle the letter of the best answer for each of the following questions. Be sure to underline key words and eliminate wrong answers.

6. If you're failing a course, you should:
   A. rank that course as your top priority.
   B. drop the course.
   C. check with the professor to ask if there is any chance you could pass.
   D. stop attending, don't study, and don't take the final.

7. On the Final Exam Planning Calendar, optional study time can be used for:
   A. additional practice for all of your exams.
   B. additional practice for your top-priority exam.
   C. preparation time for a fifth course.
   D. all of the above.

Short Answer–Essay: On a separate sheet, answer each of the following questions.

8. Why do students experience so much anxiety at the end of the semester?

9. Why do some students have difficulty taking final exams? What should they do differently?

10. How should students prepare for 25 percent, 50 percent, 75 percent, and 100 percent comprehensive finals?